MW00475974

Lord and Servant

Also by Michael S. Horton

Covenant and Eschatology: The Divine Drama

Lord and Servant:
A Covenant Christology

Michael S. Horton

WESTMINSTER
JOHN KNOX PRESS
LOUISVILLE · KENTUCKY

© 2005 Michael S. Horton

All rights reserved. No part of this book may be reproduced or transmitted in any form or by any means, electronic or mechanical, including photocopying, recording, or by any information storage or retrieval system, without permission in writing from the publisher. For information, address Westminster John Knox Press, 100 Witherspoon Street, Louisville, Kentucky 40202-1396.

Scripture quotations from the New Revised Standard Version of the Bible are copyright © 1989 by the Division of Christian Education of the National Council of the Churches of Christ in the U.S.A. and are used by permission.

Scripture quotations from the New King James Version of the Bible are copyright © 1979, 1980, 1982, Thomas Nelson Inc., Publishers. Used by permission.

Scripture quotations from The Holy Bible, English Standard Version, are copyright © 2001 by Crossway Bibles, a division of Good News Publishers. Used by permission. All rights reserved.

Book design by Sharon Adams
Cover design by Eric Walljasper

First edition
Published by Westminster John Knox Press
Louisville, Kentucky

This book is printed on acid-free paper that meets the American National Standards Institute Z39.48 standard. ♾

PRINTED IN THE UNITED STATES OF AMERICA

05 06 07 08 09 10 11 12 13 14—10 9 8 7 6 5 4 3 2 1

Library of Congress Cataloging-in-Publication Data

Horton, Michael Scott.
    Lord and servant : a covenant Christology / Michael S. Horton.
       p. cm.
    Includes bibliographical references.
    ISBN 0-664-22863-1 (alk. paper)
    1. Jesus Christ—Person and offices.   2. Covenant theology.   I. Title.

BT205.H665 2005
232—dc22
                                                       2004054947

Contents

Introduction

Lord and Servant is the second in my three-volume project whose principal burden is to take up some critical questions in contemporary systematic theology with the concrete covenantal structure of the Creator-creature relationship serving as a hermeneutical guide. This is motivated at least in part by the conviction that covenant is far more important as an architechtonic scheme in Scripture than is often recognized in dogmatics. It is not only a locus in Scripture, but the environment within which the drama of creation, fall, redemption, and consummation unfolds. To be sure, most architectonic structures are not wholly visible, and in the same way I do not intend to focus on the covenant per se at every point, but rather to see every locus in its covenantal context. Far different from a central dogma, out of which every doctrine is deduced, a framework does not overdetermine the content from the outset.

The importance of this theme has been stressed by biblical scholars from Walther Eichrodt to N. T. Wright.[1] Yet the interaction between biblical and systematic

---

1. As N. T. Wright notes in the preface to his *Climax of the Covenant* (Edinburgh: T & T Clark, 1991), xi, "The overall title reflects my growing conviction that covenant theology is one of the main clues, usually neglected, for understanding Paul." However, Wright seems unaware of the older covenant theology in this connection.

theology in this regard has been either lacking or marked by mutual suspicion. Perhaps by recovering this theme, the boundaries between biblical and systematic theology can become fluid again, as they were in the federal theology, which was at once the founding of the discipline of biblical theology while engaging in dogmatics.

THE COVENANT CONCEPT

As Eichrodt argued, "the covenant-union between Yahweh and Israel is an original element in all sources, despite their being in fragmentary form."[2] From the very beginning, the Israelites were a coalition of tribes not committed to nationalism nor bound by political aims, but who regarded themselves as "called out" by God to belong to God by means of a covenant. Thus "God's disclosure of himself is not grasped speculatively, not expounded in the form of a lesson; it is as he breaks in on the life of his people in his dealings with them and moulds them according to his will that he grants them knowledge of his being."[3] The promissory character of this covenant "provides life with a goal and history with a meaning." The arbitrariness and caprice of the gods in nature religions stands in sharp contrast to the creating, sustaining, and redeeming Lord who enters into oaths and bonds with the work of his hands.[4] Both transcendence and immanence find their proper though incomprehensible coordinates in the covenantal matrix.

Biblical-Theological Development

The concept of covenant itself derives from ancient Near Eastern treaties.[5] Pulling together a number of threads from modern discoveries, George E. Mendenhall's magisterial *Law and Covenant in Israel and the Ancient Near East* (1955) demonstrated the remarkable parallels between ancient (especially Hittite) treaties and the covenantal structure of Old Testament thought and practice.[6] Especially in the case of empires, local control was exercised through suzerainty

2. Walther Eichrodt, *Theology of the Old Testament*, trans. J. A. Baker, 2 vols., Old Testament Library (Philadelphia: Westminster Press, 1961–67), 1:36.

3. Ibid., 37.

4. Ibid., 38, 42. Gerhard von Rad writes along similar lines, arguing that canonical saving history receives its time divisions through its covenant theology (*Old Testament Theology*, trans. D. M. G. Stalker, 2 vols. [San Francisco: Harper & Row, 1962–65], 1:129).

5. For the connections to the ancient Near Eastern suzerainty treaty, see especially Meredith Kline, *Treaty of the Great King* (Grand Rapids: Eerdmans, 1963).

6. G. E. Mendenhall, *Law and Covenant in Israel and the Ancient Near East* (Pittsburgh: Biblical Colloquium, 1955); cf. Delbert R. Hillers, *Covenant: The History of a Biblical Idea* (Baltimore: Johns Hopkins University Press, 1969), 30. Cf. Kline, *Treaty of the Great King*; David Foster Estes, "Covenant," in *The International Standard Bible Encyclopedia*, ed. James Orr, vol. 2 (repr., Grand Rapids: Eerdmans, 1957), 727–29; M. Weinfeld, *"berith,"* in *Theological Dictionary of the Old Testament*, ed. G. Johannes Botterweck and Helmer Ringgren, trans. John T. Willis, vol. 2 (Grand Rapids: Eerdmans, 1975), 253–79.

treaties in which an imperial lord (suzerain) imposed obligations on the servant state and its lesser king (vassal) by oaths. It was in this way that reliable political structures were possible in a time of petty warlords, who often acted on the basis of raw power and military control, taking advantage of the instability of rising and falling, competing empires that often exhibited weak administration over the outlying fringes of their domain. The Hittite and Babylonian languages had no specific term for "covenant" or "contract," but employed the phrase "oaths and bonds."[7]

These international treaties are typically distinguished by a preamble ("thus [says] So-and-so, the great king, king of the Hatti land, son of So-and-so . . . the valiant"), a historical prologue (justifying the present and future obligation of the people on the basis of the suzerain's past action), stipulations (commands) and sanctions (blessing and curse), with formal guidelines for witnesses (the gods in the Hittite treaties) and deposit in the vassal's shrine.[8] It is worth observing that the covenant rights of the suzerain were upheld not on the basis of the vassal's judgments of his superior knowledge, justice, truth, or wisdom concerning universal principles, but as the consequence of concrete historical acts.

The "I-Thou" form contrasts with the impersonal language of contracts in modern times. It is a relationship and not merely "an objective, impersonal statement of law."[9] One simply cannot contrast legal and relational categories in this relationship. Concerning the stipulations, Delbert Hillers notes, "This section states in detail the obligations imposed upon and accepted by the vassal. . . . Every hostile action against a co-vassal is hostility against the king himself, and the king promises to take the part of the oppressed. . . . The vassal must answer any call to arms sent him by the king."[10] The technical term for this in English is *invocation*. Because of the treaty, the vassal could call upon the name of the great king and be confident of rescue. For the vassal's part, there can be no backroom alliances, no hatred of anything or anyone under the suzerain's domain, no entertainment of rumors concerning the suzerain, and the vassal must annually appear before the Hittite suzerain representing his people with a tribute/tax.[11] Obvious parallels between these ancient treaties and biblical covenants cannot detain us here.

It is important, however, to point out that the covenant concept, whether it explicitly employs the Hebrew term *bĕrît* or simply exhibits the form, is multivalent. Despite the attempts to reduce *bĕrît* to one type of arrangement (i.e., a covenant of grace), it actually encompasses a broad range of relationships. The most obvious types are the suzerainty treaty just mentioned and the royal grant, the latter ordinarily serving as an unconditional pledge of the suzerain to a vassal in view of some past performance.

---

7. Mendenhall, *Law and Covenant*, 31.

8. Hillers, *Covenant*, 25–45; cf. A. Goetze, in *Ancient Near Eastern Texts Relating to the Old Testament*, ed. J. B. Pritchard, 3rd ed. (Princeton, NJ: Princeton University Press, 1969).

9. Hillers, *Covenant*, 30.

10. Ibid., 33.

11. Ibid., 32–33.

I do not have the space here to develop these distinct lines as they emerge in Scripture, but can only summarize the widely held consensus among ancient Near Eastern scholars that such a distinction between conditional and unconditional covenants exists and can be correlated with the Sinai covenant and the Abrahamic, Davidic, and new covenants, respectively. Moshe Weinfeld summarizes a large consensus in contemporary Old Testament scholarship: "the covenant at Sinai in Ex. 24 is in its essence an imposition of laws and obligations upon the people (vv. 3–8)," while the Abrahamic and Davidic covenants "belong to the type of the covenantal grant."

> In contradistinction to the Mosaic covenants, which are of an obligatory type, the covenants with Abraham and David belong to the promissory type. . . . Although their loyalty to God is presupposed, it does not occur as a condition for keeping the promise. . . . By the same token, the covenant with the patriarchs is considered as valid for ever (*'adh 'olam*). Even when Israel sins and is to be severely punished, God intervenes to help because he "will not break his covenant" (Lev. 26:44). Just as the obligatory covenant in Israel is modeled on the suzerain-vassal type of treaty, so the promissory covenant is modeled on the royal grant.[12]

Systematic-Theological Development

While Eichrodt sought to recognize covenant as the integrating motif of biblical theology, his project was weakened by his reduction of the various covenants to a single covenant of grace. Accordingly, the unconditional-conditional distinction reflects not distinct covenants but different substrata in the history of traditions, with the priestly (happily) winning out over the Yahwist writers.[13] Dennis McCarthy, SJ, criticizes Eichrodt and others for such a univocal understanding of "covenant." "The historical relationships, and ideological differences, of the Abrahamic, Mosaic, and Davidic covenants are glossed over in the necessity to subordinate the entire Old Testament material to the one covenant of Mount Sinai."[14]

Thus it would seem that the federal theologians were justified in distinguishing not merely different emphases in one covenant, but two covenants: a law covenant and a promise covenant. The heart of the Reformation complaint was that the medieval church had turned the gospel into a new law. In other words, it had failed to properly distinguish law and gospel, command and promise, imperative and indicative. This was in no way a distinction between the Old and New Testaments, but rather ran throughout both. While we must beware exclud-

---

12. Weinfeld, "*berith*," *Theological Dictionary of the Old Testament*, 2:255, 258, 270.

13. Eichrodt, *Theology of the OT*, 1:44–59.

14. Dennis J. McCarthy, S.J., *Old Testament Covenant: A Survey of Current Opinions* (Atlanta: John Knox Press, 1972), 5. A similar move of the sort McCarthy criticizes here was made in dogmatics by Karl Barth, who argued that grace "epitomises all the gifts of God—not merely revelation, reconciliation and redemption, but also creation" (*Church Dogmatics* [hereafter *CD*], 4 vols. in 14, ed. G. W. Bromiley and T. F. Torrance, trans. Bromiley et al. [Edinburgh: T & T Clark, 1936–69], II/1:354).

ing the principle of law from the new covenant and the gospel from the old, I am following the suggestion that the biblical covenants themselves call for organization under one of those two rubrics. Our Reformation forebears were not wide of the mark, therefore, when they said, "Therefore, the law and gospel are the chief and general divisions of holy scriptures, and comprise the entire doctrine comprehended therein" (Ursinus).[15]

Of course, the Reformers were not the first to have been impressed with this paradigm of law and gospel. They themselves were influenced not only by their reading of Paul but also by Augustine's reading of the apostle to the gentiles.[16] So how did covenant theology come to identify three basic covenants in the biblical traditions? With increasing emphasis, the Reformed (federal) tradition saw in the biblical motif of covenant a way of expressing the inherent unity of God's external works in creation, redemption, and consummation. A broad consensus emerged with respect to the existence in Scripture of three distinct covenants: of redemption (*pactum salutis*), of creation (*foederus naturae*), and of grace (*foederus gratiae*). Of course, there are other covenants in Scripture (Noahic, Abrahamic, Mosaic, Davidic), but these are all seen as specific subcovenants of these broader arrangements. I will merely summarize these three overarching covenants here, without further exegetical ado, to expand on them under their appropriate topics in this volume.

An eternal compact between the persons of the Trinity, the covenant of redemption (*pactum salutis*) is represented in federal theology as the basis for all of God's covenantal activity in history. Accordingly, the Father elects a people whom he gives to the Son as their mediator and the Spirit promises to unite them to the Son. Already we glimpse the intra-Trinitarian *perichoresis* that I will more fully develop in my discussion of creation: the Father does all things in the Son and through the Spirit. Thus Trinitarian theology has always been not only a central concept but an organizing motif in the classic Reformed systems.

The two covenants executed in history are the covenants of creation and grace. Created in righteousness and ethically equipped to fulfill the task of imitating God's own "works" in order to enter his Sabbath "rest," Adam as the representative head of the human race was already eschatologically oriented toward the future. As a reward for his faithfulness to the covenant, he would lead humanity

15. Zacharius Ursinus, *Commentary on the Heidelberg Catechism* (P & R), 1. See also Michael Horton, "Law, Gospel, and Covenant: Reassessing Some Emerging Antitheses," *Westminster Theological Journal* 64, no. 2 (2002): 279–87.

16. Augustine commends the hermeneutical rules of Tichonius: "The third rule relates to the promises and the law, and may be designated in other terms as relating to the spirit and the letter, which is the name I made use of when writing a book on this subject. It may be also named, of grace and the law. This, however, seems to me to be a great question in itself, rather than a rule to be applied to the solution of other questions. It was the want of clear views on this question that originated, or at least greatly aggravated, the Pelagian heresy. And the efforts of Tichonius to clear up this point were good, but not complete. For, in discussing the question about faith and works, he said that works were given us by God as the reward of faith, but that faith itself was so far our own that it did not come to us from God" (Augustine, *On Christian Doctrine* 3.33, Philip Schaff, ed., *A Select Library of Nicene and Post-Nicene Fathers*, vol. II in *St. Augustine's City of God and Christian Doctrine* [Edinburgh: T. & T. Clark; Grand Rapids: Eerdmans, repr. 1993], 569).

in triumphant procession into the everlasting consummation, confirmed in righteousness. However, as a consequence of his disobedience and the mysterious solidarity of humanity in Adam, the sanctions of the creation covenant were invoked. In contrast to the conditional emphasis of the pre-fall covenant, however, God issues a unilateral promise to overcome the curse through the woman's offspring. This covenant of grace, carried forward by Seth and his descendants, is renewed in the Abrahamic covenant, just as the works principle in the creation covenant is renewed in the Sinai covenant. On the basis of the Messiah's fulfillment of the covenant of works (in fulfillment of his mediatorial role assigned in the covenant of redemption), the people of God are accepted on the terms of the covenant of grace.

While the covenant received considerable attention as a way of framing the economy of salvation, for instance in Irenaeus, it became the identifying motif in Reformed theology. In I. John Hesselink's words, "Reformed theology is covenant theology."[17] This new vocabulary, many thought, was more consistent with Scripture's own speech. Instead of imposing an a priori system on Scripture or deducing a system from a central dogma, covenant theology became an enormously fruitful enterprise and gave Reformed theology theological coherence it has had across its varied ethnic and generational landscape, a coherence that has become increasingly difficult to recognize in some measure because of the remarkable lack of attention and interest given to it even in Reformed seminaries.

Yet working out the implications of covenant theology into every locus remains an unfinished project, which has been somewhat eclipsed in modern theology. My own attempt to contribute to its revival assumes that it is an unfinished project—and will remain so well after these three volumes have come and gone. Mine is not an effort in repristinating: appealing to the sources of federal theology, it nevertheless eschews slavish imitation and repetition. Furthermore, my project does not assume that the federal theologians would have agreed with every development encountered in this work (they had their own significant differences among themselves, after all), nor that the adoption of a covenantal paradigm for theology will necessarily lead at every point to the same conclusions I have adopted. In *Covenant and Eschatology* I laid out the case for viewing covenant as a theological matrix in relation to hermeneutics and theological methods. With this volume, however, I am able finally to suggest in broad strokes what such a scheme might look like.

ESCHATOLOGY

The other motif that I am using as a lens through which to view the various topics of systematic theology is *eschatology*. Long before Jürgen Moltmann suggested

---

17. I. John Hesselink, *On Being Reformed* (Ann Arbor, MI: Servant Books, 1983), 57.

that eschatology be regarded not only as the last section of the system but as the warp and woof throughout, the federal (or covenant) theologians of the sixteenth and seventeenth centuries made this same argument. Eschatology has to do not only with "last things" but with the anticipation of the consummation even in the very beginning of the biblical narrative. Too often, systematic theologies have been content to draw logical connections with insufficient attention to the plot of the divine drama. However, the dramatic analogy is now receiving considerable attention, and this is no doubt due at least in part to a revival of eschatological thinking. In the intersection between history and eschatology, the progress of redemption and the inbreaking of the kingdom, lies the dynamic energy of covenant theology; thus, in the words of Dorothy Sayers, "the dogma is the drama."[18] Eschatology helps to provide the cosmic and redemptive-historical horizon without which our systematic-theological reflection, even with the covenantal lens, easily becomes distorted in the direction of an individualistic, speculative, and ahistorical theology.

So, as I have argued in the introductory volume (*Covenant and Eschatology*), *drama* is the genre best suited to such a project and *analogy* is the appropriate epistemological corollary. Throughout this book, I will work out these assumptions. My goal in this project, stretched over three volumes, is to appeal to Scripture as a script for the divine drama and to take up crucial topics and debates in contemporary theology with covenant and eschatology as hermeneutical guides. Although this project basically follows the logical order of a system (the so-called loci), it is not a systematic or dogmatic theology per se, but a series of contributions to contemporary reflection. Many topics are left unexplored, while others are given considerable attention.

Jean-Luc Marion wisely reminds us, "One must obtain forgiveness for every essay in theology."[19] Who are we, mere mortals—and "prone to wander," to "suppress the truth in unrighteousness"—who are we to speak about God? Yet to remain silent is to refuse to invoke the God who addresses us in command and promise. Theology is thereby committed to a hermeneutical rather than speculative enterprise.

In advance, I beg not only the forgiveness of God for weaknesses in this work but of friends and family who have been incautiously indulgent in giving me time, support, insights, and suggestions along the way. There are many names I could mention, but I will reduce the list to the following. To my colleagues and students at Westminster Seminary in California I owe a tremendous debt for all of the contributions mentioned above; deserving special mention is Ryan Glomsrud, my teaching assistant, who gave valuable input. I am also grateful to Daniel Braden at Westminster John Knox, and especially to Donald McKim, for

18. Dorothy Sayers, *Creed or Chaos* (New York: Harcourt, Brace, 1949), 5.

19. Jean-Luc Marion, *God Without Being: Hors-Texte*, trans. Thomas A. Carlson (Chicago: University of Chicago Press, 1991), 2.

invaluable encouragement and insight. Closer to home, I cannot fail to mention those who have provided opportunity to write before, during, and after the arrival of triplets into my family: Jeff and Carla Meberg, Winona Taylor, Barbara Duguid, Judith Riddell, and especially my father- and mother-in-law, Paul and Linda Bossman. Above all, my deepest gratitude is reserved for my best friend, soul mate, wife, and critic, Lisa, and my two-year-old son James, without whom my ruminations on human nature would lack any depth of personal reflection.

PART ONE
LORD

Chapter One

Meeting a Stranger

A Covenantal Prolegomenon

In his essay "The Two Types of Philosophy of Religion," Paul Tillich contrasts the "ontological" and "cosmological" approaches, which he characterizes as "overcoming estrangement" versus "meeting a stranger."[1] Drawing on Tillich's typology and adding a third alternative: "a stranger we never meet," I will defend "meeting a stranger" with the covenant as its site, as a summary introduction of the paradigm assumed throughout this project.[2]

---

1. Paul Tillich, "The Two Types of Philosophy of Religion," *Theology of Culture* (New York: Oxford University Press, 1959), 10. Merold Westphal's treatment in *Overcoming Onto-Theology: Toward a Postmodern Christian Faith* (New York: Fordham University Press, 2001), 238–55, first brought Tillich's essay to my attention, and I will interact with Westphal's insights below.

2. I concede from the outset that typologies are notoriously reductive, and this chapter is necessarily limited to a number of generalizations that cannot be given sufficient nuance here. Further, the term *ontological* can be understood in its most mundane sense as the study of being or reality, though particularly since Heidegger it has acquired a narrower meaning and today (after Derrida) it is largely associated with Platonism—specifically, with presence as manifestation, sameness over difference, etc. Tillich seems to use it in this narrower sense—at least Heidegger's—but is more approving of its theological usefulness.

3

TWO WAYS OF AVOIDING A STRANGER

Overcoming Estrangement (Hyper-Immanence)

Of course, Tillich does not regard his own (ontological) view as a method of avoiding a stranger. As far as he is concerned, God is not a stranger in the first place. According to Tillich, "In the first way ['overcoming estrangement' or the 'ontological' view] man discovers himself when he discovers God; he discovers something that is identical with himself although it transcends him infinitely, something from which he is estranged, but from which he never has been and never can be separated."[3] Tillich cites an example from Meister Eckhart: "There is between God and the soul neither strangeness nor remoteness, therefore the soul is not only equal with God but it is . . . the same that He is."[4] If we think of God as "'the innermost center of man which is in kinship with the Deepest Reality in the Universe'; . . . if the concept of vision is used again and again, for our knowledge of God, we are in an ontological atmosphere."[5] Tillich's own defense of the "ontological" view repeats familiar oppositions in Platonism and Neoplatonism, in spite of the significant differences between these two systems.[6] In this approach, unity, univocity, and sameness win out over plurality, analogy, and difference.

This ontological way or "overcoming estrangement" persists in the various pantheistic and panentheistic visions of modern theology according to which *we come to ourselves when we come to God.*[7] This approach represents an ontology of emanation and an epistemology of vision. Thus encountering God is nothing like meeting a stranger—a genuine other—but is more like a new awareness of a presence that is always immanent (*visio Dei*) and, at least in its liberal Protestant form, always benevolent, even benign. In Schleiermacher's words, "Turn from everything usually reckoned religion, and fix your regard on the inward emotions and dispositions, as all utterances and acts of inspired men direct."[8] "God never reveals

---

3. Tillich, "Two Types," 10.

4. Ibid., 15, citing Eckhart.

5. Ibid., 21. What then is the ontological principle? It is this: "*Man is immediately aware of something unconditional which is the prius of the separation and interaction of subject and object, theoretically as well as practically.*" Tillich adds, "The ontological approach transcends the discussion between nominalism and realism, if it rejects the concept of the *ens realissimum*, as it must do. Being itself, as present in the ontological awareness, is power of Being but not the most powerful being; it is neither *ens realissimum* nor *ens singularissimum*. It is the power in everything that has power, be it a universal or an individual, a thing or an experience" (25–26).

6. Ibid., 27–28.

7. Hegel has been rehabilitated in various theological programs, particularly in the tendencies toward dialectical historicism that we perceive in the work of Jürgen Moltmann and Robert W. Jenson. However, a more direct appeal to Plato, Eckhart, and the Platonist tradition comes from certain members of the group known by the label "radical orthodoxy," especially John Milbank, Catherine Pickstock, and Graham Ward. For a programmatic statement of this revival of Platonism, see the introduction to *Radical Orthodoxy: A New Theology*, ed. John Milbank, Catherine Pickstock, and Graham Ward (London and New York: Routledge, 1999), 3. That what we are calling the "ontological way" has many mansions is all too evident in this grouping of representatives.

8. Friedrich Schleiermacher, *On Religion: Speeches to Its Cultured Despisers*, trans. John Oman (New York: Harper & Row, 1958), 18.

himself from outside, by intrusion," wrote Teilhard de Chardin, "but from within, by stimulation and enrichment of the human psychic currents."[9] (Avery Dulles observes, "Karl Barth, for his part, dismissed Teilhard as 'a giant Gnostic snake.'")[10] In more banal forms, this approach is also dominant in the various New Age spiritualities and can be regarded as generally characteristic of popular American religion across the denominational and religious landscape.[11] It is no wonder that Feuerbach could conclude that "the religious object of adoration is nothing but the objectified nature of him who adores," so that "God is the manifested inward nature, the expressed self of man."[12] It was in reaction to this trajectory that Barth invoked Kierkegaard's "infinite-qualitative distinction" between God and humanity.[13] We are therefore authorized to speak of God only because of the *Deus dixit*—God has spoken, and has done so ultimately for his glory, not ours. "The very names Kierkegaard, Luther, Calvin, Paul, and Jeremiah suggest what Schleiermacher never possessed, a clear and direct apprehension of the truth that man is made to serve God and not God to serve man."[14] "The only answer that possesses genuine transcendence, and so can solve the riddle of immanence, is God's word—note, *God's* word."[15]

Yet even this word does not render God "haveable," as Dietrich Bonhoeffer observed in criticism of Barth.[16] Recoiling from hyper-immanence, Barth resists identifying God with any creaturely reality.[17] Although Barth regarded the covenant as an important concept, it does not seem to have mitigated his overwhelming concern to guard God's freedom as wholly other.

9. Cited in Avery Dulles, *Models of Revelation* (Garden City, NY: Doubleday, 1985), 99. He also refers to William James's description: "The mystical feeling of enlargement, union and emancipation has no specific content whatever of its own" (cited ibid., 80, from *Varieties of Religious Experience*, 325).

10. Dulles, *Models of Revelation*, 113.

11. See Harold Bloom, *The American Religion: The Emergence of the Post-Christian Nation* (New York: Simon & Schuster, 1993). A self-proclaimed Jewish gnostic, Bloom persuasively argues that American religion is essentially gnostic.

12. Ludwig Feuerbach, *The Essence of Christianity*, ed. and abridged by E. Graham Waring and F. W. Strothmann (New York: Ungar, 1957), 10–11; cf. Sigmund Freud, *The Future of an Illusion*, trans. and ed. James Strachey (New York: Norton, 1961), 21.

13. In the following comments I recognize that Barth's theology matures in the direction of the "humanity of God" (as in *The Humanity of God* [1956]), but the dialectical tension (indeed, dualism) between time and eternity is never completely overcome in the *Church Dogmatics*.

14. Barth, *The Word of God and the Word of Man*, trans. Douglas Horton (repr., New York: Harper & Bros., 1957), 196.

15. Ibid., 199.

16. Dietrich Bonhoeffer, *Act and Being*, trans. Bernard Noble (New York: Harper & Bros., 1961), 90–91.

17. Not even the historical Jesus is as such the revelation of God. See Barth, *CD* I/1:323, 406. For Barth, nature does not seem to have the inherent integrity to receive revelation: all divine-human contact must be the result of an overcoming of natural capacities (*CD* II/1:142–78). In other words, Barth pushed the *non capax* (i.e., the Calvinistic emphasis on divine transcendence) too far. Revelation is a complete and utter novum with no previous analogies. "It comes to us as a datum with no point of connection with any previous datum" (Barth, *CD* I/2:172–73). Although he never took it as far as "the stranger we never meet," the thrust of Barth's doctrine of revelation renders God "wholly other" in a sense that threatens the covenantal bond—and creaturely integrity.

But all of these debates are rather intramural in the light of the postmodern critique of theology of any kind. The suspicion of divine immediacy, "haveability," and presence is far more emphatically worked out in the phenomenology of Martin Heidegger, Emmanuel Levinas, and Jacques Derrida, among others.

A Stranger We Never Meet (Hyper-Transcendence)

To Tillich's two types, overcoming estrangement versus meeting a stranger, I would like to add a third: a stranger we never meet. If hyper-immanence avoids meeting a stranger by denying that he *is* a stranger—a genuine other, different from oneself—hyper-transcendence avoids meeting a stranger by denying access to the other. If the ontological view is given to hyper-immanence, the critical approach embraces a hyper-transcendence in which the reality of God can be neither affirmed nor denied, but can serve only as a placeholder for things like the "universal religion of morality" in contrast to an "ecclesiastical faith" (Kant), or Derrida's equivalent contrast of a "universal messianic structure" over against the actual arrival of any particular messiah.[18] If we cannot find a passable road to God, there must not be one.[19] If univocity fits with "overcoming estrangement" and analogy with "meeting a stranger," then equivocity is the epistemology of choice for postmodern skepticism.

That which Tillich defined and defended as the ontological way is now pejoratively labeled "ontotheology." The term *ontotheology* dates to Martin Heidegger, in his 1936 lectures on Schelling.[20] There, despite the widespread use that is made of his term, Heidegger is interested not in "debunking" religion, but rather in liberating theology from philosophy—specifically, a speculative metaphysics and ontology. The kind of god one gets after Descartes—the metaphysics of being, *causa sui*, and the Infinite—is finally not even a god to whom one can pray

18. The same oppositions of "messianic structure" (universal) to "an actual messiah" (particular) remain as undeconstructed in Derrida as in Kant. See Derrida, *Specters of Marx*, trans. Peggy Kamuf (New York: Routledge, 1994), 167–70.

19. This is where the two approaches converge, at least with some of the representatives of either paradigm. For example, Kant and Schleiermacher or, say, Derrida and Bultmann, share a common anthropocentric presupposition: theological statements reveal something *about* us, rather than something *to* us, but where this leads Kant and Derrida to skepticism with respect to constitutive knowledge of God, Schleiermacher and Bultmann see theological statements as bearing experiential or existential truth. Thus ironically the Kantian tradition could be taken either in the direction of the ontological way (overcoming estrangement) or skepticism (the stranger we never meet), but could never conceive of meeting a stranger on that stranger's own terms. In the history-of-religions school of the nineteenth century, theology is reduced to anthropology, psychology, or, more recently, sociology—just as Feuerbach, Marx, Nietzsche, and Freud had announced. The irony is that it was the theologians who had given flesh to their caricature, as Nietzsche was fond of reminding us. Thus religious language is *equivocal*, grounded in the attempts of specific peoples and groups (ecclesiastical faith) to express the truth of a universal morality (Kant), feeling (Schleiermacher), or sense of Justice (Derrida) that is *univocal*. With Schleiermacher, such language is expressive of religious experience and thus, as Feuerbach and his successors properly concluded, a psychological projection.

20. Laurence Paul Hemming, "Nihilism: Heidegger and the Grounds of Redemption," in *Radical Orthodoxy*, ed. Milbank et al., 95.

or sing.[21] According to Heidegger, at least, Aquinas, Luther, Calvin, Pascal, and Kierkegaard represented resources for overcoming the ontotheological project that seemed to hold theology captive especially in German idealism and its philosophy of the absolute.

For Heidegger, therefore, "'God' as thought in metaphysics is not the God of faith, but a consequence of the way metaphysics thinks transcendence."[22] But "to think God in terms of being is to impose limit and finitude on God."[23] In Zurich in 1951, replying to the question "Need being and God be posited as identical?" Heidegger replies, appealing to Aquinas, "being and God are not identical, and I would never attempt to think the essence of God through being." Heidegger adds, "If I were yet to write a theology—to which I sometimes feel inclined—then the word 'being' would not occur in it."[24]

Derrida, for his part, recognizes that the ontotheology that he particularly has in mind is that of Enlightenment rationalism, where "the determination of absolute presence is constituted as self-presence, as subjectivity."[25] Despite the ambiguity of some of his now taken-for-granted phrases, Derrida asserts, rightly I believe, that all dualisms and monisms ultimately spring from "a metaphysics whose entire history was compelled to strive toward the reduction of the trace" in favor of "full presence." This is why this history of Western thought, including Derrida's, is trapped in a circle of hyper-transcendence and hyper-immanence, I would argue. It is not presence per se that is Derrida's bogeyman, but *violence*, "an onto-theology determining the archeological and eschatological meaning of being *as presence*, as *parousia*, as *life without difference*."[26] Like Kant's categories (including God), however, Derrida's universal messianic structure must be presupposed while proscribing any particular presence of a given messiah in time.[27] Whatever his intentions, therefore, Derrida does not overcome the dualistic habits of Western thought, nor does he return the particular to pride of place.[28]

21. Martin Heidegger, *Identity and Difference*, trans. Joan Stambaugh (New York: Harper & Row, 1969), 72.

22. Hemming, "Nihilism," 96.

23. Ibid.

24. Cited ibid.

25. Jacques Derrida, *Of Grammatology*, trans. Gayatri Chakrovorty Spivak (Baltimore: Johns Hopkins University Press, 1976), 16. For a fascinating conversation between Marion and Derrida on the so-called metaphysics of presence in the Christian Neoplatonic tradition, see the first two chapters of *God, the Gift and Postmodernism*, ed. John D. Caputo and Michael J. Scanlon (Bloomington: Indiana University Press, 1999), 20–78.

26. Derrida, *Of Grammatology*, 71. This presence as parousia is "another name for death, historical metonymy where God's name holds death in check. That is why, if this movement begins its era in the form of Platonism, it ends in infinitist metaphysics. Only infinite being can reduce the difference in presence. In that sense, the name of God, at least as it is pronounced within classical rationalism, is the name of indifference itself."

27. The transcendent "One" beyond being is as essential for Derrida as it was for Plotinus in grounding all positive being. This transcendent "One," inherently indeconstructible, is Derrida's *difference*. See Conor Cunningham on this point in his *Genealogy of Nihilism* (London and New York: Routledge, 2002), 155–265.

28. For further treatment, see Michael Horton, *Covenant and Eschatology: The Divine Drama* (Louisville, KY: Westminster John Knox, 2002), 20–45.

Nevertheless, Merold Westphal sees Derrida as providing at least a useful therapy against "a Neoplatonism that denies the reality of divine alterity," which can lead only to "what I call ontological xenophobia, the fear of meeting a stranger, even if the stranger should be God."[29] In the light of this long-running critique that began, one could say, with Kant himself and culminates in Derrida, Westphal sees Christian faith as "the overcoming of ontological xenophobia." Derrida cites two sermons in which "Eckhart stresses that it is the task of the intellect to apprehend God naked: 'The intellect pulls off the coat from God and perceives him bare, as he is stripped of goodness and of being and of all names.'" (It is no wonder that Luther characterized the theology of glory as an attempt to climb up to heaven to get a glimpse of the "naked God.") Such immediacy is, of course, direct. "But if I am to perceive God without a medium," says Eckhart, "then I must just become him, and he must become me."[30]

Westphal elaborates on Eckhart's comments in the light of Derrida's critique:

> Derrida finds this kind of talk as troubling as did the church authorities. It denies the finitude we experience in what he calls "the structure of the trace": "Language has started without us, in us and before us. This is what theology calls God." There is a necessity in language that beckons "toward the event of an order or of a promise that does not belong to what one currently calls history. . . . Order or promise, this injunction commits (me), in a rigorously asymmetrical manner, even before I have been able to say I, to sign such a provocation in order to reappropriate it for myself and restore the symmetry."[31]

Neoplatonic pantheism allows for no real "otherness," but Westphal is convinced that the Christian doctrine of creation does generate precisely that transcendent space that opens up to genuine otherness: "the finite self is real" even if it is not an emanation of God's being. "Eden is heteronomy from the outset," with the possibility of estrangement (sin).[32]

> Ontological xenophobia is not just the attempt to use linkages of being to defend myself from the anxiety of meeting a stranger; it is the attempt to avoid meeting the kind of stranger whose moral presence is sufficient to undermine the ultimacy of ontological categories as such, the kind of stranger who might lead me to ask, "Is Ontology Fundamental?" and to answer my own question by exploring the possibility of "Ethics as First Philosophy."[33]

Levinas and Derrida recognize the violence against the other that hyperimmanence represents. The problem with their accounts, however, is that they

---

29. Westphal, *Overcoming Onto-Theology,* 238.
30. Ibid., 239–40.
31. Ibid., 241.
32. Ibid. So Augustine is not a Neoplatonist on this point at least: he was "converted" to God, addressed as "you." Such thought "knows that union with God can only have the form of reconciliation, and that reconciliation means the courage to meet one who has become a stranger. If we want to give a name to this faith we could hardly do better than to call it Augustinian" (249).
33. Ibid., 252.

render the other absolutely and wholly other. Suspicious of all presences as the reduction of the other to oneself (Levinas), the actual arrival of any specific God is indefinitely postponed—*a venir* (Derrida).[34] It is the aneschatology of always-deferred presence (Georges Bataille and Mark C. Taylor), a "coming" that never arrives, the ontology of the stranger we never meet.[35]

MEETING A STRANGER

What if Kant and his postmodern successors are right, as I think they are, in telling us that there is no safe path *to* God? But what if instead there is a path *from* God to us, such as the famous Emmaus road, and instead of our finding God he has caught up with us, even when we did not recognize him? In the wake of Kant's critique, those who have not taken Hegel's triumphalistic route have in fact been much like those despondent disciples: "They stood still, looking sad," as the stranger inserted himself into their conversation about the arrival that never came. "Then one of them, whose name was Cleopas, answered him, 'Are you the only stranger in Jerusalem who does not know the things that have taken place there in these days?'" (Luke 24:17–18). For them, the empty tomb was not a sign of presence but of sheer absence, without a trace.

> Then [Jesus] said to them, "Oh, how foolish you are, and how slow of heart to believe all that the prophets have declared! Was it not necessary that the Messiah should suffer these things and then enter into his glory?" Then beginning with Moses and all the prophets, he interpreted to them the things about himself in all the scriptures. (Luke 24:25–27)

Finally, when he celebrated the Supper with them, they and the rest of the disciples recognized Jesus as their risen Lord (vv. 28–35).[36] In word and sacrament they had met a Stranger.

If hyper-transcendence introduces an unbiblical *dualism* (i.e., antitheses) between the Creator and creature, eternity and time, heaven and earth, hyper-immanence collapses all *dualities* (i.e., difference) in a monistic scheme. If the paradigm of "overcoming estrangement" represents an ontology of emanation and an epistemology of vision, "meeting a stranger" articulates an ontology of genuine difference and an epistemology of the external Word, both grounded in a theology of the covenant.

---

34. See n. 13 above.

35. Mark C. Taylor, *Erring: A Postmodern A/Theology* (Chicago: University of Chicago Press, 1984).

36. Marion appeals to this second part of the Luke 24 narrative as evidence that the Eucharist is the site of revelation (*God Without Being*, 150–52). However, the Emmaus road encounter is hardly a mere prologue to revelation. It was in Christ's opening of the Scriptures and explaining them as referring to himself that the dejected disciples could respond, "Were not our hearts burning within us while he was talking to us on the road, while he was opening the scriptures to us?" (Luke 24:32).

A Covenantal Ontology

Rejection of the "ontological way" does not mean that we lack an ontology. But it is to say that recognizing a stranger, especially if that stranger should be God, is an *ethical* enterprise. We do not usually think this way, at least in the West, because we have been taught to separate epistemology from ethics, *theoria* from praxis, giving the former its own autonomous foundation. The ethical steward-ship of knowledge—the accountability for what we hear—is directly stated by Jesus in the Emmaus passage: "Oh, how foolish you are, and how slow of heart to believe all that the prophets have declared!" (v. 25). If we begin not with the metaphysics of being but with YHWH of the covenant, we ineluctably find our-selves in the world thus described as meeting a stranger.

Reflecting this suspicion of the ontological way as defined by Tillich, then, Reformation theology has always been wary of even discussing the "being" of God. It is not a "what" that we worship, but a "who"—an agent, not an essence. That is not to deny God's essence, but to recognize that this is hidden from us. Speculation yields a "what," but the biblical drama renders a "who."[37]

So, for example, concerning Calvin, B. B. Warfield noted, "He is refusing all *a priori* methods of determining the nature of God and requiring of us to form our knowledge of him a posteriori from the revelation He gives us of Himself in His activities."[38] In the *Institutes*, after a mere paragraph on the exegetical support for God's spirituality and immensity, Calvin moves hurriedly on to the Trinity.[39] "The essence of God is rather to be adored than inquired into."[40] Calvin goes so far as to assert, "They are mad who seek to discover what God is."[41] At least this far Calvin would sympathize with Heidegger's remark above, "If I were to write a theology . . . then the word 'being' would not occur in it." Early Reformed writ-ers such as Musculus repeated this approach, explicitly launching their discussion of God with the question of who God is rather than what God is.[42]

The notion of God as "supreme being" (*summum ens*) is suspended upon an ontology common in most essentials to Platonism according to which, as Gerald Bray notes, "only God has being (*ousia*)," and "everything else is a corrupt or illu-sory emanation from the 'one which is.'"[43] The scale-of-being ontology not only

---

37. Louis Berkhof, *Systematic Theology* (Grand Rapids: Eerdmans, 1941), 41: "The Bible never operates with an abstract concept of God, but always describes Him as the Living God, who enters into various relations with His creatures, relations which are indicative of several different attributes."

38. B. B. Warfield, *Calvin and Augustine*, ed. Samuel Craig (Philadelphia: Presbyterian & Reformed, 1956), 153. See further his excellent summary of this reticence in Calvin and the tradi-tion generally to explore the "whatness," pp. 139–40.

39. Calvin, *Institutes* 1.13.1.

40. Calvin, *Institutes* 1.2.2.

41. Calvin on Rom. 1:19.

42. Richard Muller, *Post-Reformation Reformed Dogmatics*, vol. 3: *The Divine Essence and Attrib-utes* (Grand Rapids: Baker, 2003), 228.

43. Gerald Bray, *The Doctrine of God* (Downers Grove, IL: InterVarsity Press, 1993), 55. Of course, simply appealing to such terms does not require prior commitment to a univocity of being, but such univocity is the native soil of the concept.

confuses the creature with the Creator (any distinction being merely quantitative); it simultaneously downgrades creation as a falling away from being in its very essence. In Scripture, however, God is not revealed as the "supreme being," but as the Creator who freely wills that which is not-God nevertheless to be related to God in all of its difference. As Kathryn Tanner reminds us, aside from the incarnation, God communicates his goods, not his being, to creatures.[44]

The covenant is the place where a stranger meets us. It is an ethical clearing that opens before us, not a preoccupation with "being" or "existence" as if we knew what it was like for God to "be."[45] Therefore, Reformed theology recognizes some of its own polemics in the postmodern criticism of modernity, yet without falling into the opposite reductionisms of an equivocal metaphysics of absence, sheer difference, and endless deferral.

Covenantal Rather than Ontological Union

Basic to my account is the sharpest possible contrast between ex nihilo creation and emanation.[46] Brevard Childs recounts that Gerhard von Rad concluded that far from relying on the ancient Near Eastern mythologies, "Israel's world-view performed a major function in drawing a sharp line of division between God and the world, and by purging the material world of both elements of the divine and the demonic. There were no avenues of direct access to the mystery of the creator emanating from the world, certainly not by means of the image, but Yahweh was present in his living word in acts of history."[47] Pagan myth allowed only two ontological options: the divine and the demonic, while biblical faith introduced the notion of a creation that is neither divine nor demonic but is affirmed in all of its difference, finitude, and materiality. The secular was good without being God. Thus while Buddhism, Platonism, and much of modern theology down to our own time locate good and evil in ontic structures, Scripture relocates that discussion to an ethical-historical site of a broken

---

44. Kathryn Tanner, *Jesus, Humanity and the Trinity: A Brief Systematic Theology* (Minneapolis: Fortress, 2001), 44.

45. In contemporary theology there are, of course, rather vague and sweeping denunciations of rival positions as "metaphysical," and I do not have the space here to treat these. In terms of defining what is meant by the so-called metaphysics of substance, William P. Alston has provided an excellent summary in "Substance and the Trinity," in *The Trinity*, ed. Gerald O'Collins et al. (Oxford: Oxford University Press, 1999), 179–201.

46. More popular in our day is panentheism, an attempt to incorporate elements of both pantheism and theism. While denying that all of reality is divine, panentheism maintains the interdependence of God and world.

47. Brevard S. Childs, *Biblical Theology of the Old and New Testaments: Theological Reflection on the Christian Bible* (Minneapolis: Fortress, 1993), 386, referring to Gerhard von Rad's essay, "Some Aspects of the Old Testament World-View," in *The Problem of the Hexateuch and Other Essays*, trans. E. W. Trueman Dicken (New York: McGraw-Hill, 1966), 144–65. In his landmark *History of Israel*, John Bright observed, "We must once again make it clear that Israel's faith did not center in an idea of God. Nevertheless, her conception of God was from the beginning so remarkable, and so without parallel in the ancient world" (John Bright, *A History of Israel*, 3rd ed. [Philadelphia: Westminster Press, 1981], 157).

covenant.[48] The cosmos is not shot through with divinity, but that does not make the cosmos evil. Finitude does not imply fault. Again Westphal is helpful in making this point:

> Henceforth, to Tillich's chagrin, religion can only have the form of meeting a stranger. . . . No doubt that is why Kierkegaard's Anti-Climacus describes "as pantheistic any definition of sin that [makes] it out to be something merely negative—weakness, sensuousness, finitude, ignorance, etc." As long as theology has only the categories of cause and effect or infinite and finite to work with, it is vulnerable to the loss of divine alterity that pantheism represents.
>   On the other hand, when the creation and fall motifs are united, the mild otherness of the former is preserved in the wild otherness of the latter.[49]

The basis for creation is not conflict (as in ancient Mesopotamian and Canaanite creation myths, as well as in Manicheism, Hobbes, Hegel, and Marx), but "covenant love," as Colin Gunton notes, and this also generates a different ethic.[50] This paradigm affirms genuine difference without succumbing either to antitheses or monism.

If the fall acutely reminds us of God's relation to us as a *stranger*, the covenant is the site where strangers *meet*. Whether in secular treaties or those associated with the biblical traditions, a covenant is "a union based on an oath" (McCarthy) or "a relationship under sanctions" (Kline).[51] Under this broad definition existed a variety of treaty forms, some of them promissory while others were strictly law covenants. One implication of a covenantal approach is that divine "presence" and "absence" are ethical and relational rather than ontological categories. "Presence" (or nearness) is synonymous with salvation and divine favor—righteousness ($\dot{s}\check{e}d\bar{a}q\hat{a}$), sabbath peace (shalom), while "absence" names the judicial curse for covenant breaking (Lo-ammi, "not my people"). We know this form of presence and absence in our own covenantal experience with marriage. Sometimes even when the spouse is physically present, he or she may be said to "not really be *there*" in the relationship. Desertion happens in the heart. It is this ethical or covenantal form of presence and absence that Scripture employs. Although, onto-

---

48. Bright, *History*, 161. The paganism of Israel's ancient neighbors exhibits a mythological cosmology which, as Bright explains, "reflected the rhythmic yet unchanging pattern of nature upon which the life of earthly society depended." Thus the cosmos is enchanted, with divinity shot through it in every part. While pagan myths were ritually reenacted in order to renew the cosmic forces, "In Israel's faith nature, though not thought of as lifeless, was robbed of personality and 'demythed.' Yahweh's power was not, in fact, primarily associated with the repeatable events of nature, but with unrepeatable historical events."

49. Westphal, *Overcoming Onto-Theology*, 246.

50. Colin Gunton, *The Triune Creator: A Historical and Systematic Study* (Grand Rapids: Eerdmans, 1998), 26. It is worth adding that both Hegel and Marx demonstrate how easily "otherness" is affirmed only on the way to sublation—i.e., the higher synthesis.

51. M. G. Kline defines a covenant as "a relationship under sanctions" (*By Oath Consigned: A Reinterpretation of the Covenant Signs of Circumcision and Baptism* [Grand Rapids: Eerdmans, 1968, 16]); cf. Dennis J. McCarthy, *Treaty and Covenant*, Analecta biblica 21 (Rome: Pontifical Biblical Institute Press, 1963), 96.

logically speaking, God is omnipresent, the real question is this: Where is God there *for us*? It is a question of security, given our knowledge of ourselves as rebels against the God who calls out, "Adam, where are you?" It is no wonder that the marital analogy figures so prominently in the biblical drama. The two become "one flesh" not in any kind of ontological synthesis, reducing the other to oneself (or vice versa), but in covenant. The sort of union that a covenantal approach entails corresponds to the analogies of marriage and adoption, in which the two becoming "one flesh" or the child being made an heir is constituted by both legal and organic solidarity, while retaining their otherness.

Divine Descent over Human Ascent

This is a retrieval especially of the doctrine of analogy as the form of the Creator-creature relationship, which is ontologically realized in the incarnation. As J. K. A. Smith argues, "the incarnational paradigm operates on the basis of an affirmation of finitude, materiality, and embodiment. In this sense, I take it to be the very antithesis of the versions of 'Platonism' which have dominated philosophy of language from the *Phaedrus* to the *Logical Investigations*."[52] But if the ontological approach, especially at its radical quasi-gnostic fringes, announces an escape from finitude, materiality, and embodiment through absorption into the "whole" (however defined), antithetical accounts are too suspicious even of any *likeness* or analogy between Creator and creature. What I am calling here a covenantal account or, in Smith's coinage, "the incarnational paradigm," is essentially analogical rather than embracing either the univocity or the equivocity of being. Indeed, humankind was created to be, in its parts and as a whole, the paradigmatic analogy of God. The prime example of this in Scripture is the familiar pattern of divine summons, "Where are you?" and the servant's reply, "Here I am."

"To think," says Levinas in agreement with Heidegger, "is no longer to contemplate but to commit oneself, to be engulfed by that which one thinks, to be involved. This is the dramatic event of being-in-the-world."[53] Thus far Heidegger's phenomenology shows great promise, according to Levinas. But in counseling us to go beyond the particular being (i.e., the other who calls) to the "horizon of being," Heidegger "rejoins the tradition of Western philosophy" rooted in Plato.

> We respond: in our relation with the other (*autrui*) is it a matter of letting be? Is not the independence of the other (*autrui*) accomplished in the role of being summoned? Is the one to whom one speaks understood from the first in his being? Not at all. The other (*autrui*) is not an object of comprehension first and an interlocutor second. The two relations are intertwined. In other words, the comprehension of the other (*autrui*) is inseparable from his invocation. . . . I do not only think that he is, I speak to him. He is my

52. Smith, *Speech and Theology: Language and the Logic of Incarnation* (London and New York: Routledge, 2002), 156.
53. Levinas, "Is Ontology Fundamental?" in *Emmanuel Levinas: Basic Philosophical Writings*, ed. A. T. Peperzak et al. (Bloomington: Indiana University Press, 1996), 4.

partner in the heart of a relation which ought only have made him present to me. I have spoken to him, that is to say, I have neglected the universal being that he incarnates in order to remain with the particular being that he is.[54]

Instead of aiming at an object, says Levinas, *prayer*—the proper mode of discourse par excellence—is "the tie with a person" expressed in the vocative.[55]

Instead of comprehending, possessing, dominating the other through vision, we invoke the other and are summoned by the other through voice. Rather than a universal horizon, there is a particular depth in the face/voice of the other.[56] To be a self is to be responsible.[57] Thus Levinas seeks to transcend ontology by shifting thought to the ethical plane. At the same time, Levinas lacks an incarnational perspective that would allow him to identify the revelation of the Other with someone or something to which he had access. In this respect, Levinas only deepens Kant's strictures against the knowability of noumena—reflecting what I have designated the paradigm of "the stranger we never meet."

By contrast, Smith rightly argues that our finitude, materiality, and embodiment, far from being obstacles to revelation, are the very conditions of its possibility. In Levinas, the radical alterity of the other does not permit access. In Jean-Luc Marion "'religious phenomenon' (as the 'saturated phenomenon') displaces and overwhelms those conditions," notes James K. A. Smith.[58] But in that case, how could there ever be a possibility of anyone receiving revelation?

> In other words, if the Wholly Other were *wholly* "Wholly Other," how would we know it even "exists"? How could any discourse concerning the Wholly Other—even about its being "beyond being"—ever be generated? And more importantly, how could any *relation* with the Wholly Other be possible, apart from its appearing *in some manner?*

Both Levinas and Marion insist on the importance of such a relation (ethical responsibility, etc.), but there can be no relation.[59] "This is where I would locate my critique of Levinas and Marion: any 'revelation' can only be received, and must be received, insofar as the recipient possesses the *condition* for its reception—otherwise, it will remain unknown."[60] The great questions that occupy theology can finally be settled only in the sphere of history and ethical action rather than metaphysics and ontological participation.

In a deeply incarnational approach, as Smith notes, "new truth comes from the outside to us as a gift."[61] "As Kierkegaard argues, such an 'equality' could only be made possible by a descent by God, and more particularly, by an incarnational

---

54. Ibid.; cf. 6–7.
55. Ibid., 8.
56. Ibid., 10.
57. Levinas, "Transcendence and Height," in ibid., 17.
58. Smith, 157.
59. Ibid., 158.
60. Ibid., 159.
61. Ibid., 161.

appearance in which God will 'show up' in terms that the finite knower can understand."[62] Thus, says Smith, "analogy is an incarnational account of knowledge. . . . Thus we are not surprised to see Derrida emphasize that 'language never escapes analogy . . . , it is indeed analogy through and through.' On my accounting, that is to conclude that language is incarnational through and through, that it never escapes incarnation as its paradigm and condition of possibility."[63] Even Aquinas spoke of our contact with God as "a matter of 'raising up' the human intellect to the level of the divine, rather than a movement of descent from the divine (ad3)."[64] Aquinas himself must be transcended, says Smith, arguing along similar lines to the Reformation traditions. God accommodates his revelation to our capacity, without surrendering his transcendence in the process.[65] While "correlational" theologies (Tillich, Rahner, McFague) threaten to reduce revelation to "cultural manifestation," theologians such as Barth and von Balthasar "ignore the historical conditions of finitude which are the condition of possibility for the reception of a revelation. An incarnational account does justice to both of these poles."[66]

Having emphasized the downward descent, I should also insert a brief mention of eschatology. A theology of the cross (divine condescension) is inert unless dialectically related to a theology of the resurrection and ascension. This is also to reintegrate christology and pneumatology. For instance, in Paul's teaching, not only has God become flesh; in so doing, and by living, dying, rising, and ascending, he, by his Spirit, has "raised us up with him and seated us with him in the heavenly places" (Eph. 2:6). Paul is not inviting them in such expressions to climb by sure-footed contemplation from weak physical and historical appearances to the beatific vision of "the One." It is not the overcoming of ontological estrangement, a new awareness of what has always been the case. Rather, says the

---

62. Ibid., 162.

63. Ibid., 164.

64. Ibid., 165.

65. Ibid., 166: "Thus the God whom no one had seen, nor could see, at any time (John 1:18) was 'beheld' (*etheasametha*) in that moment that 'the word became flesh and pitched his tent among us' (John 1:14). Thus the analogical principle whereby the difference is known by means of the same is also a fundamental incarnational principle, where the Infinite is known by means of a finite appearance, without losing its infinitude—'neither slipping away nor betraying itself.' . . . It will not be, as Marion suggests, a matter of displacing or overcoming these conditions, but rather understanding the possibility of the Transcendent condescending to such conditions without thereby undoing its transcendence."

66. Ibid. Cf. 168, 176. The debate between Barth and Brunner over general revelation reflects these very tensions. Barth's analogy with the virgin birth reveals no capacity. It creates a capacity ex nihilo. Yet, counters Smith, 167–68, 176: "Does it not begin with a created womb? In other words, is not Mary's (albeit virgin) womb nevertheless a condition for the birth of the Savior? . . . In emphasizing that Mary was utterly unable to conceive this child apart from the creative agency of God, Barth seems to confuse 'capacity' with a 'tendency' or 'predisposition.' . . . The logic of incarnation, in contrast to the mere logic of participation, moves by condescension rather than by ascension, and is rooted in a more fundamental affirmation of embodiment as an original and eternal good, rather than a remedial 'instrument' of salvation whose *telos* is disembodiment. Thus the logic of incarnation is a logic of *dona*tion, a logic of giving. . . . In short, it is because of the Incarnation that we avoid not speaking."

apostle to the gentiles, his readers were in times past "aliens from the common-wealth of Israel, and strangers to the covenants of promise, having no hope and without God in the world." But the solution is as ethically and historically embed-ded as the problem: "But now in Christ Jesus you who once were far off have been brought near by the blood of Christ." In his broken body is created "one new humanity in place of the two, thus making peace . . . through the cross" (vv. 13–16).

A Covenantal Epistemology

Neither modern accounts (by turns Kantian or Hegelian—or both at once) nor postmodern extensions of Kantian criticism can serve as reliable alternatives to a covenantal epistemology. Like Derrida, we Reformed theologians are suspicious of idols; but unlike Derrida, we recognize its summoning Shepherd and welcome his arrival. We share postmodernism's critique of the Promethean pretensions of the modern self to absolute (archetypal) knowledge, but find in the fact of reve-lation the basis for finite, creaturely (ectypal) knowledge.

Archetypal-Ectypal Theology

If anything, the Reformers went beyond Aquinas in their criticisms of the god of the philosophers. The attributes of God are set forth in Scripture, writes Calvin. "Thereupon his powers are mentioned, by which he is shown to us not as he is in himself, but as he is toward us: so that this recognition of him consists more in living experience than in vain and high-flown speculation."[67] Revealed knowl-edge is not mere "opinion," as in Plato's shadowy and imperfect realm of appear-ances, since phenomena are creations rather than emanations of God. God cannot be directly known by our climbing the scale of being, but can only be known in and through the Mediator. Calvin explained, in terms reminiscent of Heidegger's above:

> When faith is discussed in the schools, they call God simply the object of faith, and by fleeting speculations, as we have elsewhere stated, lead miser-able souls astray rather than direct them to a definite goal. For since "God dwells in inaccessible light" (1 Tim. 6:16), Christ must become our inter-mediary. . . . Indeed, it is true that faith looks to one God. But this must also be added, "to know Jesus Christ whom he has sent" (Jn. 17:3).[68]

In a very important passage Reformed scholastic Francis Turretin expands on this counsel, even taking Aquinas and the medieval scholastics to task:

> But when God is set forth as the object of theology, he is not to be regarded simply as God in himself (for thus he is incomprehensible [*akataleptos*] to us), but as revealed and as he has been pleased to manifest himself to us in his word, so that divine revelation is the formal relation which comes to be

67. Calvin, *Institutes* 1.10.2.
68. Calvin, *Institutes*, 3.2.1.

considered in this object. Nor is he to be considered exclusively under the relation of deity (according to the opinion of Thomas Aquinas and many Scholastics after him, for in this manner the knowledge of him could not be saving but deadly to sinners), but as he is our God (i.e., covenanted in Christ as he has revealed himself to us in his word not only as the object of knowledge, but also of worship). . . . Thus although theology treats of the same things with metaphysics, physics and ethics, yet the mode of considering is far different. It treats of God not like metaphysics as a being or as he can be known from the light of nature, but as the Creator and Redeemer made known by revelation. It treats of creatures not as things of nature, but of God (i.e., as holding a relation and order to God as their Creator, Preserver and Redeemer) and that too according to the revelation made by him. This mode of considering, the other sciences either do not know or do not assume.[69]

This distinction between archetypal and ectypal knowledge is the epistemological corollary of the Creator-creature distinction. Hearing the following comments this side of Descartes' "clear and distinct ideas," I find the following statement from Wolfgang Musculus (1497–1563) particularly interesting: Even the advanced believer does not attain a "plain and perfect" knowledge of "those things which concern the Majesty of God, which is so clothed and covered with inaccessible brightness, that the finest part of our mind or understanding can by no means comprehend it . . . So we stand in a profound predicament—with the most mighty and unsearchable Majesty of God on the one side, and the necessity of our salvation on the other."[70] (Derrida has correctly perceived that a discourse on religion cannot be dissociated from a discourse on salvation.)[71] The "predicament" that Musculus refers to is irreducibly ethical and soteriological, not ontological or epistemological. It is all about meeting or avoiding a stranger. These theologians not only spoke of a distinction between "our theology" (*theologia nostra*) and God's, but even distinguished eschatologically between our theology as pilgrims in the state of grace from our knowledge of God in the state of glory.

69. Turretin, *Institutes of Elenctic Theology*, vol. 1, ed. James T. Dennison Jr., trans. George Musgrave Giger (Phillipsburg, NJ: P&R, 1992), 16–17. The Reformed scholastics have been victims of the rumor that they transformed the Reformers' project by returning to the very "scholasticism" that the Reformation attacked. Not only does this fail to appreciate that similar methods and forms of presentation do not necessarily imply an identity of content. It is also anachronistic. For example, Robert C. Greer, in *Mapping Postmodernism* (Downers Grove, IL: InterVarsity Press, 2003), 34, writes, "Roughly coinciding with the advent of early Enlightenment thought, an emerging Protestant scholasticism made use of the Cartesian *Cogito* in this systematization of Reformation thought. With a sense of irony, this introduction of Enlightenment thought to the Protestant tradition reintroduced back into the church a method (the *via moderna*) that Luther had strenuously argued against. Protestant scholasticism affected the church in a number of ways, the most basic being the division of theological liberalism from conservatism." However, Protestant scholasticism actually began with the likes of Melanchthon and Calvin, and was already in decline well before Descartes's *Meditations* had begun to make a wide impact. Representing Reformed scholastics as rationalists and forerunners of the Enlightenment is a powerful geneological narrative, but without any foundation in the primary sources.

70. Cited in Richard Muller, *Post-Reformation Reformed Dogmatics*, vol. 1: *Prolegomena to Theology* (Grand Rapids: Baker, 1987), 179.

71. Jacques Derrida, "Faith and Knowledge," in *Religion*, ed. Jacques Derrida and Gianni Vattimo (Stanford, CA: Stanford University Press, 1998), 2.

The parallels between these classical epistemological distinctions of premodern Protestant systems and, for instance, the following claim of Michel de Certeau should become obvious: "Seeing is devouring"—a "white eschatology" that is blinding vision. "There are no more words if no absence founds the waiting that they articulate."[72] It is not in the intellectual logos of the self that rises to beatific vision but in the incarnate Logos who descends that the divine and human meet, and this even itself is founded on a covenant in which speech (command and promise) both marks absence and mediates presence. Even as incarnate, he remains the Word, not the Vision. He is received through the ear rather than the eye. God is a stranger indeed, but one who has met us in covenantal history. This covenant history is not simply a phenomenon of the past, but is the present location of all who have "called on the name of the Lord," which leads us to our second implication of a covenantal epistemology: *invocation*.

Invocation: Calling on the Name

God has given us his name as a pledge of his covenant faithfulness throughout all generations. "But how are they to call on one in whom they have not believed? And how are they to believe in one of whom they have never heard?" (Rom. 10:14). Faith, the habitus calibrated to our state of pilgrimage, comes by hearing, while idolatry, the result of demanding immediate presence and full vision before its time, comes by seeing (Heb. 11:1; Rom. 8:18–25). Faith rests in its object, while vision is given to restless devouring of its object until all transcendence is lost.

Still, even if faith or invocation does not devour its object, there must be content to it. As Derrida notices, even prayer assumes that there must be something that one knows about the one invoked.[73] Thus revelation cannot simply be an encounter; it must tell us something about the one encountered. It cannot be reduced to propositional content, but it also cannot be devoid of it. Theology serves the function of articulating the identity of this God so that he may be properly invoked.

I alluded earlier to Levinas's appeal to the category of invocation. This is especially interesting in the light of the familiar topic in classic prolegomena that answers the question as to what kind of knowledge theology claims to be among Aristotle's list of various types (knowledge, wisdom, prudence, technique, art). One habitus that Aristotle did not list, however, is the one that I regard as most appropriate though by no means exhaustive for theology: *invocatio*. Theology exists for this very purpose: so that believers may faithfully appeal to the God who has revealed himself and his redemptive purposes, so that he may be invoked in

---

72. Michel de Certeau, "White Ecstasy," in *The Postmodern God: A Theological Reader*, ed. Graham Ward (Oxford: Blackwell, 1997), 157.

73. See Smith's development of this point in Derrida and Levinas, *Speech and Theology*, 132–33.

trouble and praised in gratitude. This is not the "objective" knowledge possessed by detached spectators, but the personal knowledge in which we ourselves are involved in an unfolding plot, cast either as "strangers and aliens" or as "children of promise." The importance of theology lies in getting God's name right not in order simply to have the right metaphysics, much less to harness God (or rather, our projection of God) for our purposes, but in order to *call* on the actual God who is there and has made himself there for us. Invocation, as Levinas has reminded us, is the most appropriate epistemological corollary to an ontology of otherness; but with the incarnation as the ground of the covenant in which invocation takes place, God is "haveable" in a way that Levinas does not recognize.

In the context of the covenant or treaty pattern, "calling on the name" of the great king (suzerain) had to do with invocation for liberation from an invading army. Early in the story, the lines of Cain and Seth are contrasted, the latter distinguished by the announcement, "At that time people began to invoke the name of the LORD" (Gen. 4:26). This is not an act of generic piety, but a recognition early on that YHWH had revealed himself sufficiently even at this stage in redemptive history to be called upon as the suzerain in time of threat. Those who deny YHWH are foolish: "Have they no knowledge, those evildoers, who eat up my people as they eat bread, and do not call upon God?" (Ps. 53:4). The people of God's inheritance are distinguished by the fact that they call upon the name of YHWH and thereby own him as their only sovereign because of his antecedent liberation of them (Ps. 80:18; 105:1; 145:18). A recurring sign of Israel's own apostasy is that "There is no one who calls on your name, or attempts to take hold of you" (Isa. 64:7). The liberation in the last days will therefore involve a renewed invocation: "Then everyone who calls on the name of the LORD shall be saved" (Joel 2:32). Paul appeals to Joel 2:32 in Romans 10: "For, 'Everyone who calls on the name of the Lord shall be saved.' But how are they to call on one in whom they have not believed? And how are they to believe in one of whom they have never heard?" (vv. 13–14). This knowledge of God clearly comes from God, mediated through creaturely agency. Thus it is not good advice, techniques, experiences, or propositions, but good news.

The covenant people are summoned to their God's command and promise. At the heart of the theological way of knowing, then, is the hearing of an announcement so that hearers may call upon the name of the Lord. So when God reveals his name to Moses we read, "YHWH *descended* . . . and *proclaimed* the name" (Exod. 34:5). Again, the theology of divine descent corresponds to a Word proclaimed, while a theology of human ascent corresponds to a vision of one's own making (idols). The content of that revelation is that YHWH is "a God merciful and gracious" (v. 6). This was essential because "presence" by itself communicates very little in this situation. For one thing, God's presence in a given situation could be regarded as fairly trivial, since God is said to be omnipresent. Further, God's presence is not infrequently treated in Scripture as a danger as much as a blessing (Gen. 3:8; Exod. 19:21–25; 18–21; 32:9–14; Lev. 10:1–3; Isa. 6:1–5; Amos

5:18–19; Luke 8:25; Rev. 20:11). Given our ethical situation before God and the ethical connotation of God's presence in Scripture, immanence is not by itself a piece of good news. So the real question, given our ethical stance before this God, is where one can find God's *gracious* presence. The covenant of grace is the place and the Son is the mediator of this saving encounter.

THINKING IMMANENCE WITHOUT LOSING TRANSCENDENCE

The critique of ontotheology, inasmuch as it targets the god of metaphysics, together with the metaphysics of presence, is no more of a threat to Christian theology than the theologies of glory they critique that have dominated the horizon of so many modern theologies across the entire spectrum. But Levinas's search for "a thinking which does not bring transcendence back to immanence," which even he calls "an impossible demand," is fulfilled, as Smith has argued so cogently, in an incarnational phenomenology.[74]

Modernity has assured us that we are in the consummation, knowing good and evil without any ethical obligation except to be true to oneself. It is the autonomous voice or vision within, not the *verbum externum*, that we are told to heed. It is not surprising, then, that a theologian of glory like Hegel would find the faith of Israel so mundane. Vincenzo Vitiello notes, "Hegel recalls the disappointment of Pompey, who 'had approached the heart of the temple, the center of adoration, and had hoped to discover in it the root of the national spirit . . . the life-giving soul of this remarkable people . . . [only] to find himself in an empty room."[75] After generations have thought we were in the promised land of pure presence, postmodern thought has reminded us quite truly that "under the sun," we are in the desert—in Derrida's development of the concept, the *chorah*, desert of deserts.[76] Even more dogmatically in Mark C. Taylor's postmodern a/theology, the metaphor of pilgrimage is still too full of presence. In truth, says Taylor, our existence is "endless straying," "erring," and "wandering."[77] Biblical faith does not hesitate to affirm this as the form of life in this present evil age that refuses to meet a Stranger, but it treats this as an ethical rather than metaphysical problem. The pointless existence that Taylor celebrates is precisely this "empty way of life" passed down to us by our pagan ancestors from which Peter tells us we have been liberated. We may be in the desert, "exiles and sojourners" in this age (1 Pet. 1:18),

---

74. Levinas, *Basic Philosophical Writings*, 155.

75. Vincenzo Vitiello, "Desert, Ethos, Abandonment: Towards a Topology of the Religious," in *Religion*, ed. Derrida and Vattimo, 141.

76. Derrida, "Faith and Knowledge," 19–22.

77. Taylor, *Erring*, 157. This sentiment is hardly new, however, but is a constant refrain in romanticism, as in Flaubert's statement that "No great genius has come to final conclusion, . . . because humanity itself is forever on the march and can arrive at no goal" (cited by Roger Lundin, *The Culture of Interpretation* [Grand Rapids: Eerdmans, 1993], 39).

but Egypt is behind us even more fully than it was for the Israelites in the wilderness. The tomb is empty. We are not in an empty room, but seated with Christ in the Holy of Holies. It is not a time for either the beatific vision or the funeral dirge, but for the songs of Zion as we make our way to the City of God, for the Stranger of the Emmaus road and the upper room still meets us, to bring us into his Sabbath joy by his Spirit through Word and sacrament. Even if we are still in the desert rather than the promised land, it is not a desert of deserts. A theology of pilgrims will have to suffice—and does suffice, for meeting a Stranger.

Chapter Two

Strong Verbs

A God with Character

The triune God is known in his works, not in his essence. This crucial presupposition motivated the older Reformed systems to substitute a discourse on God's names for a lengthy opening chapter on God's being. So Calvin, for example: "Many take the name of God simply for God himself; but . . . I think something more is expressed by this term. As God's essence is hidden and incomprehensible, his name just means his character, so far as he has been pleased to make it known to us."[1] And because God's names and works are disclosed in the context of an unfolding narrative, the *who* of revelation had priority over the *what*. Additionally, it is perhaps useful to appeal to Walter Brueggemann's suggestion that we identify God within the rubric of testimony, particularly as outlined by Paul Ricoeur. According to Brueggemann, this narrative identity emerges grammatically, through strong verbs, which give rise to adjectives and finally to the relative stability of nouns.[2] I would add only adverbs to this scheme. For example, God judges and saves (the verbs), and does so impartially and mercifully (the adverbs),

---

1. Calvin, *Commentary on the Psalter*, 9:10, in *Calvini Opera*.
2. Walter Brueggemann, *Theology of the Old Testament: Testimony, Dispute, Advocacy* (Minneapolis: Fortress, 1997), 145–266.

so that eventually many of these actions and descriptions generate what we can legitimately construe as attributes (adjectives): a just, loving, merciful, omnipotent, omniscient, gracious God. The names, then, function as the nouns yielded by the strong verbs. Furthermore, these descriptions thus grounded in past action are tested in the present and future of Israel's history with its God, as testimony for and against YHWH arises. YHWH and Israel are both "on trial" in the covenantal drama. And because speech is itself an act, we no longer are forced to choose between "word-revelation" and "act-revelation." Among God's revelatory acts are his commands, promises, warnings, assurances, and so forth.

Once again, my purpose is not to offer a thorough treatment of the usual themes in theology proper, but to focus the covenantal model on some of the current debates. This is particularly important to observe here since I am treating a covenantal approach to the Trinity in a separate work.[3]

What does it mean to announce the triune God as the covenant *Lord?* Does this Lord-and-Servant structure simply reify once more oppressive hierarchies? Further, can the covenantal motif provide fresh insight into not only God's lordship but also relatedness? Not only in God's so-called moral or communicable but even in the incommunicable perfections, we are able to affirm, as Barth expresses it, both God's freedom *from* and freedom *for* the world.[4]

WHY *LORD?*

There are "names" and "*the* Name." Scripture introduces us to the divine names rather than the divine essence, and this is sufficient since the purpose of such revelation in the first place, as we have seen in the opening chapter, is to call upon or invoke the Lord of the covenant. Hence the prohibition against taking God's name in vain (Exod. 20:7). "It is a designation of Him, not as He exists in the depths of His divine Being, but as He reveals Himself especially in His relations" to us, as Louis Berkhof concludes.[5] Or, as Pannenberg expresses the same point, "In the Bible the divine name is not a formula for the essence of deity but a pointer to experience of his working (Exod. 3:14)."[6] God gives his name not as a window into his being or as a means of harnessing cosmic forces, but as a pledge. Thus the name is *invoked*, not decoded or used. "Everyone who calls on the name of the LORD shall be saved" (Joel 2:32, quoted in Acts 2:21 and Rom. 10:13; cf. Gen. 4:26; Ps. 18:3; 145:18; Isa. 55:6; Mal. 3:12).

Therefore, the title "Lord" (Hebrew *ʾădōnāy*), however analogical, and the name YHWH are at the heart of the biblical conception of God. To adopt any

---

3. The original draft included a labyrinthine chapter on the Trinity, which has subsequently been excised to meet the page requirements for this volume. I hope to publish it separately.

4. Barth, *CD* II/1:304.

5. Louis Berkhof, *Systematic Theology* (Grand Rapids: Eerdmans, 1941, repr. 1979), 47.

6. Wolfhart Pannenberg, *Systematic Theology*, trans. G. W. Bromiley, vol. 1 (hereafter *ST*) (Grand Rapids: Eerdmans, 1991), 360.

conception that circumvents "lordship" is to describe a religion other than the faith that knows "no other name under heaven given among mortals by which we must be saved" (Acts 4:12). It is by this name that we are rescued and in this name that every kingdom activity is effectual (Mark 9:38). In the context of bringing the Lord's "indictment against Judah," the prophet announces, "The LORD the God of hosts, the LORD is his name!" (Hos. 12:5). There is no way around this name YHWH and the title Lord, for those who belong to God: the suzerain-vassal structure of divine-human relationships is not accidental but essential. That more can be said—must be said, and in fact is said—is of course granted. But biblical faith is surely not less than this affirmation.

But is this emphasis on God as "Lord" simply a symbol that has outworn its usefulness? More seriously, has it actually legitimized an oppressive hierarchical way of thinking that inspires violence? Mary Daly raises the concern I have in mind, suggesting that in all spheres of life—the church, the home, and society—patriarchy rules because the Father rules in heaven.[7] Sallie McFague summarizes this perspective by suggesting that the picture represented in the "Hallelujah Chorus" of Handel's *Messiah* ("King of kings and Lord of lords," "for the Lord God omnipotent reigneth") is "a very dangerous one."[8]

> It creates feelings of awe in the hearts of loyal subjects and thus supports the "godness" of God, but these feelings are balanced by others of abject fear and humiliation: in this picture, God can be God only if we are nothing. The understanding of salvation that accompanies this view is sacrificial, substitutionary atonement, and in Anselm's classic rendition of it the sovereign imagery predominates. Since even a wink of the eye by a vassal against the Liege Lord of the universe would be irremediable sin, we as abject subjects must rely totally on our sovereign God who "became man" in order to undergo a sacrificial death, substituting his great worth for our worthlessness. . . . It inspires strong emotions of awe, gratitude, and trust toward God and, in ourselves, engenders a satisfying swing from abject guilt to joyous relief. Its very power is part of its danger, and any picture that seeks to replace it must reckon with its attraction.[9]

It is not even the case that the monarchical model must be supplemented with other models (such as that of parent), since its dangerous current is too strong not to pull every other model into its wake. (Parents become rulers, for example.) But do these criticisms have any significant purchase in light of the covenantal way in which the "vassal" and "suzerain" roles are actually played in the biblical drama? Is the covenant itself inherently oppressive or is it the basis for a genuine relationship between agents, if not equals?

In contrast to her own preference for the metaphor of the world as the body of God, "in the monarchical model there is no concern for the cosmos, for the

7. For a thorough treatment of this perspective see especially Mary Daly, *Beyond God the Father: Toward a Philosophy of Women's Liberation* (Boston: Beacon, 1985), 13.

8. Sallie McFague, *Models of God* (Philadelphia: Fortress, 1987), 64.

9. Ibid., 64–65.

non-human world." Further evidence of this anthropocentrism is that the monarchical model is typically tilted toward the aural over the visual in its exclusion of nonhuman creatures:

> An aural tradition is anthropocentric: we are the only ones who can "hear the Word of the Lord." A visual tradition, however, is more inclusive: if God can be present not only in what one hears but also in what one sees, then potentially anything and everything in the world can be a symbol of the divine.[10]

As we will explore in connection with creation, however, the solidarity of the human and nonhuman world is affirmed by the covenantal model of Lord-and-Servant, where the whole creation is "spoken" and "speaks back" to its Lord. Here the aural is participatory, but not in a manner that attempts, as in a vision, to master the other.

Sallie McFague summarizes her problem with the Lord-and-Servant paradigm by suggesting that the king-subject dualism of the monarchical model has generated "the cleavages of male/female, white/colored, rich/poor, Christian/non-Christian, and mind/body."[11] But if her analysis has any historical merit with respect to monarchical/hierarchical more generally, it certainly is difficult to maintain in the light of the sharp distinction between Creator and creature that this particular covenantal model maintains. If all of reality were on a single scale of being—if, in other words, being were univocal—certainly one could understand YHWH as the supreme reification of hierarchy. While he does not take the critique quite as far, Jürgen Moltmann has contributed significantly and profoundly to its development.[12] Just this sort of thinking led to political monotheism, which explains why the Roman Empire could become the *Holy* Roman Empire. Almost any and every hint of God as "Creator, Lord, and possessor of his world," whose "will is its law" and in whom "the world has its unity and peace," is taken to be an instance of hellenization when in fact it is at the heart of Israel's faith.

However, it is the Shema and not pantheistic Stoicism that emphasizes the sole lordship of YHWH as king. It is precisely Israel's narrative identity, constantly reasserted, of having been slaves liberated from bondage and taken into God's care as a community founded on a covenant rather than racial and social hierarchies that makes this God's sole kingship the basis for freedom in contrast to the nations.

It is important to remember that the point of having no other king than YHWH was to guard Israel itself from the oppressive hierarchies of the nations. The laws given to Israel defy the traditional social, economic, and racial stratifications of their neighbors. The judges applied this law. But before long, Israel

---

10. Ibid., 67.

11. Ibid.

12. Jürgen Moltmann, *The Trinity and the Kingdom: The Doctrine of God*, trans. Margaret Kohl (Minneapolis: Fortress, 1981), 192–93.

wanted a king "like all the nations" (Deut. 17:14). "Yet that the step was taken almost tentatively and, on the part of some, with great reluctance is likewise not surprising," writes John Bright, "for monarchy was an institution totally foreign to Israel's tradition."[13] Even in God's concession to a monarchy, strict limitations were to be placed on royal power: the ruler "must not acquire many horses for himself" or wives or "silver and gold . . . in great quantity for himself," and above all must school himself in the law, "neither exalting himself above other members of the community nor turning aside from the commandment" (Deut. 17:14–20). It had after all been the covenant Israel made with YHWH at Sinai that had made an earthly king of the confederacy unnecessary and perhaps even disloyal. As early as the first king (Saul), the saga of corrupt power taints Israel's history. YHWH's status as Israel's sole king was not the validation to the rise of oppressive hierarchies, but their rival. That Israel's faith in YHWH as the "great king" of the covenant can be exploited for pernicious interests says more about the endless resources of the human imagination in the service of idolatry and power than it does about any necessary correlation between this covenant relationship and oppression. Moltmann himself is somewhat equivocal, however, on these points. On one hand he claims, "The monotheistic God is 'the Lord of the world,'" in contrast to the *community* constituted by the social trinity.[14] "It is only when the doctrine of the Trinity vanquishes the monotheistic notion of the great universal monarch in heaven, and his divine patriarchs in the world, that earthly rulers, dictators and tyrants cease to find any justifying religious archetypes any more."[15]

On the other hand, however, Moltmann appears to accept the picture he had ostensibly rejected:

> Men and women are his created beings and are hence his property as well. In their naked existence human beings are completely and utterly dependent on their Creator and preserver. They can contribute nothing to what God creates, for they owe everything they are to God's creative activity. If God takes them into his service, becoming their master and lord, this is their exaltation and their mark of distinction. To be "the servant of God" raises men and women above all the rest of God's creatures.[16]

In terms reminiscent of Luther's *Freedom of the Christian*, Moltmann adds,

> For the person who is a servant of the Most High is indeed utterly dependent on his master; but he is completely free from other things and other powers. He fears God alone and nothing else in the world. He belongs to his Lord alone and to no one else. He hears his voice alone and no other voice at all. *The sole lordship of God, which the first commandment proclaims, is the foundation for the extraordinary freedom of having to have "no other gods" beside him.* This is what Paul means too when he explains freedom with the

---

13. John Bright, *A History of Israel*, 3rd ed. (Philadelphia: Westminster Press, 1981), 187.
14. Moltmann, *Trinity and the Kingdom*, 199.
15. Ibid., 197.
16. Ibid., 218.

help of the theological hierarchy of property: "All things are yours and you are Christ's and Christ is God's" (I Cor. 3.22f.).[17]

Therefore, Moltmann himself finds it necessary to appeal to the Lord-and-Servant motif, as radically reinterpreted by the biblical traditions, and even ends up arguing that this is the basis for our freedom from oppressive overlords.

Israel's national constitution was a covenant between YHWH as the Great King and the people as YHWH's servant; the tablets were housed in the ark of the covenant. The covenant is not simply one of the metaphors of God and his people, but is the concrete constitution of that relationship. But just because it is a covenant, it is a constitutional rather than an absolutist monarchy.

Moltmann is quite right to insist, "It is impossible to form the figure of the omnipotent, universal monarch, who is reflected in earthly rulers, out of the unity of this Father, this Son and this Spirit."[18] But it is precisely in Israel's unfolding narrative that one is presented with the figure of an omnipotent, universal monarch who is *not* reflected in the oppression, injustice, violence, and self-will of earthly rulers, including those then on the throne in Israel and Judah. Israel's confidence is in a great king whose universal lordship judges and casts down the despotic emperors of this world. Only the King of kings and Lord of lords can bring about an end to despots and oppressors. Jesus does not reject the lordship model but is quite happy to accept the title "Lord" and "King." But it is in his exercise of power through the cross that we recognize what we have seen all along of the Lord of the covenant. We have "crucified the Lord of glory" (1 Cor. 2:8). But in the kingdom of the risen Son, we are called to follow the law given to Israel's kings and not to lord it over others as the gentiles do (Matt. 20:25).

In these criticisms by McFague and Moltmann, the ontological paradigm delineated in my first chapter is clearly invoked, specifically by way of an appeal to panentheism, but can this approach do justice to the reality of otherness that injustice itself ignores, much less to the covenantal ontology of Scripture? While the hermeneutical circle always involves the horizon of the interpreter and therefore can never guarantee a perfect fit between language and reality, the hermeneutics of suspicion has left us too cynical. On one hand, we are able to critique the power regimes of others and yet all too typically regard our own as sanctioned by the gods (or justice, etc.). But suspicion moves in both directions. For those who believe that God meets us in personal address in and through the Scriptures, biblical language cannot be reduced to symbolized expressions of pious experience. This means that while it is certainly true that particular biblical metaphors for God will have different meanings for different groups in different times and places—sometimes liberating, sometimes jarring, sometimes reinforcing negative stereotypes—we must never forget that the traffic runs in the other direction too. What if our own presuppositions are governed by the will to power as well? After

17. Ibid., 219.
18. Ibid., 196.

all, "Christendom" has employed a variety of strategies, including democratic egalitarianism, in its will to power. Christian theology already has its own hermeneutics of suspicion in its account of the noetic effects of sin as suppressing the truth in unrighteousness (Rom. 1:18). This is done by all of us, regardless of how validated we feel in our own ideology.

It is quite possible for God's self-revelation even in terms alien or perhaps painful to us because of our experiences to transform our understanding. In pastoral ministry I have seen young people from troubled homes liberated from their concept of "father," for instance, as they came to know the Father of Jesus Christ, the Father who has elected them in unconditional grace to be, by his Spirit, joint heirs with his Son of all that he possesses. Sinful patterns of structural oppression and injustice do not invalidate biblical analogies and metaphors that draw on everyday life. Rather, they are called to account precisely as they are measured by their archetype. "God is Father," writes Aida Besançon Spencer, "not because God is masculine," since Scripture itself affirms consistently that "God is Spirit, neither male nor female. God has no form at all (as God clearly revealed to Moses in Deut 4:15–16)."[19] As Stanley Hauerwas observes, "The often-made claim that those who have had an abusive father have trouble calling God father may be psychologically true, but it is theologically uninteresting. If one sees that fatherhood is a grammar controlled by christological convictions, then those who have a troubled relation with their biological father are perhaps in the best condition to worship Trinity."[20] The same arguments obtain for the concept of lordship, as it is actually enacted in the history of YHWH and Israel, and supremely in Christ.

Even Moltmann's all-encompassing metaphor of "suffering love" can be exploited and valorized to render victims passive, as if they must simply absorb oppression and injustice, thereby sublating its destructive power in a higher redemptive synthesis. Surely many victims besides those calling from the heavenly altar cry out, "How long, O Lord!" before justice is finally done in the earth. It is by saying "Our Father" with Jesus, by the Spirit who forms in us that filial cry (Rom. 8:15–16), that we encounter a stranger who embraces us as adopted heirs of his kingdom, just as the same Spirit leads us to confess that Jesus is Lord to the glory of the Father (Phil. 2:11).

COVENANT LORD OR STOIC SAGE?

Suzerainty treaties assumed that the suzerain or lord of the covenant was independent of obligation, except to the suzerain's own aims and objectives. Once the suzerain accepts self-imposed obligations on the vassal's behalf, however, the

---

19. Aida Besançon Spencer, "Father-Ruler: The Meaning of the Metaphor 'Father' for God in the Bible," *Journal of the Evangelical Theological Society* 39, no. 3 (1996): 442.

20. Stanley Hauerwas, "Knowing How to Go On When You Do Not Know Where You Are: A Response to John Cobb, Jr.," *Theology Today* 51, no. 4 (1995): 568.

suzerain's character is on trial. The suzerain must be reliable. This is also an assumption of the biblical narrative with respect to YHWH.

The so-called incommunicable attributes specify characteristics unique to God, attributions that cannot even analogically be said to describe creatures. Since most of the biblical evidence falls on the side of God's analogical self-disclosure in the narrative of a covenant, the incommunicable attributes are understandably the most susceptible to philosophical abstraction and speculation.[21] Historically, they are also the most dependent on the *via negationis* and *eminentiae*, since they are expressions of divine transcendence—hence the recurring alpha-privative as a prefix (aseity, *apatheia*) and the superlative ("omni") prefix (omnipotence, omniscience, omnipresence). It is no doubt true that the so-called metaphysics of perfection/infinitude can easily end up justifying Feuerbach's theory of religion as projection. That which constitutes an ideal or perfect being varies, of course, and we do not achieve much in the way of identifying the God of biblical revelation by substituting a priori definitions. One important difference between the Thomist and Reformed approaches to analogy is that the latter is suspicious of the claim that we can know what God is *not* (*via negationis*) any more than we can know what God *is*, apart from God's own self-disclosure in revelation. We cannot start with our idea of perfect being, in a way of either eminence or negation.

However, the challenge for us today is patiently to attend to what the Christian tradition has meant to claim by appealing to these predicates without immediately dismissing them as a metaphysics of presence/infinitude in the light of modern philosophy (especially Descartes, Spinoza, and German idealism). The criticism of the classical Christian doctrine of God as "metaphysical" (specifically, Stoic) was launched by the Socinians in the sixteenth century and reached its zenith in the post-Kantian theologies of Ritschl and Harnack.[22] This charge has underwritten a century of modern theology, not only in neo-Protestantism but in neo-orthodoxy and in the version of the "biblical theology" movement identified especially with G. E. Wright. According to Wright, the God of systematic theology was the deity of static order, while the God of biblical theology is dynamic, a claim that seems to ignore the different objectives of theological subdisciplines (systematic theology being concerned with logical connections and biblical theology interested in organic and historical development).[23] But the

21. Cf. Francis Turretin, *Institutes of Elenctic Theology*, vol. 1, ed. James T. Dennison Jr., trans. George Musgrave Giger (Phillipsburg, NJ: Presbyterian & Reformed, 1992), 190.

22. On the Arian criticism of the orthodox doctrine as philosophical, while Arianism itself was entangled in philosophical assumptions, see Jaroslav Pelikan, *The Emergence of the Catholic Tradition (100–600)* (Chicago: University of Chicago Press, 1971), 194. The Socinians, according to Genevan theologian Francis Turretin, reproached classical theism on the same basis; viz., that "the whole doctrine is metaphysical" rather than biblical (Turretin, *Institutes of Elenctic Theology*, 191). On Harnack see his *History of Dogma*, trans. N. Buchanan et al., 7 vols. (repr., Boston: Little, Brown, 1902), 1:48ff.

23. G. E. Wright, *God Who Acts: Biblical Theology as Recital*, Studies in Biblical Theology 1/8 (London: SCM, 1952), especially 35, 81, 111.

twentieth century also witnessed the rehabilitation of the sixteenth-century Reformers in this respect, shifting the blame for "Hellenistic" theology to their systematizing successors instead.[24] In a chapter titled "Overcoming a Pagan Influence," evangelical theologian Clark Pinnock takes this well-traveled road, but with the entire classical tradition from the church fathers to current orthodoxy dismissed in one stroke as hopelessly trapped in ancient paganism.[25] This does not keep Pinnock, any more than Harnack, from reading Scripture through the lens of modern thought, especially Hegel, in addition to Teilhard de Chardin and Alfred North Whitehead, a debt that Pinnock readily acknowledges.[26] But in this case the philosophical debt is evidently justified, since "modern culture . . . is closer to the biblical view than classical theism."[27]

However, this broader thesis has been challenged. On the biblical-theological side, James Barr led the way to its demise,[28] and subsequent research has raised serious questions about its viability: in relation to Jesus (Hebrew) versus Paul (Greek)[29] and the Reformers versus the Protestant scholastics.[30] Although he himself rejects divine simplicity, immutability, and impassibility, William P. Alston demonstrates that for Aquinas and others, the whole point of affirming these predicates was to avoid any kind of substance metaphysics.[31]

But if we can discern these incommunicable attributes in the strong verbs, adverbs, adjectives, and nouns that arise out of the biblical drama, even from good and necessary consequences of such identification, an argument against the meta-

---

24. This was the working assumption of neo-orthodoxy (particularly evident in Brunner and Barth), in its attempt to rescue the Reformers while eschewing the systems of their successors. On the Reformed side, it is the controlling presupposition of T. F. Torrance, James B. Torrance, Michael Jinkins, Jack Rogers, B. A. Armstrong, R. T. Kendall, and others.

25. Clark Pinnock, *Most Moved Mover* (Grand Rapids: Baker, 2001). First, Pinnock does not seem to grant that in the Hellenistic world are many mansions: not only Parmenidean stasis, but Heraclietean flux. To reduce Hellenism to the Stoics and Plato is to ignore that even Hegel et al. appealed to important streams of Greek thought (especially Aristotle, oddly enough). Cf. Clark Pinnock, "Theological Method," in *New Dimensions in Evangelical Thought: Essays in Honor of Millard J. Erickson*, ed. David S. Dockery (Downers Grove, IL: InterVarsity Press, 1998), 197–208.

26. Pinnock, *Most Moved Mover*, 142ff.

27. Clark Pinnock, "From Augustine to Arminius: A Pilgrimage in Theology," in *The Grace of God and the Will of Man*, ed. Pinnock (Grand Rapids: Zondervan, 1989), 24.

28. James Barr, "The Old Testament and the New Crisis of Biblical Authority," *Interpretation* 25, no. 1 (1971): 24–40; cf. idem, *The Semantics of Biblical Language* (Oxford: Oxford University Press, 1961); idem, *Biblical Words for Time*, 2nd ed., Studies in Biblical Theology 1/33 (London: SCM, 1969).

29. Against the application of the Harnack thesis to the so-called Jesus vs. Paul antithesis, see the recent collection, Troels Engberg-Pedersen, ed., *Paul Beyond the Judaism/Hellenism Divide* (Louisville, KY: Westminster John Knox Press, 2001).

30. For the criticism of the Luther/Calvin vs. Lutheranism/Calvinism version, see particularly Richard Muller, "Calvin and the 'Calvinists': Assessing Continuities and Discontinuities between the Reformation and Orthodoxy," *Calvin Theological Journal* 30 (1995): 345–75; and 31 (1996): 125–60; cf. Robert Preus, *The Theology of Post-Reformation Lutheranism*, 2 vols. (St. Louis: Concordia, 1970–72). Articles and monographs by Willem van Assalt, David Steinmetz, Susan Schreiner, Irena Backus, Robert Kolb, among others, have contributed significantly to this field.

31. William P. Alston, "Substance and the Trinity" in *The Trinity: An Interdisciplinary Symposium*, ed. Gerald O'Collins et al. (Oxford: Oxford University Press, 1999), 179–201.

physics of being is not necessarily a strike against the classical Christian claim. To repeat Francis Turretin, theology "treats of God not like metaphysics as a being or as he can be known from the light of nature, but as the Creator and Redeemer made known by revelation."[32] Having said that, any claim about God—even God's existence—whether positive, agnostic, or atheistic, is metaphysical.

In contemporary theology, the backlash against ahistorical approaches especially dominant in rationalism and idealism has led to a number of challenges with which these traditional definitions must reckon. Understandably, the foil for such critiques is Greek metaphysics in general and that of Parmenides in particular, according to which the absolute is identified with stasis, immobility, pure self-presence, and the absence of all relation, immune to external circumstances and the change that plagues temporal reality. This model achieves its apogee in Stoicism, where the ideal Stoic sage (independent, self-sufficient, apathetic, and therefore untroubled) is projected onto the ultimate fountain of Reality. While we must beware of the temptation to quit ourselves of Parmenides only to rebound into the arms of Heraclitus (there are at least two Greek traditions, after all), many of the recent criticisms of traditional constructions have sought to recover the dramatic historical sense that one does find in the biblical text.[33]

Now to the claims themselves. Traditionally, Christian theology has emphasized as a corollary of the Creator-creature distinction God's independence, expressed by a cluster of predicates such as simplicity (i.e., not a composite being made up of various parts), immutability (unchangeableness), impassibility (immunity to suffering), and aseity (independence).

If we take the "strong verbs" disclosed in the narrative of the covenant trial as our starting point, nothing could be clearer to the covenant people in both Testaments than God's self-existence, independence, and uniqueness. It is basic to the transcendence of YHWH in contrast to the idols of the nations. Psalm 115:3 is typical: "Our God is in the heavens; he does whatever he pleases." Hence the recurring polemic against the idols: "To whom will you liken me and make me equal, and compare me, as though we were alike? . . . Remember this and consider, recall it to mind, you transgressors, remember the former things of old; for I am God, and there is no other; I am God, and there is no one like me, declaring the end from the beginning and from ancient times things not yet done, saying, 'My purpose shall stand, and I will fulfill my intention'" (Isa. 46:5, 8–10). YHWH is in a class by himself. There is no genus of "deity" to which he belongs, a *whatness* of which God is an instance.

> To whom then will you liken God, or what likeness compare with him? . . .
> It is he who sits above the circle of the earth, and its inhabitants are like grasshoppers; who stretches out the heavens like a curtain, and spreads them like a tent to live in; who brings princes to naught, and makes the rulers of

32. Turretin, *Institutes of Elenctic Theology,* 16–17.
33. Robert Jenson, *Systematic Theology* [hereafter *ST*], 2 vols. (New York: Oxford University Press, 1997–99). 1:66.

> the earth as nothing. . . . Have you not known? Have you not heard? The
> LORD is the everlasting God, the Creator of the ends of the earth. He does
> not faint or grow weary; his understanding is unsearchable. He gives power
> to the faint, and strengthens the powerless. (Isa. 40:18, 22–23, 28–29)

It is precisely because God—and only God—has life and sovereignty in himself
that the weak and powerless can cry out to him in their distress. Evil powers never
have the last word.

While Exodus 3:14 is inconclusive for drawing sophisticated doctrines of aseity and eternity, Revelation 1:4 (drawing, no doubt, on the LXX translation of
Exod. 3:14) at least points in the direction of something like aseity and eternity,
referring to the Son as "the one who is, and was, and is to come (*ho ōn, kai ho ēn,
kai ho erchomenos*), the Almighty." Being is not antecedent to God or a predicate
shared with creatures: "Just as the Father has life in himself, so he has granted the
Son also to have life in himself" (John 5:26). Scripture repeats the constant
refrain that the world is dependent on God, while God is dependent on no one
and no thing. Surrounded by Epicurean deists and Stoic pantheists, Paul glosses
Isaiah 40 along with some Greek poets (Acts 17:24–28). In this passage divine
transcendence is not set against immanence, but is the very presupposition for it.
The distinction between Creator and creature is not an ontological opposition:
it is precisely in God's independence and freedom from contingency that a hab-
itable space is opened for the freedom of contingent reality. If the world is not
God's body, it is certainly God's house. This reverses panentheism: "God indwells
all," not "all indwells God"; thus God is necessarily independent and yet contingently related to the world covenantally. The necessary relations of the Trinity
cannot be univocally applied to the God-world relationship.

Perhaps among the most conclusive arguments for God's infinite perfection
and independence is that nothing can be given to him or done for him by a creature that demands reimbursement: "For from him and through him and to him
are all things. To him be the glory forever. Amen" (Rom. 11:34–36). The human
analogy here is once again the suzerainty treaty: the suzerain owes nothing to the
vassal but freely and sovereignly establishes a relationship of genuine, if hierarchical, mutuality. To assert absolute perfection, then, is to recognize that God is free
of all limitations and containments (1 Kgs. 8:27). It is not even that he is infinitely
extended in space (*pace* Spinoza) but that he *transcends* space (and, as I will argue,
time)—even as God *indwells* both more fully (repletively) than any creature.

All created reality is contingent upon the necessary existence of God without
being swallowed up in that necessity. As Herman Bavinck notes, this "unbounded,
limitless, absolutely undetermined, unqualified" view of God is irreconcilable
with pantheism ancient and modern: Babylonian, Hellenistic, Neoplatonist, kabbalistic, and Spinozistic.[34] Possessing every virtue in an absolute degree, perfect,
God's infinitude is qualitative, not quantitative; intensive, and extensive; posi-

---

34. Herman Bavinck, *The Doctrine of God*, trans. William Hendriksen (Grand Rapids: Eerdmans,
1951), 152.

tive, not negative.[35] God's infinity cannot mean that he can be anything or every-thing (*pace* Ockham and Hegel), unbounded and absolutely undetermined, because his attributes are descriptive of his being itself. In other words, God is bound by his nature, but only by his nature. But just so, God is bound to us (bet-ter, has bound himself to us) by a free decision to enter into covenant with us and with the whole creation. God is not free to act contrary to such covenantal guar-antees because doing so would entail the violation not only of his decision but of his nature, particularly his faithfulness. God's infinite perfection is his greatness: "Great is the LORD, and greatly to be praised; his greatness is unsearchable" (Ps. 145:3). All of these biblical references to God's incomparable perfection have concrete historical events as their frame of reference. In the prophets, for exam-ple, YHWH invites the covenant people to a trial of the gods: can they speak and act as YHWH has done? "Their idols are like scarecrows in a cucumber field, and they cannot speak; they have to be carried, for they cannot walk. Do not be afraid of them, for they cannot do evil, nor is it in them to do good. There is none like you, O LORD; you are great, and your name is great in might" (Jer. 10:5–6).

God can be wholly identified with his revelation without being entirely reduced to it: this is the point of analogy and incarnation, and it is the point of the doctrine of aseity. In every identification, God is always *that and yet not that.* While the absolute and the personal are antithetical concepts in ancient Greek paganism and in modern (idealist) philosophy, they find their unity in the God of Israel.[36]

Since there is no predicate of being that God and creatures univocally share, God's freedom is qualitatively and not simply quantitatively different from our own. This is where Barth's affirmation of both freedom *from* (transcendence) and freedom *for* (immanence) is crucial: "But freedom in its positive and proper qual-ities means to be grounded in one's being, to be determined and moved by one-self."[37] This once more affirms God's self-determination and aseity.[38] But it must not be defined only negatively (independence *from* conditions), but positively—as God's unique freedom to enter into fellowship and so freely to will to be conditioned.[39] The purely negative likely originates in a Neoplatonism in which to enter into such fellowship is a sign of less being.[40] It is not a generic freedom that we then apply to the gods or God, but the freedom proved in Jesus Christ.[41] To say that God is *a se*, "we say that (as manifest and eternally actual in the rela-tionship of Father, Son and Holy Ghost) He is the One who already has in Him-self everything which would have to be the object of His creation and causation

35. Ibid.

36. I. A. Dorner, *Divine Immutability: A Critical Reconsideration*, trans. Robert R. Willliams and Claude Welch (Minneapolis: Fortress Press, 1994), 84–85.

37. Barth, *CD* II/1:300–301.

38. Ibid., 302.

39. Ibid., 303.

40. Ibid.

41. Ibid.

if He were not He, God. Because He is God, as such He already has His own being."[42]

On no point is the challenge to a traditional understanding of divine perfection more forcefully elaborated today than the concept of *impassibility*. Traditionally regarded as an implication of divine perfection, the notion of God's immunity to suffering is now frequently seen rather to be an implication of a certain presupposition of perfection defined by Greek metaphysics rather than by Scripture.

T. E. Fretheim's *Suffering of God* was formative in raising this question in biblical theology. The biblical writers, he argued, used the metaphor not only in an emotive sense but as "reality depicting."[43] (The contrast of metaphor with "reality-depicting language" already assumes a fundamental misunderstanding of language, I would argue.)[44] Fretheim recognizes the twin dangers of agnostic equivocity and rationalistic univocity. We are dealing with metaphors, he realizes. Nevertheless, they need to be taken seriously as revealing something important about God's very nature; otherwise, why call them revelation at all?[45] But, as Childs observes, Fretheim assumes "that a biblical metaphor always arises from the projection of human experience to a depiction of the divine. . . . A. Heschel (*The Prophets*, II, 51f.) correctly senses the problem when he writes: 'God's unconditional concern for justice is not an anthropomorphism. Rather, man's concern for justice is a theomorphism.'" While in the history of religions, Fretheim might be right, "according to Israel's scriptures this is blasphemy. God, not man, is the only creator."[46] Second, Childs judges that Fretheim's "organismic image" of the mutual interdependence of God and humans is more indebted to process thought than to the dynamic movement of revelation.

> God is self-contained: "I am Yahweh" (Ex. 6.2). "I am who I am" (3.14). There is none like him (Ex. 8.10; 15.11; Ps. 86.8). He is God alone (Deut. 4.35; II Kings 19.15). His love is everlasting (Jer. 31.3). God does not from necessity need Israel (Ps. 50.10ff.), but rather willed not to exist for himself alone. In full freedom for his own purpose, God loves unconditionally with an utterly sovereign love. James' witness is fully Jewish in depicting God as "the Father of lights with whom there is no variation or shadow due to change" (1.17; cf. Job 28.24; Ecclus. 42.18–20; Wisd. 1.5ff.).[47]

Although as "living God," and not a static concept, God suffers with and for his people (Isa. 63:9), the fact remains that "God is God and not human (Hos. 11.9),

---

42. Ibid., 306.

43. T. E. Fretheim, *The Suffering of God: An OT Perspective*, Overtures to Biblical Theology (Philadelphia: Fortress, 1988), 7.

44. In addition to the many sources to which I appeal in the hermeneutical discussions in *Covenant and Eschatology*, I would single out Colin Gunton, *The Actuality of Atonement: A Study of Metaphor, Rationality, and the Christian Tradition* (Grand Rapids: Eerdmans, 1989).

45. As we will see below, this argument is prominent in what has come to be called "open theism" in evangelical theology, especially in its critique of immutability.

46. Childs, *Biblical Theology*, 357.

47. Ibid.

yet he has become 'God with us' (Isa. 8.10)."[48] And he is God-with-us not only in the incarnation, but already in anticipation of the incarnation as creator, sustainer, liberator, and lord.

In the nineteenth century, kenosis was a christological category. In other words, as Dorner pointed out, the Lutheran *communicatio idiomatum* (communication of attributes), whereby the attributes of Deity were said to be communicated to the humanity of Christ, was now reversed: the Logos became finite.[49] While I will interact with this form of divine self-emptying in another place, the interesting development that concerns us here is that kenosis has now become a category applied to the being of God even apart from the incarnation. God is either absolute or personal: that is the false dilemma of nineteenth-century idealism that continues to be pressed in contemporary debates. But such views tend to make the incarnation merely an instance of a general phenomenon that goes on quite well without it. Furthermore, they fail to take into account that as covenantal, God's relation to the world is just as much an ontological fact as it is in rival accounts, but as such it underscores the important truth that God enters into covenants rather than being constituted in his very being by them.

No one has provided a more thorough criticism of impassibility in systematic theology along these lines of a general divine kenosis than Jürgen Moltmann. He asks, "How can Christian faith understand Christ's passion as being the revelation of God, if the deity cannot suffer? . . . If God is incapable of suffering, then—if we are to be consistent—Christ's passion can only be viewed as a human tragedy."[50] "If, in the manner of Greek philosophy, we ask what characteristics are 'appropriate' to the deity, then we have to exclude difference, diversity, movement and suffering from the divine nature."[51] "The absolute subject of nominalist and Idealist philosophy is also incapable of suffering; otherwise it would not be absolute," so we are working with Greek, nominalist, and idealist philosophy as the conceptual fund for the traditional doctrine.[52]

Yet however impassibility (along with simplicity and aseity) might have been formulated in nominalism and idealism, these affirmations were strenuously maintained by the ecumenical church until recently, quite apart from these modern developments. The demise of this consensus occurred with the advent of absolute idealism. Moltmann argues that patristic theology clung to impassibility in theory (contrary to its liturgical and devotional praxis) "for two reasons": to protect the Creator-creature distinction, and to hold out salvation as conferring "immortality, non-transience, and hence impassibility too" by participation in his eternal life.[53] The ancient formulation knew only the false choice between "essential incapacity for suffering" and "a fateful subjection to suffering."

48. Ibid., 358.
49. Dorner, *Divine Immutability*, 43–44.
50. Ibid., 21–22.
51. Moltmann, *Trinity and the Kingdom*, 21.
52. Ibid.
53. Ibid., 23.

> But there is a third form of suffering: active suffering—the voluntary laying
> oneself open to another and allowing oneself to be intimately affected by him;
> that is to say, the suffering of passionate love. In Christian theology the apa-
> thetic axiom only really says that God is not subjected to suffering in the same
> way as transient, created beings. It is in fact not a real axiom at all. It is a state-
> ment of compassion. It does not exclude the deduction that in another respect
> God certainly can and does suffer. If God were capable of suffering in every
> respect, then he would also be incapable of love.[54]

Moltmann approaches here what I call the analogical proviso, even allowing that
the "apathetic axiom only really says that God is not subjected to suffering in the
same way as transient, created beings," which he is quite willing to accept. "God
does not suffer out of deficiency of being, like created beings. To this extent he
is 'apathetic'. But he suffers from the love which is the superabundance and overflowing of his being. In so far as he is 'pathetic.'"[55]

But is Moltmann consistent with this analogical proviso or qualification? He
develops his account out of the relationship in which God "makes himself a partner in a covenant with his people."[56]

> Creation, liberation, covenant, history, and redemption spring from the
> pathos of God. This therefore has nothing to do with the passions of the
> moody, envious or heroic gods belonging to the mythical world of the sagas.
> Those gods are subject to destiny because of their passions. But the divine
> passion about which the Old Testament tells us is God's freedom. It is the
> free relationship of passionate participation. . . . Of course the images of
> Yahweh as Israel's friend, or father, or mother, or her disappointed lover are
> just as anthropomorphic as the notions of an ardent, jealous, angry, or erot-
> ically craving God. But what these images are trying to express is missed by
> the person who holds "apathy" to be the only characteristic that is "appro-
> priate" for the deity.[57]

Appealing to the mystical, kabbalistic, and speculative traditions, Moltmann
treats the incarnate Christ almost as a cipher for God's eternal kenotic being: "If
Christ is weak and humble on earth, then God is weak and humble in heaven.
For 'the mystery of the cross' is a mystery which lies at the centre of God's eternal being"—and not simply at the center of God's eternal plan.[58] Moltmann so
identifies revelation (the economy) with God's being (in himself) that despite his
criticisms of Barth for substituting an absolute Subject for the three persons, his
own move is strikingly similar. According to Sabellianism (modalism), it is the
Father (as the only divine person) who suffers. While Moltmann is not a modal-
ist, the same question could be put to his project: What is it that the Son uniquely
brings to the God-world relationship?

54. Ibid.
55. Ibid.
56. Ibid., 25.
57. Ibid., 25–26.
58. Ibid.

The historical passion is not so much the culmination of a divine plan as it is a window through which we see what is in fact an eternal event—this despite Moltmann's otherwise persuasive and pervasive critique of Parmenides and Plato. "If we follow through the idea that the historical passion of Christ reveals the eternal passion of God, then the self-sacrifice of love is God's eternal nature."[59] The Christ event does not seem to be a contingent (and therefore genuinely historical) eschatological intrusion, but is necessary to God's inner being. It is not simply that God's mercy, grace, compassion, and kindness are eternal attributes: the cross itself, or at the very least, the event (not just the possibility) of suffering and self-sacrifice are predicates of God's nature. The cross is not something that might not have happened: "Self-sacrifice is God's very nature and essence."[60]

While I cannot explore this point more fully now, one wonders if the theodicy represented here can be correlated not only with Scripture but with the experience of suffering that Moltmann himself has known quite closely. How can a victim of the Holocaust, for example, concede, "Suffering love overcomes the brutality of evil and redeems the energy in evil, which is good, through the fulfillment which it gives to this misguided passion"?[61] Moltmann says that "the process of evolution is the process of redemption through suffering love."[62] This requires us to regard God's love in the creation and sustenance of the world as "*suffering* love" rather than unconditional love. It therefore calls into question, as much as the pagan view Israel opposed, not only the goodness of God but the goodness of creation as creation. What is the source of suffering in creation (and thus in God)? The Son, the Spirit—eventually the other that is the world? Moltmann speculates that "if God is already in eternity and in his very nature love, suffering love and self-sacrifice, then evil must already have come into existence with God himself, not merely with creation, let alone with the Fall of man."[63] Rather than embrace a dualistic cosmology such as Manicheism, with good and evil grounded in two opposing gods, Moltmann synthesizes these oppositions within the very being of God himself.[64] Again we should be aware that in the history of metaphysics dualism and monism often depend on each other for their strength. Thus Moltmann approves G. A. Studdert Kennedy's conclusion: "God, the Father God of Love, is everywhere in history, but nowhere is He Almighty."[65]

Developing the theme of divine sorrow, Moltmann appeals to the early-twentieth-century Spanish mystic Miguel de Unamuno, who discovered "the mystery of the world and the mystery of God," viz., that "Christ's death and

59. Ibid., 32.
60. Ibid.
61. Ibid.
62. Ibid.
63. Ibid., 34.
64. Ibid.
65. Ibid., 35. G. A. Studdert Kennedy's book, *The Hardest Part* (London: Hodder & Stoughton, 1918), came out about the same time as Barth's *Epistle to the Romans*. "In fact," Moltmann judges, "it deserved even greater attention than Barth's book, for the theology of the suffering God is more important that the theology of the God who is 'Wholly Other.'"

struggle on Golgotha reveals the pain of the whole world and the sorrow of God. . . . Hegel, Kierkegaard ('the brother from the North'), Schopenhauer and Jakob Böhme helped him to formulate this insight to his."[66] Unamuno's "theology of the infinite *sorrow* of God" affirms this sorrow as the "quintessence of his picture of Christ. The Christ despairing in his agony on the cross is for him the only true picture of Christ."[67] This is in contrast to "the God of the logician" who, "arrived at by the *via negationis*, knew neither love nor hate." A God who does not suffer does not really live.[68] It would seem that the categories provided by nineteenth-century speculative philosophy press Moltmann to choose between the "absolute" and the "personal." Given the interdependence of God and the world via the history of suffering, "It is not only that we need God's compassion; God also needs ours. . . . The deliverance of the world from its contradiction is nothing less than God's deliverance of himself from the contradiction of his world."[69] Standing beneath Velázquez's crucifix, Unamuno "had an idea that reaches the limit of radical boldness: 'Is this the atoning God, who wants to clear his conscience of the guilt, the reproach of having created man, and at the same time evil and suffering?'" Suffering and God's sorrow "is not merely a contradiction in God's world," Unamuno concluded. "It is bound up with that; but it is also a contradiction in God himself. . . . He contents himself with a pointer to Jakob Böhme's idea about there being a 'dark side' to God."[70] But in the dialectic of mediation, this "dark side of God" is sublated into a higher synthesis. Hegel's speculative Good Friday yields to Easter overcoming.[71]

> If, then, the reason for the mystery of human freedom is to be found in God himself, then we must assume a movement, a passion, a history— yes, even a "tragedy in God" himself. That is why Berdyaev, pointing to Jakob Böhme's idea about a "dark nature in God," talks about "the possibility of tragic destiny for the divine life." . . . "The divine life itself in a deep and mysterious sense is history. It is a historical drama, a historical mystery play." In saying this he takes up Schelling's attempt to translate the concept of the theogonic process out of mythology into philosophy. . . . Berdyaev believes that it is an irony of thought that the "disciples of consistent monism" should fall victims to dualism instead of escaping it. . . . In actual fact, therefore, without dualism it is impossible to state the monistic position at all.[72]

Yet Moltmann, like Berdyaev, does not seem to recognize that his own proposal remains deep within the dualistic discourse that surrenders to monism after all. Despite the analogical proviso that preserves the Creator-creature distinction

---

66. Moltmann, *Trinity and the Kingdom,* 36.
67. Ibid., 37.
68. Ibid., 38.
69. Ibid., 39.
70. Ibid., 40.
71. Ibid., 42.
72. Ibid., 43–44.

while affirming real relatedness, Moltmann surrenders to univocity.[73] The drama of history, with tragedy as well as comedy, is the very life of God in its becoming.

Not surprisingly, then, "Perfection of Christ's cross," Moltmann concludes, "makes 'the metaphysical historical' and 'the historical metaphysical.'"[74] For Berdyaev, as for Moltmann, not only is God's freedom reduced to suffering; this suffering freedom, one may legitimately infer, is not only internal but anterior to God. Suffering freedom is abstracted from God and divinized when we read, "but freedom has no origin; it is an ultimate frontier. But because freedom exists, God Himself suffers and is crucified."[75] Although Moltmann concedes the mysterious aspect of evil, his impatience with that mystery seems to demand a resolution, and he finds it in a combination of kabbalism, modern pantheism, and dialectical historicism—all the while trying to hold on as much as possible to the analogical proviso, but finally without success.

In recent discussions of impassibility (like other incommunicable attributes), readers are pressed to make a decision between false alternatives. This point comes into sharper focus in open theism's treatment of the classical doctrine of divine impassibility, which it incorrectly defines as the inability to experience or feel emotion. If God were exactly identical to every representation we come across in Scripture, could we not justly conclude that he is, for instance, capricious: "Kiss the son, lest he be angry and you perish in the way, for his wrath is quickly kindled" (Ps. 2:12)? As we have seen above, Moltmann seems more aware of the dangers in entirely rejecting the analogical proviso just at this point.[76] In this psalm, God is depicted as mocking his enemies with sardonic laughter. But do we really want to ascribe this univocally to God's being rather than to recognize it as a sober comparison of a great king undisturbed by the pretenses of human power? I have yet to discover among open theists an argument in favor for God's rage being understood in the same univocal terms as his repentance.

There is also enough similarity to what we experience as love to say "God is love" (1 John 4:8), but love is obviously different in the case of the one who loves in absolute freedom than for creatures whose experience of love is always related to some form of dependence and reciprocity. This very point seems implied in the same chapter: "In this is love, not that we loved God but that he loved us and sent his Son to be the atoning sacrifice for our sins. . . . We love him because he first loved us" (1 John 4:10, 19). In other words, here God's love is the ultimate reality and human loves are analogies: human love is a theomorphism.

Surely this dialectic play of analogies is comparable to the narrative representation of God as repenting and yet affirming, "I am not a mortal that I should

73. Ibid., 45.
74. Ibid., 47.
75. Ibid.
76. Ibid., 4: "God experiences people in a different way from the way people experience God. He experiences them in his divine manner of experience." It is interesting that Moltmann approaches the analogical proviso most nearly whenever he is faced with the representations with which he is uncomfortable (viz., anger, wrath, impatience, jealousy) but loses sight of it whenever elaborating more sympathetic divine outbursts.

repent" (1 Sam. 15:29). Jealousy is praised in God (Exod. 20:5; 34:14; Deut. 4:24), while it is condemned in creatures (1 Cor. 3:3; Gal. 5:20), so clearly "jealousy" cannot mean exactly the same thing in God and creatures. God is described as uprooting the Israelites "in furious anger and great wrath" (Deut. 29:28), and yet "his anger is but for a moment, and his favor is for a lifetime" (Ps. 30:5). All of these diverse analogies must be taken seriously within their specific redemptive-historical context and then interpreted in the light of the rest of Scripture. The anger that God condemns in us (Prov. 29:11, 22; 22:24; 1 Cor. 13:5) is different from the anger that fills him with holy wrath, whatever similarities there may be. Neither Moltmann nor the representatives of open theism give any significant space to the wide range of divine pathos. Even if we were to adopt their univocal attribution of emotion to God, we would be left with a monopathetic deity whose only pathos is suffering love or, in Pinnock's expression, creative love. But can this do justice to the scores of passages in which God not only feels our pain but inflicts it? What of God's hatred, vengeance, jealousy, and wrath? Even if they were to make a serious appearance in these proposals, such predications would be quickly absorbed into the higher synthesis.

John Sanders, an advocate of open theism, judges,

> The desire not to speak about God anthropomorphically simply seems correct. After all, just about everyone takes the biblical references to the "eyes," "arms" and "mouth" (anthropomorphisms proper) of God as metaphors for divine actions, not assertions that God has literal body parts. But some go further, claiming that the anthropopathisms (in which God is said to have emotions, plans or changes of mind) are not actually to be attributed to God.[77]

Yet it is precisely the desire to speak anthropomorphically and to recognize it as such that defines an analogical approach. But further, why would we make an arbitrary distinction between analogies of being and analogies of feeling? This is not to reject predications of emotion to God (as classical theism has tended to do), but it is also not to say that emotions are predicated univocally of God and humans. If all predicates applied to God and creatures must be regarded as analogical, that would include references to God's sardonic laughter at his enemies in Psalm 2 or his grief at the disobedience of covenant partners. Perhaps, to attain consistency, one should speculate with Moltmann that God has tear ducts.[78] Pinnock does take this next logical step, speculating concerning God's embodiment beyond the incarnation.[79] This is a good example of how God's transcendence

---

77. John Sanders, *The God Who Risks: A Theology of Providence* (Downers Grove, IL: InterVarsity Press, 1998), 20.

78. Moltmann, *The Crucified God*, trans. R. A. Wilson and John Bowden (New York: Harper & Row, 1974), 222.

79. Pinnock, *Most Moved Mover*, 33–34. He cites Mormon theologian David Paulsen, among others, for support and appeals to Mormon criticisms of divine incorporeality as well as other classical attributes (ibid., 35n31 and 68n11).

itself is at stake in these debates, and how the denial of divine simplicity easily leads to a rejection of divine spirituality. But short of making the move to affirm divine corporeality, there seems to be no theoretical reason to separate attributions of particular emotions from attributions of particular limbs and organs.[80]

I do not have the space here to pursue this important point further.[81] Nevertheless, renewed attention to this particular formulation of divine impassibility would seem to be called for on both sides of this debate.

B. B. Warfield's treatment of divine emotion contrasts sharply with the picture that one obtains from many of the recent caricatures especially of Reformed orthodoxy and also warns us against formulations of the traditional view that begin with philosophical presuppositions of what is appropriate for God rather than attending closely to the biblical narrative. We are told, Warfield says, "that God is, by the very necessity of His nature, incapable of passion, incapable of being moved by inducements from without; that He dwells in holy calm and unchangeable blessedness, untouched by human sufferings or human sorrows forever,—haunting

> The lucid interspace of world and world,
> Where never creeps a cloud, nor moves a wind,
> Nor ever falls the least white star of snow,
> Nor ever lowest roll of thunder moans,
> Nor sound of human sorrow mounts to mar
> His sacred, everlasting calm."

But Warfield replies,

> Let us bless our God that it is not true. God can feel; God does love. We have Scriptural warrant for believing that, like the hero of Zurich, God has reached out loving arms and gathered into His own bosom that forest of spears which otherwise had pierced ours. But is not this gross anthropomorphism? We are careless of names: it is the truth of God. And we decline to yield up the God of the Bible and the God of our hearts to any philosophical abstraction. . . . We may feel awe in the presence of the Absolute, as we feel awe in the presence of the storm or of the earthquake. . . . But we cannot love it; we cannot trust it. . . . Nevertheless, let us rejoice that our God has not left us by searching to find Him out. Let us rejoice that He has plainly revealed Himself to us in His

80. In a written response as part of a seminar on divine impassibility with Professor Nicholas Wolterstorff at Yale University in 1997, Marilyn Adams has observed: "It seems to me that human suffering could be a reason for Divine compassion without being an efficient cause of it." Adams captures what is really at stake here: "If something other than God causally affects God, however, God can't be the first cause of every change, unless Divine passibility is just an indirect approach to Divine self-change. . . . If God could be totally or even nearly overcome by grief within God's Divine nature, God would not only fail to have an ideal Stoic character (which those of us who flirt with passibility can live with), God's providential control might be jeopardized. Do crucifixion, earthquakes, and eclipses signal that God has 'lost it' in Divine rage and grief?"

81. See Paul Helm, "The Impossibility of Divine Passsibility," in *The Power and Weakness of God*, ed. Nigel Cameron (Edinburgh: Conference in Christian Dogmatics, 1990), 123, 126.

Word as a God who loves us, and who, because He loves us, has sacrificed Himself for us.[82]

Whatever weaknesses that might attend criticisms and counterproposals, there can be little doubt that some traditional interpretations of God's otherness have been freighted with assumptions that are alien to the biblical canon. For example, given the enormous consensus of patristic writers on these points, John of Damascus was hardly going out on a limb when he wrote, "The Deity, then, alone is motionless, moving the universe by immobility."[83] The language is clearly that of Aristotle's unmoved mover. So too is his defense of simplicity with the argument that "difference introduces strife."[84] God's most proper attribute is aseity.[85] But to suggest that any attribute is more "proper" than another is to contradict simplicity. These writers were not consistent with these statements, however, emphatically teaching creation, providence, the incarnation, and other demonstrations of God's solidarity with and in the world. Nevertheless, their philosophical assumptions, however implicit, could at times blunt the force of the Christian story, just as Heraclitean (i.e., Hegelian) speculations often overdetermine contemporary exegesis. Reformed orthodoxy has been correct in its rejection of divine immunity to emotion and motion.

I. A. Dorner has offered the intriguing observation that in the metaphysics of the ancients, particularly Plato and Aristotle, God was so transcendent that no interaction with the world was conceivable. This provoked the crude anthropomorphism of Greek mythology, in which the gods are curiously human—with greater capacities, to be sure, but filled with the virtues and vices common to us all. We have never quite gotten beyond this, Dorner says, in the modern rivalry between deism and pantheism, hyper-transcendence and hyper-immanence.[86] Classical theism has displayed at least a tendency toward the former, and much of contemporary criticism may be an overreaction in the other direction. God, it is true, is *other* than the world. But unless we affirm just as emphatically that God has fully involved *himself*, and not only an *appearance* of himself, in our world of time and space, the most important features of the Christian proclamation must be either surrendered or at least said tongue-in-cheek. While analogies and anthropomorphisms do not yield univocal access to God's being, they do communicate truth.

The Stoic doctrine of *apathēs/apatheia* is flatly denied by the Christian tradition wherever the latter asserts God's free involvement in the world. Moltmann

82. B. B. Warfield, *The Person and Work of Christ*, ed. Samuel G. Craig (Philadelphia: Presbyterian & Reformed, 1970), 570–71. I am grateful to Professor John Frame for pointing out this reference.

83. John of Damascus, "An Exact Exposition of the Orthodox Faith," *A Select Library of Nicene and Post-Nicene Fathers of the Christian Church*, 2nd Series, vol. 9, trans. S. D. F. Salmond (Grand Rapids: Eerdmans, 1973), 2.

84. Ibid., 4.

85. Ibid., 12.

86. Dorner, *Divine Immutability*, 82f.

is right when he says that we cannot read the passion narratives and conclude that God is aloof and unaffected by us. While some ancient and medieval Christian writers evidence a wariness toward attributing emotion to God, at least in etymological terms God's impassibility referred not to an inability to relate or to feel, but to an inability to *suffer*. For the ancients, "emotions" referred mainly to the temperamental moods of the gods, not to feeling or experience per se. This is one of those cases in which the English cognate does not match the Greek or Latin. We assume that *passio* is simply passion, but *suffering* was the precise definition in antiquity.[87] This is true even for John of Damascus, whose citations above might make us skeptical. As Gerald Bray points out, "Apatheia, as John of Damascus understood it, meant the inability to suffer, i.e., impassibility in the strict sense. The emphasis was not on tranquility in a state of indifference, but on the sovereignty of God."[88]

If we say that God is *not* intrinsically affected by the world, what are we to make of the intimacy of that personal relationship that God is represented as having with his creatures? Yet if we say that God *is* intrinsically affected by the world, how can we continue to say that God is perfect and independent of created reality? The answer proposed here is to recognize that although God exists independently of creation, he freely chooses to enter into a genuine relationship with the world. In this freedom *for* creaturely reality, God is genuinely affected, although in any given case this is to be understood in an analogical rather than a univocal sense. Is he moved to compassion? Yes, but not as we are. This is the analogical proviso that even Moltmann affirms and yet finally surrenders in working out the implications of his view.

By way of response to such criticisms of impassibility, Kevin J. Vanhoozer offers a suggestive way forward. He begins by summarizing the traditional account. Although Augustine moved beyond the Platonic view that the gods, lacking nothing, cannot love (referring to God's love as "gift-love: agape"), he nevertheless held with the Stoics the belief that "*pathos*—any emotional event that 'disturbs' reason and joy—has no place in the life of the only wise God."

> Importantly, Aquinas does not believe that God *responds* to the good in a thing by loving it, but rather that God's love for a thing is the *cause* of its goodness. On the traditional view, then, God metes out good but takes neither joy nor delight in the good he brings about (for this would make God's joy conditional on something in the world). That in which God takes delight turns out to be his own exercise of benevolence. . . . God, says Aquinas, is like a stone column to which humans stand in relation. The column may be on our left or our right, in front or behind us, but our relation to the column is in us, not in the column. Similarly, we may experience

87. Richard Muller, "Incarnation, Immutability, and the Case for Classical Theism," *Westminster Theological Journal* 45 (1983): 27: "The scholastic notion of God as immobile does not translate into English as 'immobile'—as one of the many cases of cognates not being fully convertible—but as 'unmoved.'"

88. Bray, *Doctrine of God*, 98.

> God's mercy or his wrath, but it is not God who changes, only our relation to him. "What changes is the way we experience the will of God" [Richard Creel]. . . . This is a most important analytic point: impassibility no more means impassive than immutability means immobile. God may be unmoved (transcendent: unsusceptible to worldly causes), but he is nevertheless a mover (immanent: active and present in the world).[89]

If Vanhoozer is correct in his interpretation of Aquinas, then it is difficult to know what to make even of the benediction that God pronounces on creation. Does God's loving make the creation lovely? Or does God love the creation because in it, as a result of his work, he sees its intrinsic value? Even with the analogical proviso, it is difficult to square the creation narrative, not to mention the so-called nature psalms, with the view that God does not *respond* to the creation. I will expand on this communicative view of the God-world relation in another place, but already I should affirm that God's goodness and love as the cause of the goodness and loveliness in the creature in no way mitigates the responsive delight that God shows in the work of his hands.

The analogy of a stone column only exacerbates the impression that this is a woefully inadequate approach to this question. In the view of relational theism, "God and the world are . . . partners—a suggestion that would have probably horrified most classical theists."[90] We should observe, however, that this suggestion would not have horrified covenant theologians, who nevertheless did not reduce God's being to God's relations. "For classical theism, God's love is a matter of his sovereign will, of benevolence: willing and acting for the other's good," whereas "the panentheist suggests that God's love is more a matter of affective empathy ('I feel your pain')."[91] "A picture of God as causal agent holds classical theism captive," which makes it "difficult to reconcile divine love with the notion of personal relation."[92]

This analysis of the dilemma seems justified. Strictly speaking, causes do not have to be personal, and they typically bear connotations of physical action of one object upon another. "One way beyond the classical theism-panentheistic impasse is, I suggest, to see God as a *communicative* agent."[93] God's communication is perfect (Isa. 55:11), never empty but always effective.[94] Further, "The good God wills for human beings is communion. . . . God's love is best viewed neither in terms of causality nor in terms of mutuality but rather in terms of communication and self-communication. . . . What God brings about in communicative action is *understanding*, as well as its precondition, faith."[95] Jesus as the

---

89. Kevin J. Vanhoozer, *First Theology: God, Scripture and Hermeneutics* (Downers Grove, IL: InterVarsity Press, 2002), 74–76.

90. Ibid., 87.

91. Ibid., 89–90.

92. Ibid., 90.

93. Ibid.

94. Ibid.

95. Ibid., 91.

Word is God's supreme communicative act. "To communicate is to impart, to give something to another."[96]

> God loves his people largely by bringing about understanding (and faith) through his communicative action. This is not simply a matter of conveying information but of making promises, issuing commands and giving warnings, as well as comforting and consoling. The crucial point is that God brings about understanding (faith, hope, comfort and so on) not through manipulation but precisely in a manner that is appropriate for persons with reason, will, imagination and emotions. The question of God's "openness," in regard to communicative theism, is whether God's relation to his people can be genuinely loving if God is unaffected by the communicative acts of his human interlocutors.[97]

Though surprising perhaps, this view can affirm impassibility, if it is properly defined—as indicated by reference to Jesus' impeccability. Borrowing on an analogy suggested by Augustus Strong for the latter, Vanhoozer argues,

> Jesus was sinless yet subject to real temptation in the same way that an invincible army is subject to attack. Something similar, I believe, may be said for divine impassibility. . . . God feels the force of his people's suffering: "I have seen the affliction of my people who are in Egypt, and have heard their cry because of their taskmasters; I know their sufferings" (Ex 3:7). Yet as Jesus feels the force of temptation without sinning, so God feels the force of the human experience without suffering change in his being, will or knowledge. Impassibility means not that God is unfeeling but that God is never *overcome* or *overwhelmed* by passion. . . . God genuinely relates to human persons via his communicative action, but nothing humans do conditions or affects God's communicative initiatives and God's communicative acts.[98]

Even evil and sin are comprehended in God's eternal decree; therefore, not even these can be said to condition God's will or acts. Further, Vanhoozer's construction of this argument is Trinitarian: "the Son and Spirit are means of the Father's communicative action."[99]

In a variety of ways, that which the tradition at its best has wanted to affirm is retained, yet by means of a more explicitly relational (communicative) conception. If we supplement this account with the notion of covenant, we can perhaps find more suitable ways of defending God's independence and perfection than traditional formulations have been able to do on the basis of a purely causal understanding of the God-world relationship. In the covenant God establishes with creatures, there is real partnership, but always in analogical rather than univocal relations. Recent criticisms of impassibility rarely succeed in challenging the dominant causal paradigm; they simply insist that the causal impact should

96. Ibid.
97. Ibid., 92.
98. Ibid., 93.
99. Ibid., 94.

run in both directions and often have difficulty resisting the temptation to see our acting upon God and God's causal action upon us in univocal terms. This is not to eliminate the category of cause from theological discourse, but to question its usefulness as an all-encompassing paradigm within which the divine-human relationship should be interpreted. Thus I will appeal to this communicative approach at a number of points throughout this volume.

Finally, what are we to make of the attribution of *immutability* to God? As with impassibility, a lot depends on the definition. According to critics of the doctrine, immutability is equivalent to immobility. In reducing the classic doctrine of God to Aristotle's "unmoved mover," Clark Pinnock simply calls it the "immobility package."[100] At least since Dorner, there has been an attempt to forge a distinction between God's moral attributes, which cannot change, and God's being, which is conditioned to some degree by the world. Adherents of this thesis range from more conservative presentations (such as Dorner's) to more radical versions (such as process theology). But can a covenantal paradigm, underscoring the analogical character of all theological predication, avoid such a dualism between God's character and being?

What is it then exactly for God to be moved? If we knew the answer to that, would we not have univocal (archetypal) knowledge of God's being *in esse*? There is an appropriateness to analogies that must not be given short shrift in order to save God from his own revelation, and yet analogies are not an exact fit between sign and reference. In Scripture the virtue in not being "moved" lies in the assurance that God is trustworthy (Ps. 16:8; 21:7), while for the Greeks it meant that immobility—pure stasis—was a supreme mode of being.

While Robert W. Jenson has represented his own antipathy toward the simplicity-impassibility-immutability complex as a classic example of Lutheran christology (i.e., allegedly hyper-Cyrillian) as opposed to the Reformed maxim that the finite cannot comprehend the infinite (*finitum non capax infiniti*), things cannot be so easily resolved. No less a Lutheran theologian than Gerhard O. Forde has responded to Jenson's criticism of immutability precisely by reaffirming an "unaccommodated" Luther.[101] His rejoinder to Jenson could equally apply to Moltmann: "When Martin Luther issued his frightening dictum to Erasmus and stated that God, hidden in majesty, has not bound himself to his word but kept himself free over all things, he was, I think, insisting on the impossibility of simply collapsing God into Jesus."[102]

---

100. Clark Pinnnock, *Most Moved Mover*, 78. Even in the most pristine expressions of "scholastic Calvinism," Aristotle's Unmoved Mover is explicitly summoned for refutation. In addition to Warfield one could cite, for example, his predecessor Charles Hodge, *Systematic Theology*, vol. 1 (1871; repr., Grand Rapids: Eerdmans, 1946), 391.

101. The reference to "unaccommodated" I have taken from similar criticisms by Richard Muller of the many illegitimate uses to which Calvin has been put by contemporary theologians in *The Unaccommodated Calvin: Studies in the Formation of a Theological Tradition* (New York: Oxford University Press, 2000).

102. Gerhard O. Forde, "Robert Jenson's Soteriology," in *Trinity, Time, and Church*, ed. Colin Gunton (Grand Rapids: Eerdmans, 2000), 136.

In Luther's theology the attributes of divinity such as divine necessity, immutability, timelessness, impassibility, and so forth, function as masks of God in his hiddenness. That means that they function on the one hand as wrath, as attack on human pretense, and on the other hand as comfort, as backup for the proclamation. However, they never simply go away, and a systematic theology can't make them do so. They keep coming back to terrify "the conscience." So much ought to be obvious by now. Attempts to settle accounts with the immutability of God, for instance, are legion. Yet they never finally work, not for lack of erudition usually, but for failure to use the proper weapons. Luther knew that no one can tear the mask from the face of the hidden God, but he also knew from the eschatological perspective that there was ultimate comfort in the divine names. . . . "If God were not immutable," Luther asks, "who can believe his promises?" . . . The "mutability" of God in the Son gets its pathos from the fact that the one who won't change nevertheless does so because of the personal union and the *communicatio idiomatum*. The God who can't die nevertheless does so. If one simply erases the immutability systematically, the mutability flattens out to be self-evident. God threatens to become just a patsy who is enriched by sharing our misery.[103]

Forde is not alone in concluding that Jenson is here, and at other points, inconsistent in his formulations.[104] It is not Luther but Hegel whose shadow looms large over these proposals.

Yet even Jenson concedes, "We may strive to free ourselves of pagan antiquity's metaphysical prejudice, according to which God is intrinsically impassible. But the religious impulse itself, without which we would not worry about God in the first place, will never desist from offense at God's self-presentation as a victim. God must be powerful and sweep all before him, else why do we need him?"[105] Thus there must be some sense in which God as covenant Lord is free *from* as well as *for* creation.

How then might we build a doctrine of God with the timber of strong verbs leading to adverbs and nouns? In that narrated identity of God in Scripture there emerges a number of direct claims and legitimate inferences that justify at least the conclusion that despite the anthropomorphic analogies that render a real actor in a historical drama, God cannot be overwhelmed by surprise, since his knowledge is perfect and encompasses the past, present, and future (Job 37:16; Ps. 139:1–6, 16–18), including the free acts of creatures (Exod. 7:1–7, 14; 8:15, 19; 9:12, 35; 10:1–2; 11:1–3, 9; 1 Sam. 23:10–13; Isa. 42:9; Acts 2:23; Rom. 8:28; 9:16; Eph. 1:11). Although God can be opposed, ultimately he cannot be overwhelmed by opposition (Dan. 4:17–37; Exod. 15:1–23; 8:11; Ps. 22:28–31; 47:2–8; 115:3; 135:5–21; Jer. 27:5; Acts 17:24–26; Rom. 9:17–21; Rev. 11:15–19). And although God can be present in a particular place and time, he cannot be overwhelmed by such circumscription (Ps. 139:7–12). The focus of the biblical testimony seems to

103. Ibid., 137.
104. See George Hunsinger, "Robert Jenson's *Systematic Theology*: A Review Essay," *Scottish Journal of Theology* 55, no. 2 (2002): 161–200.
105. Ibid., 138, citing *ST* 1:234.

be on the proscription of any limitations on God's attributes, not of God's capacity to genuinely relate.

Similarly, while God participates in the joy and sorrow of his people, without which the moral attributes of God would be empty, he is never overwhelmed by distress. Thus narratives in which God is represented as impatient or enraged reveal the seriousness with which God takes transgression of his covenant, but they provide no univocal description of God's being in itself. God is never overwhelmed with distress because God is more unlike than like us. This is treated as welcome news for those for whom God not only has compassion but also reserves anger: "I will not execute my fierce anger; I will not again destroy Ephraim; for I am God and no mortal, the Holy One in your midst, and I will not come in wrath" (Hos. 11:9). The same is assured in Malachi 3:6: "For I am the LORD, I do not change; therefore you are not consumed, O sons of Jacob." God's immutability is surely to be distinguished from any Greek concept of immobility, yet God's independence from the world is maintained precisely in and with his involvement in it. Only because God does not change, despite constant reprisals from his creation, can there be confidence to face each day without the threat of immanent disaster.

"To whom will you liken me and make me equal, and compare me, as though we were alike?" (Isa. 46:5; 55:8–9; Num. 23:19; 1 Sam. 15:29; Hos. 11:9). The fact is that *God* has compared himself to humans, as though we were alike—and yet (the analogical proviso) God retains his transcendence. Although truly known in his revelation, God cannot be contained by it (*finitum non capax infiniti*). To take analogies seriously is not to take them univocally. Scripture is no less analogical when it says that God does not repent than when it represents him as doing just that. Models are metaphors, and rather than being alternatives to "reality-depicting" language, they are the very means of indicating reality. This is as true in the natural sciences as in theology.[106]

Despite his incomprehensibility, God wills to enter into a relationship with his creatures. The covenant is the context in which that becomes possible. God enters into worldly relations, yet without simply collapsing Jesus into God, revelation into the divine essence, the immanent into the economic Trinity, the eternal decree (things hidden) into its temporal execution (things revealed). Let us turn for a moment to examples of this covenantal (analogical) discourse, particularly as touching on this debate. Since I have raised the question of immutability as part of the constellation of attributes traditionally predicated of God (and under contemporary criticism), I will interact at this point especially with the claims of what has come to be called "open theism," especially within recent evangelical discussions. I have already referred to some of its representative writings.

The obvious examples have to do with God relenting and repenting. Both, open theists contend, demonstrate that God is *not* immutable, independent, or

---

106. See Janet Martin Soskice, *Metaphor and Religious Language* (Oxford: Oxford University Press, 1984).

omniscient—at least as these terms have been historically understood.[107] In 1 Samuel 15:11, for example, God regrets having made Saul king, and yet in verse 29 we read, "Moreover the Glory of Israel will not recant or change his mind; for he is not a mortal, that he should change his mind." Neither God's nature nor his secret plan changes, and this is why believers can be confident that "if we are faithless, he remains faithful—for he cannot deny himself" (2 Tim. 2:13; cf. Mal. 3:6, to the same point). So what changes if not God's secret plans? It is his revealed plans that change: the judgment that he has warned that he will bring upon the people is averted—precisely as God had predestined before the ages. The dynamic give-and-take so obvious in the history of the covenant must be distinguished from the eternal decree that Scripture also declares as hidden in God's unchanging and inaccessible counsel (Eph. 1:4–11).

These are not two contradictory lines of proof texts, one line pro-openness, the other pro-classical theism. Rather, they are two lines of analogy acting as guardrails to keep us on the right path. There is real change, dynamic interaction, and partnership in this covenant (*Deus revalatus pro nos*). At the same time, God is not like the human partner in that he does not repent the way the latter repents: God transcends the analogies (*Deus absconditus in se*) even while revealing himself in and through them. With Scripture, we speak on one hand of the fall as contrary to God's revealed will and yet comprehended in God's secret plan (Rom. 8:20–21). In this view, we need not have the difficulty with the "repentance" passages the way open theists seem, by their silence, to be burdened by the "nonrepentance" passages. Against both hyper-Calvinism and openness theology, we need not reduce everything to either the eternal decree of the hidden God or the historical covenant of the revealed God.[108]

An analogical account provides a paradigm in which both God's independence from and relatedness to creaturely reality may be seriously affirmed without resolving the mystery in a false dilemma. Although Moltmann is an exception, Jenson, Pinnock, and Sanders all reflect an impatience with paradox that goes hand in hand with their impatience with analogy.[109] This rationalistic tendency can be seen, ironically, on both sides of the debate, by both defenders and critics

---

107. According to open theists, God knows everything that can be possibly known, which excludes the decisions and actions of free creatures. I leave it to the reader to determine whether this stretches or breaks any identification with *omni*science.

108. Pinnock and his colleagues may not approve the Reformed account of double agency, but their repeated misrepresentation of this tradition as "omnicausality" and the elimination of human partnership in the covenant is a perennial weakness of their rhetoric. This notion of double agency is not the incursion of philosophy, but is a good and necessary inference from such numerous passages. In the familiar Joseph narrative, the same event—Joseph's cruel treatment by his brothers—has two authors with two distinct intentions: "You meant it for evil, but God meant it for good" (Gen. 50:19–20 NKJV). Peter offers precisely the same rationale for the crucifixion: "You with your wicked hands. . . . But he was delivered up according to God's foreknowledge" (Acts 2).

109. For example, Hunsinger notes concerning Jenson, "Again and again, throughout his career, he has vilified paradox as a 'pious mystery-mongering of the vacuity'; by means of paradox, he believes, 'we communicate nothing whatever' [*Triune Identity*, 126]. . . . This criticism, it seems, underlies Jenson's resort to rationalistic metaphysics" (Hunsinger, "Review Essay," 199).

of classical theism, where certain predicates are either affirmed or denied in a univocal sense.

Yet, despite calls to trade abstract for concrete description of God, many of the critics of traditional affirmations of God's independence do end up speaking of transcendence and immanence in quite abstract, static, and general terms. Some of their expressions appear to be timeless ideas drawn from the familiar antitheses of ancient and modern dualism (and dualistic monism), and this often leads to false dilemmas. We worship either a God who does not want to "control everything, but to give the creature room to exist and freedom to love," or "an all-controlling despot who can tolerate no resistance (Calvin)"; the latter gives the false impression that Calvin held this position.[110] Further, we must choose between a God who is "immobile" (a "solitary monad") and the "living God" who is dependent on the creation for his happiness.[111] That is important, since the very title of Pinnock's book suggests that the position he is criticizing is little more than a religious gloss on Aristotle's Unmoved Mover. But since we have already seen that immobility is in no way required by immutability, we need not repeat those arguments here.

However much in this respect the Christian doctrine sounds similar to Aristotle's Unmoved Mover, the differences are greater. Charles Hodge, for example, reminds us that in the classical view God is immutable, "but nevertheless that He is not a stagnant ocean, but ever living, ever thinking, ever acting, and ever suiting his action to the exigencies of his creatures, and to the accomplishment of his infinitely wise designs." Far from speculating how this is so, which extreme representations on both sides of this debate are often tempted to do, he adds,

> Whether we can harmonize these facts or not, is a matter of minor importance. We are constantly called upon to believe that things are, without being able to tell how they are, or even how they can be. Theologians, in their attempts to state, in philosophical language, the doctrine of the Bible on the unchangeableness of God, are apt to confound immutability with immobility. In denying that God can change, they seem to deny that He can act.[112]

Immutability must not be confused with immobility, and there is unanimity here among the various Reformed dogmatics.[113] In a similar vein, Cornelius Van Til writes,

110. Pinnock, *Most Moved Mover*, 4.
111. Ibid., 6.
112. Hodge, *Systematic Theology*, 1:390–91.
113. Ibid., 392. Here Hodge criticizes in particular some statements of Augustine to that effect, charging that he speculated beyond the limits of exegesis. But modern theology is far more indebted to philosophical assumptions, he charges. "We must abide by the teachings of Scripture, and refuse to subordinate their authority and the intuitive convictions of our moral and religious nature to the arbitrary definitions of any philosophical system." Bavinck concurs: "The fact that God is immutable does not mean that he is inactive: immutability should not be confused with immobility" (*Doctrine of God*, 151).

> Surely in the case of Aristotle the immutability of the divine being was due to its emptiness and internal immobility. No greater contrast is thinkable than that between the unmoved *noesis noeeseoos* of Aristotle and the Christian God. This appears particularly from the fact that the Bible does not hesitate to attribute all manner of activity to God. . . . Herein lies the glory of the Christian doctrine of God, that the unchangeable one is the one in control of the change of the universe.[114]

YHWH is therefore not a solitary monad lost in self-contemplation, a Buddha-like figure who closes his eyes to the world in order to contemplate his own bliss. But he is also not a creature contained in and circumscribed by the reality that he has created apart from himself. That which Douglas Farrow has said in criticism of Robert Jenson's view can also be applied to that of Moltmann and open theism: "It is an imposition on the biblical narrative, as on dogmatic tradition, to suggest that the God who has decided not to be God without us is therefore only God by being God with us."[115]

On one hand, we must avoid the conclusion that God is untouched or unmoved by creaturely suffering. Otherwise, the analogies carry no freight and the ominous fears of our having yielded to a god behind the God revealed in Jesus Christ are justified. Are we not therefore justified in saying that God experiences opposition to his loving designs, but not as we do? That he experiences time, but not as the passing of moments experienced by us? That he poses possibilities for humanity and his covenant people, but not merely as one person cooperates with another in human experience? Before we react too quickly to the concerns raised by Moltmann, Pannenberg, Jenson, and others, we must recognize that there is an impassibility tradition that is motivated by Greek philosophy and that has undoubtedly infected certain accounts of the doctrine in Jewish and Christian theology. For example, Moltmann cites Maimonides: "'God is free from passions; He is moved neither by feelings of joy nor by feelings of pain.' Spinoza followed the same line when he propounded the thesis that 'God neither loves nor hates.'"[116] A genuinely Christian theology cannot make these claims, but neither can it embrace a univocal identity between divine and human emotions and dependency. Whatever we are to say in defense of God's immunity to being overtaken, we must come to terms with the two fronts of the challenge: the criticism not only of God's transcendent freedom but of his covenantal relation and very personhood as well.

On the other hand, we must avoid the conclusion that God is overwhelmed or conditioned in his eternal nature or will by that which he has created, which depends at every moment on his free and unconditioned sustenance. Beyond this, we could speculate perhaps on what is "worthy" or "appropriate" of God's nature, by appealing to one metaphysical scheme or another, but to that extent

114. Cited by Muller, "Incarnation," 30.
115. Douglas Farrow, "Robert Jenson's *Systematic Theology*, Three Responses," *International Journal of Systematic Theology* 1, no. 1 (1999): 91.
116. Moltmann, *Trinity and the Kingdom*, 26.

we lose our connection with the God of Israel who confronts us as a stranger—and, in fact, a judge, apart from Christ. Idolatry is what happens when we project our own ideals of perfection onto the metaphysical map.

In contrast to both Parmenidean permutations of divine bliss and Heraclitean versions of divine flux, biblical hope inserts the eschatological category of *shalom*. While this is certainly not Stoic immobility and *apatheia*, it is nevertheless peaceful existence, but the kind of peace defined by God in the analogy of Israel and its theocratic laws and supremely in Christ's proclamation of the kingdom: the absence of strife, suffering, evil, and unrighteousness. It is even named Sabbath *rest*, not because there is no movement but because there is no departure from the proper relation to God; not because there is no passion, but because the passion of God's own abundant life and joy constantly revitalizes and refreshes its inhabitants. If God indwells the Sabbath (and if he does not, how can he bring us into it?), then he is already enjoying everlasting peace, joy, righteousness in the triune fellowship of perfect giving and receiving, loving and being loved. God not only enjoys this Sabbath reality in its fullest measure already, but is working to bring it about for us. In answer to criticism for healing on the Sabbath, Jesus replied, "My Father is still working, and I also am working" (John 5:17). That working is indeed a struggle, but one in which YHWH finally triumphs because no purpose of his can be thwarted. It is precisely because God is independent and unconditioned in his Sabbath reign that he is *able* to bring hope to victims and victimizers, and it is precisely because God has freely entered into a covenantal relation with the creatures that we can trust that he is *willing* to do so. This brings us to the communicable or moral attributes.

QUALIFIED LORDSHIP

While the "incommunicable" attributes (i.e., those predicates in which there is not even an analogical relationship to human traits) are of crucial importance in articulating a biblical account, they do not receive the concentrated focus that the "communicable" (or moral) attributes have in the biblical drama. Not surprisingly, Calvin in his *Institutes* only mentions in passing God's incommunicable perfections, since this verges on speculation concerning God's essence: "The scriptural teaching concerning God's infinite and spiritual essence ought to be enough, not only to banish popular delusions, but to refute the subtleties of secular philosophy. But even if God to keep us sober speaks sparingly of his essence, yet by those titles that I have used he both banishes stupid imaginings and restrains the boldness of the human mind."[117]

I group these communicable attributes under the heading of qualified lordship to underscore the point that God's power is bound to his nature, against the nominalist trajectory in modern theology that reduces God's perfections to an

---

117. Calvin, *Institutes* 1.13.1.

omnipotence (absolute power) that is bound simply to God's will. Calvin writes, for instance, that God's just will governs all, yet "not, indeed, that absolute will of which the Sophists babble, by an impious and profane distinction separating his justice from his power."[118] In the wake of nominalism, modernity has identified freedom with the will, but whether this blind and arbitrary freedom is predicated of God or humans, it depersonalizes freedom by divorcing it from the character of the willing agent. Such extreme libertarian views undermine any genuine reliability between agents, which is the presupposition of a covenant. But if God's will, rather than an independent faculty with pure liberty, is simply the outward expression of his character, then not even God can act contrary to his own moral dispositions. Freedom, for God and for humans, is a natured liberty—that is, a liberty to be—to will in accordance with one's essence. There is no such thing as absolute power or abstract willing. (This, by the way, is another use for the much maligned and much abused doctrine of simplicity.)

First, God's lordly freedom is qualified or, better, given its moral direction by God's knowledge and wisdom. It is not simply that God has more thoughts, better thoughts, or deeper thoughts, but that his *way* of knowing is his own, never identical at any point with creaturely knowledge: "For my thoughts are not your thoughts, nor are your ways my ways, says the LORD. For as the heavens are higher than the earth, so are my ways higher than your ways and my thoughts than your thoughts" (Isa. 55:8–9). Indeed, Paul's excursus on God's freedom in election leads to the doxology, "O the depth of the riches and wisdom and knowledge of God! How unsearchable are his judgments and how inscrutable his ways! 'For who has known the mind of the Lord?'" (Rom. 11:33–36). Secrecy is a divine prerogative that, like his glory, he will not concede to any creature (Deut. 29:29). God knows our thoughts exhaustively (Ps. 44:21; 94:11), but God's thoughts are inaccessible to us apart from revelation.

But God's knowledge and wisdom are particularly evident in the history of redemption, as the context of Paul's doxology above (Rom. 11:33) underscores. God's wisdom is seen in the revelation of the mystery of Christ in these last days, a wisdom that reduces human speculation and erudition to foolishness (1 Cor. 2:7; Col. 1:16; Eph. 3:10–11). "In Christ we have also obtained an inheritance, having been predestined according to the purpose of him who accomplishes all things according to his counsel and will" (Eph. 1:11). God's knowledge and wisdom, then, are not abstract concepts but are predominantly demonstrated in the service of God's covenant of redemption—that is, in the unfolding mystery of God's purposes in Christ. It is this wisdom and knowledge that God reveals to his prophets (Amos 3:7; Isa. 42:9). In fact, Christ is himself the content of that wisdom and knowledge (1 Cor. 1:30). The Father himself has no higher or more prized knowledge than his knowledge of the Son, and the Spirit is satisfied to keep his mission in the economy within the confines of this revelation of Christ.

---

118. Calvin, *Institutes* 1.17.2; cf. CR XXXIV. 339f: "What the Sorbonne doctors say, that God has an absolute power, is a diabolical blasphemy which has been invented in hell."

We particularly witness God's knowledge and wisdom in his displays of power. God's omnipotence, Dorner notes, far from being an antagonist to, is necessary for, our own freedom.[119] This requires a Trinitarian conception, for although omniscience, omnipotence, and omnipresence are predicated equally of the three persons, God never works simply upon the world but also within it, as that world is continually spoken forth in the Son and is effectively shaped by the Spirit. Pannenberg draws together omnipotence, omniscience, and omnipresence, and he makes a good case for this: "No power, however great, can be efficacious unless present to its object. Omnipresence is thus a condition of omnipotence. But omnipotence shows what omnipresence by the Spirit actually means."[120] John of Damascus made a similar point: "For He saw all things before they were, holding them timelessly in His thoughts; and each one conformably to His voluntary and timeless thought, which constitutes predetermination and image and pattern, comes into existence at the predetermined time."[121] Omnipresence is the rationale for this:

> For He is His own place, filling all things and being above all things, and Himself maintaining all things. Yet we speak of God having place and the place of God where His energy becomes manifest. . . . And His sacred flesh has been named the foot of God. The Church, too, is spoken of as the place of God: for we have set this apart for the glorifying of God as a sort of consecrated place wherein we hold converse with Him.[122]

Confusing this omnipotence with tyranny is the result of misunderstanding God's power "in antithesis to others who have no power." Tyranny strives after omnipotence, but its striving betrays its resentment for not being omnipotent, says Pannenberg.

> This object of its power is an outside precondition of its own activity. But the power of God has no precondition outside itself. One of its features is that it brings forth that over which it has power. Only as the Creator can God be almighty. For this reason the scriptures consistently relate what they say about God's omnipotence to references to his creative work. . . . Only the Creator can awaken the dead, and resurrection from the dead shows what it means to be Creator.[123]

Divine omnipotence does not entail the "occasionalism" (perhaps better identified as omnicausalism) that haunts the sophisticated philosophical theologies of Malebranche and Jonathan Edwards and the popular piety of many for whom secondary causes are unnecessary. For instance, Edwards maintained that all things are done by God "in the immediate exercise of his power."[124] But if God

---

119. Dorner, *Divine Immutability,* 147.
120. Pannenberg, *ST* 1:415.
121. John of Damascus, "Exact Exposition," 12.
122. Ibid., 15.
123. Pannenberg, *ST* 1:416.
124. Jonathan Edwards, *Scientific and Philosophical Writings,* ed. Wallace E. Anderson, Works of Jonathan Edwards 6 (New Haven, CT: Yale University Press, 1960), 214.

worked directly and immediately in every event, omnipotence would indeed mean the impossibility of genuine creaturely freedom.

God need not surrender the slightest degree of Creator freedom (sovereignty) in order to secure creaturely freedom (responsible agency). The assumption that in order for humans to be free God must limit his own freedom rests upon a univocity of being; but if being is analogical, then there is no common reservoir of freedom to be rationed; instead, there is Creator freedom and creature freedom. At no point are these freedoms univocal, and yet their analogical relation is sufficient to ground covenantal partnership. Once again the covenant reminds us that God's sovereignty, though infinite and by definition incapable of being limited (even self-limited), appears to us *in Christ* not as blinding majesty but as a reliable bond and oath to save and preserve us. God's power is tethered not only to his knowledge, wisdom, love, goodness, and justice, but also to his covenant.

Closely related to God's wisdom and knowledge is his veracity, which is even more closely tied to the covenantal context and, more specifically, to the trial that involves Israel and YHWH in the interchanging roles of judge, defendant, and witness, testimony and countertestimony mediated by the prophets. In the Old Testament the words ʾĕmet, ʾĕmûnāh, and ʾāmēn frequently occur in the context of these covenant lawsuits, and the New Testament carries this forward in the person of Christ, as the culmination of the cosmic trial, appealing to *alētheia* and its cognates, with Jesus Christ as the hypostasis of truth itself (John 14:6). YHWH *is* truth: in an ethical sense (Num. 23:19; Rom. 3:4; Heb. 6:18) and in a logical sense (knowing how things really are). God's covenant faithfulness (*ḥesed*) is the glue that holds all these concepts together. God will be true to reality because he who is necessarily the truth is the creator of reality and the judge of its perversions. Like God's other attributes, goodness and love are revealed in the context of strong verbs leading to nouns, in the context of a trial. We join the gallery of onlookers to this trial, for example, in Jeremiah 12, where the prophet declares, "You will be in the right, O LORD, when I lay charges against you; but let me put my case to you. Why does the way of the guilty prosper? Why do all who are treacherous thrive?" (v. 1).

A further implication of God's simplicity is not only that we cannot abstract God's will from his nature; we cannot single out our favorite attribute as the most essential and force the diverse representations of God's character to surrender to a concept. This is particularly true when we attempt to articulate God's love. It is especially in our day not a far stretch from "God is love" to "Love is God." In interpersonal relationships, love has become the rationalization for every disloyalty, infidelity, and self-seeking act. When our desire for the other is determined by what we can acquire or possess, love becomes lust and its object becomes an idol and, when it fails to deliver, a demon to be conquered—a threat to one's very existence.

What makes God's love so comforting, therefore, is not only the obvious point that it has not been twisted into lust but the more basic fact that this is so precisely because God's love is unconditioned by anything in the creature. This is not the case, of course, in the intra-Trinitarian communion, where the Father derives his very fatherhood from the eternal generation of the Son and the realization of his purposes through the eternal procession of the Spirit. In this eternal exchange, no one is ever let down. There is no Stoic refusal of entrusting one's happiness to the other. Once more the Trinitarian formulation of God's attributes is key, as Pannenberg remarks in his correction of Jüngel ("God is he who eternally loves himself"): "If, however, the one loves self in the other instead of loving the other as other, then love falls short of the full self-giving which is the condition that the one who loves be given self afresh in the responsive love of the one who is loved."[125] This is the weakness of the Augustinian-Thomistic formulations in which God's impassibility is understood as entailing God's love of the other only as a means of loving himself.

But precisely because this perfect exchange determines God's own happiness, he does not need the world in order to be the loving God. Conditioned only by the perfect love of the persons of the Trinity, God's love reaches out to create, sustain, and even redeem human persons who have not only failed to return love adequately but have become, in Augustine's apt phrase, curved in on themselves. The independence of God in all of his incommunicable attributes returns once again to underscore the sheer givenness of God's love. It is not out of a craving for what he lacks, an insufficiency in his being, or a necessity imposed upon him, but out of an overflowing abundance of ecstatic love that we continue to exist, much less to be drawn out of ourselves, made extroverts, reconciled to God and one another. A god who depends on the creation at any point for his being or will can never love in freedom: as the object of such a god's desire exercises its freedom in opposition to his desire, the creature thus made an idol becomes the object of intense resentment and hatred.

God's goodness is not a counterweight to other attributes that seem in our distorted conceptions to be inimical to it, such as sovereignty, justice, and wrath. On no occasion has God exercised his power, satisfied his holiness, or displayed his righteous anger in a way that violated his goodness. Our confidence in God's goodness, whether we recognize it explicitly or not, depends upon his lordship over evil and suffering, his righting of all wrongs, and his putting an end to all that stands in the way of our redemption and free communion with him.

Beyond God's universal goodness in creation and providence, if ever we were tempted to abstract God's sovereignty, justice, wrath, or righteousness from God's goodness, we are redirected to the cross, where we behold with unparalleled clarity the triumph of God's goodness in the face of Christ, who cries out, "It is finished." If we are ever in doubt as to how far God will go with his goodness, in view of the hostility with which it is resisted, we read, "God so loved the world that he gave his only Son" (John 3:16). As Barth cautions, it is not a "general conception" of love that is definitive here, but the specific act of God in Jesus

125. Pannenberg, *ST* 1:426.

Christ.[126] "God is love" is therefore never to be abstracted from the total divine nature. God's love is essential to his being, notes David Tracy.

> However, if this classic Johannine metaphor "God is love" is not grounded and thereby interpreted by means of the harsh and demanding reality of the message and ministry, the cross and resurrection of this unsubstitutable Jesus who, as the Christ, disclosed God's face turned to us as Love, then Christians may be tempted to sentimentalize the metaphor by reversing it into "Love is God." But this great reversal, on inner-Christian terms, is hermeneutically impossible. "God is love": this identity of God the Christian experiences in and through the history of God's actions and self-disclosure as the God who is Love in Jesus Christ, the parable and face of God.[127]

Yet it is particularly in light of human sinfulness that we can affirm that "there is no one good except God alone" (Mark 10:18). God exercises a charity toward all he has made (Ps. 145:9, 15–16), even those who return to him evil for good (Matt. 5:45). God's goodness is extravagant to the point of what we typically regard as folly, naiveté, and an overly tolerant indulgence toward others. Yet it is the hallmark of God's generous liberality toward us. Again, as with the other attributes, God not only loves or possesses love as a property, but *is* love (1 John 3:1). God loves absolutely and without any compulsion from the object of his love (John 3:16; Matt. 5:44–45; John 16:27; Rom. 5:8). This unconditionedness of God's character once again, far from inhibiting our trust in a God-with-us, firmly grounds it.

As is the case with the other attributes, grace and mercy are not static potentialities, but fully realized actualities of God's nature. Once again it is the strong verbs announcing God's acts in redemptive history that reveal this character. B. A. Gerrish notes that according to 2 Timothy 1:9–10, "God's grace has *appeared*. . . . 'Grace,' for [Paul], means more than a divine attribute: it refers to something that has happened, entered into history," as in John 1:17: "Grace and truth came (*egeneto*) through Jesus Christ."[128] We should add 2 Timothy 1:9–10, "This grace was given to us in Christ Jesus before the ages began, but it has now been revealed through the appearing of our Savior Christ Jesus, who abolished death and brought life and immortality to light through the gospel." *This* is how we know that God is gracious. Indeed, it is how we define grace itself: through election, covenant, incarnation, and redemption.

In one sense, perhaps, grace and mercy, like wrath and judgment, should not be regarded as divine attributes (at least absolute attributes), since they presuppose fault, and God would be God even if there were no opportunity to have mercy.

---

126. Barth, *CD* II/1:352.
127. David Tracy, "Trinitarian Speculation and the Forms of Divine Disclosure," in *The Trinity: An Interdisciplinary Symposium on the Trinity*, ed. Stephen T. Davis, Daniel Kendall, SJ, and Gerald O'Collins, SJ (Oxford: Oxford University Press, 1999), 285–86.
128. B. A. Gerrish, "Sovereign Grace: Is Reformed Theology Obsolete?" *Interpretation* 57, no. 1 (2003): 45.

Yet even in the intra-Trinitarian communion prior to creation, or in the prelapsarian relation with Adam and Eve, "God is gracious and full of compassion." Whether he has an occasion to show mercy, being a merciful God, "gracious and merciful, slow to anger, and abounding in steadfast love" (Joel 2:13), belongs to God's eternal character. One could even argue that because of God's eternal decree, in the intra-Trinitarian covenant of redemption (*pactum salutis*), God has always been gracious and merciful, as when Paul says in the text already cited (2 Tim. 1:9–10) that God's grace "was given to us in Christ Jesus before the ages began." In this sense, the Father has always elected in grace, the Son has always been the mediator of that grace, and the Spirit has always been the pledge and deliverer of that grace. Nevertheless, this eternal decree is a free decision on God's part. God was free to redeem or not to redeem (an essential presupposition of the very ideas of grace and mercy): "I will have mercy on whom I have mercy, and I will have compassion on whom I have compassion" (Rom. 9:15, quoting Exod. 33:19).

Appealing to Polanus and other Reformed scholastics, Barth defines grace as "the distinctive mode of God's being in so far as it seeks and creates fellowship by its own free inclination and favour, unconditioned by any merit or claim in the beloved, but also unhindered by any unworthiness or opposition in the latter— able, on the contrary, to overcome all unworthiness and opposition."[129] What Barth opposes is viewing grace as an intermediary substance rather than God's own gift of himself. Grace is not a third "thing" mediating, but is Jesus Christ. *God* is gracious to us.

> Grace denotes, comprehensively, the manner in which God, in His essential being, turns toward us. . . . Now this means that grace is a being and action of God upon which no one and nothing has any claim; [God] owes nothing to any counterpart. . . . Grace means redemption.[130]

The gift that God gives in grace is none other than himself:

> We must not follow Roman Catholic dogma . . . in making an *a priori* and decisive definition of grace as a supernatural gift, and then proceeding to characterise it as a third element mediatorial between God and His creatures. Grace is certainly a gift—and indeed a very supernatural gift. In fact it epitomises all the gifts of God—not merely revelation, reconciliation and redemption, but also creation. But it is a gift—and this must be our *a priori* definitive description—in so far as the Giver, i.e., God Himself, makes Himself the gift, offering Himself to fellowship with the other, and thus showing Himself in relation to the other to be the One who loves.[131]

There is much in Barth's treatment that is of value. In fact, his definition of grace is an important improvement on the usual understanding of grace as sim-

---

129. Barth, *CD* II/1:353.
130. Ibid., 354–55.
131. Ibid., 353–54.

ply "unmerited favor." "Grace means redemption," he rightly says. "It is always God's turning to those who not only do not deserve this favour, but have deserved its opposite."[132] In fact, "Grace itself is mercy."[133] But then it is all the more alarming to suggest that creation itself is an act of redemption and that humankind simply *as* human deserves condemnation. But just because of this definition, how can it be applied to every divine act toward the world?

Grace cannot be comprehensive of God's being turned toward us in the act of creation, for example, since there is no ethical fault. While creation is an act of divine condescension and therefore a gift that is not deserved, it is also not an act of mercy. It is true, of course, that God's creation of the world and us in it is in no way conditioned by us, but that does not make it gracious. Adam and Eve were not created out of any external obligation, and so it is an utterly free decision; but this is condescension, love, and goodness rather than grace and redemption. Barth has not slipped into inconsistency in this formulation. He emphatically maintains that grace presupposes sin.[134] However, a supralapsarian version of predestination allows eternity to swallow the horizon of the covenant's historical unfolding: "before" and "after" lose their ontological status. "Where grace is manifest and effectual, it is always a question of the misery of man."[135] Grace is "how God loves."[136] But what if we were to apply this to the intra-Trinitarian life? Furthermore, what has happened to goodness, love, the desire for fellowship with creatures, condescension? Are these not sufficient as the basis for a covenantal relationship with pre-fallen creatures?

Theology needs desperately to recover a sense of God's kindness and generosity, which belong properly to the order of creation even prior to and distinct from the specific sort of kindness and generosity that is shown to sinners in their misery. Even the intra-Trinitarian relationship is defined by grace in Barth.[137] But how can *de*merit (part of Barth's own definition) possibly be predicated of the divine persons? In this connection, it is because grace is a "turning to," but his other definitions of grace above have to be figured in as well. It would seem that for all of the talk of the triumph of grace, this actually weakens the coinage while also surrendering the space for creation simply to be itself, as God created it, without being redeemed.

Not only are love and grace simply identical, according to Barth; so too are grace and holiness. "We are not, then, making any crucial change of theme when we go on to speak of God's holiness. We are merely continuing to speak of God's grace."[138] Again, what is the import of that statement if we take it together with his definition of grace as God's gift of himself not only to those who do not

132. Ibid., 356.
133. Ibid., 369.
134. Ibid., 355.
135. Ibid., 371.
136. Ibid., 357.
137. Ibid., 358.
138. Ibid., 359.

deserve it but who deserve its opposite? "In grace God turns to others and simultaneously in holiness is true to himself. . . . To say grace is to say forgiveness of sins; to say holiness, judgment upon sins."[139] What is so peculiar about this is that Barth himself had earlier stated so emphatically that traditional approaches to God's attributes failed to see each perfection in its distinct character. Yet here (as elsewhere), grace is not only correlated with holiness and holiness with judgment upon sins, but grace *is* condemnation! This is far from a genuinely dialectical view. Grace, rather, should be seen as an attribute that God displays in the unconditional freedom of his response to human fault. It is shown to covenant-breakers. It is not that this event creates or activates a divine attribute, but that it provides the occasion for its demonstration.

With God's *holiness* we are once again deep in the covenantal territory, especially when correlated with God's covenant love/faithfulness (*ḥesed*). Holiness is treated in Scripture as a marker both of God's ontological distinction from creation and his ethical distinction from fallen humanity. Thus when God elects Israel, calling Abram out of Ur, he "makes holy" that which is itself profane. The cutting ceremonies that God commands (circumcision, the sacrifices, and the wider cultic life of the theocracy such as dietary and sanitation laws) enact this decisive separation of God's people from the world. While the nations inhabit an enchanted cosmos filled with numinous gods and supernatural forces, Israel knows as holy only YHWH and its own election by YHWH. Barth rightly comments, "The holy God of Scripture is certainly not 'the holy' of R. Otto, a numinous element which, in its aspect as *tremendum*, is in itself and as such divine. But the holy God of Scripture is the Holy One of Israel."[140]

Closely related to God's holiness is his glory or majesty: *kābôd*, which is itself closely related to the Spirit as God's Shekinah-presence among his people and, one day, throughout the earth. We catch a glimpse of this in Isaiah's vision:

> In the year that King Uzziah died, I saw the Lord sitting on a throne, high and lofty; and the hem of his robe filled the temple. Seraphs were in attendance above him; each had six wings: with two they covered their faces, and with two they covered their feet, and with two they flew. And one called to another and said: "Holy, holy, holy is the LORD of hosts; the whole earth is full of his glory." The pivots on the thresholds shook at the voices of those who called, and the house filled with smoke. And I said: "Woe to me! I am lost, for I am a man of unclean lips, and I live among a people of unclean lips; yet my eyes have seen the King, the LORD of hosts!" (Isa. 6:1–5)

The vision thus far provoked fear, as every encounter with the God of holiness does, as when Peter responds to Jesus' filling of his nets with fish, "Go away from me, Lord, for I am a sinful man" (Luke 5:8). An otherwise joyful event is ominous

139. Ibid., 360.
140. Ibid.

because it measures the gulf separating Peter from that stranger who is calling him to his side. Holiness and glory become synonymous in these events, where human beings realize that they are in the presence of the Shekinah-Glory that filled the temple and yet was shrouded behind the veil.

This holiness must be read by us through the lens of the gospel; otherwise, it becomes a blinding glory, an overwhelming presence that reduces sinful creatures to death. That is precisely where Isaiah's vision leads. Having been commissioned to pronounce God's "woes"—the verdict of the covenant lawsuit—against others, he now finds himself trapped under the weight of God's blinding glory: "Woe to me! I am lost, . . . yet my eyes have seen the King, the LORD of hosts!"

> Then one of the seraphs flew to me, holding a live coal that had been taken from the altar with a pair of tongs. The seraph touched my mouth with it and said: "Now that this has touched your lips, your guilt has departed and your sin is blotted out." Then I heard the voice of the Lord saying, "Whom shall I send, and who will go for us?" And I said, "Here am I; send me!" (vv. 6–8)

Only in Christ are the unholy made holy, elected and separated out of the world as the temple that his glory fills. The New Testament in no way contradicts this distinction between holy and profane, but rather God's holiness widens to include gentiles, so that the previous distinctions of "clean" and "unclean" are no longer canonical (i.e., in force) for the new covenant community (Acts 10:9–48). Thus, as we have seen with other attributes typically associated with God's transcendence, God's holiness is not only a marker of God's distinction from the creation but of God's driving passion to make the whole earth his holy dwelling.

God's holiness and righteousness express ethical perfections that are not always easy to translate into the intellectual and practical habits of modernity. The noun "holiness," *qōdeš*, comes from the verb *qādaš* (to cut or separate). Once again this holiness is better seen in action than abstractly contemplated. This "cutting" or "separating" lies at the heart of Israel's most important cultic practices: circumcision, the ceremonial separation of even vessels to be used in the tabernacle and temple, the ceremonial legislation governing "clean" and "unclean" animals, all indicating the solidarity of the whole people as separated out of the world to belong to YHWH, to share in his holiness and righteousness. There are no significant departures from this understanding of holiness in the New Testament expression (*hagiazō/hagios*). God's holiness refers to both his ontological transcendence (Creator-creature distinction) and his ethical incomparability, but also to his immanence in taking to himself a people who, unholy in themselves, are acceptable in Christ, "who became for us wisdom from God, and righteousness and sanctification and redemption" (1 Cor. 1:30).

Righteousness has been one of the most widely debated predications with respect to its meaning, especially in the Old Testament. Some time ago Eichrodt noted, "It is a decided obstacle to any attempt to define the concept of divine righteousness, that the original significance of the root *ṣdq* should be irretrievably lost."[141] The predominant use is for right behavior. "When applied to the conduct of God the concept is narrowed and almost exclusively employed in a forensic sense. God's ṣᵉdāqā or ṣedeq is his keeping of the law in accordance with the terms of the covenant."[142] This is not the distributive justice of Roman law, though, which is too formal and abstract to describe Israel's thought. Eichrodt follows Cremer's groundbreaking work, which identifies righteousness with showing right relationship between persons. It is closely related to mišpāṭ, "justice," and (following Cremer), is a *iustitia salutifera*.[143]

In the Psalter, righteousness and mercy (ḥesed) go together as well. Righteousness involves centrally God's dogged determination to bring about his purpose in spite of human sin. *"The maintenance of the fellowship now becomes the justification of the ungodly*. No manner of human effort, but only that righteousness which is the gift of God, can lead to that conduct which is truly in keeping with the covenant."[144]

Therefore, as Barth notes, the connection between righteousness and mercy is closer than Bernard of Clairvaux's description ("the two feet of God").[145] Yet we cannot simply collapse righteousness into mercy, as Ritschl does.[146] But nowhere in this discussion does Barth allow a divine exercise of righteousness that is not simultaneously merciful. God's righteousness includes the concept of *"iustitia distributiva*, a righteousness which judges and therefore both exculpates and condemns, reward and also punishes. . . . But as mercy and grace and love it is now a righteousness which condemns and punishes."[147] This avoids the error of both orthodoxy and Ritschl, Barth surmises.[148] However, we must not deduce an understanding of righteousness in Scripture from fears of where it might lead. Ṣdq and its cognates appear in the context of judgment and wrath as well as justification and deliverance.

Thus closely related to righteousness and holiness, not to mention the wrath that can "flare up in a moment" in the face of breaches, is that interplay in history among God's jealousy, wrath, and patience. As with wrath, jealousy strikes most of us as unworthy of God particularly because of its associations in our experience of human vice. As wrath generally connotes in our parlance a thirst for revenge or the temper tantrums of the powerful against the weak, jealousy is almost universally regarded as a negative human trait. But instead of jettisoning jealousy or attempting to "translate" it into (i.e., accommodate it to) our own experience, the biblical representation of God's jealousy can open us up to a new understanding of the term that challenges and potentially heals our experience.

141. Eichrodt, *Theology*, 1:240.
142. Ibid.
143. Ibid., 241.
144. Ibid., 247.
145. Barth, *CD* II/1:380.
146. Ibid., 382.
147. Ibid., 391.
148. Ibid.

As Dorner remarks, "The divine jealousy is one that is holy and not one that is envious."[149]

It is probably not too much of an exaggeration to suggest, with Robert Jenson, "In the Scriptures . . . it is first among the Lord's attributes that he is 'a jealous God.'"[150] While political toleration is a benefit of democratic culture, YHWH ranks religious pluralism enemy number one in his stipulations for his covenant people, as enshrined in the Decalogue. The sole lordship of YHWH, as we have seen, is the presupposition of biblical faith, and it is carried forward into the fuller revelation of YHWH's identity as applied to Jesus Christ. "I am the way, and the truth, and the life. No one comes to the Father except through me" (John 14:6). "Therefore God also highly exalted him and gave him the name that is above every name, so that at the name of Jesus every knee should bend, in heaven and on earth and under the earth, and every tongue should confess that Jesus Christ is Lord, to the glory of God the Father" (Phil. 2:9–10). God has raised Jesus from the dead. Therefore, "There is salvation in no one else, for there is no other name under heaven given among mortals by which we must be saved" (Acts 4:12). God is jealous for his own name and for the people who call on his name and are called by his name. God will not give his glory to another.

Jealousy in humans is a perversion because it implies a right that does not belong to us. We hoard possessions, and to the extent that even relationships, creatures, and other people can become possessions rather than being acknowledged as genuine others, our jealousy confirms our oppressive stance. But God does possess the world and everything in it by right of creation and daily sustenance. Nevertheless, he exercises covenant lordship by giving rather than possessing, by sacrificing rather than hoarding, by spending rather than saving his wealth. It is God's jealousy for his people that underscores his love and eventuates in their salvation. God's jealousy is his zeal. Like a devoted spouse or parent, God is passionately committed to his covenant. Nothing distracts him from it. He works all things together for the good of those who love him, "who are the called according to his purpose" (Rom. 8:28). The famous prophecy of the Messiah in Isaiah 9 concludes, "The zeal of the LORD of hosts will do this" (v. 7). It is jealousy or zeal for God's name and God's house that consumed the psalmist (Ps. 119:139), a passage recalled by the disciples in relation to Jesus' cleansing of the temple (John 2:17). Such jealousy or zeal is the opposite of the fickle character of the human covenant partner. Isaiah tells God that he longs for the day when the whole earth recognizes "your zeal for your people" (Isa. 26:11).

Similarly, God's wrath presupposes a particular historical situation and not any caprice in God's nature. Despite the moral revulsion that modern assumptions of autonomy and justice sometimes evoke, the biblical texts offer abundant testimony to the possibility and reality of God's wrath in history. If God were *only* love or if every other attribute had to be surrendered in a given conflict with it, the entire

---

149. Dorner, *Divine Immutability*, 178.
150. Jenson, *ST* 1:47, referring to Exod. 34:14.

narrative would be determined by long-suffering and patience. But that is quite evidently not the case, and no theoretical construction that one might substitute in those wide open spaces can make the story say otherwise than what it says.

I cannot pursue here the diverse reasons why the wrath of God is so difficult to maintain in prosperous democracies, even though it is a prominent theme, along with the supporting themes of God's justice and righteousness. At least since Amos's day, the comfortable have had trouble with a God of justice, while the weak have been empowered by it. While it is true that "the wrath of God is revealed from heaven against all ungodliness and wickedness of those who by their wickedness suppress the truth" (Rom. 1:18), judgment is delayed by God's long-suffering in order to bring about his saving purposes (2 Pet. 3:9), even if this is taken as evidence that there is no final reckoning (vv. 1–10). God risks being misunderstood as neither good nor just, in order to redeem. We have already referred to Jeremiah's protest: "You will be in the right, O LORD, when I lay my charges against you; but let me put my case to you. Why does the way of the guilty prosper? Why do all who are treacherous thrive?" (Jer. 12:1). It is a complaint that the sufferers, not the satisfied, lodge against God. For them, the problem is not with a God of judgment and wrath, but with a God who waits too long to act.

While our own experience is inescapable in mediating how we hear such words as *judgment* and *wrath*—viz., an abusive father or husband, a horrendous dictator, an ideological crusader, the shrill discourse of entertainment politics—we should allow the possibility of hermeneutical transformation. If we allow for this, we will see that God's judgment is precisely the threat to all human violence and oppression. As with the biblical imagery of king and kingdom, lord and servant, power and weakness, the very hope of healing our distorted master narratives and metaphors is thwarted if we dismiss them rather than listen to what this narrative drama does with, to, and through them. The theology of the cross and resurrection does not respond to the will to power so evident particularly in the modern West by denying power or resigning itself to this-worldly injustice for the sake of an otherworldly peace (which was precisely Nietzsche's no doubt well-founded caricature of the cultural Christianity of his day). On the contrary, as Miroslav Volf argues, the Word of God inserts a new power into the matrices and structures of earthly regimes.[151] Beyond this, a crucial feature in any discussion of God's wrath and judgment is eschatology, in the light of which we are able to recognize the various judgments in redemptive history as proleptic "intrusions" of the last judgment that issues in the everlasting Sabbath. God does not pour out his wrath in one static, eternal moment, but "stores up wrath" for the last day, occasionally anticipating it in discrete moments of apocalyptic judgment. While God's nature is eternal and unchanging, the way in which God expresses his nature in history is oriented to a particular place in the unfolding story.

---

151. Miroslav Volf, "Theology, Meaning, and Power," in *The Future of Theology: Essays in Honor of Jürgen Moltmann*, ed. Miroslav Volf, Carmen Krieg, and Thomas Kucharz (Grand Rapids: Eerdmans, 1996), 109.

It is through this narrative, covenantal, and eschatological account of God's wrath that we can distinguish the appropriateness of God's wrath, executed through human agency in a kingdom of glory (by anticipation in the theocracy), and the wholly inappropriate longing for—perhaps even the illusion of personally executing—God's wrath in this age.

The answer to self-righteous religious violence is not to deny the wrath of God, but it is to put wrath where (in God's hands) and when (on the last day) the biblical drama puts it. Sinners—even Christian ones—are not qualified to call fire down on other sinners. The absence of this eschatological dimension is doubtless at the heart of religious violence, whether it is the Christian crusaders fancying themselves the armies of Israel driving out the Canaanites and ushering in God's final judgment, or radical Islamists acting as Allah's warriors. Christianity is not distinguished by apathetic sentimentalism masquerading as a religion of tolerance and love, which would smother the cry of the victims, but by a recognition that only YHWH is just and the final reckoning belongs to him alone. God is also spoken of as long-suffering or patient (Exod. 34:6; Ps. 86:15; Rom. 2:4; 9:22; 1 Pet. 3:20; 2 Pet. 3:15). Again, these predicates are applicable only in a context of covenantal breach. One should not imagine the persons of the Trinity patiently enduring one another's transgressions, nor those of creatures without fault.

It is important that our understanding of God's love and wrath not be nicely "balanced," which ordinarily amounts in our context to the conclusion that when God's holiness and justice bump up against his love in a given situation, love trumps wrath. If the biblical story does not let us make that simplistic move, it also does not allow us to see God as capricious, as if God could display wrath unjustly. As it is God's love that moves him to compassion for sinners, it is God's holiness, righteousness, and justice that move him to wrath when that which and those whom he loves are threatened. It is in the covenant that Israel is assured that God will not utterly cast them off despite their covenant breaking. In the light of the human propensity to sin, they realized that it is only because of the covenant of grace that they can rely on God's mercy. Apart from God's just anger, mercy and grace have no meaning, as has become all too familiar in the prevailing therapeutic deity of popular religion.

As I have argued, it is not only God's incommunicable attributes, but also his communicable ones, that express both God's transcendence and immanence. Furthermore, these attributes must all be taken together as facets of our understanding of God. I have indicated key places where Brueggemann's illuminating pattern of strong verbs leading to adverbs and adjectives, and finally established in nouns, yields a composite description of a noncomposite God. Neither sovereignty nor love, power nor compassion, wrath nor long-suffering, justice nor mercy is divine. Rather, the triune God is God and has identified himself in these ways to elicit our trust and our own *ḥesed* or covenant faithfulness.

Chapter Three

A Glorious Theater

Triune Lordship in Eternity,
Nature, and History

The drama that discloses the work of the triune God in history begins in the eternal relationship of the divine persons (the covenant of redemption), executed in the temporal covenants of creation and grace. This underscores the closest possible bond between God and a world that is ontologically other. While the concept of covenant cannot carry the entire burden for an account of the God-world relationship, it provides a context in which both otherness and union, transcendence and immanence, can be concretely articulated. In the covenant of redemption (the eternal intra-Trinitarian *pactum*) we recognize the closest possible relationship between the immanent and economic Trinity, the eternal decree and the temporal execution of God's works *ad extra*. In the covenant of creation, nature is affirmed in its integrity: neither divine nor demonic, bearing its own capacities for "answering back" to the creative speech of the triune God. Nature and history, far from being either rivals to God or emanations of Deity, become in their own way and with their own particular capacities the place where we meet a stranger. Therefore, says Calvin, "let us not be ashamed to take pious delight in the works of God open and manifest in this most beautiful theater."[1]

---

1. Calvin, *Institutes* 1.14.20.

66

ACT ONE: COVENANT LORD IN NATURE

While there are dualistic ontologies (viz., Manicheism), the most pervasive non-Christian views of reality, in both the East and the West, tend to be some form of dualism that is ultimately sublated into a higher monism. For example, in *Enuma elish*, Plato, and Hegel, despite their great differences, all of reality is ultimately one, with higher and lower (or antithetical) forms of existence, corresponding to spirit/eternity/unity and matter/time/difference, respectively. In the ancient cosmogonic myths (as well as in the Christian heresies of Gnosticism and Manicheism) the created world is generally depicted as a piece of reality that arose out of disaster, evil, and chaos, while the divine spark somehow remains in the mind of the fallen self. (As Hans Jonas's postscript to *The Gnostic Religion* famously, or infamously, suggests, modern existentialism's "thrownness of being" shares remarkable affinities with ancient Gnosticism.)[2] But more broadly, our Western culture for centuries now has split reality apart into the "body" (material creation generally), which is inert and acted upon, manipulated and exploited, and the "soul" or "heart," which is free, irrational, and connected to the cosmic heartbeat. Enlightenment and Romanticism remain codependent rivals well into the so-called postmodern era.

It is against these habits of thought that Israel's God is said to create a cosmos ex nihilo. To repeat Childs's summary, Gerhard von Rad concluded that far from relying on the ancient Near Eastern mythologies, "Israel's world-view performed a major function in drawing a sharp line of division between God and the world, and by purging the material world of both elements of the divine and the demonic. There were no avenues of direct access to the mystery of the creator emanating from the world, certainly not by means of the image, but Yahweh was present in his living word in acts of history."[3] Emanation gives rise to mythologies of eternal return, while biblical faith in the creation gave rise to history. Once more the contrasting typologies of "meeting a stranger" versus "overcoming estrangement" are brought into view.

The Greek version of pagan cosmology continued to cast its spell even over some early Christian reflection, particularly where mediated by the Jewish scholar and Middle Platonist Philo. For example, Origen maintained that creation was eternal because an immutable God could not have a new relation to anything. God must have been eternally a creator and, therefore, creation must be eternal.[4] But making creation necessary to God's being (Origen) is no less foreign to Scripture than making redemption so (Moltmann). As the covenant of redemption is the site for the relative necessity of incarnation, the covenant of creation is the

2. Hans Jonas, *The Gnostic Religion: The Message of the Alien God and the Beginnings of Christianity,* 2nd ed. (Boston: Beacon, 1958); Edwin Yamauchi, *Pre-Christian Gnosticism: A Survey of Proposed Evidences,* rev. ed. (Grand Rapids: Baker, 1983); Giovanni Filoramo, *A History of Gnosticism* (Oxford: Basil Blackwell, 1990).

3. Childs, *Biblical Theology,* 386. See von Rad's essay "Some Aspects of the Old Testament World-View."

4. Origen, *De principiis* 2.4.

site for the *relative* necessity of the world. The existence of the world is not necessary in consequence of God's being, but rather it is God's free intra-Trinitarian determination. This is not a nominalist thesis, however, since it affirms that any divine determination must be consistent with God's character, without the stronger claim that in order to be so God is necessarily obligated by his very nature to create or provide redemption. Furthermore, as we shall see, although Origen's view comports better with modern science even up to and including Einstein, it is in the process of being radically reversed in the contemporary scientific consensus, which increasingly stresses a temporal beginning as well as evident signs of contingency. Although science can hardly be expected to prove ex nihilo creation, its current paradigm is nonetheless consistent with it.

In the classical alternatives that the apostle to the gentiles encountered in Athens, the God-world relationship was seen either in terms of hyper-immanence (Stoic pantheism) or hyper-transcendence (Epicurean deism), the former rendering God and the world equally necessary while the latter regarded divine agency unnecessary at least for the continuation and preservation of nature. This has been repeated with variations in the modern era, particularly since Spinoza and Kant, respectively. The freedom of God *and* the otherness of creation were lost in the bargain, as I have argued in the first chapter.

Absolute Beginning

"In the beginning God created the heavens and the earth." So, significantly, begins the historical prologue of the creation treaty. After all, it is at this place where God's triune life reaches out ecstatically in openness to that which is other than God. As Barth has reminded us, creation is the outer side of the covenant (although—crucially, he rejected the older division between a covenant of creation and a covenant of grace). This theological point is further supported if the creation narrative is viewed as the historical prologue of the covenant itself, not one of the many cosmological myths or explanations of the world's beginning. Given the way the first two chapters of Genesis are often abstracted from their covenantal context in modern debates on human origins, this is an important point.

The syntax of Genesis 1:1 can be taken either as a relative clause (i.e., as the beginning of the specific history to be narrated) or as an absolute clause (i.e., as the beginning of the creation).[5] Whatever analogies there might be between human creation and divine *creatio continua*, the choice of the technical verb *bārā'* to designate this initial act of God in ex nihilo creation underscores its uniqueness to God.[6] "Lexical investigations are here of little help," Jenson rightly

---

5. Childs, *Biblical Theology*, 111: "On the one hand, the strength of taking verse 1 as a relative clause is supported by its parallel to Ancient Near Eastern conventional formula used of the initial temporal phrase. On the other hand, Eichrodt ('In the Beginning') has mounted a strong case for the absolute use of the term by a careful study of related terms which clearly depict an absolute beginning (Isa. 40.21; Prov. 8.23, etc.)."

6. Ibid.

observes, "because Scripture reserves the verb translated 'creates' (*barah*) [*sic*] for this one use; 'creating' is something only God does."[7]

But how this absolute beginning comes about is just as crucial. While causal analogies are not entirely absent, the dominant ones are communicative. This follows the pattern of intra-Trinitarian processions, I would argue. In other words, instead of debating *causal* relations in the Trinity (particularly as they relate to the *filioque* controversy), which frequently end in charges of subordinationism and modalism, we are in fact on better exegetical ground to think of *communicative* relations: the Father speaking the Son in the Spirit. (This also circumvents the Western tendency to reduce the Spirit to a "bond" between the Father and Son and therefore to a principle instead of a person.)

Analogically, the triune God *speaks* a cosmos into being in the Son and by the Spirit, and with this statement the chasm separating the biblical understanding of creation from the cosmologies of the nations is measured. Israel knows only the duality of Creator and creation, and even here there is no inherent antithesis despite difference. A repeated refrain in the polemics against the gods of the nations is that there is no cosmic or ontological dualism: equally ultimate principles of good and evil. YHWH is Lord. Diversity is not a fall from being, but the measure of creative bounty: "O LORD, how manifold are your works! In wisdom you have made them all; the earth is full of your creatures" (Ps. 104:24). Also underscored is God's universal lordship in nature as well as history, and over the world, not just Israel. Israel's God is the universal Lord and not *a* lord circumscribed by geography, blood, and ideology, nor indeed even the chief of a given pantheon of deities. "Israel's testimony about Yahweh as Creator is fully embedded in Israel's larger covenant testimony," says Brueggemann. "As Israel believes that its own life is covenantally ordered, so Israel believes that creation is covenantally ordered; that is, formed by continuing interactions of gift and gratitude, of governance and obedience."[8] This expresses the "relentless ethical dimension."[9] That the story of God's covenant with *Israel* emerges out of the story of God's covenant with *creation* underscores the integral relationship between the universal and the particular. The contrast explored in the first chapter between "overcoming estrangement" and "meeting a stranger" is once more relevant.

The so-called nature psalms give further insight into Israel's unique testimony to a God who creates everything "by the word of his mouth." Psalm 33 is especially interesting in this regard, Brueggemann notes, "because of its assertion that Yahweh creates by utterance: 'By the word of the Lord the heavens were made, and all their host by the breath of his mouth. . . . For he spoke, and it came to be; he commanded, and it stood firm' (vv. 6, 9)."[10] The same Lord who "sent out his word and healed [the Israelites], and delivered them from destruction"

7. Jenson, *ST* 2:5.

8. Walter Brueggemann, *Theology of the Old Testament: Testimony, Dispute, Advocacy* (Minneapolis: Fortress, 1997), 158–59.

9. Ibid., 158.

10. Ibid., 154.

(Ps. 107:20), sent out his word to create the world and everything in it: Israel's redeemer is the creator. The "living and active" word that brings salvation (Heb. 4:12) is the same word spoken in the beginning. It is God's performative utterance that creates, sustains, redeems, and consummates. Thus YHWH is the Alpha-Creator and Omega-Consummator.[11]

Reading the story canonically, we can say that the Father issues the summons, the Son obeys it on behalf of creation, and the Spirit brings the creation thus summoned and shaped to its appointed goal. Therefore, the debate in biblical scholarship over *Wortbericht* (word) as opposed to *Tatbericht* (act) as the source of God's creative work is rendered a false dilemma. God's active agency in creation, as in his other works, is his speech-act. The Father who eternally speaks forth the Son in the Spirit speaks the world into existence through the Son and the Spirit. The communicative dance of God and world exhibits marks of being a large-scale analogy for the intra-Trinitarian life—although (*pace* Moltmann, Jenson, and others) it always remains an *analogy*.

"The mighty one, God the LORD, speaks and *summons* the earth from the rising of the sun to its setting" (Ps. 50:1). This is unmistakably covenantal language. The great king speaks, and the servant obeys: "For he spoke, and it came to be; he commanded, and it stood firm" (Ps. 33:9). Creation already bears the indelible imprint of covenant; it is itself a charter. There is not first a creation and then a covenant. Nature "speaks back" its praise to the God who has "spoken forth." Thus, as Brueggemann observes, "Creation has within it the sovereign seriousness of God, who will not tolerate the violation of the terms of creation, which are terms of gift, dependence, and extravagance. Thus for those who refuse the doxology-evoking sovereignty of Yahweh, creation ends on an ominous warning."[12]

It is to this covenant that the natural world gives its testimony (as in Psalm 19), and YHWH even calls upon the natural world to testify both for (Gen. 15:5–6; 8:22; 9:8–17; Matt. 2:10) and against (Matt. 24:28; 27:45; Acts 2:20) his covenant people in history. While the natural elements are called upon as *gods* by the nations in their suzerain-vassal treaties, in Israel they are called upon as created *witnesses* to the triune God's effective purposes.

Once again, the God-world relation cannot be reduced to causal analogies but must be supplemented with the communicative agency that the texts themselves highlight. "It is by God's speech that the relation with his creation is determined," says Brueggemann.

> God "calls the world into being" (cf. Rom. 4:17; II Pet. 3:5). . . . The way of God with his world is the way of language. God speaks something new that never was before. As God's "speech-creature," the world is evoked by this summoning God who will have his way. . . . There is no doubt that [Genesis] *utilizes older materials*. It reflects creation stories and cosmologies of Egypt and Mesopotamia. However, the text before us transforms these

---

11. I draw this terminology from M. G. Kline.
12. Ibid., 156.

older materials to serve a quite new purpose, a purpose most intimately related to Israel's covenantal experience. . . . Israel is concerned with God's *lordly intent*, not his *technique*. . . . It is news about a transaction which redefines the world.[13]

"The effect of this understanding of creation," according to Childs, "was to desacralize the world by removing all demonic and mythical powers from it and by subordinating them to the sole power of the one creator. Similarly in the New Testament Jesus exercised supreme power over the spiritual powers, and in his conquering of the demons demonstrated his control as creator."[14]

The most controversial aspect of this conception is that creation resulted from an absolute beginning ex nihilo. The heart of this claim is that the original creation had its source in God's command. God did not merely manipulate preexisting matter into discrete forms but called into existence everything that he was to subsequently shape into specific things and viable systems of life.

Once more we must recall that the context of Genesis is a piece of polemical theology: God's assertion of his sovereignty over and against the gods of the nations as Israel's suzerain. It is Israel's God who created all that exists.[15] The world is dependent on YHWH for its creation and preservation, but YHWH in no way depends on the world. This is the confession of faith against the idols of the nations all the way down to Paul's day: "The God who made the world and everything in it, he who is Lord of heaven and earth, does not live in shrines made by human hands, nor is he served by human hands, as though he needed anything, since he himself gives to all mortals life and breath and all things" (Acts 17:24–25).

But does this require ex nihilo creation? Brueggemann shares the tentativeness of some biblical scholars with respect to this doctrine. Evidence in the biblical traditions, he argues, is as late as 2 Maccabees.

> Other texts, perhaps even Gen 1:1–2, permit but do not require such a reading. . . . And if not *ex nihilo*, then we are bound to conclude that Israel understood Yahweh's activity of creation to be one of forming, shaping, governing, ordering, and sustaining a created world out of the "stuff of chaos," which was already there. Unlike some speculative traditions, Israel evidences no interest or curiosity about the origin of the "stuff of creation." It is simply there as a given, which Yahweh then addresses in a lordly fashion.[16]

If Brueggemann is right, Israel was not merely, as he suggests, agnostic about the question of the origin of created reality, but actually affirmed, as he does, that

13. Walter Brueggemann, *Genesis*, Interpretation (Atlanta: John Knox Press, 1982), 24, 26.

14. Childs, *Biblical Theology*, 399.

15. Gunton, *Triune Creator*, 127, refers to Claus Westermann, *Genesis 1–11*, trans. John J. Scullion (Minneapolis: Augsburg, 1984), 16–17. "What distinguishes the priestly account of creation among the many creation stories of the Ancient Near East is that for P there can be only one creator and that all else that is or can be, can never be anything but a creature."

16. Brueggemann, *Theology of the Old Testament*, 158.

God was merely the organizer of preexisting matter. Brueggemann thus merges creation and providence: God's agency in creation is indistinct from the continual creative work of God in nature.

This tendency to confuse creation and providence becomes even more apparent when Brueggemann includes evil in the very fabric of creation itself. He believes Israel assumed that the world that is there, including "vexation, trouble, and destructiveness that appear to be untamed and on the loose," are just created givens for Israel.

> We may say that all such evil is the result of sin, but Israel resists such a conclusion, if by sin is meant human failure. Evil is simply there, sometimes as a result of human sin, sometimes as a given, and occasionally blamed on God. Jon Levenson has made a powerful case that there is on the loose in the world, according to Old Testament texts, something untamed and destructive that has still not been brought under the rule of Yahweh. While it is promised that Yahweh will prevail over such counterpowers, it is clear that Yahweh has not yet gained such mastery and does not now prevail. Fredrik Lindstrom has shown, moreover, how in many psalms such deathliness makes headway in the midst of Israel only when and where Yahweh is absent, neglectful, or inattentive.[17]

However, two points should be noted by way of response. First, it is one thing to say that "evil is simply there" in the world as Israel knows it and another to suggest that it is there in the world as nobody, including Israel, has known it since the fall. In the biblical beginning, pains are taken to emphasize—over against the cosmological dualism of pagan thought—God's direct involvement in and sovereignty over all of reality, the goodness of creation, and the absence of evil. In this opening act, the narratives of creation stress, in antithesis to the creator-creature confusion of the nature religions, the fiat origin of creation as good and the subsequent fall of humankind into sin as a result of Adam's disobedience. It is a fall that takes place in history and not in nature itself, as the biblical witness, especially in the Psalms, continually attests. The subsequent narrative structure of creation, fall, redemption, and consummation that we find in both Old and New Testaments is founded on these first chapters of Genesis. Brueggemann says that psalms such as Psalm 146 remind us "that Yahweh's creating work is not raw power but is a work that intends and provides well-being precisely to the oppressed, the hungry, prisoners, the blind, the bowed down, the righteous, strangers, widows, and orphans (cf. Prov 17:5)."[18] We may legitimately infer God's concern for those considered "nothings" by the world from God's creating work. And certainly this work is never "raw power," but it remains the case that Psalm 146 is describing God's providence and redemptive purposes rather than creation in the beginning.

Second, while there are numerous examples of the covenant people crying out in their distress against circumstances over which they know that God is ultimately

17. Ibid., 159.
18. Ibid., 155.

sovereign, even calling God to account for his mysterious ways, I know of not a single text where *evil* is "occasionally blamed on God" in a fallen creation. It is Israel's YHWH who is unlike the nations precisely in that there is not some other principle of sovereignty "loose in the world . . . something untamed and destructive that has still not been brought under the rule of Yahweh." Isn't this, after all, the point in the plagues where YHWH asserts sovereignty over all mysterious forces personified as deities? It is one thing to debate this point about "something untamed" in relation to providence, but to regard evil as a principle at work in creation *as* creation verges on the Manichean dualism that Israel's neighbors would have recognized in a more primitive form. To argue that evil exists as a "counterpower" to YHWH at least requires nuance, since it was Israel's simultaneous witness that evil as an ethical opposition to God's rule was real and that it was nevertheless under the limitations imposed by God, as the book of Job famously attests. But still, this is to make a point about providence, not creation. When creation and fall are collapsed, and evil is located in the primordial elements (the "ontological way") rather than in the breaking of a covenant (ethical estrangement), the threat of the cosmic dualism to which I have alluded remains serious.

Third, while criticism of an absolute beginning used to be to some degree motivated by the view that it was irreconcilable with modern science, the emerging scientific consensus no longer sustains that objection.[19]

Whatever the presuppositions of Brueggemann's view, it cannot be reconciled with the biblical account. As Childs argues,

> According to the structure of [Genesis 1] it is out of the question to suggest that creation resulted from a reforming of chaos (*contra* Welker, "Was ist 'Schopfung'?," 209ff.). The biblical author set the act "in the beginning" to establish that God's creation was not to be understood merely as a "constitutive relationship," or an expression of a "mode of being" characterizing creator and creature. Rather, creation marked the beginning of time, the start of an ongoing history, and the moment of origin before which there was no such reality apart from God. Moreover, God pronounced his workmanship good and blessed it. The creation rested in its perfection; no further work was needed.[20]

This should not be taken to mean that no further work was needed for the flourishing and progress of creation, but is simply to distinguish the original creation from its providential development and sustenance.

Creation is not only a distinct act of God in the beginning, but a free one, recognizing again Barth's important point that divine freedom is not only freedom

---

19. The warfare between science and religion, though often overplayed in the light of more recent conflict, has hampered attempts of ordinary Christians and scientists to see the value of each other's different research programs and methods. Harvard astrophysicist Owen Gingerich is correct: "Philosophical problems aside, the Bible is thoroughly historical in its outlook, a chronicle of particular events of a people who covenanted with God. The scientific picture was not in the first place historical" ("The Universe as Theater for God's Action," *Theology Today* 55, no. 3, 307). Cf. Holmes Rolston III in the same issue, 425.

20. Childs, *Biblical Theology*, 385.

from, but freedom *for*. Unlike a work of art, legitimately created for its own pleasure, God had a further goal in view for the earth: the covenant. "He formed it to be inhabited" (Isa. 45:18). In *Enuma elish*, the ancient Babylonian creation myth, for example, the creation of the world results from a family quarrel. In the cosmic battle, Father Apsu and Mother Tiamat are slain, Tiamat's corpse torn into two parts to create the universe. The other gods were forced into servitude to the victors, but when they cried out to the king of gods, Marduk, humankind was created from the blood of the rebellion's ringleader to take the rebel gods' place in menial service. The oppressive burden of serving self-indulgent deities was now shifted from the defeated gods to humans.[21] Despite clear parallels in form, the biblical creation story is polemically charged in denunciation of such worldviews. The world is not God nor a part of God nor an emanation of God, but it is also not the "stuff" created out of conflict, rebellion, strife, and evil. The creation is "very good" even if it is not even close to being divine.

Appealing to Paul Ricoeur's contrasts between the Babylonian creation myth and the Bible, Colin Gunton points up the remarkable differences between a primordial violence that underwrites the violence of kings and conquerors and the biblical creation account as founded in covenant love.

> The biblical view that the creation has its origins in the covenant love of God is thus a way of understanding the world different in principle from both the myths of the ancient world and much of the Greek philosophy that has its roots in them. Consequently . . . it generates a different ethic: a different way of inhabiting the world and treating its inhabitants. The continuing importance of this contrast of world-views is to be found in the fact that the view of creation as deified conflict is perpetually renewed in human culture, most recently perhaps in Hegel and Marx, as well as in many of their disciples.[22]

Similarly, Jenson, appealing to Basil, contrasts the historical emphasis of the Genesis narrative on an absolute beginning with the mythological cosmologies:

> Genesis' story is not a myth, for it does not in fact tell us anything about what things were like when there were not things. Its "*tohu webohu*" [darkness and void] is not an antecedent nothingness-actuality like the Great Slime dismembered by Babylonian Marduk, nor yet an eternal egg or womb or pure potentiality of primal matter. The fathers were clear about this: "The heretics say, 'But there was also the darkness . . . over the deep.' Again new occasions for myth. . . ! 'The deep' is not a fullness of antithetical powers, as some fantasize, nor is the darkness an original and evil force arrayed against the good." Genesis' reference to emptiness and formlessness, and the darkness and "waters" of chaos, is not to a presupposition of creation but to the inconceivable beginning of creation, made inconceivable by the absence

---

21. See Alexander Heidel, *The Babylonian Genesis*, 2nd ed. (Chicago: University of Chicago Press, 1963); idem, *The Gilgamesh Epic and Old Testament Parallels* (Chicago: University of Chicago Press, 1949).

22. Gunton, *Triune Creator*, 26.

of presuppositions. Augustine reads Genesis precisely: "You have made all times; and before all times only you are, nor does time antecede itself."[23]

The *rûaḥ* of God is *the Spirit*. "If this phrase were to be translated 'wind from God,' as some modern versions do, again the narrative would be mythic," but such a translation just indicates the translators' prejudice. There is no reason to believe that by *rûaḥ 'ĕlōhîm* the Spirit of God was not intended.[24] It is by his Spirit that God creates—"and not from anything" in the creation (2 Macc. 7:28). In the two accounts in Genesis, it is clear that creation comes into being as a history.[25]

The necessary implication of this view is that God created the world for his own glory, and not out of any need or necessity within his own being (*pace* Meister Eckhart and even some of the tendencies in Arminian accounts or the more recent panentheistic proposals). Again, covenantal participation replaces an emanationist scheme of participation and the world is given its own legitimate space. While in my own experience many popular Christian treatments of this question focus on some *lack* in God (his desire for fellowship, company, etc.), the doctrine of ex nihilo creation, emphasizing as it does the sheer freedom of God in the matter, consequently finds the reason for creation in God's *abundance*. Therefore, the motive of creation is sheer *agapē*. God did not have to "create space" for us, as if he is somehow so expansive that his existence might threaten his creation unless he restricted himself. Rather, says Paul, in a subversive appeal to a Greek poet, "in him we live and move and have our being" (Acts 17:28). This underscores the oddity in Moltmann's formulation already encountered to the effect that God must experience a kenosis of his being in order to give creation space within him. Ironically, the biblical picture is *more* affirmative of divine immanence when it recognizes a Creator-creature distinction that nevertheless challenges any intrinsic antithesis. We find in the independent God of perfect aseity and trinity the amplitude of being sufficient to support all nondivine life, including the forms that God has chosen to create. The difference (variety) that is affirmed in God as good (i.e., the three persons) is the basis for the affirmation of difference in the God-world relationship. God created the world for his own glory, the final end for everything that God does. It brings God pleasure and honor to create nondivine creatures, some of them with the requisite capabilities to respond to him in a loving and purposeful relationship. Jenson rightly insists that we cannot substitute God's love for his glory as the motive and final end of creation. It is a "disastrous" move and "is doubtless one cause of late modernity's degradation of deity into a servant of our self-help."[26] The Creator-creature relationship entails divine sovereignty, which invocations of "free will" cannot finally subvert.[27] It is not competition between God's will and mine, since his is absolute and mine is contingent, so that there is

23. Jenson, *ST* 2:11, citing Basil's *Hexaemeron* 2.4.
24. Ibid., 11–12.
25. Ibid., 14.
26. Ibid., 18.
27. Ibid., 22.

"no arithmetic within which a decision by me is one less for him or vice versa."[28] Only because the biblical God has this kind of divine freedom are his creatures able to have creaturely freedom.[29] Freedom is not predicated univocally of God and humans, but analogically.

This doctrine of ex nihilo creation underscores, among other things, the freedom of God *from* as well as *for* creatures: "In the beginning God created the heavens and the earth" (Gen. 1:1). The psalmist declares, "Before the mountains were brought forth, or ever you had formed the earth and the world, from everlasting to everlasting you are God" (Ps. 90:2). The cosmos is not God's body, but the effect of God's creative summons—an other whose difference is not an obstacle to, but rather the prerequisite of, its relation to God. Furthermore, creation is not divided between antithetical "heavenly" and "earthly" realms, since even "the heavens are the work of your hands" (Ps. 102:25). The divide is between Creator and creature, not between heavenly and earthly, spiritual and material, and so forth, and even here it is a distinction, not an intrinsic antithesis. While we do not know what God was doing before creation (Augustine and Calvin answered, "Creating hell for curious persons"[30]), we do know that God has been "always working" (John 5:17). God's existence before the creation could not therefore have been inactive. James Orr rightly concluded that this question turns on the relation of time to eternity and the realization that "God's eternity is no indefinitely extended time, but something essentially different, of which we can form no conception."[31] This creation implies no change in God, since it is not God who is created.

Creation ex nihilo means not that creation is uncaused but that God brought it into existence without any preexisting material. Everything but God exists contingently, by God's will and action. "By faith we understand that the worlds have been framed by the word of God, so that what is seen has not been made out of things that already existed" (Heb. 11:3). It is this powerful word that is spoken by God into nonexistence in the opening chapter of Genesis, and it is this pattern of ex nihilo creation that serves as a constant parallel for the "new creation" language that follows in redemptive history.

A World of Difference

The doctrine of creation ex nihilo allows us to say that although materiality, temporality, contingency, and change are unworthy of *God*, they are worthy and dignified aspects of *creaturely* existence. Here we discover a duality to end all dualism. The other can be completely different *and* good. The whole Greek (especially Platonic) dualism between spirit and matter, eternity and time, immutability and mutability, the intellectual and the sensual, rests on this emanationist theory in which all of reality participates in a single scale of being.

---

28. Ibid.
29. Ibid., 22–23.
30. Calvin, *Institutes* 1.14.1.
31. Cited in Berkhof, *Systematic Theology*, 131.

Many today suppose that a sharp distinction between Creator and creature leads necessarily to an abuse of the environment. Consequently, pantheistic or panentheistic metaphysics are seen as the only hope for ecological concern. Yet can this Creator-creature confusion allow nature its own integrity and its own relatively independent status? Why must nature be either divine or demonic? "And at the time of this writing," Jenson observes, "academically and church-politically powerful 'feminist/womanist/mulierist theology' oddly supposes that any 'dualism' of God and creature is 'patriarchal.'"[32] However, it is precisely this Creator-creature duality that Israel's God puts in the place of the cosmic dualisms of the nature religions. Monism cannot account for diversity. Difference and oth-erness become merely so many different facets of the same. Much of postmod-ern thought, in its impatience with dualism, risks falling into similar kinds of monism that have already plagued modernity, simply reversing the privileged terms. It is not that there is no foundation for the critique of an erroneous oppo-sition of humans to the environment (an opposition that itself derives in part from a Platonic anthropology), but that if genuine plurality is to be affirmed without setting up ontological antitheses, it is just this *differential* duality between Creator and creation—positively construed—that is able to subvert the *anti-thetical* dualisms that pit various forms of creation against one another.

In a monistic scheme there is no way to talk about how creaturely attributes might be entirely proper and fitting for creatures but not for their creator. But for Christians, such differences are attributed to the Creator-creature distinction (ex nihilo creation), rather than to the inherent antitheses of spirit and matter, grace and nature, and the like. As Barth reminds us,

> The differentiation of the divine happening from the non-divine does not coincide in Holy Scripture with the distinction between nature and grace, soul and body, inner and outer, visible and invisible. On the contrary, the event of revelation as described for us in Scripture has everywhere a natural, bodily, outward and visible component—from the creation (not only of heaven but of earth), by way of the concrete existence of the people of Israel in Palestine, the birth of Jesus Christ, His physical miracles, His suffering and death under Pontius Pilate, His physical resurrection, right down to His coming again and the resurrection of the body.[33]

To confuse God with a generic "absolute spirit" as opposed to nature is to iden-tify the Creator with the creation, since the "spiritual world," even at its "high-est pinnacles," is also a creation and not divine.[34] "Indeed the peak of all happening in revelation, according to Holy Scripture, consists in the fact that God speaks as an I, and is heard by the thou who is addressed. The whole con-tent of the happening consists in the fact that the Word of God became flesh and

---

32. Jenson, *ST* 2:6.
33. Barth, *CD* II/1:265.
34. Ibid., 256–57.

that His Spirit is poured out on all flesh."[35] God is God without us, but freely chooses to be our God—and thereby we exist.

Among the practical benefits of this doctrine is the realization that the good, the true, and the beautiful do not have to be justified in terms of their ontological participation in spirituality or divinity, but as divine creations that bear a divine benediction. There is a real sense in which they are good in themselves, and not just to the extent that they participate in eternal forms, even if that form should be "God." More Aristotelian than Platonic, the question is whether created things or persons do what they were created to do—including humans, which points once more to an ethical commission (stewardship) from God rather than to a patronizing relationship of "higher" to "lower" forms of life. The ecological implications are obvious as well, since reality is divided between Creator and creature, not higher and lower forms of being.

Key to the ex nihilo doctrine of creation is the conviction that creation has its own space—not that it is independent of God, much less a rival to God, but that it is different from God and yet affirmed in that difference. It does not emanate from God as rays from the sun. I would even go further and suggest, contrary to Barth and most of contemporary theology on this specific point, that the proper category for understanding the basis of creation is not grace but *condescension*. Is this going too far in allowing the simultaneous affirmation of creation's difference from God and goodness as such? I would argue that if grace is already the foundation for creation in the historical economy (granting that it is the basis, of course, in the eternal decree), and grace is the mercy God shows to sinners, then creation *as creation* cannot be considered good. This choice is based first of all on a strict definition of grace as not only unmerited but demerited favor. As we have seen, Barth himself affirms this definition of grace as that which God shows in view of transgression (i.e., synonymous with mercy), but argues consistently that God has had mercy on creation from the very beginning. Yet if mercy is only given in response to fault, a weak doctrine of creation results. This point requires further elaboration.

One of the crucial motives for asserting that creation is based upon God's goodness, freedom, and condescension rather than on God's grace is that it affirms the reality and integrity of nature as creation. Despite different formulations, both traditional Roman Catholic teaching and most Protestant interpretations since Barth have argued that the grace of God in Jesus Christ is the foundation of creation. According to the former, ever since Origen, creation was regarded as possessing not only the potentiality for corruption (which, of course, I would affirm), but was suspended between higher and lower realms, concentrated in the dualism between the intellectual contemplation of the eternal and unchanging Good and the temporal and fluctuating passions.[36] Despite signifi-

---

35. Ibid., 257.

36. Of course, the Platonic-Philonic-Plotinian influence predates Augustine. Origen is a notable example: "It is the custom of sacred Scripture, when it wishes to designate anything opposed to this gross and solid body, to call it spirit, as in the expression, 'The letter killeth, but the spirit giveth life,' where there can be no doubt that by 'letter' are meant bodily things, and by 'spirit' intellectual things, which we also term 'spiritual'" (*De principiis*, 1.1.2, 242).

cant agreement with the patristic consensus concerning the weakness of human nature being located in the body and its passions, Augustine also criticized Platonism, insisting that it is the corruption of the body by sin and death, not the body itself, that is to be blamed.[37] However, he does argue that Adam's sustenance—and therefore that of the created order—depended at every moment not on the integrity of freedom in created righteousness, but on a *donum superadditum*, a gift of grace added to nature.[38] It is not difficult to conclude that human and, more generally, creaturely, integrity was therefore lost when this *donum* was removed, as Augustine himself implies. Aside from problems of theodicy, this understanding cannot help but obscure the significance of what God was doing by creating a world that was truly the product of his lordly hand while nevertheless letting it "stand on its own two feet," as it were. Thus the significance of ex nihilo creation is blunted.

In Barth's formulation, Christology—and not simply Christology, but one in which eternity at certain moments threatens to engulf time, Divinity humanity, Creator creature, and redemption creation—takes the place of the *donum superadditum*, but with similar results. While I wholeheartedly affirm Jesus Christ as the ontological grounds of creation, I would want to argue that it is because of the fact that in the intra-Trinitarian covenant of redemption he assumes the office of mediator, fulfilling in history the covenant of works broken by Adamic humanity and only in this way—"by becoming obedient to the point of death" (Phil. 2:8), administering salvation leading to consummation in what is, for us, a covenant of grace. Calvin has been erroneously interpreted through a Barthian lens to advocate that the whole historical economy can be reduced to redemption. John Heywood Thomas's assessment is right on the mark: "I do not dispute that for [Calvin] all God's work is revealed in Christ in so far as it is in his face that we see all those comfortable truths of our salvation, including predestination. Yet I defy anyone to read the opening chapters of the *Institutes* and not agree that for Calvin the creation is logically distinct from and prior to our salvation."[39] Thus the cry of Reformation theology must not only be "Let God be God," but "Let creation be creation." Protology and eschatology precede soteriology. There is a time in history prior to sin and redemption yet short of consummation.

Creation Eschatology

This interpretation not only draws ex nihilo creation and the goodness of original creation in darker lines; it offers a more thoroughgoing eschatology of creation. Creation as a distinct work of God had a definite beginning and ending. Yet the Sabbath waited. This is the import of the analogical pattern of "six days" followed by an everlasting "seventh day." Once more, eschatology precedes

---

37. Augustine, *The City of God*, ed. David Knowles (New York: Penguin, 1972), 550–53.

38. See Leo Scheffczyk, "Concupiscence," in *Sacramentum Mundi: An Encyclopedia of Theology*, ed. Karl Rahner, SJ, et al., vol. 1 (New York: Herder & Herder, 1968), 403–5.

39. John Heywood Thomas, "Trinity, Logic and Ontology," in *Trinitarian Theology Today: Essays on Divine Being and Act*, ed. Christoph Schwöbel (Edinburgh: T & T Clark, 1995), 75.

soteriology. Even prior to the narrative of fall and redemption, there is the narrative of creation and consummation: the goal of creation as confirmation in righteousness and participation in the everlasting shalom, God's own justice and peace. Instead of seeing temporal existence as an imperfect copy or shadow of eternal ideas, it is recognized as dependent yet distinct. For Origen, the alpha-point and omega-point of eschatology are the same: restoration to the original state.[40] Augustine's eschatology is not very eschatological, preoccupied as he was with eternal ideas in God's mind. But according to the biblical drama, it is not a return to Eden and a lifting of the curse that eschatology announces but a welcome into the royal sabbath of God's reign in history and nature.

Drawing upon important features of covenant theology, Meredith Kline has written extensively on the remarkable strategy employed in the two creation narratives of Genesis 1 and 2.[41] Rather than attempt a report on the chronology of origins, "these chapters pillage the pagan cosmogonic myth—the slaying of the dragon by the hero-god, followed by celebration of his glory in a royal residence built as a sequel to his victory."[42]

> God sets forth his creative acts within the pictorial framework of a Sabbath-crowned week and by this sabbatical pattern he identifies himself as Omega, the One for whom all things are and were created, the Lord worthy to receive glory and honor and praise (cf. Rev. 4:11). It is the seventh day of the creation week, the climactic Sabbath to which the course of creative events moves, that gives to the pattern of the week of days as a whole its distinctive sabbatical character, and it is then in the unfolding of the significance of the Sabbath day that the disclosure of the Omega name of God will be found.

This interpretation is supported by the internal structure of the two narratives themselves, focusing as they do on the appointment of the various vassal-kings to rule the spheres placed under their charge:

> Within the first three day-frames is described the origin of three vast spheres over which rule is to be exercised. . . . The fourth day-frame depicts the creation of the sun and moon and their royal appointment "to rule over" the day and night, the realms described in the parallel first day-frame. Their rule is expressed in their defining of the boundaries of their realm as they "separate" the light and darkness (Gen. 1:16–18). Then the fish and the birds of day five, the lords of the waters below and the sky above, the realms of the parallel second day-frame, are given the blessing-commission to enter into possession of their domains to their utmost limits. The terms that describe their commission—to be fruitful, to multiply and fill (Gen. 1:22)—anticipate the royal mandate that was to be given to man. The sixth day-frame introduces those who are to rule over the dry land of the parallel third day—

40. Origen, *De principiis* 1.6: "For the end is always like the beginning."

41. Meredith G. Kline, *Kingdom Prologue: Genesis Foundations for a Covenantal Worldview*, vol. 1 (Overland Park, KS: Two Age Press, 2000), 26–31.

42. Particularly in view here is the Babylonian Gilgamesh epic, to which I referred above.

land animals and man. The lordly beasts are authorized to serve themselves of the natural tributary produce of their land-realm (Gen. 1:30), a prerogative they share with man (Gen. 1:29).

Of course, the pairing of creaturely realms with their respective rulers does not end with the human creature:

> Even during the pageant of the creature-kings in the narrative of days four through six, their royal splendor is paled by the surpassing glory of the Creator-King who commands them into existence, identifies them in his fiat-naming of them, and invests them with their subordinate dominions. And then when the creation apocalypse has reached the vice-regency of the God-like creature-king of the sixth day, and moves beyond it, we observe the glory of all the creature-kingdoms of all six days being carried along as a tributary offering within the gates of the Sabbath day to be laid at the feet of the Creator-King, now beheld in the brilliance of his epiphany as Sabbath Lord. . . . Man is king over creation, but he is a vassal king, he reigns as one under the Creator's authority, obligated to devote his kingdom to the Great King.[43]

This interpretation, fortified by recent studies in ancient suzerainty treaties of the Near East, represents a powerful polemic against the idols of the nations that Israel must confront. This creation narrative, therefore, constitutes the historical prologue of the creation treaty that asserts YHWH's sovereignty. It also exhibits the unmistakably covenantal character of creation itself.

Kline's "framework" interpretation of Genesis 1 and 2 fits well with the concerns raised by those who see Barth's treatment of these chapters as underplaying "the way in which Genesis brings the non-human creation into the covenant." "We need," says Gunton, appealing to Andrew Linzey's analysis, "more than an extended exegesis of Gen. 1.26f, and in particular a broader treatment of the topic, if we are really to make more satisfactory use of the concept of the imago dei."[44] Kline's interpretation provides that wider context in which the whole creation participates in a covenant that is administered by humanity as the guardian and viceroy of the great king. The covenant with all of creation after the flood (Genesis 9) is just as encompassing. Not only are humans addressed with the renewed command, "Be fruitful and multiply" (v. 1); God's oath reads, "As for me, I am establishing my covenant with you and your descendants after you, and with every living creature that is with you, the birds, the domestic animals, and every animal of the earth with you, as many as came out of the ark" (vv. 9–10). The rainbow will be a sign to God. "When the bow is in the clouds, I will see it and remember the everlasting covenant between God and every living creature of all flesh that is on the earth" (v. 16). In this eschatology, the fate of the earth rests penultimately in human hands but ultimately on God's fidelity. The earth does not exist for humans to exploit, but is rather the theater of God's glory and

---

43. Kline, *Kingdom Prologue*, 18–30.
44. Gunton, "Trinity, Ontology and Anthropology," in *Persons, Divine and Human*, ed. Christoph Schwöbel and Colin Gunton (Edinburgh: T & T Clark, 1991), 58.

the analogy of God's own Sabbath rest, which humankind fell short of entering and therefore of bringing creation in its train.

The God-World Relation: Trinity and Mediation

As the intra-Trinitarian communion has been dynamic, ecstatic, and relational, God's creation of the world is just as personal. "The universe," as E. J. Carnell put it, "is ordered by personal interest, not logic."[45] The Logos by whom the worlds were made is not a silent principle or semidivine emanation, but the second person eternally spoken by the Father in the Spirit. According to Berkhof, the first thing to be said about creation is that it is "an act of the triune God." "Though the Father is in the foreground in the work of creation (1 Cor. 8:6), it is also clearly recognized as a work of the Son and of the Holy Spirit. The Son's participation in it is indicated in John 1:3; 1 Cor. 8:6; Col. 1:15–17, and the activity of the Spirit in it finds expression in Gen. 1:2; Job 26:13; 33:4; Ps. 104:30; Isa. 40:12, 13."[46] Instructive in the light of our earlier discussions concerning the Trinity, Berkhof adds,

> The second and third persons are not dependent powers or mere intermediaries, but independent authors together with the Father. The work was not divided among the three persons, but the whole work, though from different aspects, is ascribed to each of the persons. All things are at once *out of* the Father, *through* the Son, and *in* the Holy Spirit. In general it may be said that *being* is out of the Father, *thought* or the *idea* out of the Son, and *life* out of the Holy Spirit. Since the Father takes the initiative in the work of creation, it is often ascribed to Him economically.[47]

When we think of the Father as the agent in creation, the Son in redemption, and the Spirit in sanctification, it is easy to lose this sense of their mutual cooperation in every work. In particular, creation can be as easily conceived in monistic terms (as the work of the Father) even where the Trinity is formally affirmed. Thus I have taken Calvin's advice: instead of coordinating the Father, the Son, and the Spirit with creation, redemption, and sanctification, I view the Father as the beginning, the Son as the ground, and the Spirit as the effectiveness of God's communicative agency in every external work.

We have already seen the witness of a number of biblical passages to God's creation of the world as communicative rather than purely causal. I might add Calvin's statement that the Spirit's brooding over the waters in creation "shows not only that the beauty of the universe (which we now perceive) owes its strength and preservation to the power of the Spirit but that before this adornment was added, even then the Spirit was occupied with tending that confused mass."[48] By

45. E. J. Carnell, *Christian Commitment: An Apologetic* (New York: Macmillan, 1957), 247.
46. Berkhof, *Systematic Theology*, 129.
47. Ibid.
48. Calvin, *Institutes* 1.13.14.

the way, Calvin is not here denying an absolute beginning, but recognizing on the basis of the Genesis account the *tōhû wābōhû* (darkness and void) between the initial fiat and the formation of matter into its diverse kinds. "For it is the Spirit who, everywhere diffused, sustains all things, causes them to grow, and quickens them in heaven and earth . . . in transfusing into all things his energy, and breathing into them essence, life, and movement, he is indeed plainly divine."[49] Commenting on Psalm 33:6, Calvin writes, "But although the Psalmist sets the word of God and the breath of his mouth in opposition both to all external means, and to every idea of painful labour on God's part, yet we must truly and certainly infer from this passage, that the world was framed by God's Eternal Word, his only begotten Son."[50]

Subtly but significantly different in the long run is Augustine's treatment of the Trinity's external works (*opera ad extra*), according to which the distinct actions of each person are often subordinated to a more basic unity. Calvin speaks of the external works as done by each person *together with* the others. In the incarnation, for example, the three members are involved, but not in the same way. Yet diversity is apparently there for *our* benefit, not as real as the one action of the Godhead. "Wherefore," says Augustine, "although in all things the Divine Persons act perfectly in common, and without possibility of separation, nevertheless their operations behoved to be exhibited in such a way as to be distinguished from each other, *on account of the weakness which is in us, who have fallen from unity into variety*."[51] Still under the sway of Neoplatonism at this point—despite his strong commitment to ex nihilo creation—Augustine reflects a broader tendency in Christian theology to think of unity as basic and diversity as accidental. Like his doctrine of the Trinity, his understanding of creation at this specific point can only undermine the equal ultimacy of unity and trinity in God and reduce the diversity in creation to a "falling away" from primal unity. The diversity of actions, much less the persons themselves, appears at least in this expression to belong to the realm of appearance—how things look to us—rather than a revelation of God's ontological plurality.

It is only by recovering a more thoroughgoing Trinitarian theology that one can offer a view of creation that prizes plurality and unity together without reducing one to the other. Among Christians in the natural sciences, one discerns a clash between those who identify divine agency in creation with intervention and those who insist that God has so gifted creation with its own intrinsic potential that intervention is not required. In some ways, however, this is a perpetuation of the false alternatives of hypersupernaturalism (philosophically known as "occasionalism") and deism. But would not a biblical theology of creation—specifically, a covenantal view—affirm both truths that God has equipped nature with

49. Ibid.

50. Calvin, Commentary upon Psalm XXXIII, in *Commentary on the Book of Psalms*, trans. James Anderson, vol. 1 (repr., Grand Rapids: Baker, 1996), 542–43.

51. Augustine, Letter XI, to Nebridius, 389, "Letters of St. Augustine," in *A Select Library of the Nicene and Post-Nicene Fathers*, vol. 1, 229–31 (emphases added).

its own giftedness and that none of this potential can be purposefully realized without the Father's continual speaking of his Word in and through the work of the Spirit?

In a purely causal account, the one God acts *upon* the world, but in a Trinitarian view, the three persons are seen to be acting *within* it, bringing about some effects through a causal action, but many (perhaps most) through in-forming and drawing out created capacities. A theology of mediation rightly sees the Son and the Spirit as the two hands of the Father within creation, giving shape and effect to the Father's speech. According to Calvin, for example, "it is the Spirit who, everywhere diffused, sustains all things, causes them to grow, and quickens them in heaven and in earth."[52] In the words of the Reformed scholastic Venema, the "beauty, harmony, and motion" of creation are attributed to the Spirit's work. This fits well with John of Damascus's phrase, "the Word filling it and the Spirit perfecting it."[53]

I would add the covenant to the Trinity as a necessary corollary for this mediation. Everyone is looking for the nexus between transcendence and immanence. In the pantheistic turn with Schelling, Hegel, and Schleiermacher, the key idea is God's ontological unity with the world and the self, and some contemporary theologies are often simply variations on this theme. But the *covenant* is the proper site. Not even the incarnation suffices at this point, because it is a unique instance of the ontological unity of Creator and creature. Furthermore, the incarnation itself is a covenantal event in which the Lord and servant of the covenant is one person. For the rest of us, the God-world bond is not ontologically but covenantally constituted. Neither independence (deism) nor absorption (pantheism), but *relation*: it is ethical, not ontological. The world is not divine, demonic, or illusory. It is neither God's emanation nor God's enemy. It is an other that God creates as a partner for ethical communion. It is not in God's *being* that God is "conditioned" by creatures, but in God's *covenant*. This is perhaps a better distinction than that between *deus in se est* and *pro nobis*; not only is it more concrete but also, because of that fact, we do not have to wonder about a "God" behind "God." In the covenant, God has pledged *himself*. Each person of the Trinity has pledged to perform the unique actions that bring about their own intra-Trinitarian pact. It is not a general statement that God is one thing in revelation (economic Trinity) and another in reality (immanent Trinity). The doctrine of analogy cannot be allowed to give way to equivocity. It is the covenant that keeps the relation between God's hiddenness and revealedness from slipping. Only when God is seen to be active not only as "first cause" but as the immanent Life who gives a particular shape to nature, mediated through the particular persons of the Godhead, are we able to preserve God's freedom from and freedom for—and, I must add, freedom *within*—the world. This is the communicative and covenantal shape of Trinitarian mediation.

52. Calvin, *Institutes* 1.8.14.
53. John of Damascus, "Exact Exposition," 18.

Thus the omnipotence that we recognize in God's creation of the world is the power of mutual cooperation among the Father, the Son, and the Spirit. In Jenson's expression, "We are 'worked out' *among* the three."[54] Jenson and Pannenberg rightly insist that the Logos is not a silent partner, a Platonic Idea transferred to the divine mind.[55]

> The Spirit is *Spiritus Creator* as he frees the Father from retaining all being with himself, and so frees what the Father initiates from being the mere emanation it would have been were the Father God by himself. . . . We may think of the Spirit's particular word in the creating conversation as: "*Let there be* . . . ; and that is good."[56]

The concept of the creation as an analogy of the inner-Trinitarian *koinōnia* has the merit not only of teasing out the implications of the covenant of redemption, but also of showing that the eternal archetype is not an idea in the one God's mind, but the Son himself, which can only be realized in and through the Spirit. Yet it is the Son who became incarnate and therefore the Son alone who is the ontological bridge between Creator and creature. Hence it is surprising to read in Moltmann, "It is the powers and energies of the Holy Spirit that bridge the difference between Creator and creature, the actor and the act, the master and the work—a difference which otherwise seems to be unbridged by any relation at all."[57] If the Spirit rather than the Son is seen as this ontological bridge, it is easy to slip into an emanationist rather than incarnational paradigm, as Moltmann himself seems to evidence in his attempt to reconcile pantheism and theism, giving a pneumatological spin on the Neoplatonic doctrine of emanation.[58]

In such approaches, even in the name of plurality, monism wins out. This is especially true in Hegel's system, as Graham Ward observes: "The final synthesis . . . is a victory for the immanent—for the other, the outside, is seen to belong fundamentally to the inside. The positive work of negation, then, leads to wholeness; the many belong to the One: *Geist* ('spirit' or 'mind') knows itself." It is "a difference now overcome."[59] Despite his intentions, real difference is surrendered to a final synthesis in Moltmann's account. We yet again encounter the difference between meeting a stranger and overcoming estrangement, with Moltmann reflecting the latter's influence.

---

54. Jenson, *ST* 2:25.

55. Ibid., 7–8; Pannenberg, *ST* 2:41–42.

56. Jenson, *ST* 2:26.

57. Moltmann, *Trinity and the Kingdom*, 113.

58. Ibid.: "A trinitarian doctrine of creation is able to absorb the elements of truth in the idea of creation as God's 'work' and in the notion of creation as a divine overflowing or 'emanation'. The Holy Spirit is 'poured out'. The metaphor of emanation belongs to the language of pneumatology. It is therefore wrong to polemize continually against the neo-Platonic doctrine of emanation in considering the Christian doctrine of creation. Creation in the Spirit has a closer relationship to the Creator than the act has to the actor or the work to the master. All the same, the world is not 'begotten' by God, as is the Son, who is one in essence with the Father."

59. Graham Ward, "Introduction," in *The Postmodern God: A Theological Reader*, ed. Graham Ward (Oxford: Blackwell, 1997), xxvii.

The doctrine of ex nihilo creation allows us to hold to both divine transcendence and immanence, since the God who is in no way a part of the world or dependent on the world nevertheless created and inhabits it, filling its every nook and cranny with his presence: over, for, and within the world. God is involved in every facet, and yet he also gives to creation its own relative independence and freedom, even to be fruitful and multiply, to bring forth vegetation and children, everything "after its kind," with rich diversity. The fruitfulness of creation is not always the result of God's direct action in the world. The Father does not only command, "Let there be light" (Gen. 1:3); he also summons, "Let the earth put forth vegetation: plants yielding seed, and fruit trees of every kind on earth that bear fruit with the seed" (v. 11). The result was that "The earth brought forth vegetation" (v. 12). This summons and response allows for neither pantheism nor deism. The very fact that God created fruit to have its own seed, its own means of propagating, analogous to human generation, shows that God was not interested in creating a world without its own inherent, generative capacities—its own space. Similarly, God commanded, "Let the waters bring forth swarms of living creatures," summoning them to "be fruitful and multiply" (vv. 20, 22); "Let the earth bring forth living creatures of every kind" (v. 24). Far from entailing ecological exploitation, ex nihilo creation and the Creator-creature distinction actually allow space for the world to be itself, with its own unfathomable finite possibilities given in the creation. It is by his "two hands," the Son and the Spirit, that the Father directs this potential to its intended end in the Sabbath rest. Yet there is in this mediation a "letting be" that never surrenders the otherness of God and creatures.

Not only is the intra-Trinitarian exchange described by Scripture in terms of the Father eternally speaking forth the Son and spirating the Spirit and, in redemptive revelation, the Son bearing verbal witness to the Father and the Spirit to the Son. Even in creation there is this recurring theme of the natural world being uttered into existence and sustained daily by the triune God, with that creation answering back in covenantal response: "The heavens are telling the glory of God; and the firmament proclaims his handiwork. Day to day pours forth speech, and night to night declares knowledge. There is no speech, nor are there words; their voice is not heard; yet their voice goes out through all the earth, and their words to the end of the world" (Ps. 19:1–4). The psalmist moves easily back and forth between the testimony of nature and that of God's historical revelation (vv. 7–14). The Son is not only the Father's speech in redemption, but "in him all things in heaven and on earth were created, things visible and invisible, whether thrones or dominions or rulers or powers—all things have been created through him and for him. He himself is before all things, and in him all things hold together" (Col. 1:16–17; cf. John 1:3).

I have argued that a Trinitarian account of creation entails a covenantal approach in which communicative action would be paramount. For example, it could go a long way toward elaborating the theme of the Son as the eternally begotten Word, in contrast to the platonizing Logos Christologies of traditional theology that often persist in not so traditional theologies as well. As I have discussed earlier at some length, Tillich contrasted two fundamental approaches to the philosophy of religion: the ontological approach (overcoming estrangement) and what I have been calling the covenantal-ethical approach (meeting a stranger). According to the former, which Tillich himself advocated, creation returns to the ahistorical origins of ancient mythology. "The doctrine of creation is not the story of an event which took place 'once upon a time.' It is the basic description of the relation between God and the world," answering the question of human finitude.[60]

By contrast, I would argue that the import of the doctrine of creation is neither philosophical (whether of an idealist or existentialist variety) nor scientific, although there are clearly implications for both. I would concur with Berkhof's suggestion: "The doctrine of creation is not set forth in Scripture as a philosophical solution of the problem of the world, but in its ethical and religious significance, as a revelation of the relation of man to his God."[61] Once more, in other words, we are talking about meeting a stranger rather than overcoming estrangement, a covenantal relationship rather than an emanation or an expansion and/or contraction in the being of God.[62] As the sciences have shown in recent times, our words can grasp something real about the world itself. So too theology, but, as Gunton reminds us, only a truly Trinitarian theology of creation can overcome Plato and Kant.[63] And maybe even Hegel.

60. Paul Tillich, *Systematic Theology* (Chicago: University of Chicago Press, 1967), 1:60.
61. Berkhof, *Systematic Theology*, 126.
62. See especially Moltmann, *Trinity and the Kingdom*, 99–113.
63. Gunton, *Triune Creator*, 156–57.

PART TWO
SERVANT

Chapter Four

"Here I Am"

A Covenantal Anthropology

Just as the "ontological way" concentrates on the *being* (the what) more than the *agency* (the who) of God, its anthropological corollary is to ask what it is that makes humans different and unique, which typically comes down to locating the divine-human identity in the intellectual-spiritual essence. Consequently, the *imago Dei* in much of Christian theology has been regarded as the site of immediate communion and even ontological participation between Creator and creature. It is the intellect/soul that participates in the heavenly side of the register and distinguishes human beings from animals. The soul/spirit/intellect is the true self, transcending its finite embodiment.

Modernity at least since Descartes was dominated by a notion of the self that was constrained by a metaphysics of presence. Yet a line is often (and not entirely without warrant) drawn from Augustine to Descartes in this respect. Among others, Charles Taylor provides a reliable summary of this complex relationship, so I will not pursue it here.[1] Returning more directly to classical rather than biblical

---

1. Charles Taylor, *Sources of the Self* (Cambridge, MA: Harvard University Press, 1989). See also Phillip Cary, *Augustine's Invention of the Inner Self: The Legacy of a Christian Platonist* (New York: Oxford University Press, 2000).

categories, modernity has radicalized and secularized this ontotheological enterprise, especially with the addition of a sharp emphasis on autonomy. Personhood
thus became reduced to knowing, duty, feeling, striving, overcoming, authentic-
ity, and so on. Otherness, relatedness, ethical responsibility, embodiment—and
covenant (which gives concrete form to these other categories)—were irrelevant
to such discourse. The image of God was a question about the introspective rather
than ecstatic self, a corollary to Augustine's psychological approach to the Trinity.[2] "For not in the body but in the mind was man made in the image of God,"
said Augustine.[3] A subtext running through this chapter is something like the
typologies of meeting a stranger versus overcoming estrangement as applied to
anthropology.

In all of its modern forms, the "ontological way" involves *disengagement*, to
borrow Taylor's term, despite attempts to resituate the self in "lived experience,"
through language, culture, and history. What we fail to see is a corresponding
biblical-theological effort to resituate selfhood in the "lived experience" of the
covenant and eschatology. Dilthey correctly discerned that in the empiricism and
idealism of the Enlightenment period, "No real blood runs in the veins of the
knowing subject that Locke, Hume and Kant constructed."[4] Regardless of the
classical and modern roots of this approach to our question, I hope that this proposal will provide an alternative paradigm for anthropology over against the more
Neoplatonic rivals and their secularized successors without running into the arms
of a reactionary reductionism (viz., seflhood reduced to relations or language) in
which Michel Foucault's prediction is realized that "man" is about to be "erased
like a face drawn in the sand at the edge of the sea."[5]

My goal in this chapter is to relate the covenantal theme of lord and servant
to anthropology, specifically, the image of God. I approach this topic in terms of
two concentric circles: humanness more generally and the *imago* specifically,
identifying the character of the *imago Dei* in its context of covenant and eschatology. I then suggest some ways in which this perspective might interact fruit-
fully with some recent approaches to the problematic status of the "postmodern
self." Covenant and eschatology do not exhaust the meaning of the human, but
significantly contextualize and orient it.

2. Augustine should not bear the entire burden, since the identification of the *imago* with the
intellect within a basically Platonic scheme was the common inheritance of patristic thought. Cf.
Gregory of Nysssa, *A Select Library of Nicene and Post-Nicene Fathers*, 2nd series, ed. Philip Schaff and
Henry Wace, vol. 5 (Grand Rapids: Eerdmans, 1972), 390–442.

3. Augustine, *Commentary on John's Gospel*, XXIII, 19.

4. Cited by Anthony Thiselton, *Interpreting God and the Postmodern Self: On Meaning, Manipulation and Promise* (Edinburgh: T & T Clark, 1995), 47.

5. Michel Foucault, trans. Alan Sheridan-Smith, *The Order of Things: An Archaeology of the
Human Sciences* (New York: Random House, 1970), 387. Let's not forget that modernity was never
wholly individualistic (viz., Spinoza, Hegel, Fichte, Schopenhauer, Marx, Freud). Furthermore, postmodernity celebrates atomistic individualism as often as communitarianism. In both modernity and
postmodernity are many mansions.

THE SELF AS SERVANT

According to Stanley Grenz, the Reformation in general and Calvin in particular represent "the birth of the relational *imago*."[6] While it was hardly their intention to prepare the ground for a wholly relational understanding of personhood, there can be little doubt that Calvin and his theological heirs have contributed significantly to the discussion before us and that they have done so with a willingness both to appropriate and to critique the tradition they had inherited from the patristic and medieval periods. Rather than speculate on whether the image of God was a quality that was somehow attached to the mind or soul of human beings, the Reformers gave greater attention to the concrete relationship between God and humans as revealed in Scripture. In their wake, the theologians of these Reformation churches went even further in situating their understanding of human nature before and after the fall in terms of covenant theology.

COVENANT

As we have seen, the mature covenant theology typically advanced three covenants: an eternal, intra-Trinitarian covenant of redemption, and two covenants made between God and human beings, executed in time. The covenant of creation (also designated the covenant of "works," "nature," or "law") was the natural state in which Adam and Eve were created and under which humanity "in Adam" stands condemned by the original covenant curses.

The *protoeuangelion* (Gen. 3:15—the first announcement of the gospel), however, announces a gracious covenant. Without setting aside the original covenant, God promulgates a covenant of grace in anticipation of the second Adam whom he will send. As the tree of life was the sacrament of the covenant of creation, Adam and Eve are clothed sacramentally in animal skins by God to prefigure "the Lamb of God who takes away the sin of the world" (John 1:29). Through Abraham, God gives greater clarity to this gracious covenant by swearing unconditional loyalty to Abraham for the sake of his seed, identified by the apostle Paul as Jesus Christ (Gal. 3:16), and ordains circumcision as the sign and seal of its old covenant administration, with baptism as its new covenant sacrament of incorporation (Matt. 28:18–20; Mark 16:15–16; Col. 2:11–12).

Thus, even after the fall, human existence remains intrinsically covenantal, even though it is divided between Cain's proud city (Gen. 4:17–24) and the City of God represented by Seth, whose descendants are distinguished by their invocation of the Great King for their salvation: "At that time people began to invoke the name of the LORD" (v. 26). Those who do not invoke God or embrace his

6. Stanley Grenz, *The Social God and the Relational Self* (Louisville, KY: Westminster John Knox, 2001), 162.

covenant of grace are "in Adam" under the original covenant, yet upheld by common grace despite their being strangers to the divine promises announced in the covenant of grace. Intrinsic to humanness, particularly the *imago*, is a covenantal office or commission into which every person is born; it is therefore, as an equally universal phenomenon, the basis for God's righteous judgment of humankind even apart from special revelation (Romans 1 and 2). This is to say that "law"—in particular, the divine covenant-law—is natural, a *verbum internum* (internal word) that rings in yet is not identical to the conscience. The covenant of creation renders every person a dignified and therefore accountable image-bearer of God.

Even the fall did not eradicate the original revelation of God's righteous law to the conscience; indeed, to this day this law-covenant is in force: "Now we know that whatever the law says," whether written on the conscience or on tablets, "it speaks to those who are under the law, so that every mouth may be silenced, and the whole world may be held accountable to God" (Rom. 3:19). The law brings no hope of relief, but only the knowledge of breach (v. 20). The gospel, by contrast, is entirely foreign to the human person in this natural state. It comes as a free decision on God's part in view of the fall and can be known only by a *verbum externum* (external word), an astounding announcement proclaimed that brings hope and confidence in our standing before God (vv. 21–26).

For the biblical writers at least, What is it to be human? is ultimately a narrative-ethical rather than a metaphysical-ontological question. This is not to assume that my account avoids its own ontological/metaphysical scheme (the impossibility of which is insufficiently appreciated, as I have previously argued). Yet it means that these presuppositions at least strive to be grounded in the concrete revelation of God and humanness as we pick out the characters in the biblical drama and its didactic notations rather than starting with ostensibly universal givens of anthropological science. Neither the Creator nor creation can be named apart from the drama of creation, fall, redemption, and consummation.

Eschatology

The notions of covenant and eschatology are closely intertwined in biblical theology. Both are oriented toward promise and fulfillment. Furthermore, both eschew any ontological dualism. As the covenant idea in Scripture excludes a nature-grace antithesis by emphasizing instead the ethical antithesis (sin-grace), biblical eschatology similarly concentrates its antithesis between "flesh" and "Spirit" in terms of "this present aeon" and "the aeon to come," respectively. It is this world *in its ethical rebellion* that is under divine judgment, and it is this same world—"far as the curse is found"—that will be finally liberated when the work of the second Adam has finally resulted in the Spirit's consummation of all things in him. Thus both body and soul are included in this image-bearing task and only in a psychosomatic unity enjoy the consummation in Jesus Christ.

According to this eschatological perspective I am proposing by extending the logic of the older Reformed theologians and in profound continuity with Irenaeus and the Cappadocians, creation was not the goal, but the beginning, of God's purpose for humankind specifically and the natural world generally. As Geerhardus Vos reminds us, the particular covenantal and eschatological orientation found in Scripture is thoroughly concerned with the ethical and personal sphere, not with abstract metaphysics and ontology. "The universe, as created, was only a beginning, the meaning of which was not perpetuation, but attainment." Thus eschatology is prior to soteriology: creation began with a greater destiny lying before it.[7] Creation was the stage, the "beautiful theater," for God's drama, not an end in itself.

This has obvious implications for the concept of human immortality. While human death should not be regarded merely as "a characteristic of frail, temporal creation,"[8] Moltmann is nevertheless right to point out, on the basis of God's command to be fruitful and multiply, "that human beings were mortal from the beginning."[9] Miroslav Volf correctly sees in Moltmann's construction a classic debate between Eastern and Western approaches, with the categories of corruption and completion and the paradigm of sin and redemption, respectively.[10] However, by recognizing that creation even before the fall was awaiting its completion under Adamic dominion, and that this consummation included the conferral of immortality as well as indefectibility, covenant theology is able to integrate both of these strands—the eschatological and the soteriological, immortality and redemption. Thus conceived, death did not come as a consequence of mere human finitude nor was immortality a human possession from the beginning (especially not in virtue of an immortal soul). Immortality was a goal, not an origin; the tree of life was a prospect, not a presupposition, of human existence. Prior to the fall, Adam and Eve lived between the two trees: entering everlasting Sabbath (the blessing of the consummation) and everlasting death (the curse of sin). "You shall surely die" (curse). Eden was a trial.

As human beings are therefore by nature covenantal, they are also constitutionally prospective, even utopian, despite the distorted ways in which fallen humanity seeks to win its glorification apart from and even against God. The fact that Adam and Eve were representatively created in God's image and yet were to attain the perfection and consummation of that image in the future gives to

7. Geerhardus Vos, *The Eschatology of the Old Testament*, ed. James T. Dennison Jr. (repr., Phillipsburg, NJ: Presbyterian & Reformed, 2001), 73–74: "The universe, as created, was only a beginning, the meaning of which was not perpetuation, but attainment. . . . Eschatology aims at consummation rather than restoration. . . . It does not aim at the original state, but at a transcendental state of man."

8. Jürgen Moltmann, *The Coming of God: Christian Eschatology*, trans. Margaret Kohl (Minneapolis: Fortress, 1996), 78.

9. Ibid., 91.

10. Miroslav Volf, "After Moltmann: Reflections on the Future of Eschatology," in *God Will Be All in All*, ed. Richard Bauckham (Edinburgh: T & T Clark, 1999), 249–50.

human personhood both a retrospective and anticipatory eschatological identity. This fact becomes crucial to the account of personal identity that I elaborate below in terms of dramatic narrative emplotment.

PERSON AND IMAGE

While personhood cannot be made to consist in relations, the actual existence of persons cannot be comprehended apart from them. To be created in God's image is to be called persons in communion.[11] That *koinōnia* consists originally in the covenant of creation, in which all of humanity participates in Adam as its representative.

"Here I Am"

Robert Jenson has compared God and humans along the lines of hearing rather than seeing. God is "a conversation, a fugue, a personal event." Therefore,

> to be, as a creature, is to be mentioned in the triune moral conversation, as something other than those who conduct it. Western intellectual history has for the most part continued the Greek tradition for which "to be" meant to have form and so to appear and be seen, whether with the body's or the mind's eye. But there plainly is another possibility: that to be is to be *heard of;* and it is this interpretation that is demanded by the doctrine of creation.[12]

For Thomas Aquinas (and the Protestant scholastics), the language of relation is archetype and ectype—images.

> But if God's creating word is an actual utterance and not an unspoken mental form actualized by the will, the matter cannot be construed quite in this way. Creatures have being precisely as God transitively says, "Let there be . . ." Therefore insofar as "being" says something *about* God or creatures, "being" must after all be univocal rather than analogous. And yet there must be some break between "God is" and "Creatures are"; the force of Thomas's insight remains. Perhaps we may adopt categories from J. L. Austin and suggest: "x is" is univocal in its "locutionary sense," in what it says about x, but equivocal in its "illocutionary force," in what is done when it is said. Just so the utterance is indeed constituted in a kind of analogicity, which may indeed be finally much like that posited by Thomas.[13]

---

11. See Colin Gunton, "Trinity, Ontology and Anthropology," in *Persons, Divine and Human,* ed. Christoph Schwöbel and Colin E. Gunton (Edinburgh: T & T Clark, 1991), 47–61. At the same time, I find such arguments as those employed by Harriet A. Harris (against a purely relational ontology of person) compelling ("Should We Say that Personhood Is Relational?" *Scottish Journal of Theology* 51, no. 2 [1998], 222–23).

12. Jenson, *ST* 2:35–36. He is influenced in this by Franz K. Mayr, "Philosophie im Wandel der Sprache," *Zeitschrift für Theologie und Kirche* 61 (1964): 439–91.

13. Jenson, *ST* 2:38.

Before getting to my main point by way of response, I should first suggest that the weakness of Jenson's argument lies in his presupposition of selfhood reduced to relations: God as "a fugue, a conversation, a personal event." It is one thing to say that the triune God is three persons—even three identities, as Jenson prefers—engaged in an eternal fugue, and quite another to say that God just *is* a fugue, a conversation, a personal event. I realize that this is question-begging: it is hardly the case that Jenson has missed a major flaw in his argument. Rather, he holds consistently to the strong view of the relational self. If God just *is* a conversation, there is no reason to believe that the Son and the Spirit are divine partners unless and until the Father freely wills to engage them. This is the logical conclusion that Jenson himself seems to adopt.

But the strengths of Jenson's further argument, particularly with respect to human identity, are worth considering in connection with this topic. In various places, Jenson explores what theology might look like if it adopted the metaphor of hearing over that of seeing—a quite typical move in Reformation theologies. I have also defended this prejudice throughout this project, though not yet with this application. While Jenson himself, in the quotation above, comes to the edge of identifying divine and human persons in terms of "being spoken of" rather than "being" (with visual connotations), only to (happily) back away from it, it does seem congenial to the covenantal approach I am pursuing to suggest that human "being" is the result of our being *said* by someone else—God. In this case, to be is to be mentioned.[14] Again we have to be careful not to take this as a general principle *coram hominibus*, since it can easily lead to the suggestion that one's status as a person is dependent on whether one is talked about. The marginalized are not only those whose voice we do not hear but those about whom we do not speak. Nevertheless, the point stands as applied to God's creative agency (*coram Deo*), which in fact judges our speech.

If we extend this reflection, we could say—and this brings us in line with an argument to be made below—human beings are those who reflect God's image not chiefly in who they *are* essentially but in how they *reply* ethically. Though determined *as* human persons by the mere fact of their creation as God's image, their *realization of the purpose* of their personhood depends on whether they correspond to God's intentions. Here we could interject Aristotle for a moment: "good" is teleologically defined. A good watch is one that tells time well. Similarly, the creation was pronounced good by God at every stage precisely because it "answered back" appropriately. Each facet of creation, grouped under the various creature kingdoms, functioned as it was ordained in the declaration, "Let there be *x*." The sun, we might say, did not "talk back," but fulfilled its destiny. Fulfilling their design was identified in ethical and aesthetic terms. So when humans were created, the superlative benediction was God's evaluation of the "answering back" that he heard.

Even if we do not have exegetical warrant for this conclusion from the creation narratives themselves, we do find it in the explicit biblical motif of the servant of

14. Ibid., 2:348.

YHWH as the one who answers back to the divine commission, "Here I am"; "Behold, let it be done unto me according to your word." Thus human existence is human regardless, but it is "very good" insofar as humans answer back according to the purpose of their existence. Human personhood is analogous to divine personhood in its ecstatic character. There is a fundamental dispossession that such an understanding entails, in sharp contrast to the possessed self that we find especially in modern (Cartesian and idealist) anthropologies. There is something to the fact that Descartes developed his cogito by isolating himself from society, divesting himself (so he thought anyway) of all previous historical reflection, while the biblical understanding of persons arose in the context of historical, covenantal drama. "Here I am," I shall argue, as an answer to the other, is diametrically opposed to the autonomous self that is the product of one's own introspective reflection. We cannot begin to think that we really know ourselves until we know someone other than ourselves. In Trinitarian terms, as Jenson explains,

> It is in virtue of the Son's triune role that the creating command is a word with a definite content. . . . We will then say: to be a creature is, in christological respect, to be a revelation of God's will. In the more dramatic and therefore more accurate language we found in Luther, to be a creature is to be a "created word" from God.[15]

Before I offer a constructive proposal, let me stake out the development of the doctrine of the *imago* within the Reformed tradition specifically, since the older theologians offer some surprising insights that we often miss in contemporary discussions.

The dialectical character of Calvin's thought is finally receiving deserved attention.[16] His dim view of fallen humanity must be measured against his sometimes astonishing respect for created humanity.[17] Utterly essential for Calvin—and instructive for us—is the refusal to locate the slightest weakness or defect in humanity that might make the fall and consequent need for redemption necessary from the start. "For the depravity and malice both of man and of the devil, or the sins that arise therefrom, do not spring from nature, but rather from the corruption of nature."[18] This he distinguishes from the "Manichean error." "For if any defect were proved to inhere in nature, this would bring reproach upon

15. Ibid., *ST* 2:45; cf. Gunton's critique of Jenson in *The Promise of Trinitarian Theology*, 2nd ed., 118–36.

16. See especially in this regard Kilian McDonnell, OSB, *John Calvin, the Church, and the Eucharist* (Princeton, NJ: Princeton University Press, 1967).

17. Calvin concurs with Aristotle's reference to humankind as a "microcosm" because "he is a rare example of God's power, goodness, and wisdom, and contains within himself enough miracles to occupy our minds, if only we are not irked at paying attention to them" (*Institutes* 1.5.3). He praises "the human body" as "ingenious" (1.5.2). Yet in all this, humanity is "struck blind in such a dazzling theater" (1.5.8). When we catch a glimpse of the "burning lamps" shining for us in God's works, including ourselves, we smother their light (1.5.14). The dialectic here moves between the exquisite character of nature and the equally unfathomable ruin of that nature to which humans are inclined.

18. Calvin, *Institutes* 1.14.3.

[God]."[19] Contrary to the Augustinian tradition's notions of concupiscence and the *donum superadditum*, Calvin regards the human *as* human in remarkably positive terms. Nature *as* nature is in no need of supplemental grace for its perfection but is already oriented toward the perfection that is within Adam's power to attain. "Finally, we shall learn that in forming man and in adorning him with such goodly beauty, and with such great and numerous gifts, he put him forth as the most excellent example of his works."[20] What then constitutes the "image"?

First, the proper seat of the image-likeness (Calvin judges Hebrew *ṣelem* and *dĕmût* to be synonymous) is the soul, but he goes beyond the earlier tradition in attributing its glory to the whole person.[21] Consequently, "there was no part of man, not even the body itself, in which some sparks did not glow."[22] For this reason, "it would be foolish to seek a definition of 'soul' from the philosophers," he says, and to make this definition then the basis for our understanding of the *imago*.[23]

Second, the true nature of this image "can be nowhere better recognized than from the restoration of his corrupted nature." Adam was alienated from God. "Therefore, even though we grant that God's image was not totally annihilated and destroyed in him, yet it was so corrupted that whatever remains is frightful deformity. Consequently, the beginning of our recovery of salvation is in that restoration that we obtain through Christ, who also is called the Second Adam for the reason that he restores us to true and complete integrity."[24] The willful distortion of this image is a measure both of its ineradicable status and human depravity, and thus redemption is at least in part understood in terms of "putting on" Christ: "Put on the new self, created after the likeness of God" (Eph. 4:24).[25] The understanding of "image" is therefore not to be sought through speculation on the meaning of *ṣelem* and *dĕmût* in Genesis, but by learning from eschatology the identity of the second Adam in whom the image is fully expressed: "Now we see how Christ is the most perfect image of God; if we are conformed to it, we are so restored that with true piety, righteousness, purity and intelligence we bear God's image."[26] Calvin rejects both Augustinian speculations concerning a "trinity" of the soul as well as Neoplatonic "emanation," "as if some portion of immeasurable divinity had flowed into man."[27]

Like Calvin, the Reformed scholastics appeal to the classical (Aristotelian) identification of humanity as a sort of microcosms, displaying in a signal manner God's external works. God's likeness in humanity, according to Mastricht, is "that conformity of man whereby in his own way (i.e., as a creature) he reproduces

19. Ibid., 1.15.1.
20. Ibid., 1.14.20.
21. Ibid., 1.15.3.
22. Ibid.
23. Ibid., 1.15.6.
24. Ibid., 1.15.4.
25. Ibid.
26. Ibid.
27. Ibid., 1.15.5.

the highest perfection of God."[28] It is therefore ethical rather than metaphysical: hearing and obeying God's word spoken, not a matter of locating the ontological point of contact between divine and human being. "For the understanding of the Reformed Church doctrine of the divine image in man," Heppe relates, "it should be noted that it is thoroughly connected with man as such, indeed with the entire man, with his entire spirit-body being."[29]

Peter Martyr Vermigli, characteristic of the tradition, follows Calvin's analysis quite closely, insisting that the proper interpretation of the image will have to look to Christ and our renewal in him by the Spirit. It is not that we are no longer human after the fall, but that we abuse our office in self-interest. In our fallen condition, we no longer exercise proper dominion, but "exercise tyranny over things instead." From the very beginning, the *imago* is not only teleologically but eschatologically oriented. "The image of God is the new man, who understands the truth of God and desires its righteousness. So Paul has taught us, when he writes to the Colossians: 'Put on the new nature, which is being renewed in the knowledge of God, after the image of its Creator.'"[30] We may be renewed in the image of Christ, but Christ is "the primary and true image" of God.[31]

The only reference that we find in the Heidelberg Catechism identifies the image with the "true righteousness and holiness" in which Adam was created (Q. 6).[32] The Westminster Confession elaborates along the same lines, adding the inscription of God's law on the conscience "and power to fulfill it; and yet, under a possibility of transgressing being left to the liberty of their own will, which was subject unto change." In addition to this natural law and liberty, there was the special command "not to eat of the tree of the knowledge of good and evil" (chap. 4). A speculative anthropology suspended on the framework of ontological participation is therefore in eclipse for these writers.

According to Heppe,

> Cocceius (*Sum. theol.* XVII) finds the divine image not in the "substance of the soul," nor yet in the "faculties of the soul," nor yet in the "*imperium* which man had over the living," but in the *rectitudo* which he explains (para. 22) as moral reciprocity with God in all a man's parts, in the soul of course as the *hegemonikon* and in the body and limbs as the *skeuos*. Similarly Heidegger (VI, 19), Braun (I, ii, 15), Riissen (VI, 60), etc.[33]

Others see the *imago* in the *dominio*, but even this remains an ethical obligation imposed upon humankind rather than a tyrannical lordship. According to Ver-

28. Heinrich Heppe, *Reformed Dogmatics*, rev. and ed. Ernst Bizer, trans. G. T. Thomson (London: Allen & Unwin, 1950), 232.

29. Ibid.

30. Ibid.

31. Ibid., 44.

32. "God created man good and in his image, that is, in true righteousness and holiness, so that he might rightly know God his Creator, love him with his whole heart, and live with him in true blessedness, praising and glorifying him."

33. Heppe, *Reformed Dogmatics*, 232.

migli, it renders man "a kind of representative (vicar) of God."[34] Thus long before the criticism of substance metaphysics and ontological dualism, the Reformed tradition generally—even more persistently than Calvin—directed discussion of the *imago* away from the usual assumptions of Christian Platonism toward a more ethical conception.

As we will see below in our concluding interaction with Lutheran dogmatics, the *definition* of the image is all-important in deciding whether it has been wholly abolished after the fall. Ursinus reflects a Reformed consensus in carefully distinguishing the sense in which this image is lost and retained: "But after the fall, man lost this glorious image of God."[35] Yet he hastens to add, "There were, however, some remains and sparks of the image of God still left in man, after his fall, and which even yet continue in those who are unregenerated," which include the rational soul and will, knowledge of the arts and sciences, "traces and remains" of civic virtue, "the enjoyment of many temporal blessings," and some measure of stewardship rather than tyranny over other creatures. However, what is lost are the most important things belonging to the image: true knowledge of God, his will and works; the regulation of affections and actions in accordance with God's law; a genuine stewardship over creation; and a true happiness in this life and the next. In spite of this breach of the covenant of creation, however, God has promulgated the covenant of grace:

> God the Father restores this image through the Son; because he has "made him unto us wisdom, righteousness, sanctification, and redemption" (1 Cor. 1:30). The Son, through the Holy Spirit, "changes us into the same image, from glory to glory, as by the Spirit of the Lord" (2 Cor. 3:18). And the Holy Ghost carries forward and completes what is begun by the Word and the use of the Sacraments.[36]

So, for Ursinus, "the image of God is not to be sought in the sole substance of the soul, but particularly in the virtues and gifts with which it was adorned by God in creation."[37]

From these writers we learn that the image is chiefly rectitude, the law written on the conscience. This underscores the point that the law is not to be understood as simply an external list of rules imposed on those who are already constituted as human persons on some other (autonomous) basis, but as that righteousness that defines both God and God's works. As with God himself, the law does not simply stand over against the creature as a heteronomous authority, but belongs to the creature's own identity. The law of God and image of God are

---

34. Ibid., 233. But the view that came to dominate (via Melanchthon) was a distinction between the substance (in the personal nature of man) and the actual endowments (original righteousness). Despite a formal rejection of the semantic difference between "image" and "likeness," this approximates the patristic distinction.

35. Zacharias Ursinus, *The Commentary on the Heidelberg Catechism*, trans. G. W. Williard (Phillipsburg, NJ: Presbyterian and Reformed Publishing Co., 1852), 32.

36. Ibid., 32–33.

37. Heppe, *Reformed Dogmatics*, 233.

therefore two sides of the same coin. Even Christ can be said to be the incarnate law of God as the archetypal divine image, since he perfectly *represents* this will as God and *fulfills* this will as human. It is not, therefore, a question of some inner faculty or quality in the soul or mind, nor a matter of a supernatural gift added to nature. This original rectitude is lost, but not the knowledge of God's law entirely. Nevertheless, this is not a saving knowledge for human beings: "Knowledge of natural law did not make them better," says Vermigli, "because even if the law is known it cannot change us nor give us strength to act rightly; therefore, we must run to Christ."[38] The law was a sufficient revelation for God's covenant with humankind in rectitude; the gospel is only economically necessary afterward due to human fault.

Obviously, the Reformed and Lutheran theologians were drawing on similar resources, though with different conceptual tags. In fact, drawing upon Luther and the Lutheran scholastics, Robert Jenson makes a point that is very similar to the point I am making through the Reformed scholastics: God's command upholds human community.

> This "use" is often identified with natural law "written in the hearts" of all humans. And for Martin Luther himself, whose drastic use of this concept is a chief incitement of the following, to live in the world and to be "under the law" are the same thing; God's rule by the gospel in the church and his rule by his law in the world are then God's two "regimes," his two ways of establishing his will *ad extra*.[39]

It is not that law and gospel are set against each other as abstract opposites, but that they are distinguished according to their different functions (and, I would add, economies and covenants).

> Therefore if we humans address one another at all we speak law. For, as we have seen, every address somehow opens a future, and only rarely and unreliably can address be promise. Since we are finite we can take on ourselves only a tiny part of the conditions for the futures we hold out to others, and not even so reliably; for those we address there can be no firm barrier between, for example, the promise, "I will find you some food," and the law, "Sorry, friend. I did my best. But you know, you really should pull yourself together."[40]

"Thus all our speech to one another finally somehow obligates; 'law' is the necessary discourse of all community," and it is rooted in God's say-so, his command.[41] Autonomy is thereby excluded: we exist because we are addressed. "If we exist because we are addressed by God and if we have our specific identity as those who respond to God, then we do not possess ourselves."[42] So "it is

38. Vermigli, cited by ibid., 24.
39. Jenson, *ST* 2:62.
40. Jenson, *ST* 2:62.
41. Ibid., 63.
42. Ibid.

not only our salvation that is accomplished by God's address, but our being as such."[43]

Not surprisingly, given their own way of making these points, the early Reformed theologians included the covenantal dimension of the *imago*:

> Mastricht (III, ix, 33): "Original righteousness was conferred on Adam not as a private but as a public person, or what is the same thing, in Adam on the whole of human nature, whence it would have been transmitted to all his posterity. But this original righteousness is not a substance as Illyricus used to rave, but a quality diffused as it were through all the substance, and so common to body and soul, to the mind, also to the will and the affections."[44]

So despite some lingering effects of the more Neoplatonic bent of the patristic and medieval tradition on Calvin's thought, he and his theological colleagues and successors came to clearly affirm the psychosomatic unity of the image. More recently, John Murray reflected this consensus: "Man is bodily, and, therefore, the scriptural way of expressing this truth is not that man has a body but that man *is* body. . . . Scripture does not represent the soul or spirit of man as created first and then put into a body. . . . The bodily is not an appendage."[45]

It is noteworthy that although the Reformed scholastics follow the older tradition in distinguishing the soul as the proper seat of the image, their emphasis on the goodness of nature as nature and humanness as human keeps them from the nature-grace dualism that marks and mars so much of the medieval synthesis. "As flesh and spirit (taken physically) are disparates, not contraries," explains Turretin, "so also are the appetites, inclinations and habits of both in themselves. The repugnancy now found in them arises accidentally from sin."[46] In this way, anthropology was clearly articulated with a discourse of ethics rather than ontology or metaphysics as such. Difference does not imply strife (much less antithesis), and sin cannot be attributed to any aspect of human nature that is ostensibly weaker or more susceptible to fault.

As we make our way through a covenantal-eschatological approach to the vexing question of human personhood by specifying within that larger question the character of the *imago*, we might begin by distinguishing between what we may call prerequisites for image-bearing and the *imago* proper. This is the broader concentric circle encompassing the narrower circle of the *imago* proper.

43. Ibid., 68.
44. Heppe, *Reformed Dogmatics*, 240.
45. John Murray, *Collected Writings of John Murray*, 4 vols. (Carlisle, PA: Banner of Truth, 1976), 2:14.
46. Cited in Heppe, *Reformed Dogmatics*, 468. This echoes Peter Martyr Vermigli: Based on Gen. 9:4, he argues that "the blood is the soul." This represents a metonymy: "Since the blood is a sign of the soul's presence, it may be called the soul itself . . . I do not offer this as if I accept it as the reason why God gave that commandment [against eating the blood of animals], but to indicate the communion of man's soul with the body" (*The Peter Martyr Library*, vol. 4: *Philosophical Works*, trans. and ed. Joseph C. McLelland (Kirksville, MO: Sixteenth Century Essays and Studies, 1996), 42.

IMAGE AND EMBASSY

With these developments in mind, we are better prepared to offer a constructive analysis and proposal for identifying the character of the image. Extending the logic of covenant theology beyond its traditional limits, I will argue that the *imago Dei* is not a property of a particular faculty of the human person. At the same time, I seek to avoid the opposite reductionism that renders the *imago* nothing more than relational. To argue this position, I will distinguish between *prerequisite attributes* of humanness that make human beings suitable candidates for bearing the divine image and the nature of the *image itself.*

Prerequisite Characteristics for Human Image-Bearing

The Platonic rooting of the *imago* in reason has had disastrous effects, as recent criticisms have highlighted. Furthermore, there is not a hint in Scripture of the oft-repeated theological axiom that human likeness to God has to do with a shared "spirituality," since the concept of ex nihilo creation blocks any emanationist scheme with its chain of being. Since human spirituality is also created rather than a divine emanation, the human soul is no more to be identified with God than the human body.

While my proposal rejects any identification of the image of God with any faculty or substance, mental or physical, can there be any doubt that human beings are uniquely suited among the creation to be covenant partners with God? And can we not point out fairly obvious prerequisites such as certain natural capacities for deliberative reason, intentional relationality, moral agency, and linguisticality? Yet none of these capacities exists prior to the covenant of creation, but all are already presupposed by it. Suffice it to say that human personhood requires these characteristics if it is to be construed as *covenantal* personhood, and yet the *imago*, properly considered, cannot be identified with these. Rather, as I will argue, the image is to be understood in this account as an office or embassy, *a covenantal commission with an eschatological orientation.* To be sure, there are ontological features that distinguish humanity from the rest of creation, but these do not define the *imago* itself.

This approach necessarily directs our attention away from the inner quest, out toward a conception of the self that is inseparable from, though not reduced to, its external relations in a specific "form of life" defined by mutual obligations. Covenant is the language game of the human way of being in the world. Although Calvin himself did not sufficiently develop this aspect of his thought, covenant theology is unthinkable apart from a basic commitment to relational categories. Even if Grenz's suggestion cited above concerning the "birth of the relational self" in the Reformation (and especially Calvin) is exaggerated, it is nevertheless true that A. N. Whitehead's famous quip, "Religion is what the individual does with his own solitariness," is far removed from any view of the self as oriented covenantally.[47]

---

47. A. N. Whitehead, *Religion in the Making* (New York: Meridian, 1960), 16.

The Image of God

So far I have outlined essential features of a covenantal anthropology as touching the subject of human personhood generally. I now turn to what I regard as "the image proper." I will argue that the image, properly speaking, is constituted by the following four characteristics: sonship/royal dominion, representation, glory, and prophetic witness.

Sonship/Royal Dominion

At least part of the significance of the *imago* as "image" and "likeness" is that it is the royal investiture of a servant-son. In his person and work, Jesus Christ receives in the place of fallen Adam his royal investiture in the seventh day as the image-son of God. Thus this aspect of the *imago* (as others) must be allowed to emerge as we think the first and second Adams together.

At this point we should add as a parenthetical remark that it is not the biblical doctrine of creation that has led to the oppression of nonhuman as well as human creation, but the reality of sin that the biblical doctrine of the fall describes. Childs expresses this point well: "If the Bible rejects viewing the world as an object to be possessed and exploited, it also strongly resists all attempts to blur the fundamental distinction between God and the world."[48] To say that "the earth is the LORD's" is to say two things: that the earth is not *God* and that it is not *ours*. It is precisely because "the earth is the LORD's and the fullness thereof" that human beings (a) take their place with the rest of nature as creatures and (b) recognize their commission to be stewards of God's world, not consumers and exploiters of what they take to be their own possession. I am reminded of Vermigli's comment above that it is the fall that transforms human dominion (conceived as stewardship) into tyranny. Only because there is a creator and judge who stands outside human technology can we say that exploitation will not finally go unchecked. Dietrich Bonhoeffer underscores this point:

> This freedom of dominion directly includes our tie to the creatures who are ruled. The soil and the animals whose Lord I am are the world in which I live, without which I am not. . . . It bears me, nourishes me, and holds me. But my freedom from it consists in the fact that this world, to which I am bound as a lord to his servant, as the peasant to his soil, is subjected to me, that I am to *rule* over the earth which is and remains my earth. . . . It is by no other commissioned authority except that given by the Word of God to man—which thus uniquely binds and sets him over against the other creatures.[49]

Technology gives us the illusion that we rule, but the very opposite is actually the case.

---

48. Childs, *Biblical Theology*, 400.
49. Dietrich Bonhoeffer, *Creation and Fall: A Theological Interpretation of Genesis 1–3*, trans. John C. Fletcher (London: SCM, 1959), 39.

> We do not rule because we do not know the world as God's creation, and because we do not receive our dominion as God-given but grasp it for ourselves. There is no "being-free-from" without "being-free-for." There is no dominion without serving God. . . . From the very beginning the way of man to the earth has only been possible as God's way to man. . . . Man's being-free-for God and the other person and his being-free-from the creature in his dominion over it is the image of God in the first man.[50]

The Platonic interpretation of the *imago* easily allows for an irresponsible ecological ethic, however unintentionally. John of Damascus is just as Platonic in his anthropology as Augustine, for example.[51] Along this path, we locate our nearness to God in our distance from creation, instead of in our participation in it as stewards. A covenantal *imago* is desperately needed to challenge rationalistic and dualistic accounts. John of Damascus adds, for example, "For the phrase 'after His image' clearly refers to the side of his nature which consists of mind and free will, whereas 'after His likeness' means likeness in virtue so far as that is possible." So humans stand "midway between greatnesss and lowliness, spirit and flesh: for he is spirit by grace, but flesh by overweening pride: spirit that he may abide and glorify his Benefactor, and flesh that he may suffer, and suffering may be admonished and disciplined when he prides himself in his greatness."[52] Accordingly, community is determined by sameness, not difference (as in covenant):

> Man, it is to be noted, has community with things inanimate, and participates in the life of unreasoning creatures, and shares in the mental processes of those endowed with reason. For the bond of union between man and inanimate things is the body and its composition out of the four elements: and the bond between man and plants consists, in addition to these things, of their powers of nourishment and growth and seeding, that is, generation: and finally, over and above these links man is connected with unreasoning animals by appetite, that is anger and desire, and sense and impulsive movement.[53]

But by lodging the commonality of the human and nonhuman creation in the lowest common denominator of essential qualities, otherness is not truly respected. If, however, it is the covenant that brings them together, the relationship of humans to their fellow creatures and to their environment is as appreciative of difference as of similarities.

The dominion, therefore, rests on God's commission and not on distinguishing predicates of the human essence. This offers tremendous potential for overcoming some of the theological presuppositions that are often overlooked in criticism of the alleged Judeo-Christian foundations for ecological violence.

50. Ibid., 38.
51. John of Damascus, "Exact Exposition of the Orthodox Faith," 29–37.
52. Ibid., 31.
53. Ibid., 32.

Brueggemann reminds us that throughout its employment in the biblical narrative, this dominion is that of a shepherd-king (Ezekiel 34). "Moreover, a Christian understanding of dominion must be discerned in the way of Jesus of Nazareth (cf. Mark 10:43–44). The one who rules is the one who serves. Lordship means servanthood. It is the task of the shepherd not to control but to lay down his life for the sheep (John 10:11)."[54]

Despite superficial similarities, the royal sonship motif in Genesis 1:26–28 differs significantly from ancient Egyptian and Mesopotamian myths. For instance, while the king in these myths is represented as the royal son of the chief deity—an incarnation, in fact, of the deity—Adam and Eve were never regarded by the Jews as a divine incarnation. Furthermore, this royal investiture in Genesis included all human beings, "male and female," and not just a single ruler.[55]

As Meredith Kline notes, the three principal elements of likeness that are evident in all their redolence when the royal son appears are the following: the images of the temple (dominion, kingship), the ethical commission (the foundations of the temple are justice, equity, truth, righteousness, holiness, goodness), and glory (physical beauty).[56] "To be the image of God is to be the son of God."[57] Similarly, Phyllis Bird observes that while *selem* by itself tells us nothing, "The *selem ʾĕlōhîm* in Genesis 1 is, accordingly, a royal designation, the precondition or requisite for rule."[58] This interpretation, Bird argues, fits well with the parallel passage in Psalm 8, where coronation language and dominion language once more converge.

This sonship-likeness is seen most clearly, of course, in Jesus Christ, of whom Adam was himself a proleptic reflection. It is essential to recognize that in this sense the incarnate Lord of the covenant is its servant, and as the new Adam his royal sonship-likeness is not the same as his eternal Sonship. In his humiliation, he must attain this sonship-likeness—this royal image—on behalf of his brothers and sisters. This is how we might understand references such as Psalm 2:7 and 89:26, repeated in Hebrews 1:5: "To which of the angels did God ever say, 'You are my Son; today I have begotten you'?" In John's Gospel especially, Jesus' fulfillment of this destiny of royal sonship is repeatedly underscored (cf. John 5:17–21). I will explore this in chapter 6.

54. Walter Brueggemann, *Genesis,* Interpretation (Atlanta: John Knox Press, 1982), 33.

55. Phyllis A. Bird, "'Male and Female He Created Them': Gen. 1:27b in the Context of the Priestly Account of Creation," *Harvard Theological Review* 74, no. 2 (1981): 144: "The genius of the formulation of Gen 1:26 may be seen in its use of a common expression and image of Mesopotamian (-Canaanite) royal theology to counter a common image of Mesopotamian (-Canaanite) anthropology, viz., the image of humanity as the servant of the gods, the dominant image of Mesopotamian creation myths. The language that describes the king as one who stands in a special relationship to the divine world is chosen by the author of Genesis 1 (perhaps under influence of Egyptian wisdom tradition) to describe humanity as a whole, *adam qua adam,* in its essential nature."

56. Meredith G. Kline, *Images of the Spirit* (Eugene, OR: Wipf & Stock, 1999), 35.

57. Ibid., 36.

58. Bird, "Male and Female," 140.

Representation

To speak of the image of God as representation is to place it in the realm of judicial commission (ethical relationship) rather than, as in the more traditional understanding, a mirror of the divine essence (ontology). It refers not so much to a correspondence in attributes (even the so-called communicable ones), but to an official embassy—for which humanity is nevertheless suited by created nature. I will also develop this more fully in later chapters.

Glory

While royal sonship, representation, and mutuality find ample support in Scripture, perhaps the theme most closely attached to the relevant passages is that of "glory" (*kābôd*).[59] It is this notion that best ties together both Testaments and indicates the closest connection between covenant and eschatology especially in relation to anthropology.

Pillaging the ancient cosmogonic myths, the creation narrative recounts the Great King's completion of his cosmic house, then filling it with his Glory-Spirit as his own holy dwelling. One of the gains in this account is a greater integration of christology and pneumatology, as the Glory of God is identified directly with both the Spirit and the Son, and indirectly/reflectively with those whom the Spirit engenders by breathing into them the breath of life, rendering human beings prophetic witnesses to the Glory they reflect. Adam and Eve were created as temples of the same glory-Spirit identified in Genesis 1:2. As Adam is represented as having been created by a "divine inbreathing" of the Spirit, Mary was told, "The Holy Spirit will come upon you, and the power of the Most High will overshadow you; therefore the child to be born will be holy; he will be called Son of God" (Luke 1:35). In inaugurating his new creation, Jesus breathed on the disciples, saying, "Receive the Holy Spirit" (John 20:22). Individual believers and the corporate church are therefore re-creations in the image of Christ, the true temple filled with the glory-Spirit.

All of this serves, retrospectively, of course, to illuminate the Genesis narrative. "As Genesis 2:7 pictures it, the Spirit-Archetype actively fathered his human ectype," showing that "image of God and son of God are thus twin concepts," as the birth of Seth in Adam's image seems to confirm (Gen. 5:1–3).[60]

> The eternal, firstborn Son furnished a pattern for man as a royal glory-image of the Father. It was in his creative action as the Son, present in the Glory-Spirit, making man in his own son-image that the Logos revealed himself as the One in whom was the life that is the light of men. Not first as incarnate

59. Ricoeur also observes that Paul's development of the *imago Dei* theme (for instance, in 2 Cor. 3:18) anchors itself not in the Old Testament notion of creation in the image of God (Gen. 1:26) but in the Old Testament motif of glory (*Figuring the Sacred*, 267–68). There is a lot of exegetical support for such a view, and this underscores how the importance of the *imago Dei* concept in Scripture will be determined by corollaries or constituent aspects of the image rather than direct statements concerning the image as such.

60. Kline, *Images of the Spirit*, 23.

Word breathing on men the Spirit and re-creating them in his heavenly image, but at the very beginning he was quickening Spirit, creating man after his image and glory.

It is "a making of man in the likeness of the Glory-Spirit."[61] It is no wonder, then, that the Son sends the Spirit to inaugurate a new creation on the pattern of his own glory both as God and the glorified new Adam.

The eschatological and the protological are thus coordinated with each other, as when Paul states, "Thus it is written, 'The first man, Adam, became a living being'; the last Adam became a life-giving Spirit. . . . Just as we have borne the image of the man of dust, we will also bear the image of the man of heaven" (1 Cor. 15:45, 49). In 1 Corinthians 11:7, as Grenz notes, "the apostle connects the *imago dei* with the concept of the divine glory (*doxa*). The way was paved by the Old Testament, most directly by the declaration in Ps. 8:5 that God has crowned humankind with 'glory and honor.'"[62] This protological image, though effaced and marred by human sin, will be eschatologically fulfilled in the new creation: the one who created us in his image by his Spirit in the beginning will re-create us in the same image by the same Spirit in the end. Thus Christ identifies himself as no less than the Creator and Consummator, "the Alpha and Omega, the beginning and ending, the first and the last" (Rev. 1:8), "the faithful witness" to God's covenant (Rev. 1:5). The church is then the temple built according to the likeness of the heavenly City. The church witnesses to Christ: that is its glory-image, and in its glorified state this witness is vindicated.

All of this serves to show the inextricable link among covenant, eschatology, and the judicial-official character of the divine image.[63] Again, this glory is ethical-official, rather than corresponding to a particular essence in the human constitution. "As image of God, man is a royal son with the judicial function appertaining to kingly office. The renewal of the divine image in men is an impartation to them of the likeness of the archetypal glory of Christ."[64]

In drawing together these various strands, we can say that the creation of humankind represents the appearance of the image-bearing "son" (adopted, not a divine incarnation), although investiture in the royal office is in a sense already eschatologically oriented at creation toward its consummation. In other words, Adam has not yet assumed the throne under God in the Sabbath glory. Now those who even after the fall still bear an official glory are re-created to reflect the ethical glory of the Son in the power of the Spirit. (See 2 Cor. 3:7–18; 4:4–6; with the investiture figure of "putting on Christ," in Eph. 4:25; Col. 3:10; Rom. 13:14; Gal. 3:27; 1 Cor. 15:53; 2 Cor. 5:2ff.) Ricoeur therefore is justified in seeing *union* with Christ and not the *imitation* of Christ as the New Testament

---

61. Ibid., 23–24.
62. Grenz, *Social God*, 205.
63. "Nuclear to the divine Glory," says Kline, "is its official-functional aspect: it is the glory of royal-judicial office" as well as "an ethical dimension" (*Images of the Spirit*, 27).
64. Ibid., 28.

successor to the Old Testament prophetic idea: the summoned subject of the prophetic narratives is "the christomorphic self."[65] It is a re-creation by the Spirit after the archetypal image of the eternal Son of the Father (Rom. 8:29–30).

Related also to this covenant-bearing glory-image is the concept of "name." Adam and Eve are both named by God (a clear indication of their equality in creation and as image-bearing officers), while Adam is given the prior task of naming the animals. Similarly, believers are "named 'sons of God,' just as people customarily are surnamed after the name of their forebears."[66] This "naming" practice is also a treaty-making practice, as we have seen. "The name 'Christian' is a covenantal identification for the servant-son people of the new covenant."[67] That we are not only created but created-in-covenant, and that we are named, both in creation (Adam) and then in redemption (Christ), undermines all notions of autonomous self-creation. The federal or covenantal nature of this redemption (as well as creation) undermines all anthropological individualism. Anthony Thiselton also indicates the significance of this communicative act of naming in determining the biblical concept of selfhood: "In a distinctively theological sense the biblical text . . . may be said to address the selfhood of the reader with transforming effects. It thereby gives the self an identity and significance as the recipient of loving and transforming address. In this sense, it 'names' the self."[68] In baptism, Christ claims believers and their children, writing his name on their foreheads, setting them apart for himself as images of his glory. To bear the name of God is to bear the glory of God, which is to say, the Spirit of God. Kline adds here,

> The equivalence of the bearing of God's name and the bearing of God's image appears strikingly in Revelation 22:4. Here, in the midst of the description of the glorified covenant community, renewed after the image of the Lord, it is said: 'They will see his face and his name will be in their foreheads.' . . . To say that the overcomers in the New Jerusalem bear the name of Christ on their forehead is to say that they reflect the glory of Christ, which is to say that they bear the image of the glorified Christ.[69]

The creature thus named is a prophetic witness, authorized to declare God's word of command and promise. It is important to recognize that in Adam humankind, like Moses with his disobedient fellow travelers on the verge of the

---

65. Paul Ricoeur, *Figuring the Sacred* (Minneapolis: Fortress, 1995), 268.

66. Kline, *Images of the Spirit*, 54. Kline here elaborates the significance of the priests' vestments as themselves "tabernacle-temple replicas of the Glory theophany," as "the tabernacle-vested priest bears the name of Yahweh on his head. The idea is that these persons and things are holy. . . . The church's bearing of Christ's new name is exponential of its new nature as the new city-temple, the priest-bride arrayed in tabernacle-glory, the image of the Glory-Spirit-Lord, the glory of the bridegroom-Son."

67. Ibid., 55.

68. Ibid., 63.

69. Ibid., 54.

Jordan, never entered the Sabbath consummation and therefore does not yet possess the glorification that royal investiture indicates. "As originally created, man was not yet endowed with this [physical] form of Glory-likeness. Physical glorification might only be contemplated in eschatological hope."[70] Adoption is only finally and fully realized for us in our bodily resurrection and glorification (Rom. 8:23).

Prophetic Witness

Although something of the witnessing character of the image has been mentioned, I should add a bit more to this important aspect. As Kline observes,

> The lives of the prophets caught up in the Spirit were prophecies of the eschatological destiny of mankind re-created in God's image. . . . In the beginning man was created in the image of God by the power of creative fiat after the paradigm of the theophanic Glory-Spirit. In redemptive history the reproduction of the image of God in the new mankind takes place through the mediatorial agency of Jesus Christ, in whom the divine Glory became incarnate. He is the paradigm of the Glory-image and he is the mediator of the Spirit in the process of replicating the divine likeness.[71]

Pentecost then, as a new creation, is nothing less than "a redemptive recapitulation of Genesis 1:2 and 27."[72] "In the command of the voice from heaven, 'Hear him,' Peter perceived [Acts 3:22ff.] the ultimate application of the Deuteronomic requirement that Israel obey God's prophet (Deut. 18:18). That was God's own identification of Jesus as *the* prophet like unto Moses."[73] The preincarnate Son, as "angel of the covenant" (Mal. 3:1; Zechariah 3), "was that archtetypal prophet behind the human prophet paradigm."[74] Through the descent of the Glory-Spirit at Easter and Pentecost, the "new creation" has dawned, equipping those once "dead in trespasses and sins" (Eph. 2:1; cf. Ezek 37:1–15) to be witnesses to the ends of the earth. The Son witnesses to the Father and both the Father and the Spirit witness to the Son, as the Spirit sent by the Son makes of fallen office-bearers a resurrected prophetic priesthood. Kline observes, "In 2 Corinthians 3 and 4, Paul describes the Christian's transformation into the image of the glory of the Lord in terms of Moses' transfiguration. . . . According to 2 Corinthians 3 and 4, for Christ to re-create the church in his divine likeness is to create a prophet-church."[75] "Christ is the original light; the church which he creates in his likeness is a reflective light," a "prophetic witness."[76] The Son has witnessed to what he has seen and heard in the heavenly council—the paradigm for the Old Testament prophets who, unlike the false

70. Ibid., 61.
71. Ibid., 63–64.
72. Ibid., 70.
73. Ibid., 81–82.
74. Ibid., 83.
75. Ibid., 84.
76. Ibid., 85.

prophets, have "stood in the council of YHWH," even as the disciples stood in the council during the ministry of Jesus. John received his apocalypse by being taken into God's council through a vision. Now Jesus' disciples are to witness to what they have seen and heard as they have stood for these three years in that same council with the incarnate Lord himself among them. The Spirit is then sent to make us witnesses as those who have entered into the Holy of Holies through the mediation of Christ.

In Revelation 11, "The figures in whom the likeness of Christ is reproduced are expressly denoted as witnesses (v. 3) and prophets (vv. 10, 18) and their mission is described as one of prophesying (v. 3), prophecy (v. 6), and testimony (v. 7)."[77] Now all believers enter the Holy of Holies (with their high priest) and are prophets in the Spirit, wearing the garments of the Spirit as a bride adorned for her husband. Yet the visible church is the bride of Christ, not yet the wife. The confirmation in righteousness and the consummation of the glory-image that constitutes royal investiture await believers in hope.

That the image necessarily involves—even centrally—the ethical dimension is evident in the close connection it bears with the repetition of God's work and rest in the seven-day pattern. Yet this is true only in the liminal state of the already–not yet, as believers—together with the whole creation—await their own resurrection from the dead and royal entrance into confirmed righteousness. The glorification (what the Eastern church calls theosis), already partly realized in the possession of the Holy Spirit as a down payment, will be the full psychosomatic investiture of each believer "male and female" as a royal "son." This may be why Paul (Rom. 8:18–25) puts an eschatological spin on adoption, deferring its full accomplishment until the whole creation is able to participate with redeemed humanity in the Sabbath enthronement of God.

Although the whole earth will be full of the glory of God, human beings are central in this construction for theological reasons. The so-called anthropocentrism of the Bible is due to the centrality of the covenant between God and his people, not any abstract cosmological conception. In other words, it has a specific theological orientation and is not meant to be treated as an all-encompassing description of natural history or the relation of humankind to its environment. Just as in the eschatological fulfillment of Israel's embassy as the center from which the glory of God fills the earth, the eschatological goal of human mediation of God's glory in a restored image-bearer is the drawing of all created reality into the Sabbath consummation.

I hope to have shown also in the preceding section how christology informs our understanding of these themes without collapsing protology into soteriology. Having allowed a space for the essential (ontological) constitution of human beings as prerequisite conditions for a covenantal relationship, my conclusion is that the image of God in humankind is itself official rather than essential, ethical rather than ontological, eschatological rather than metaphysical.

---

77. Ibid., 91.

"HERE I AM": THE RELATIONAL
AND PRAXIS-ORIENTED SELF

Arguing for a "praxis-oriented self, defined by its communicative practices, oriented toward an understanding of itself in its discourse, its action, its being with others, and its experience of transcendence," Calvin O. Schrag draws together insights from narrative approaches that are, as I have already indicated, quite congenial to my proposal.[78] In step with similar approaches by Charles Taylor, Alisdair MacIntyre, Paul Ricoeur, and others—all of whom share important affinities with Martin Heidegger's analysis at certain points—Schrag seeks to disentangle personhood from the "what" question initiated by Descartes to the "who" question, "putting us in quest not of an abstract universal nature but rather of a concrete and historically specific questioner. The question about the who thus becomes a question about the questioner."[79] I have already argued for this approach in relation to God. Similarly, instead of the question, What is it to be human? the question becomes, Who am I?[80] We have seen earlier that this narrative approach stands in sharp contrast with the "mute and self-enclosed" individual of modernity. Instead, "The who of discourse is an achievement, an accomplishment, a performance, whose presence to itself is admittedly fragile, subject to forgetfulness and semantic ambiguities."[81] Thus the question "Who is speaking?" is about *ipse*-identity, while the atomic weight of silicon is an *idem*-identity question.[82] The subject of *ipse*-identity is a temporalized self of a given narrative. "The self that has nothing to remember and nothing for which to hope is a self whose identity stands in peril," according to Schrag.

This would seem to lend support to my view that being eschatologically oriented to the future—indeed, a better world—is intrinsic to humanness.

> The story of the self is a developing story, a story subject to a creative advance, wherein the past is never simply a series of nows that have lapsed into nonbeing, but a text, an inscription of events and experiences, that

---

78. Calvin O. Schrag, *The Self after Postmodernity* (New Haven, CT: Yale University Press, 1997).

79. See Martin Heidegger, *Being and Time*, trans. Joan Stambaugh (Albany, NY: SUNY Press, 1996), 108ff.

80. Schrag, *Self after Postmodernity*, 13. It is worth noting that Psalm 8 does not ask, "What is man?"—an abstract metaphysical question—but "What is man *that you are mindful of him*?" It is a rhetorical question about the psalmist's own existential sense of smallness (probably not only in cosmological but also ethical terms).

81. Ibid., 33. I would add, of course, *sin*, as Watson's remarks above clearly mark. Schrag does not include theological reflections and his account is clearly weighted toward human autonomy. At the same time, he does indicate the significance of self-identity as achievement, something to be won or lost. While it is certainly true that justification of the ungodly is a gift and in no way "an achievement, an accomplishment, a performance," Eberhard Jüngel (like Barth) seems to reduce human identity to soteriology without remainder ("On Becoming Truly Human," in *Theological Essays II*, ed. J. B. Webster, trans. Arnold Neufeldt-Fast and J. B. Webster [Edinburgh: T & T Clark, 1995]). This is where, once again, a covenantal model seems to provide more conceptual space for a wider body of exegesis on this topic.

82. Schrag, *Self after Postmodernity*, 36.

stands open to new interpretations and new perspectives of meaning. Correspondingly, the future is not a series of nows that has not yet come into being. The future of narrative time is the self as possibility, as the power to be able to provide new readings of the script that has already been inscribed and to mark out new inscriptions of a script in the making.[83]

In this narrative construction, the self is neither wholly self-determined (either rationally or volitionally) nor wholly determined by the past or by the present but is relatively open to the future.[84] Created by the Word and upheld by the Word, the human person is eschatologically oriented by nature to the Word that calls from the future. Even our fallen distortion of that Word into fatalism, determinism, utopianism, etc., is evidence of this ineradicable orientation. Further, "The communalized self is *in* history but not *of* history. It has the resources for transcending the historically specific without arrogating to itself the unconditioned and decontextualized vision of the world."[85] Schrag draws on Julia Kristeva's suggestive expression for the self as "a subject on trial" (*sujet en proces*).[86] Here, as in Ricoeur's hermeneutics of testimony, narrative easily meets covenant: "As Kristeva reminds us, the subject constitutes itself at the same time as speaking and agentive subject against the backdrop of an ethos and a body politic of common goals and institutional involvements."[87]

Although Schrag's account is not explicitly theological, it bears closer affinities with the biblical orientation than the traditional, more Neoplatonic (i.e., "ontological") approach. Nowhere in Scripture is the question of human identity asked or answered in the abstract, but only in terms of the covenantal—which is to say, ethical—commission that takes an explicitly narrative construction. Echoing the structure of ancient Near Eastern treaties, biblical covenant making begins with a historical prologue that contextualizes the subsequent stipulations and sanctions. Thus it is never a question of bare ethics—timeless, eternal moral truths—but of a particular form of existence that arises from a concrete narrative emplotment: "I am the LORD who brought you up out of Egypt." The opening narratives of Genesis suggest the same for the creation covenant. Walther Eichrodt's judgment that "the covenant-union between Yahweh and Israel is an original element in all sources," even the earliest, is shared more widely across the landscape of biblical scholarship than ever before.[88] It is the *promissory* character of this covenant that "provides life with a goal and history with a meaning."[89]

---

83. Ibid., 37.
84. "The failure to distinguish between 'context-conditioned' and 'context-determined' has ushered in a profound confusion on matters of the degree and quality of transcendence required for making moral judgment and submitting critiques of culture" (ibid., 107).
85. Ibid., 109.
86. Ibid., 40. See Julia Kristeva, "The System and the Speaking Subject," in *The Kristeva Reader*, ed. Toril Moi (New York: Columbia University Press, 1986), 24–33.
87. Schrag, *Self after Postmodernity*, 41.
88. Walther Eichrodt, *Theology of the Old Testament*, trans. J. A. Baker, 2 vols., Old Testament Library (Philadelphia: Westminster Press, 1961–67), 1:36.
89. Ibid., 1:37.

Modern anthropology is even a far remove from this biblical mentality in its addition of autonomy to inwardness.[90] It is in the context of being a covenantal creature ("a little lower than the angels," endowed with "glory and honor") that the psalmist, lost in the immensity of the cosmos, rediscovers his bearings, his "Here I am" that gives him a place of narrative significance that would otherwise elude him (Psalm 8). Eberhard Jüngel comments,

> Biblical texts certainly do not address people about themselves without at the same time addressing them about something else. This is a decisive clue for the proper understanding of the true humanity of human persons. It is only as the human "I" is addressed not only about itself, but rather addressed in such a way that it is simultaneously claimed by something outside itself, that one is really speaking about the human "I" as such.[91]

What I appreciate about Schrag's particular construction of a more nuanced narrative approach is that he, like Ricoeur, refuses to surrender personhood to either relations or the cogito. "The we-experience and the I-experience are more intricately entwined," he rightly urges, "than has been acknowledged by proponents of either the social doctrine of the self or the individualist doctrine. . . . The point is that both these doctrines trade on a common mistake of sundering the undivided portion of world-experience and then reifying the abstracted components."[92] For a host of reasons that I have already elaborated, Christian theology cannot do without both sides of such lived experience.

I have conveniently left out aspects of Schrag's account that I find inconsistent with my own proposal. However, his approach does help to indicate the direction in which a covenantal account of human personhood might be construed. In such an account, the modern notions of selfhood that pivot on autonomy are resolutely challenged even more vigorously than Schrag would allow. We have happily witnessed the deconstruction of the Cartesian subject, but equally reductionistic reactions have filled the void. I would suggest that the "we-experience" that is essential to our consciousness of ourselves, at least in connection with the topic before us, is constituted at least theologically by the covenant. First, the covenant of creation renders us responsible to the divine Other and therefore to all human others and indeed to the entire creation, whose care has been entrusted to us. Second, rightly ordered selfhood is constituted by the covenant of grace, administered by the covenant Lord together with his people through Word and sacrament in the power of the Spirit. Any account that takes sufficient note of the wide range of biblical teaching will have to appreciate both aspects of this "we-experience" without reducing one to the other.

The covenant of creation provides the basis for the unity of the human race, and even after the fall the features of this original human creatureliness are not

---

90. Grenz, *Social God*, 98.

91. Jüngel, "On Becoming Truly Human," 220. Despite appreciation on key points of Jüngel's theological anthropology, my account obviously differs in our understanding of "true humanness."

92. Schrag, *Self after Postmodernity*, 79–80.

in any way altered, but are employed in ways that are ethically subversive of their original intention. The covenant of grace similarly determines human existence, but this time does relate entirely to the sphere of redemption, christology, and ecclesiology. It is at this point that we recognize the shape not of true humanness (ontologically considered), *pace* Barth, Jüngel, Zizioulas, et al., but of the properly oriented and experienced true humanness (covenantally considered).[93] It is here that synergism is excluded: we are fallen image-bearers who need to be rescued, no longer innocent covenant partners who can cooperate in the mission of leading creation into its consummation. Only by being reconciled to God in Jesus Christ by the power of the Spirit working through the means of grace in the church can covenant-breakers be constituted covenant-keepers and be kept in that covenant until one day the image of God is finally not only perfectly restored but confirmed in everlasting righteousness.

In the Pauline eschatology, both "I-experience" (*ordo salutis*) and "we-experience" (*historia salutis*) are fully integrated, without surrendering to an exclusively social or individual understanding of self-identity. The experience of the covenantal self emerges not only in the narrative unity of one's own life, but the narrative unity of all the lives lived in the history of God's covenant people. That life is told by God back to us as we find ourselves in the drama of creation, fall, redemption, and consummation. In fact, Ricoeur singles out Israel "because 'no other people has been so overwhelmingly impassioned by the narratives it has told about itself.'"[94] As this drama evolves and incorporates us, we find ourselves not merely imitating characters in the story, but being scripted by the Spirit as characters in its unfolding plot. Even gentiles can be written into the script no longer as "strangers and aliens" but as "children of Abraham." While we are not masters or self-constituting and self-constructing authors of our own identities, we are nevertheless partners in the covenant and therefore contribute meaningfully to its development. This represents a dialectical development of self-identity in which the reply "Here I am" reflects the acceptance of the terms of that covenantal selfhood.[95]

---

93. Among the chief dangers of a dualistic ontologizing of creation-fall-redemption is the tendency seen, for example, in Athanasius, Augustine, and Barth to exchange a natural rectitude-human depravity problematic for a Neoplatonic being-nothingness one. For Athanasius, the fall made the human race "turn back again according to their nature; and as they had at the beginning come into being out of non-existence, so were they on the way to returning, through corruption, to nonexistence again" (*On the Incarnation*, trans. Sister Penelope Lawson [New York: Macmillan, 1946], 8). For much of the patristic and medieval tradition, "nothingness," "corruption," and "natural state" become virtually synonymous, leaving the state of nature ambiguous at best.

94. Cited by Dan R. Stiver, *Theology after Ricoeur: New Directions in Hermeneutical Theology* (Louisville, KY: Westminster John Knox, 2001), 172.

95. It may be worth noting that this "Here I am" formula brings nothing to the table that might be considered worthy of God's favor. In other words, it is nothing less than faith itself. The Westminster Larger Catechism expresses this well: "Faith justifies a sinner in the sight of God, not because of those other graces which do always accompany it, or of good works that are the fruits of it; nor as if the grace of faith, or any act thereof, were imputed to him for justification; but only as it is an instrument, by which he receiveth and applieth Christ and his righteousness" (Q. 73, *Book of Confessions* [Louisville, KY: Office of the General Assembly, Presbyterian Church (U.S.A.), 1991], 7.183).

Although space does not allow an exegetical treatment of this theme, a lot could be said at this point about the recurring feature of this response. "Here I am" (Hebrew *hinnēh*, "behold," plus *nî*, "me"), and its New Testament equivalent (Greek *idou*, "behold," plus *egō*, "me"), is the typical marker of covenantal response on the part of God's servants. In fact, the flight of Adam and Eve from the divine call, "Adam, where are you?" (Gen. 3:9), is contrasted with the "Here I am" of Abraham, Moses, Samuel, Isaiah, Mary, and Jesus. After the angel's auspicious announcement, Mary declares, "Here am I, the servant of the Lord; let it be with me according to your word" (Luke 1:38). It is noteworthy that Jesus announces his triumphant arrival in heaven with the words, "Here am I [*idou egō*] and the children whom God has given me" (Heb. 2:13b).[96] As humanity was created as a word from God, it was intended to respond to God's speaking by repeating back God's word as its own. The "answering back" in the first instance was the creation itself, but it was meant to be the continual response, though expressed in countlessly diverse ways.

All of this underscores the point made above, that the self is a situated, narrated subject, an agent who, like God, is known from his acts and not from his essence. But the human self is not merely situated in a hermeneutically sealed cultural-linguistic bubble; it is able to be drawn out of a purely mundane, chronological, and immanent context of self-identity to be written into a script that cuts across all times and places through the vertical "intrusions" of the Spirit. The biblical narrative seems to support Schrag's suggestion that the question, What is humanness? should be substituted with the query, Who am I? It is in the context of the covenant that this question can even be properly asked, much less answered from a theological perspective. "The self's commitment to something," writes Dan Stiver, "provides a kind of self-constancy that also provides an answer to the question of identity."[97] In this way narrative (resting on the indicative of God's mighty acts) and ethics (the imperatives that delineate the "reasonable service" offered "in view of the mercies of God," Rom. 12:1–2) become integrated without reducing one to the other.

Thus the covenantal self is, to borrow Ricoeur's phrase, "the summoned subject in the school of the narratives of the prophetic vocation."[98] These "narratives of vocation" constitute the self-identity of the prophet, and we should bear in mind that this vocation may be understood in the narrower sense (biblical prophets) and in the broader sense (the general office of all human beings in creation and of all believers in redemption).

Even Colin Gunton reflects the tendency in recent theologies to emphasize the relational character of personhood, and to do so in reference to being

---

96. I appreciate the able assistance of my seminary colleague in Old Testament, Bryan Estelle, for confirming my intuitions along this path and bolstering its grammatical basis.

97. Stiver, *Theology after Ricoeur*, 175–76; cf. Ricoeur, *Figuring the Sacred*, 170.

98. Ricoeur, *Figuring the Sacred*, 262. According to Ricoeur, the narratives of prophetic vocation include three phases: confrontation with God, an introductory speech of divine self-identification ("I am the God of your father Abraham"; "I am who I am," etc.), and then finally the "decisive word can be pronounced: 'I send you,' 'go and say to them . . .'" (265–66).

properly related to God, to the point of saying, "we are persons insofar as we are in right relationship to God."[99] Yet he still wants to maintain both "otherness and relation" as the two poles of personhood. Otherness, I would argue, is what I am getting at when I insist on the priority of person to relation. But Gunton continues, "In the first place, we are persons insofar as we are in right relation to God. Under the conditions of sin, that means, of course, insofar as the image is reshaped, realised, in Christ. . . . To be in the image of God therefore means to be conformed to the person of Christ."[100] He does acknowledge the important place for protology as well as eschatology, but finally the latter seems to win out over the former: "In all of this, John Zizioulas' point that *person* is an eschatological concept must constantly be borne in mind. To say that is to say that personhood is being that is to be realised, and whose final realisation will come only when God is all in all. And yet . . . that need not be taken to undermine the fact that it is also, and without inconsistency, a protological concept."[101] With this reminder of protology, Gunton seems to add a nuance to his earlier point: "To be in the image of God is at once to be created as a particular kind of being—a person—and to be called to realise a certain destiny."[102]

It is that last statement that I would affirm, over against his earlier ones. Being a human person is not itself dependent on the realization of conformity to Christ and restoration of the *imago*. The most resolute atheist is just as truly God's image-bearer, and therefore responsible, as anybody else. It is an indelible status, commission, and office, and unlike the elected official who is caught with his or her hand in the till, no person is relieved of that office. Instead, it witnesses against each of us, even as it also demands respect for all human life regardless of one's relation to God in Christ.

Just as the Creator-creature distinction gives a real, though relative, independence to the world, the covenant of creation ensures that personhood belongs to every human being not by virtue of being united to Christ by faith but by virtue of being created by the Father, in the Son's image, through the agency of the Holy Spirit in the beginning. It is not the case that unbelievers are not truly "persons" in the theological (or any other) sense, since they too stand in a personal covenantal relation to God, though under the terms of that original covenant of creation.

Throughout this chapter I have assumed the historicity of Adam and Eve. Apart from a historical Adam (whatever account by which one arrives at this claim), the anthropology assumed by biblical writers all the way up to Paul's contrast of the two Adams—not as mythical figures or religious symbols but as the historical loci of judgment and justification—is meaningless. It is rendered meaningless not because everything that a religion wants to affirm has to be in the form of historically reliable assertions, but because the Bible itself presents the fall in the genre of realistic narrative and the ethical and doctrinal statements in subse-

99. Gunton, "Trinity, Ontology and Anthropology," 58.
100. Ibid., 58–59.
101. Ibid., 60.
102. Ibid., 61.

quent Scripture (including references to this history by Jesus) make the historicity essential rather than accidental, particularly in the contrast of the two Adams. Instantaneous creation of Adam and Eve is not explicitly required by the text or its subsequent interpretation, but the historicity of a first human couple with whom God entered into covenant is indispensable to theology at significant points in almost every locus. After noting that Hegel, Schleiermacher, Ritschl, Bultmann, Reinhold Niebuhr, and Barth all denied the historicity of Adam, replacing it with the story of Jesus as the paradigm of truly actualized personhood, Childs correctly perceives that this move can only be made without serious attention to exegesis: the "problem" is modern, not biblical.[103]

To conclude then, it is not only a narrative that renders a self, but the face of the other in binding address. Who am I? I am one who exists as a result of being spoken by God. Furthermore, I am one of God's covenant children whom he delivered out of Egypt, sin, and death. I am one who has heard his command but not fulfilled it, one in whom faith has been born by the Spirit through the proclamation of the gospel. In Derrida's words, drawing upon Levinas,

> Language has started without us, in us and before us. This is what theology calls God. . . . Order or promise, this injunction commits (me), in a rigorously asymmetrical manner, even before I have been able to say *I*, to sign such a provocation in order to reappropriate it for myself and restore the symmetry. That in no way mitigates my responsibility; on the contrary. There would be no responsibility without this *prior coming (prévenance)* of the trace, or if autonomy were first or absolute. Autonomy itself would not be possible, nor would respect for the law . . . in the strictly Kantian meaning of these words.[104]

Because human beings are by nature created in covenant with God, self-identity itself depends on one's relation to God, even if one denies any such relations or is not rightly related to God in Christ. There is no "autonomous self," as some forms of postmodern thought have rightly concluded, although this has often meant that there is therefore no "self" at all. But this conclusion only follows if the premises of modernity are correct in the first place. In denying that they are, Christian theology is able to go deeper in its deconstruction of modern autonomy and further in its reconstruction of biblical claims about the relational *imago*. Even when that relation is denied or its truth suppressed, the narrative within which a life is plotted remains ineluctably God-centered. No one can escape the reality of God in his or her experience, because there is no human existence that is possible or actual apart from the ineradicable covenant identity that belongs to us all, whether we flee the summons or reply, "Here I am."

103. Childs, *Biblical Theology*, 593.
104. Derrida, "How to Avoid Speaking: Denials," in *Derrida and Negative Theology*, ed. Harold Coward and Toby Foshay (Albany, NY: SUNY Press, 1987), 99.

Chapter Five

"Adam, Where Are You?"

Trial of the Covenant Servant

Having briefly outlined some of the most central features of a covenantal anthropology, I turn now to a discussion of the fall in terms of the great trial, the solidarity of all human beings in the fallen condition, and the story of Israel as a play-within-a-play: the trial of Israel as recapitulating more locally the universal trial of humanity and God in the covenant relationship.

THE COURTROOM

First of all, if the world is a theater or a stage, as Calvin and Shakespeare among other notables have told us, then the play is a courtroom drama. Like Hamlet's play-within-a-play, the story of Israel can be read as a condensed version of the original covenant with humankind. But it can also be read in the other direction: humankind's creation, fall, and redemption can be seen as a play within Israel's larger narrative plot.[1] In either case, we are set before a great trial in which

---

1. Both strategies seem well-grounded exegetically, as long as the traffic is allowed to move in both directions. N. T. Wright, however, seems suspicious of any universal horizon in the Scriptures and reduces all references to this horizon to Israel itself. "We cannot, in particular, discuss the

120

we ourselves are actors and not just audience. Of course, the courtroom analogy is not the only one that is employed: the parent-child relationship is just as obvious and therefore we should not play the relational and the legal off of each other but recognize that they are both integral to a covenantal account. Adoption is a simultaneously legal and relational event. The New Testament builds on the Old Testament interpretation of history as the story of a covenant made and a covenant broken. Jacques Lacan has written, "That tradition alone pursues to the end the task of revealing what is involved in the primitive crime of the primordial law."[2]

FALSE WITNESS

Second, the category of false witness emerges already in these beginning chapters of the Bible. The Son and the Spirit are true and faithful witnesses in this cosmic trial, as are the nonhuman creatures and created elements that are repeatedly called on for testimony in his behalf. But there is also a false witness: the one who would be identified in relation to his persecution of God's people, the one who "accuses them day and night before our God" (Rev. 12:10). He is "a liar and the father of lies" (John 8:44). Once the angelic chief under God in heaven, he has become the false witness par excellence, father of false witnesses on earth. This is seen clearly in the familiar story of the fall in Genesis. Against the Creator's clear instruction, which put the entire garden at the disposal of humankind except for the fruit of one tree, the serpent first misinterprets God's stipulation ("Did God say, 'You shall not eat from *any* tree in the garden'?" Gen. 3:1). When this fails, he asserts directly that Eve and Adam will not die but will in fact be like God, autonomous and self-sufficient to determine good and evil for themselves (vv. 4–5).

"The decisive point," notes Dietrich Bonhoeffer, "is that this question suggests to man that he should go behind the Word of God and establish what it is by himself, out of his understanding of the being of God. . . . Beyond this given Word of God the serpent pretends somehow to know something about the profundity of the true God who is so badly misrepresented in this human word." The serpent claims a path to the knowledge of the real God behind the Word.[3] It is not atheism that is introduced by the serpent but religion, says Bonhoeffer.[4]

> The wolf in sheep's clothing, Satan in an angel's form of light: this is the shape appropriate to evil. "Did God say?", that plainly is the godless

relation of Adam to universal sin, and hence certain key passages, i.e., Romans 1:18ff.; 3:23; 5:12; and 7:7ff., cannot be handled here [in relation to universal sin]" (N. T. Wright, *The Climax of the Covenant: Christ and the Law in Pauline Theology* [Edinburgh: T. & T. Clark, 1991], 26).

2. Jacques Lacan, "The Death of God," trans. D. Porter in *The Postmodern God: A Theological Reader*, ed. Graham Ward (Oxford: Blackwell, 1997), 41.

3. Dietrich Bonhoeffer, *Creation and Fall*, 66.

4. Ibid., 67.

question. "Did God say," that he is love, that he wishes to forgive our sins, that we need only believe him, that we need no works, that Christ has died and has been raised for us, that we shall have eternal life in his kingdom, that we are no longer alone but upheld by God's grace, that one day all sorrow and wailing shall have an end? "Did God say," thou shalt not steal, thou shalt not commit adultery, thou shalt not bear false witness . . . did he really say it to me? Perhaps it does not apply in my particular case? "Did God say," that he is a God who is wrathful towards those who do not keep his commandments? Did he demand the sacrifice of Christ? I know better that he is the infinitely good, the all-loving father. This is the question that appears innocuous but through it evil wins power in us, through it we become disobedient to God. . . . Man is expected to be judge of God's word instead of simply hearing and doing it. . . . When man proceeds against the concrete Word of God with the weapons of a principle, with an idea of God, he is in the right from the first, he becomes God's master, he has left the path of obedience, he has withdrawn from God's addressing him.[5]

Indeed, the "I" in the "Here I am" that puts the covenant servant at the disposal of the suzerain becomes turned in on itself, demanding autonomy. In the process, Adam and Eve became false witnesses along with the serpent. In this exchange, Eve rebuffs the serpent's distortion of God's command, but even she adds to the command, ". . . or touch it" (Gen. 3:3). Further, she and Adam take it upon themselves to determine what is good or harmful for them (v. 6). They wanted to be "like God" even though they were already created analogies of God. But analogy was not enough, either for ontology (they wanted to be divine) or epistemology (they wanted to have archetypal knowledge). In short, they wanted to climb up to heaven themselves, instead of receive God as God had descended. "Then the eyes of both were opened, and they knew that they were naked; and they sewed fig leaves together and made loincloths for themselves" (v. 7).

Knowing that they were on trial and had now come under the sanctions of the creation covenant, they became false witnesses by covering up their nakedness and fleeing from God's presence. "I heard the sound [voice] of you in the garden," Adam answered God, "and I was afraid, because I was naked; and I hid myself" (vv. 9–10). This will now be the tragic response of the human conscience in the presence of God. The Israelites gathered at the foot of Sinai, filled with terror by the divine words, entreated Moses, "You speak to us, and we will listen; but do not let God speak to us, or we will die" (Exod. 20:19). Moses even replies by calling this a trial (v. 20). Isaiah, caught up in a vision of God in holy splendor, could only reply, "Woe is me! I am lost" (Isa. 6:5). It was this same terror that gripped Peter's conscience when, after Jesus calmed the storm, he could only bring forth the words, "Go away from me, Lord, for I am a sinful man" (Luke 5:8).

Read as an echo of the prophet's critique of the conquest and monarchy, Adam's first sin was not in eating the forbidden fruit but in failing to drive the false witness from the garden in the first place. Instead of cleansing God's temple-garden as God's

5. Ibid., 68.

faithful servant and son, Adam even allowed Satan entrance into the sanctuary. This will be a constant refrain in the story of Israel as well, as the idolatry of the indigenous people is tolerated and even embraced by the covenant people—because the kings were unwilling to drive evil, oppression, and idolatry out of the land.

The covenantal structure of creation and the probationary trial that ensues underscores the ethical character of this situation. Rather than serving as God's witness, adding verbal testimony to the witness of the whole creation, Adam took the witness stand against God. He perjured himself against the witness of creation, including his own high office. As Augustine describes his own participation in Adam's fall, "I inquired what wickedness is and I did not find a substance but a perversity of will twisted away from the highest substance, you O God, towards inferior things."[6] In short, it is ethical, not ontological, although Augustine shared the more general patristic tendency to identify "inferior things" with temporal creation per se. It is not because of any inherent weakness or fault in creation itself to which this fall or its empirical effects (sin, evil, and judicial death) can be attributed. Rather, it is through an act of will that perverts that which is good, twists that which is noble, suppresses that which is righteous, turning all of God's gifts against God in open rebellion.

Adam's role as false witness bears relation not only to God but to the whole creation, since he is the official image-bearer who represents the natural world before God. The creation had been placed at human disposal in a state of integrity, with a commission to be a steward of the environment. But now this power too is twisted by a perversity of will. We are reminded of Peter Martyr Vermigli's point from the last chapter: humankind has now exercised tyranny rather than stewardship.

Pain in childbirth is not an abstract sanction, but is directly connected with the fact that with each new life brought into the world breaks forth fresh opposition to God's lordship and the freedom of covenantal obedience and fellowship. It is also joyful, to be sure, because God has not abandoned humanity to its own devices. Creation remains upheld by God's hand. Yet childbirth is a mixed blessing. It involves pain not only at the beginning but in the middle and at the end. Similarly, the curse imposed on Adam and the ground is commensurate with the fruitlessness and "vanity" that life now bears for human experience. Created to have dominion over the earth in order to bring forth its fruitfulness, humankind itself turns its back on those who turned their back on their covenant Lord. "Adam is dead before he dies," writes Bonhoeffer. "Man *sicut deus* is dead, for he has cut himself off from the tree of life, he lives out of his own self and yet he cannot live. He must live and cannot live. That means he is dead."[7] Paul employs this very language of humanity in Adam being "dead in trespasses and sins" (Eph. 2:1).

Adam blamed Eve, Eve blamed the serpent, and the serpent blamed God. At the end of the day, everybody blamed God, and ever since, so do we. In ancient

6. Augustine, *Confessions* 7.15.22.
7. Bonhoeffer, *Creation and Fall*, 88.

as in modern dualism, the problem of evil is identified with created nature in an effort to externalize sin by attributing it to the "other"—"the woman you gave me," the nonhuman creation, but ultimately God. Shifting the issue from our own sin to God (viz., by attributing evil to creation itself) is one of the sources of dualism, ancient and modern. Instead, we must shift the ground back to covenantal transgression rather than ontological fault. As Cornelius Van Til observed,

> Man is not in Plato's cave. . . . Man had originally not merely a capacity for receiving the truth; he was in actual possession of the truth. The world of truth was not found in some realm far distant from him; it was right before him. That which spoke to his senses no less than that which spoke to his intellect was the voice of God. . . . Man's first sense of self-awareness implied the awareness of the presence of God as the one for whom he had a great task to accomplish.[8]

Truth is a covenantal and therefore an ethical concept.

It is this emphasis on unbelief interpreted as covenant breaking that links soteriology and epistemology, with Romans 1–3 as the *locus classicus*. In Adam we have all become false witnesses. As Merold Westphal observes, the "hermeneutics of suspicion" has "its true home in the Pauline teaching about the noetic effects of sin, the idea that in wickedness we 'suppress the truth' (Romans 1:18)."[9]

FALSE REPRESENTATIVE

Third, this courtroom trial presents the accused in the most radical relation to justice—not to abstract justice but to the personal righteousness in which humankind was created and by which it was to enjoy unbroken communion with God in a consummated Sabbath. The accused are discovered fleeing the scene of the crime, covering up the evidence. After this, all human beings will be born into the world, "dead through the trespasses and sins" and "by nature children of wrath" (Eph. 2:1, 3). Driven deeper into the brush, ever more determined to suppress the truth, "There is no one who is righteous, not even one; there is no one who has understanding, there is no one who seeks God." Paul adds in his litany especially from the Psalms,

> "All have turned aside, together they have become worthless; there is no one who shows kindness, there is not even one." "Their throats are opened graves; they use their tongues to deceive." "The venom of vipers is under their lips." "Their mouths are full of cursing and bitterness." "Their feet are swift to shed blood; ruin and misery are in their paths, and the way of peace they have not known." "There is no fear of God before their eyes." (Rom. 3:9–18)

---

8. Cornelius Van Til, *Defense of the Faith* (Philadelphia: Presbyterian & Reformed, 1955), 90.
9. Merold Westphal, *Overcoming Onto-theology*, 105.

Through the law that was once given as the way to everlasting life there is now because of sin only the expectation of death and judgment. The law announces this to everyone who is under it, whether in its written form or as it has been inscribed on the conscience, "so that every mouth may be silenced, and the whole world may be held accountable to God" (Rom. 3:19).

Because of this original covenantal relation and revelation, there is, as in Aldo Gargani's vivid expression, "the nostalgia for God of every living person."[10] This nostalgia drives us to idolatry and suppression of the truth—a theology of glory that judges by appearances—rather than to the arms of God through the revelation of his Son—a theology of the cross that judges by God's promise. Once more, it is important to note that the covenantal and eschatological appeal to such categories (theology of glory vs. theology of the cross) is not abstract or static. There was every reason in the world for an original theology of glory: ascending the ladder of obedience through trial to the point of obtaining the prize of eternal life and shalom on behalf of the whole creation. It is this revelation that is natural and remains natural, to the human conscience. It is presupposed in every theology of glory, in every national or ideological metanarrative of progress and enlightenment, and in every moral philosophy. Yet, following Adam's course, it is now not by obedience to the Word but by twisting or suppressing God's Word that the upward ascent is attempted. Ignoring the fall, this theology of glory is the revelation of the law still ringing in the conscience, with the false witness of the human agent answering back in self-confident autonomy, always trying to defer the inevitable verdict. After the fall, a theology of glory is a refusal to face the crisis and receive redemption from outside oneself, one's group, one's ideology, or one's power.

The accusation, however it is rebuffed, rationalized, therapeutically suppressed, or ignored through distraction, rings in the conscience and, as psychologist Robert Jay Lifton observes, drives our sense of guilt for a fault whose source seems forever ambiguous.[11] Thinking that their problem was merely shame rather than guilt, Adam and Eve covered themselves with loincloths, and ever since we have found ourselves incapable—or rather, unwilling—to accept the radical diagnosis of our own depravity. We can talk about evil outside us—the "others," whoever they may be; evil places, structures, forces, and principles. But, like the religious leaders whom Jesus challenged, we refuse to locate evil within ourselves (Matt. 12:33–37; 15:10–20; 23:25–28).

THE SENTENCE

Fourth, the accused, after blaming each other for the fault, now face their sentence (Gen. 3:15–16). In all of these sanctions, the generous giving and receiving

---

10. Aldo Gargani, "Religious Experience," in *Religion*, ed. Jacques Derrida and Gianni Vattimo (Palo Alto, CA: Stanford University Press, 1996), 132. See also his great Chekhov quotation on 132–33.

11. Robert Jay Lifton, "The Protean Style," in *The Truth About the Truth: De-Confusing and Re-Constructing the Postmodern World*, ed. Walter Truett Anderson (New York: Putnam's Sons, 1995), 130–31.

embedded in God's natural order will yield to strife, control, exploitation, and manipulation at every level. Finally, instead of being confirmed in righteousness and everlasting life, Adam and his posterity will return to the dust (v. 19). This is a description of the fall, not, as in the pagan cosmogonic myths, of creation itself.

Guilt, strife, and vanity seem to be the dominant terms in this sentence. Instead of being eschatologically oriented toward Sabbath life with God, one another, and the whole creation, we grow increasingly aware that we are "being toward death" (Heidegger). But this is not "natural." This play was not intended to be a tragedy. There is no tragedy in God—no "dark side," since only good comes from God, "in whom there is no variation or shadow of change" (Jas. 1:17)—but only Sabbath fulfillment that God longed to share with creatures.

Even some of the church fathers, still too much in the grip of Platonism, located guilt, strife, and vanity not in ethical fault but in some ontological aspect of creaturely existence.[12] Similarly, Jean-Luc Marion tends to identify vanity not only with postlapsarian creation, but with creation itself, even citing Romans 8:20 without any reference to sin, although sin is the context of that verse: "The totality appears, in fact, both as such but also as vain, only because it first appears as creation: 'creation was subjected to vanity [*mataiotēti*] says Paul (Rom. 8:20)."[13] Vanity "strikes the world as soon as the world finds itself taken into view—envisaged—by another gaze than its own, under the gaze," which puts the status of the world in question "by subjecting it to a gaze that comes from elsewhere, the placement of suspension" affecting the whole world, as Ecclesiastes reminds us.[14]

As seems to be the case among the circle of theologians identified under the rubric "radical orthodoxy," Marion's doctrine of sin (ethics) gets lost in ontological abstraction. He interprets Romans 1 and 2, for instance, in the following terms: distance is established, but instead of this inviting the return of the gaze that recognizes God as God, human thought became "vain" and idolatrous.[15] What is "Vanity, vanity, all is vanity" is the same creation that God pronounced "good and beautiful."

> The same distance designates the same world as vain or as "beautiful and good," according to whether the gaze perceives the distance through one pole or the other: from the world, on the fringe that opens it to the excess of a distance, the totality appears to be struck by vanity; from the inaccessi-

---

12. Typical in this respect is John of Damascus, "Exact Exposition of the Orthodox Faith." Angelic nature "is not susceptible of repentance because it is incorporeal. For it is owing to the weakness of his body that man comes to have repentance" (19). Paradise: "Free from passion . . . free from care and to have but one work to perform, to sing as do the angels, without ceasing or intermission, the praises of the Creator, and to delight in contemplation of Him and to cast all our care on Him" (29). "The tree of life, on the other hand, was a tree having the energy that is the cause of life, or to be eaten only by those who deserve to live and are not subject to death" (29).

13. Jean-Luc Marion, *God Without Being*, trans. Thomas A. Carlson (Chicago: University of Chicago Press, 1991), 122.

14. Ibid., 128–29.

15. Ibid., 130.

ble point of view of God, at the extremes of distance, the same world can receive the blessing that characterizes it in its just dignity.[16]

It is from "the gaze of charity" that "the 'goodness' of the gazed at" comes, not from the intrinsic integrity of a creation formed by God yet distinct from him. Consequently, "Vanity comes from the boredom of man."[17] But precisely insofar as a theology of sin is missing from Marion's interpretation, his existential analysis of the human condition refracted through the Preacher is thin. *Why* are we bored with life—even its very best? Why is all of our toil after wisdom, riches, fame, even godliness "a chasing after wind"? The author of Ecclesiastes is describing life east of Eden, after the fall, where things are not as they should be. There is something far more sinister than boredom at work here, and the writer discovers this only when he asks the "God" question:

> I have seen the business that God has given to everyone to be busy with. He has made everything suitable for its time; moreover he has put a sense of past and future into their minds, yet they cannot find out what God has done from the beginning to the end. I know that there is nothing better for them than to be happy and enjoy themselves as long as they live; moreover, it is God's gift that all should eat and drink and take pleasure in all their toil. I know that whatever God does endures forever; nothing can be added to it, nor anything taken from it; God has done this, so that all should stand in awe before him. . . . Moreover I saw under the sun that in the place of justice, wickedness was there, and in the place of righteousness, wickedness was there as well. . . . Again I saw all the oppressions that are practiced under the sun. Look, the tears of the oppressed—with no one to comfort them! On the side of their oppressors there was power—with no one to comfort them. And I thought the dead, who have already died, more fortunate than the living, who are still alive; but better than both is the one who has not yet been, and has not seen the evil deeds that are done under the sun. (Eccl. 3:10–4:3)

The very text to which Marion appeals offers a deeper—and darker—interpretation of human existence. Boredom is evidence, not the crime itself. The Preacher concludes: "The end of the matter; all has been heard. Fear God, and keep his commandments; for that is the whole duty of everyone. For God will bring every deed into judgment, including every secret thing, whether good or evil" (12:13–14). There is no note of the gospel struck in his conclusion of the matter, but what is clear is that the "eternity" that God has set in the heart of humanity is his law, the covenant of creation. Transgression of that covenant is the root of all human woe.

As the interpretation of sin unfolds in redemptive revelation, we encounter again an ethical-covenantal rather than ontological concept: meeting a stranger rather than overcoming estrangement. Kierkegaard rather than Hegel understood this interpretation of tragedy. It is not from the human condition as such—finitude,

---

16. Ibid., 131.
17. Ibid., 132.

for example—but from the human condition "under the law," in bondage to sin, death, and condemnation, that we begin to meet the Stranger whose approach we hear in the distance, "although he is not far from each of us" (Acts 17:27).

SOLIDARITY IN ADAM: THE COVENANT OF CREATION

The theme of covenant solidarity, otherwise regarded as congenial to relational and communal views of the self, is nevertheless put to the test when it involves collective human *guilt*. Francis Watson reminds us that this corporate aspect of self-identity is not always felicitous. "The intersubjective matrix which forms individual, related persons also simultaneously *de*forms them."[18] This "down" side to covenant solidarity that one finds in the federal theologians is largely absent from most treatments of social personhood.

This is the place to elaborate my definition of the covenant of creation, also identified variously in federal theology as the covenant of works, law, or nature. According to the federal theologians themselves, the covenant of creation/works–covenant of grace scheme was a further elaboration of the Reformation's broader law-gospel distinction.[19] In creation (and in the institution of the theocracy at Sinai), law as the basis for the divine-human relation is wholly positive. Misunderstandings emerge when we read Paul's polemic against "law" (contrasted with "promise") as a problem with "law" per se (e.g., Bultmann, Käsemann, et al.) and therefore read into all accounts of law-covenants the indictment of "legalism." According to Paul, no one will be justified by "works of the law," not because there has never been an arrangement in which that was possible (i.e., creation), but because *since the fall* (which the history of Israel recapitulates), all of humanity (including Israel) is now "in Adam." It is not being under the law that is the problem directly, but being found in Adam and especially in Israel (guardian of the law) a *transgressor* of the law. But can one be legitimately sentenced under a law unless the stipulations and sanctions were clearly present and understood? If one is under "the curse of the law," then one is under a covenant of law, since in the biblical understanding a curse is a covenantal sanction. It is difficult to conceive under what conditions humanity could be justly held responsible for Adam's fall, or even how each person can be accountable for his or her own faults, apart from a prior arrangement that constituted such actions as transgressions, with appropriate sanctions ensuing.

Even in Genesis 1–3 one can recognize the features of a covenant: a historical prologue setting the stage (Genesis 1–2), stipulations (2:16–17) and the sanctions

---

18. Francis Watson, *Text, Church and World: Biblical Interpretation in Theological Perspective* (Edinburgh: T & T Clark, 1994), 110. See also Paul Ricoeur, *Figuring the Sacred*, trans. David Pellauer (Minneapolis: Fortress, 1995); especially chap. 20; idem, *Oneself as Another*, trans. Kathleen Blamey (Chicago: University of Chicago Press, 1992).

19. See Michael Horton, "Law, Gospel and Covenant," *Westminster Theological Journal* 64, no. 2 (2002): 279–88.

(2:17b), over which Eve and the serpent argue (3:1–5), and which are finally carried out in the form of judgment (3:8–19). It is only after this fateful decision that an entirely new and unexpected basis is set forth for human destiny (3:21–24). It would appear that these elements are present, albeit implicitly, in the creation narrative. Adam is created in a state of integrity with the ability to obey God completely, thus rendering a suitable human partner. Further, God commands such complete obedience and then promises, upon that condition, the *right* to eat from the tree of life. It was the prize awaiting the successful outcome of a trial. While creation itself is a gift, the entrance into God's Sabbath rest was held out as the promise for loyal obedience in the period of testing. Just as YHWH the great king endured the "trial" of creation and came out at the other end pronouncing victory and entering his Sabbath enthronement, his earthly ectype-vassal was to follow the same course. Genesis 1–3, and their canonical Christian interpretation, have an eschatological rather than simply existential orientation.

As further confirmation, the presence of the Sabbath at the end of the "six-day" workweek-trial holds out the promise of everlasting confirmation in blessedness. This pattern is not the imposition of an arbitrary law, but the image-bearer's reflection of God's own journey from creation to consummation. If Adam should default in this covenantal relationship, he would "surely die," and we learn from the subsequent failure of Adam that this curse brought in its wake not only spiritual but physical, interrelational, and indeed environmental disaster.

A canonical reading of this episode brings into still sharper focus the corporate and representational character of Adam's covenantal role. Not only was he in covenant with God; all of humanity is represented as being in covenant with God by virtue of participating federally in Adam. Indeed, all of creation was in some sense judged in Adam (Gen. 3:17–18; Rom. 8:20). It is with this simultaneously legal and relational background in mind that Paul makes his well-known statements on the imputation of Adam's sin as the corollary of the imputation of the second Adam's righteousness (esp. Romans 5).[20] One simply cannot contrast this covenantal understanding as legal versus relational, or in corollary terms, Latin over Eastern. The same emphases may be found in Irenaeus, who not only affirms an Adamic covenant but distinguishes between an "economy of law" or "law of works" (which he associates with Adam in the prelapsarian situation, and then again in the "Mosaic economy" or "legal dispensation") and a "Gospel covenant."[21] John of Damascus adds, "It was necessary, therefore, that man

---

20. This approach also rejects the stance often taken since the 1950s to set the so-called relational against the legal categories of the divine-human relationship. "Covenant" is an inherently legal relationship.

21. Irenaeus, "Against Heresies," 4.25, from *The Ante-Nicene Fathers,* ed. Alexander Roberts and James Donaldson (repr., Grand Rapids: Eerdmans, 1989), 5.16.3, p. 554; 4.13.1, p. 24; 4.15.1; 4.16.3, pp. 25–26; cf. Ligon Duncan, "The Covenant Idea in Irenaeus of Lyons," a paper presented at the North American Patristics Society annual meeting, May 29, 1997 (Greenville, SC: Reformed Academic Press, 1998); Everett Ferguson, "The Covenant Idea in the Second Century," in *Texts and Testaments: Critical Essays on the Bible and the Early Church Fathers,* ed. W. E. March (San Antonio, TX: Trinity University Press, 1980).

should first be put to the test (for man untried and unproved would be worth nothing), and being made perfect by the trial through the observance of the command should thus receive incorruption as the prize of his virtue."[22] In the West, Augustine also clearly anticipates the covenant of works/grace scheme, as in his comment that "The first covenant was this, unto Adam: 'Whensoever thou eatest thereof, thou shalt die the death,'" and this is why all of his children "are breakers of God's covenant made with Adam in paradise."[23]

There are additional texts that appear to take into account just such an arrangement. Appeals have been made to Hosea 6:7, where it is said of Israel, "Like Adam, they have broken my covenant" (cf. Job 31:33, where "as Adam did" is the most likely translation). As a theocracy typological of the eschatological paradise of God, Israel's *national* existence was a repetition of the covenant of creation; hence the comparisons drawn by the biblical writers to Adam and the original creation.[24] Israel was called to see itself as a new theocratic garden of God's presence and as a new creation in the sense of representing humanity before God—all of this typological of the true Israel, the faithful Adam, who is also the true heavenly temple and everlasting Sabbath of God.

As with the Adamic covenant, the Sinaitic covenant is conditional. If Israel is faithful, the people "may dwell long in the land the LORD your God is giving you." Thus Israel's tenure in the land, like Adam's, is conditional—although, in the former case God's *goodness* was presupposed, while in the latter, God's *grace* (Deut. 7:7–11). Precisely the same terms and sanctions apply: Do this and you will live long in the land and enter into my Sabbath rest. As with his appeal to the two Adams for double imputation, Paul draws on the analogy of two mountains and two mothers to contrast the covenant of works (law) and the covenant of grace (promise) (Galatians 3 and 4).

But for our purposes here, it is important to notice, as Mastricht points out, that the principle of works is strenuously maintained in Scripture. The "works of the law" demand "most punctilious obedience ('cursed is the man who does not do all the works therein')." "Synonyms of the covenant of works are extant in the NT Rom. 3.27 (where is the glory? It is excluded. By what manner of law? Of

22. John of Damascus, "Exact Exposition," 43.

23. Augustine, *City of God* 16.28, trans. Henry Bettenson, ed. David Knowles (New York: Penguin, 1972), 688–89. In fact, Augustine elaborates this point in considerable detail in these two pages, contrasting the creation covenant with the covenant of grace as we find it in the promise to Abraham.

24. While this parallel is drawn by a number of writers, it is given a thorough description and analysis in Herman Witsius (1636–1708), *The Economy of the Covenants* (Escondido, CA: den Dulk Christian Foundation, 1990). For a more contemporary summary, see Charles Hodge: 'Besides this evangelical character which unquestionably belongs to the Mosaic covenant ['belongs to,' not 'is equivalent to'], it is presented in two other aspects in the Word of God. First, it was a national covenant with the Hebrew people. In this view the parties were God and the people of Israel; the promise was national security and land prosperity; the condition was the obedience of the people as a nation to the Mosaic law; and the mediator was Moses. In this aspect it was a legal covenant. It said 'Do this and live.' Secondly, it contained, as does also the New Testament, a renewed proclamation of the covenant of works" (*Systematic Theology* [Grand Rapids: Eerdmans, 1946], 117–22).

works? Nay: but by a law of faith) Gal. 2:16 (knowing that a man is not justified by the works of the law save through faith in Jesus Christ . . . because by the works of the law shall no flesh be justified)."[25] Only in this context, says Mastricht, can we possibly understand the role of Jesus Christ as the "fulfiller of all righteousness."

> Heb. 2.14–15 (since the children are sharers in blood and flesh, he also in like manner partook of the same; that through death he might bring to nought him that hath the power of death, that is, the devil). . . . If you say the apostle is speaking of a covenant not in Paradise, but the covenant at Sinai, the answer is easy, that the Apostle [sic] is speaking of the covenant in Paradise so far as it is re-enacted and renewed with Israel at Sinai in the Decalogue, which contained the proof of the covenant of works.[26]

If one objects that these passages merely demonstrate the opposite conclusion—that one cannot be justified in a covenant of works—these theologians reply that it is only humanity after the fall (i.e., humanity as sinful) that cannot be justified by works. Adam, however, was in a state of rectitude, perfectly capable of acceding to the divine mandate. As created, Adam and Eve's delight was to do the will of God. To refuse *in principle* the possibility of Adam's fulfillment of the covenant of works (or creation) is to challenge the state of rectitude (not mere innocence) in which the race was created. In addition to the exegetical arguments, Mastricht adduces the intrasystematic importance of the doctrine.[27]

Olevianus, coauthor of the Heidelberg Catechism, sees in the original covenant's prohibition the essence of the whole law—love of God and neighbor.[28] Once more, then, we are cautioned not to pit love against law, since the law's very summary is to love God and one another (Matt. 22:38, 40). Law and love are typically contrasted in contemporary theology and in popular thought. But the theology of covenant brings these together. In his research on the covenant theme in Israel, Delbert Hillers observes that the people are *commanded* to love. "We have heard these words so often that their doctrine does not seem surprising, but we need to remember that one theory of love, of very potent influence, has held that duty and love are incompatible. Here they are nearly identified."[29] As in the secular treaties, "The relation that exists between 'brothers,' that is, equal partners in a treaty, is 'love,'" but is also the way a suzerain (like Pharaoh) expresses his relation to his vassal-subjects.[30]

25. Heppe, *Reformed Dogmatics*, rev. and ed. Erst Bizer, trans. G. T. Thompson (London: The Wakeman Trust, 1955), 90.

26. Cited by ibid., 289–90.

27. Ibid.: "To very many heads of the Christian religion, e.g., the propagation of original corruption, the satisfaction of Christ and his subjection to divine law Rom. 8.3–4 (what the law could not do, in that it was weak through the flesh, God, sending his own Son in the likeness of sinful flesh and for sin, condemned sin in the flesh, that the requirement of the law might be fulfilled in us, who walk not after the flesh, but after the Spirit) Gal. 3:13 (Christ redeemed us from the curse of the law, having become a curse for us . . .), we can scarcely give suitable satisfaction, if the covenant of works be denied."

28. Heinrich Heppe, *Reformed Dogmatics*, 294.

29. Hillers, *Covenant*, 153.

30. Ibid.

> Love here is in part the language of emotion, in part the language of inter-
> national law. . . . To say then that "Love the Lord your god" is ultimately
> legal language is not to take it out of the realm of emotion but only to say
> that the legal concept shapes the emotional term. To love is to set one's sin-
> cere affections on the covenant Lord and to give this affection its expression
> in loyal service. . . . The Sinai covenant offered little grounds for optimism,
> but some hope could be garnered from the promise to Abraham. "When
> you are in distress and all these things have overtaken you, in the latter time,
> then you will return to Yahweh your god and hearken to his voice, for Yah-
> weh your god is a merciful god who will not let you down or destroy you,
> and who will not forget the covenant with your fathers, that which he swore
> to them" ([Deut.] 4:31).[31]

We can really begin to understand love only when we come to know God in this
history of the covenant, as *ḥesed—covenant* love. In this state Adam could expect—
for himself and his covenant heirs—royal entrance into the consummation, the
Sabbath rest of God himself, and everlasting confirmation in righteousness. In the
words of the Formula Consensus Helvetica, "the promise annexed to the covenant
of works was not just the continuation of earthly life and felicity," but of a confirmation in righteousness and everlasting heavenly joy.[32]

A final argument in favor of the covenant of creation is supplied by Cocceius,
in terms of *conscience* (Rom. 2:15), a point that Calvin had repeatedly emphasized in relation to the law. By nature human beings know that they have offended
God's friendship and communion. All of this presupposes an original relationship that has been breached.[33] Cocceius sharply rejects the nominalist covenant
theology of the late Middle Ages, which stressed God's absolute power (*de potentia Dei absoluta*). By covenanting with his creatures, God assured them that he
too had bound himself to act in certain ways that could be relied upon. Heppe
relates, "Cocceius is therefore (XXII, 39) zealous against the *Scholastics* [i.e., late
medieval nominalists], who by an appeal to the 'absolute lordship of God' assert,
that if He willed God could abandon even a perfectly obedient man and the holy
angels to eternal damnation."[34] God's covenantal lordship is a reliable relationship of genuine freedom and partnership. Because God's sovereignty is exercised
in the context of such a freely chosen bond, creatures do not have to fear an arbitrary exercise of raw omnipotence—the sort of despotic power that Israel's neighbors had come to accept as normal. The covenant of creation is an arrangement
that is suited to the intelligence, wisdom, and virtue of the human creature.[35]
Humanity, as created by God, was big enough, we might say, for the relationship.

It is therefore premature to insert into the creation covenant an element of divine
graciousness, strictly speaking. To be sure, God's decision and act to create constitute a "voluntary condescension" (Westminster Confession 7.1), as is his entrance

31. Ibid., 154–55.
32. Heppe, *Reformed Dogmatics*, 295.
33. Ibid., 286.
34. Cited ibid., 288, from Cocceius, *Summ. Th.* XXII, 23–24, 27–28.
35. Ibid.

into a covenantal relationship with creatures. Nevertheless, if "grace" is to retain its force as divine clemency toward those who deserve condemnation, we should speak of divine freedom, love, wisdom, goodness, justice, and righteousness as the governing characteristics of creation. Grace and mercy are shown to covenant-breakers and reflect the divine commitment to restore that which is fallen.

It is within this framework, then, that Reformed theology understood the active obedience of Jesus Christ, emphasizing the significance of his humanity in achieving redemption for his covenant heirs.[36] The priority of law in the covenant of creation establishes that God cannot acquit the guilty nor simply forgive sinners. In the context of the covenant of creation, the law must be perfectly satisfied, either personally or representatively. Again, this is not simply a legal hoop through which God created humankind to jump in order to satisfy his love of justice. Quite the contrary: God delights in *ḥesed* more than sacrifice (1 Sam. 15:22; Ps. 51:16–17; Isa. 1:11; 19:21; Hos. 6:6; Matt. 9:13; Rom. 12:1; Eph. 5:2; Phil. 4:18; 1 Pet. 2:5). Obedience is a sacrifice of thanks, while forgiveness is a sacrifice for sin. While the latter cancels debts, only the former renders an appropriate covenantal response. Forgiveness may be primarily juridical, but God's requirement in the covenant of creation was a life that answered back in faithfulness to its creator. Precisely as *natural* to humankind, the moral law was not an external authority imposed from without expressing abstract commands, but the expression of God's own personal character that he communicated, albeit analogically, to his image-bearer. To reflect God is therefore to be righteous, holy, obedient—a covenant servant, defined as such by the covenant charter (Hos. 6:7; Isa. 22; 24:5; Jer. 33:20, 25; 31:35–37).

Original Sin

But our collective human estrangement takes the form of what at least the Western church has identified as original sin. No doctrine is more crucial to our anthropology and soteriology and yet no doctrine has been more relentlessly criticized ever since it was articulated. In prosperous "developed" nations, it is not chiefly the problem of evil but the problem of abundance that makes it difficult to maintain a strong view of sin. In the 1970s secular psychologist Karl Menninger demanded to know, *Whatever Became of Sin?* while a popular preacher in the Reformed tradition, Robert Schuller, wrote *Self-Esteem: The New*

---

36. The Fourth Gospel once again especially underscores the "fulfilling of all righteousness" that is central to Jesus' mission. Jesus himself uses the language of a victorious second Adam, an obedient and loyal covenant servant, who has come "not to do my own will, but the will of him who sent me" (John 6:38), who always does what his Father says and who can say at the end of his obedient probation, "I have accomplished everything you have given me to do" (John 17:4). The hauntingly familiar words from the cross, "It is finished," take on fresh significance in its light, as does the rending of the temple curtain, through which humanity is now invited to enter into the Sabbath land and eat from the tree of life. In fact, the statement immediately preceding the last cry from the cross is, "After this, Jesus, knowing all things were now accomplished, that the Scripture might be fulfilled, said, 'I thirst!'" (John 19:28).

Reformation, in which he denounced the traditional doctrine of sin as damaging to the ego.[37]

Harnack called original sin "an impious and foolish dogma."[38] That, however, was before two world wars. Not surprisingly, the postwar years allowed a fresh reappraisal of the classical doctrine of original sin. Reinhold Niebuhr correctly surmised, "The Christian doctrine of sin in its classical form offends both rationalists and moralists by maintaining the seemingly absurd position that man sins inevitably and by a fateful necessity but that he is nevertheless to be held responsible for actions which are prompted by an ineluctable fate."[39] As the natural theology par excellence, Pelagianism was the anthropological assumption of Kant's thought.[40] It remains one of the most powerful currents in the popular assumptions of North America, which Dietrich Bonhoeffer has aptly described as "Protestantism without the Reformation."[41]

To be sure, not all criticisms of the doctrine of original sin are motivated by Pelagian assumptions, but neither are they motivated by Pauline ones—not that Paul developed the exegetical basis for original sin de novo. The same assumptions are articulated in the Psalms (Ps. 51:5, 10; 143:2), the prophets (Isa. 64:6; Jer. 17:9), and in the Gospels (John 1:13; 3:6; 5:42; 6:44; 8:34; 15:4–5) and Catholic Epistles (Jas. 3:2; 1 John 1:8, 10; 5:12). But more basically, the doctrine of original sin may be seen to arise from two principal sources: the covenant itself as the biblical paradigm for relating divine-human relations, and the narrative of the fall from an original state of integrity. Citing examples from Second Temple Judaism, Childs concludes, "Judaism shared the view that human sin derived from Adam (IV Ezra 3.7; Sifre Deut. §323)."[42]

One of the clearest examples of early Jewish belief in original sin is in 2 Esdras:

> The same fate came upon all: death upon Adam, and the flood upon that generation [of Noah]. . . . For the first man, Adam, burdened as he was with an evil heart, sinned and was overcome, and not only he but all who were descended from him. So the weakness became inveterate, and although your law was in your people's hearts, a rooted wickedness was there too; thus the good came to nothing, and what was evil persisted . . . behaving just like Adam and all his line; for they had the same evil heart. (2 Esd. 3:10, 20–22, 26)

---

37. Robert Schuller, *Self-Esteem: The New Reformation* (Waco, TX: Word, 1982). That Menninger does not profess a religious faith and Robert Schuller is ordained in the Reformed Church in America is one of the ironies of contemporary American religion.

38. Adolf von Harnack, *History of Dogma*, vol. 5, trans. Neil Buchanan (Boston: Little, Brown, 1899), 217.

39. Reinhold Niebuhr, *The Nature and Destiny of Man* (New York: Charles Scribner's Sons, 1964), 241.

40. Kant, "Religion with the Boundaries of Mere Religion," in *Religion and Rational Theology*, trans. and ed. Allen W. Wood and George Di Giovanni (Cambridge: Cambridge University Press, 1996), 148, 150; Ricoeur, *Figuring the Sacred*, 84–86.

41. Robert Jenson cites Bonhoeffer's quip in his own criticism of American theology in his *America's Theologian: A Recommendation of Jonathan Edwards* (New York: Oxford University Press, 1988), 54.

42. Childs, *Biblical Theology*, 579.

These statements are in the context of explaining God's ways with Israel in exile: the point is that Israel itself is "in Adam," and the first disobedience is lodged deep within the history of God's own people. The similarities to Paul's treatment, especially in Romans 1–3, are striking.

Whatever the arguments against original sin, modern individualism cannot be used as a legitimate refutation. The concept of solidarity—human solidarity in Adam and Israel's in Abraham and Sinai—is basic to the biblical worldview, however alien to our own. It follows, then, that if it is the case that Adam has failed to carry out his commission as the servant-king of YHWH, all of those who are "in Adam" are implicated as well, just as the people represented by the vassal in the Hittite treaties would share in the threatened sanctions in the case of a breach.

At this point, everything turns on what kind of credit we give to the historical narrative and whether we are willing to speak, as not only Genesis 3 but subsequent Scripture does, of the human condition "before" and "after" the fall. We return once more to the scandal of particularity that challenges not only this doctrine, but the entire thesis assumed by the biblical writers that the universal can be determined by the particular. Whatever problems we have with Adam's fall as the particular event giving rise to a general account of the human plight, we will also face with the second Adam as its solution. "Who then were Adam and Eve?" We might say, with Robert Jenson, "They were the first hominid group that in whatever form of religion or language used some expression that we might translate 'God,' as a vocative."[43] Barth and Brunner affirm that humanity is somehow "in Adam," but denying the historical fall, they can only lodge this fact in God's eternal predestination. Barth insists, "the guilt and punishment we incur in Adam have no independent reality of their own but are only the dark shadows of the grace and life we find in Christ."[44] If one does not take Adam (i.e., the human *as human*) seriously, it is difficult to see how one will conceive a due appreciation of Jesus Christ as the historical fulfillment of Adam's original task. For Barth, it appears that "Adam" represents a mere copy, appearance, shadow of the eternal Form (Christ), the latter swallowing the former.

This approach that I am taking admittedly requires a counterintuitive reversal: instead of beginning with universal metaphysical questions about human nature in the abstract, we begin with Adam and Israel and allow ourselves to be told who we really are. Having said this, what are we to make of the traditional doctrine of original sin? If the image of God in humankind (image and likeness) is understood primarily in terms of some faculty (soul, mind, will) of the self, original sin will probably locate sin in an ostensibly weaker faculty (viz., the body, passions, or more recently, genes). The element of solidarity is not absent from Augustine's classic account, but the main emphasis falls on the metaphysics of inheritance. While those debates may have important theological contributions,

---

43. Jenson, *ST* 2:49.
44. Karl Barth, *Christ and Adam: Man and Humanity in Romans 5*, trans. T. A. Smail (New York: Harper & Bros., 1957), 36.

even to our doctrine of original sin, they are hardly the most obvious questions raised by the biblical passages treating the topic. Solidarity, at least in my understanding of covenant theology, is primarily a matter of representation—federal and organic rather than ontological and metaphysical union. Obviously, we are once again "meeting a stranger" rather than "overcoming estrangement" in this approach. Thus, while questions about the substance of "human nature" and the means of passing it down through the generations are not irrelevant, they are at least not the main point. One might affirm what Scripture means by humanity being in Adam without being required to endorse a particular theory of how that happens. Again I refer to Jenson: "The difficulty with the classical proposal is its use of the notion of 'human nature': this in itself suggests an impersonal something that makes humans human and the alteration of which would imply an alteration in the definition of humanity."[45]

Instead, the emphasis should fall not on a faculty or principle that we all share in common, but the sheer fact that we *are* in common; that is, we are in covenant. Although Jenson does not appeal to this category, he makes essentially the same point:

> Humanity is finally one diachronically extended community, and that community and we in it are idolatrous, lustful, unjust and despairing. Moreover, we just so are compelled to posit a "fall" of humankind, occurring within created time. . . . The story told in the third chapter of Genesis is not a myth; it does not describe what always and never happens. It describes the historical first happening of what thereafter always happens; moreover, had it not happened with the first humans it could not have happened at all, since then the first humans would have been omitted from an "encompassing deed of the human race." We may one last time pose the question: Who were Adam and Eve? And in this context the answer must be: the first community of our biological ancestors who disobeyed God's command.[46]

The fall in which we all participate is "the presence of the past."[47]

Solidarity in Adam illustrates that covenant is not simply a metaphor for a relationship but *is* the relationship between God and creation. No one is an island. The presumption of entering a room by oneself, closing the windows, and starting from scratch in order to find out the truth about ourselves, as Descartes attempted, is an illusion—and a deadly one. We are all part of the *Wirküngsgeschichte* (effective history) of the curse and the pervasive effects of the fall. The past is present not only among us but within us. The covenant consciousness that we all share by virtue of our humanity carries with it ever since the fall the ineradicable consciousness of our existence as breach, alienation, and transgression.

According to Walter Brueggemann, however, Genesis 3 does not support the idea of a fall into sin.

45. Jenson, *ST* 2:149–50.
46. Ibid., 150.
47. Ibid., 355.

The text is commonly treated as the account of "the fall." Nothing could be more remote from the narrative itself. . . . In general, the Old Testament does not assume such a "fall." Deut. 30:11–14 is more characteristic in its assumption that humankind can indeed obey the purposes of God. . . . If one were to locate such a pessimistic view of human nature in the Old Testament, one might better look to the tradition of Hosea, Jeremiah, and Ezekiel than here. Frequently, this text is treated as though it were an explanation of how evil came into the world. But the Old Testament is never interested in such an abstract issue.[48]

By way of response, I should say first of all that "how evil came into the world" is hardly an abstract issue. It is treated concretely and historically by Israel, including in Genesis 2:4–3:24, not abstractly and speculatively. Second, Brueggemann is quite right to suggest that Genesis has a relatively high view of human potential *as created*. This I have assumed in my treatment of the covenant of creation: the integrity of human nature as nature. But who can deny that the narrative here offered moves transitionally from creation to fall? That is simply how the story reads: there is a "before" and "after." Reformed theology has therefore emphasized simultaneously the radical integrity of human nature as created and the radical depravity of human nature as fallen.

Further, this passage, Brueggemann tells us, is not about the origin of death in the world as punishment for sin.[49] We cannot even enlist Paul for this: "Paul's argument [in Rom. 5:12–21] is not concerned with an analysis of the origin of evil, sin, or death, but with the proclamation of good news. In Paul's work, Genesis 2–3 is not used for the presentation of a problem, but for proclamation of the gospel." In fact, "such questions are no part of biblical testimony and are of no interest to genuine faith."[50] Yet later in his reflections on this passage, Brueggemann asserts,

> The scene becomes a trial [!]. . . . The speech of the indicted [!] couple is revealing, for it is all "I." Therein lies the primal offense [!]: "I heard . . . , I was afraid . . . , I was naked; I hid. . . . I ate. . . . I ate" (3:10–13). Their own speech indicts [!] them. It makes clear that their preoccupation with the Garden/er, with his vocation, his permission, his prohibition, has been given up. Now the preoccupation is "I." . . . Life is turned back on self.[51]

But this is a fine Augustinian reflection on the passage that he otherwise refuses as part of its scope. "There is, of course, talk here of sin and evil and death" after all. "But it is understated talk. The stakes are too high for reduction to propositions. The story does not want to aid our theologizing. It wants, rather, to catch us in our living. It will permit no escape into theology."[52] Such comments naively

48. Walter Brueggemann, *Genesis,* Interpretation (Atlanta: John Knox Press, 1982), 41.
49. Ibid., 42.
50. Ibid., 43.
51. Ibid., 49.
52. Ibid., 50.

assume that when Brueggemann interprets the narrative, he is not asserting theological propositions, yet even he cannot get away from the language of "trial," "indictment," "the primal offense," and life "turned back on self."

In our day, it is not only Pelagianism on one hand and a suspicion of "church theology" on the other but a therapeutic understanding of human rights, criminal justice, and social relations that challenges the traditional understanding of sin. A sentimental theology has emerged in the context of changing concepts of jurisprudence in which there is no place for any form of justice that is not exclusively ameliorative and healing for the perpetrator as well as the victim. As the rights of the convicted often weigh more heavily than the rights of the offended party, our concept of sin as transgression against God's personal righteousness and our own ethical commission are surrendered to therapeutic models of behavioral modification. Although its roots may not always be Pelagian, its conclusions cannot but yield a sentimental moralism in the place of a robust contrast of condemnation and justification. Law professor Jean Bethke Elshtain has, in fact, pointed to the loss of the sense of God's holiness and human sinfulness as part of the underlying rationale for a sentimentalism that undermines the very notion of human justice.[53]

Moltmann simply challenges the Pauline and patristic teaching at this point:

> The Fathers of the church consistently followed the rabbinic and Pauline doctrine: suffering and death are the divinely appointed *punishment for human sin.* "The wages of sin is death" (Rom. 6:23). . . . This reduction of suffering and death to sin means that the beginning of salvation is seen as being the forgiveness of sins. Human redemption then takes place in two steps: sin is overcome through grace, in Christ's sacrificial death on the cross; the consequences of sin—suffering and death—are overcome by power, through the future resurrection of the dead.
> . . . Clement of Alexandria, Origen and Theodore Mopsuestia disputed the casual connection. They taught that death belonged together with the creation of man as finite being. It is therefore not a consequence of sin, and not a divine punishment either. . . . Augustine and the Latin Fathers, on the other hand, traced all forms of suffering and death back to sin, reducing the doctrine of redemption to juridical form into the doctrine of grace.
> Of course there is a connection between sin and suffering. . . . This misery is already inherent in the sin itself. That is why the sinner is not really a wrongdoer who has to be punished in addition. He is something pitiable, and we must have compassion on him.[54]

But this assumes that sin is only something in which we are passive victims, hardly a doctrine likely to evoke personal responsibility for our own contributions to the lovelessness that we show to others. But is it not adding insult to injury to suggest that God imposes further penalties than the sin itself entails? Is

---

53. Jean Bethke Elshtain, *Augustine and the Limits of Politics* (Notre Dame, IN: University of Notre Dame Press, 1995); cf. the interview with Elshtain by Ken Myers in the Mars Hill Audio Journal, vol. 64 (September/October 2003).

54. Moltmann, *Trinity and the Kingdom,* 49–50.

punishment for sin itself a crime? Moltmann bravely takes the next step toward lodging sin in created nature itself: "Experience of suffering goes far beyond the experience of guilt and the experience of grace. It has its roots in the limitations of created reality itself. If creation-in-the-beginning is open for the history of good *and* evil, then that initial creation is also a creation capable of suffering, and capable of producing suffering."[55]

As in the logical leap from the premise that the act of creation is *consistent* with God's loving nature to his conclusion that it is therefore *necessary*, Moltmann here makes a creation *capable* of producing suffering into a creation that *includes* suffering and evil in its very existence. We read a string of speculations deduced from a certain therapeutic concept of justice known almost exclusively to modernity: "For love there *is* only 'innocent' suffering, because anyone who loves cannot look on at the other person's suffering any longer—he wants to overcome it."[56] As a consequence, "Suffering as *punishment for sin* is an explanation that has a very limited value. . . . The interpretation of Christ's death on the cross as an atoning event in the framework of the question of human guilt is the central part of this universal significance; but it is not the whole of it, or all its fullness."[57] In rightly contending that the question of guilt "is not the whole of it," Moltmann does not even seem to allow that it is part of it.

Moltmann's account is weakened not so much by what it affirms but by what it leaves out of the equation. A pietistic understanding of sin, Moltmann correctly observes, has emphasized the aspect of individual offense against God often to the detriment of the full-orbed view of sin as both individual and corporate, personal and structural. A fundamentalist understanding of sin has reduced the sinful condition to sinful acts and has consequently narrowed its concept of sin typically to those acts that *other* people commit. For many in such circles, one is only a sinner, never sinned against, and thus the complicated web of sin that makes people simultaneously perpetrators *and* victims is often reduced to simplistic moral assertion. This, however, is hardly a besetting sin of fundamentalists alone.

Moltmann is also correct to remind us that any Christian doctrine of sin has to be articulated in the light of its cosmic dimensions, which leads to the eschatological triumph of God over sin and death not only for human beings but for the whole creation that groans even now for its liberation. Yet Moltmann's account of sin is also reductive, and consequently much of what he has to say about God's eschatological triumph amounts to little more than the realization of ideal social structures (particularly, democratic socialism). But are we really noble savages distorted by evil social structures, as romanticism has insisted?

There is no doubt that an exclusively juridical concept of the fall cannot account for a host of passages, particularly those that emphasize the reality of systematic and institutional violence. But theology desperately needs some larger

55. Ibid., 51.
56. Ibid.
57. Ibid., 52.

paradigm within which to relate the judicial or legal and the relational and cosmic aspects. Covenant provides just such a model. Representing the backlash against juridical concepts, Christoph Schwöbel insists, "As the opposite of faith sin is to be interpreted not primarily as an offence committed against a law, as the transgression of a commandment. It is primarily the violation of a relationship, the relationship between God the creator and his human creatures."[58] But this is an example of the false dilemma that the covenant motif resolves, for in it the legal and relational are inseparable. As terms such as *redemption* and *adoption* reflect, there is an indispensably legal aspect to the particular kind of relationship in view. At the same time, this relationship cannot be reduced to the legal any more than marriage can be reduced to a piece of paper. Despite the one-sidedness of his comment, Schwöbel rightly warns us against reducing sin to legal categories without remainder. Sin is not only "the opposite of faith," as he suggests—it is also an offense against God's law. Yet, as Luther's Small Catechism reminds us, the root of all sin is the refusal to trust. This again underscores what is central to the covenant: without trust, there can be no fidelity (trustworthiness, reliability). Without faith, there cannot be works.

It is the definition of sin that generates such radically different construals of redemption. As Robert Jenson notes, "The only possible *definition* of sin is that it is what God does not want done. Thus if we do not reckon with God, we will not be able to handle the concept; without acknowledging God, we can—though perhaps not for long—speak meaningfully of fault and even of crime but not of sin."[59] With such a serious doctrine of sin, we cannot help but see even religion as one of its expressions, as Barth so forcefully argued: "Our self-respect demands, on top of everything else, . . . access to a superworld. Our deeds want deeper foundations, transcendent recognition and reward. Our lust for life covets also pious moments and prolongation into eternity."[60] Barth feels the force of Feuerbach's critique of religion and, contrasting religion with the revelation of Christ, uses that critique to define religion as idolatrous projection:

> We come to our own rescue and build the tower of Babel. In what haste we are to soothe within us the stormy desire for the righteousness of God! And to soothe means, unfortunately, to cover up, to bring to silence. . . . The longing for a new world has lost all its bitterness, sharpness, and restlessness, has become the joy of development, and now blossoms sweetly and surely in orations, donor's tablets, committee meetings, reviews, annual reports, twenty-five-year anniversaries, and countless mutual bows. The righteousness of God itself has slowly changed from being the surest of facts into being the highest among various ideals, and is now at all events our very own affair. . . . You may act as if you were God, you may with ease take his righteousness under your own management. This is certainly pride.[61]

58. Christoph Schwöbel, "Human Being and Relational Being," in *Persons, Divine and Human*, ed. Christoph Schwöbel and Colin Gunton (Edinburgh: T & T Clark, 1991), 148–49.

59. Jenson, *ST* 2:133.

60. Translation of ibid., 136, from Barth, *Der Romerbrief,* 2nd ed. (Munich: Chr. Kaiser, 1922), 20.

61. Barth, *Word of God and Word of Man,* 14–16.

Religion is one of the chief ways we cover up our shame without actually dealing with the guilt that gives rise to it. We project a god who will satisfy our suppression of the truth about ourselves. "Idolatry is not an accident," Jenson notes, "as if some of us just happened to hit on wrong candidates for deity."[62]

While enlightened modernity exhibits a Pelagianism that alternates between the serious tempo of a confident march and the nihilistic beat of self-indulgent consumerism, biblical faith cannot be sung without the blue note, the minor key. It is not all blues, of course, but without it there is no hope. Blues is not nihilism—it is not opposed to hope. On the contrary, it is the unceasingly happy and upbeat jingles we hear in the supermarket or, with increasing frequency, at church, that correlate with a denial of the reality of sin, evil, and pain and therefore deny to their consumers any longing for something profoundly redemptive. Nihilism is to be found in the anesthetizing environment of the mall or the megachurch. Upbeat popular culture, feeding on images of the beautiful, well-adjusted, pleasant, happy, young, and vigorous, ignores the brutal reality of life that is the very condition for hope and its trigger mechanism. Blues music is notoriously difficult to transpose into notations on a page, because it stretches and bends notes. The parallel to life as interpreted by Scripture is obvious.

With few exceptions, modern liberalism and fundamentalism have misunderstood the essential character of sin, sometimes in similar ways—for instance, through implicit or explicit assumptions of human goodness and the reduction of sin to actions rather than a condition. The usual explicit criticism of original sin, however, has always been some version of Kant's categorical imperative: "'ought' implies 'can.'" Both too easily locate sin externally, although one can also discern a tendency to emphasize either the self as sinned-against (liberalism) or sinner (fundamentalism). But the mystery of sin is more complex than this false choice.

Writing in the face of the most obvious examples of human sin in the twentieth century, Reinhold Niebuhr reflected deeply on this complexity in *The Nature and Destiny of Man*. He appeals to Calvin:

> Wherefore as Plato has been deservedly censured for imputing all sins to ignorance, so also we must reject the opinion of those who maintain that all sins proceed from deliberate malice and pravity. For we too much experience how frequently we fall into error even when our intentions are good. Our reason is overwhelmed with deceptions in so many forms.[63]

Although he does not adopt every detail of the classical doctrine, Niebuhr shares Pascal's view, which he cites from the *Pensées*, 434: "Certainly nothing offends us more rudely than this doctrine, and yet without this mystery, the most incomprehensible of all, we are incomprehensible to ourselves."[64] In modern

---

62. Reinhold Niebuhr, *The Nature and Destiny of Man*, 2 vols. in 1 (New York: Scribner's, 1949), 137.
63. Cited ibid., 242, from Calvin, *Institutes* 2.2.25.
64. Cited ibid., 243.

forms, Pelagianism persists, for example in the notion of "cultural lag" as that which holds back progress.

> It is not surprising that wherever essentially classical views of man prevail, as for instance in both secular and Christian modern liberalism, the bias toward evil should be defined as residing not in man's will but in some sloth of nature which man has inherited from his relation to the brute creation. This remains true even when, as in the thought of men like Schleiermacher and in the theology of the social gospel, this sloth is attributed to the institutions and traditions of history rather than purely to sensual passion or to the finiteness of the mind.[65]

According to Walter Rauschenbusch, sin is transmitted primarily through institutions.[66] "The argument by which this is done has not varied from the day of Augustine's critics."[67]

> Schleiermacher significantly makes no distinction between sin and the consciousness of sin. "We must insist on the fact," he writes, "that sin in general exists only insofar as there is consciousness of it." Pelagianism in short ascribes all sins to "deliberate malice and pravity," to use Calvin's phrase.[68]

But the problem is that neither Pelagianism (generally characteristic of modern liberalism) nor semi-Pelagianism (which he identifies with Roman Catholic theology) offers a profound enough account of human corruption, which history and experience demonstrate all too well.

> The truth is that, absurd as the classical Pauline doctrine of original sin may seem to be at first blush, its prestige as a part of the Christian truth is preserved, and perennially re-established, against the attacks of rationalists and simple moralists by its ability to throw light upon complex factors in human behaviour which constantly escape the moralists.[69]

For example, one cannot really say that the persecution of Jews is necessarily in every case motivated by malicious intent. For the Nazi, in fact, it is commitment to ultimate virtues and values that justify violence. Are we to absolve the Nazi of responsibility "merely because his choice is not consciously perverse"?[70]

But Niebuhr also takes issue with traditional formulations, both Catholic and Protestant, in ways that fit well with my treatment. The Catholic doctrine, which Niebuhr identifies as "Semi-Pelagian," distinguishes pure nature (*pura naturalia*) and the *donum superadditum*.[71] Original righteousness was lodged in the latter, a

---

65. Ibid., 246.
66. Cited ibid., 246 n. 3, from Rauschenbusch, *A Theology of the Social Gospel* (Louisville, KY: Westminster John Knox, 1997), 67.
67. Ibid., 247.
68. Ibid.
69. Ibid., 249.
70. Ibid.
71. Ibid., 247–48.

gift added to nature—a gift that has been forfeited by the fall. But "pure nature" is left virtually unaffected by the fall. The uneasy conscience is evidence of an original righteousness that Roman Catholic theology, with its distinction between a pure nature untouched by sin and an original righteousness wholly lost, does not allow. "An uneasy conscience which is not fully conscious of itself is the root of further sin, because the self strives desperately to ward off the *dénouement* of either remorse or repentance by accusing others, seeking either to make them responsible for the sins of the self, or attributing worse sins to them."[72]

In different ways, the Catholic and more radical Protestant doctrines of original sin (such as Luther's) deny this original righteousness as continuing in some sense, however depraved, in the conscience. Moralists, however, reject this moral depravity in the name of freedom. Yet "the ultimate proof of the freedom of the human spirit is its own recognition that its will is not free to choose between good and evil. . . . Man is most free in the discovery that he is not free."[73] Calvin, according to Niebuhr, is the via media between the Roman Catholic view of an unsullied "pure nature" and a Lutheran denial of the persistence of an original righteousness. Human nature is corrupt in every part, but humankind still bears the divine image and with it the conscience that both recognizes the truth and yet suppresses that truth in unrighteousness.[74]

Furthermore, the universal sense of sin is confirmed in human experience, contrary to its denial in theology, says Niebuhr. "The sense of a conflict between what a man is and ought to be finds universal expression, even though the explanations of the conflict are usually contradictory and confused." This universal experience disproves any theory that denies humankind "any knowledge of the good which sin has destroyed."[75] "In Catholicism the Fall means the loss of something which is not essential to man and does not therefore represent a corruption of his essence," while Protestantism sometimes goes too far in seeing the image as destroyed. "It is impossible to do justice to the concept of the image of God and to the perfection of that image before the Fall without making a distinction between the essential nature of man and the virtue of conformity to that nature."[76] I have already argued this point in my distinction between the fact of being an image-bearer (common to all people) and its eschatological realization in Christ (in the covenant of grace). The uneasy conscience even Luther saw as

72. Ibid., 256.
73. Ibid., 258, 260.
74. Ibid., 269.
75. Ibid., 266. However, this universal experience common to all people is left without historical grounding in Niebuhr. The idea of original perfection lost is crucial, says Niebuhr, even though he is quick to place "the fall" in the category of myth. In other words, theologically, the doctrine based on a historical fall can continue to carry its freight unhindered by the denial of its concrete basis. This is the weakness of Niebuhr's account. Consequently, he says, "The consciousness and memory of an original perfection in the self-as-transcendent must not be regarded as the possession of perfection. . . . Perfection before the Fall is, in other words, perfection before the act" (277–78). Thus "the fall" functions in Niebuhr (as in Barth and Brunner) as something like a Kantian transcendental.
76. Ibid., 266.

the point of contact between God and fallen humans.[77] It cannot therefore be missing or wholly obliterated, but rather distorted and twisted.

As Niebuhr saw so evidently, there are crucial ethical and cultural implications of one's theology of sin. The self-righteousness against which Paul strove in Romans 1–3 is reproduced in liberal Christianity today. "The greatest sin of moralistic Christianity is its tendency to encourage the assumption that men are as good as the ideals of justice and love which they entertain."[78] It is only by upholding both the reality of that sense of original righteousness as present, though sinfully suppressed, in human nature even after the fall, that we begin to see its vanity and self-righteousness. "We have seen that the original righteousness or perfection is present with sinful man as 'law,'" which is "derived from man's essential nature."[79]

> There is therefore no uncorrupted natural law, just as there is no completely lost original justice. . . . The confidence of medieval Catholicism in the ability of an unspoiled reason to arrive at definitive standards of natural justice thus became the very vehicle of the sinful pretensions of the age. The social ethics of Thomas Aquinas embody the peculiarities and the contingent factors of a feudal-agrarian economy into a system of fixed socio-ethical principles.[80]

But Lutheranism and Barth are too "relativistic" on the other side.[81] We need a "more dialectical analysis of the function of reason"—not as innocent as in the Catholic doctrine, but not as wholly depraved as to be absent or inoperative, as in some Protestant views.[82] In this dialectic, the self-as-subject reasons according to conscience, acknowledging the law and making moral judgments based on it, while at the same time the self-as-agent of action excuses its own sin and prejudices.[83] Reason "is both a servant of sinful self-love and an organ of judgment upon it." Calvin's assessment, standing between the Roman and Lutheran view, is most in accord with this dialectical nature of fallen reason.[84]

Whereas Pelagians, ancient and modern, pit freedom against the doctrine of original sin, and Augustinians often accept this antithesis by virtually denying the former, Niebuhr rightly insists that, ironically, human freedom is nowhere better understood and affirmed than in its bondage to sin. "The original righteousness which sinful man has supposedly lost is in reality present with him as the ultimate requirement of his freedom."[85] There is a freedom that calls, but is finally abused or distorted. "All simple moralism, which assumes that the law of

---

77. Ibid., 274.
78. Ibid., 279.
79. Ibid., 280.
80. Ibid., 281.
81. Ibid., 283
82. Ibid., 284.
83. Ibid.
84. Ibid., 285.
85. Ibid., 286.

life needs only to be stated in order to be obeyed, is refuted by the response of the rich young ruler to this demand: 'He went away sorrowful for he had great possessions.'"[86] This story yields at least two important conclusions: human beings know the ultimate requirements of their nature, and they are "not ready to meet these requirements once they are defined."[87]

> Both modern liberalism and modern Marxism are always facing the alternatives of moral futility and moral fanaticism. Liberalism in its pure form usually succumbs to the peril of futility. It will not act against evil until it is able to find a vantage point of guiltlessness from which to operate. This means it cannot act at all.[88]

Again somewhat ironically, whereas a strong affirmation of human sinfulness is often seen as morally debilitating (and indeed can be, if one denies any vestige of reason and conscience), it is actually Pelagianism that paralyzes action, vacillating between fanaticism and futility.

While Niebuhr's understanding of the Roman Catholic and Lutheran views may be open to some dispute, his analysis reflects the Reformed concern to deny, on the one hand, the Roman Catholic distinction between "pure nature" (uncorrupted by the fall) and a "super-added gift" of original righteousness (wholly removed by the fall) and, on the other hand, an extreme Protestant denial of the *imago Dei* in fallen humanity. I would argue that it is the covenant of creation (also called the covenant of works/law/nature) that provides the concrete basis for this approach, offering an affirmation of the persistence of the original creation as well as of the persistence after the fall of human corruption and suppression of that original constitution of its moral nature.

More recently, but also out of deep firsthand experience with human corruption, Miroslav Volf speaks of a "contrived innocence" in affluent modern societies, giving rise to "a glaring incongruity: in a world so manifestly drenched with evil everybody is innocent in their own eyes."[89] Similar to Niebuhr's appeal to Calvin's analysis of sin as involving both intentional violation and victimization, Volf says, "In *The Fall to Violence* Marjorie Suchocki argues that there is 'an intertwining of victim and violator through the very nature of violation.'"[90]

> The violence ensnares the psyche of the victim, propels its action in the form of defensive reaction, and—robs it of innocence. She writes, "To break the world cleanly into victims and violators ignores the depths of each person's participation in cultural sin. There simply are no innocents."[91]

86. Ibid., 287.
87. Ibid., 288.
88. Ibid.
89. Miroslav Volf, *Exclusion and Embrace: A Theological Exploration of Identity, Otherness, and Reconciliation* (Nashville: Abingdon, 1996), 79.
90. Cited in ibid., 147.
91. Ibid., 80.

But this is the point that the doctrine of original sin has tried to make, and its demise leaves us trapped within the cycle of blame that perpetuates exclusion and violence.

> In the wake of modernity's belief in progress, the doctrine was progressively dismantled. As Bernhard-Henri Levy rightly argued in *Dangerous Purity*..., the stubborn shadows of modernity, produced in part precisely by modernity's blind optimism, call for a judicious retrieval of the doctrine of original sin.... Solidarity in sin underscores that no salvation can be expected from an approach that rests fundamentally on the moral assignment of blame and innocence. The question cannot be how to locate "innocence" either on the intellectual or social map and work our way toward it.[92]

This doctrine should undermine our tendency to exclude on the basis of moral performance.

> A particular evil not only "inhabits" us so that we do what we hate (Romans 7:15); it has colonized us to such a thoroughgoing extent that there seems to be no moral space left within the self in which it could occur to us to hate what we want because it is evil. We are ensnared by evil not only with full consent, but without a thought of dissent and without a sigh for deliverance.[93]

Volf even relates original sin to the covenant concept: "And behind the tumult of 'making' and 'breaking' lies an anthropological constant: human beings are *always already in the covenant* as those who have *always already broken the covenant.*"[94]

Natural and Moral Ability

A corollary of the arguments above that human beings are by definition covenantal creatures and image-bearers is that being a human person therefore is not dependent on being related to God in rectitude.[95] This itself gives rise to another corollary: the distinction between natural and moral ability. This distinction, which is prominent in the Reformed systems, is the very thing that Niebuhr seems to have in mind with his own distinction above between the self-as-subject (acknowledging right and wrong) and the self-as-agent in action (justifying oneself while blaming others).

Developed particularly by Reformed theology in the seventeenth-century debates, and rigorously explored by Jonathan Edwards in his *Freedom of the Will*,

---

92. Ibid., 84.
93. Ibid., 90–91.
94. Ibid., 153.
95. I might add to my earlier citations the following from Jenson: "We are counterparts of God as we believe in the Resurrection, and so in the *homoousia* of Jesus and his Father" (*ST* 2:72). As with John Zizioulas and similar suggestions along these lines, the logic here leads to restrictive, if not dangerous, anthropological conclusions. We must distinguish between the realization of the *goal* of our humanity and the *fact* of being human.

this distinction holds that while the fall has made humanity captive to sin, it has nevertheless not eradicated the faculties or attributes that make us truly human. The Reformers indicated something similar in their distinction between "things heavenly" and "things earthly": before God, we have nothing to bring to the table, while before other human beings we may be regarded as virtuous, and so regard others. Conflation of these categories may be one reason why some critics of total depravity understandably recoil at the suggestion that human beings are utterly unworthy of praise in any sense. The kind of righteousness that was vitiated in the fall, then, is not civic righteousness—the remnants of that original righteousness that continue to make some semblance of justice possible even in a fallen world. Unbelievers as well as believers are able to hear that part of God's Word (i.e., command) as a compelling duty. It is the ground of human community—the law of love that we cannot eradicate, regardless of how hard we try to suppress and distort it in order to justify ourselves. Apart from that other part of God's Word (i.e., promise, specifically, the gospel), however, there can be no reply to that command that is directed first of all to God in faith as "Here I am." This is the "new heart" that not only the gentiles but the Israelites themselves needed if they were to respond faithfully to God's covenant commands and promises (Jer. 31:31–34).

Everyone has the *natural* ability to render God faithful obedience, but after the fall we are "sold into slavery under sin" (Rom. 7:14), our *moral* ability held captive not to a foreign army but to our own selfishness, idolatry, greed, and deceit. "There is no one who is righteous, not even one; there is no one who has understanding, there is no one who seeks God" (Rom. 3:10–11). This is not simply hyperbole: even when we pretend to seek God, we are running from the God who is actually there. If the self-help sections of the average bookstore are any indication, we are, like Paul's Athenian audience, "very religious in every way" (Acts 17:22). But God is not worshiped; he is used. "Spirituality" no less than atheism suppresses the specificity of the God revealed in Scripture.

That we are still God's image-bearers and consequently possess all of the requisite *natural* ability for relating to God and others in covenant faithfulness, and that this is even realized in our sense of duty to the rule of law, renders us culpable (Rom. 1:18–2:16). The fault lies not in that we *cannot* but that we *will not* turn from our sin to the living God (John 8:44). Captive to sin, "in Adam," we are nevertheless willing accomplices to our own imprisonment (Rom. 5:12). Only when God seizes us and ends our captivity are we truly free to be the human beings that we are (John 8:36).

Finally, the story of the fall concludes with a stay of execution. On the heels of the announcement that the woman's seed will triumph over the serpent is the surprising event of God's grace. It is the beginning of the covenant of grace: "And the LORD God made garments of skins for the man and for his wife, and clothed them" (Gen. 3:21). Reading the Bible canonically, we cannot help but see in this gracious dispensation glimpses of "the Lamb of God who takes away the sin of the world" (John 1:29). The scene does not end there, however. Nor does the great trial of the covenant.

But for now in the story, we pick up with humanity barred from paradise, tilling the soil "east of Eden." Already in the following chapter we are introduced to Cain's fratricide of Abel over the former's jealousy that his brother's animal sacrifice was accepted by God, while "for Cain and his offering he had no regard" (Gen. 4:5). As a prelude to this story, Eve announces with Cain's birth, "I have produced a/the man with the help of the LORD" (v. 1). The lack of a definite article in the ancient text makes interpretation difficult; we are especially dependent on the context. While "a man" is certainly possible, it would make more sense in the light of the unfolding narrative to see Eve as exclaiming that she had brought forth the offspring who had been promised to her—the one who would crush the serpent's head and lift the bondage of the curse. She could not have known then that far from being the "messiah," her firstborn son would be recorded as the Bible's first murderer. Yet even after the crime, God protects Cain and allows him to build a city and to produce descendants who eventually distinguish themselves as leaders in various cultural endeavors. Just at the point where this genealogy of Cain and the erection of his proud city are recounted (vv. 17–24), we read, by contrast, that another child was born to Adam and Eve. Eve "named him Seth [meaning 'appoint'], for she said, 'God has appointed for me another child instead of Abel, because Cain killed him.' To Seth also a son was born, and he named him Enosh. At that time people began to invoke the name of the LORD" (vv. 25–26). From this point on, two cities rise in history: the one identified by violence, oppression, injustice, sin, and pride—as well as, let it be noted, cultural and technological advance; the other identified by that last sentence announcing Enosh's birth: "At that time people began to invoke the name of the LORD." The obvious covenant language of invoking the name—and not just any name, but *the* name—is striking.

The ensuing biblical narrative does not attempt to produce either a comprehensive chronology or a genealogy but rather hits the highlights of redemptive history between Adam and Abraham. Noah is represented as a descendant of Seth, and his family too branches out into various nations that will figure prominently in Israel's history. At least one of the points in the narrative is that the promise is always threatened, always hanging by a thread. Disobedience marks the human race at every turn, and just when it seems that there is no one left who will be God's faithful covenant servant, God's grace prevails and a new candidate appears. Intermarriage between the two "cities" threatens to weaken the line of covenant succession to the vanishing point, and the people of Babel, the successor to Cain's proud city, raise a tower "reaching to the heavens" in order to establish a name for themselves in history by consolidating a centralized empire in the region. While, as we have noticed in relation to Cain, God's common grace has made the building of the secular city possible, such a proud and concentrated effort of human self-assertion had to be resisted; and while they were building a tower to the heavens, the Spirit of God descended to scatter the people and confuse their languages. We too have seen in our recent history that the greatest atrocities are committed in the name of totalizing ideologies in the service of a grand, ostensibly humanitarian scheme. By decentralizing the power, wealth, population, and technology through linguistic differentiation, instead of destroying the city, God restrained the devastating potential of evil.

All of this is meant to introduce us to the line of Noah, Shem, and Terah, father of Abram.

"ISRAEL, MY BELOVED"

So decisive is the call of Abram in Genesis 12 that it initiates the history of Israel and renders all that has preceded it a mere prologue to that story. Bavinck goes so far as to conclude that special revelation begins with the call of Abram.[96] All of this antedates its inscription, of course, which modern scholarship is finally beginning to allow.

> The narrative of creation and the deluge, monotheism and the worship of Jehovah, the laws and ceremonies of the cultus, the reminiscences of paradise and the expectations of the future, the idea of the Messiah and the Servant of Jehovah, and all the eschatological conceptions, are much older than the literary documents wherein they are mentioned. Babel does not lie behind the Bible, but behind the Scriptures lies the revelation which begins with the origin of the human race, continues in the tribes of the Sethites and Semites, and then flows on in the channel of the Israelitish covenant towards the fullness of time.[97]

The prophets, psalmists, Jesus, and the apostles

> all teach us unanimously and clearly that the content of the divine revelation does not consist primarily in the unity of God, in the moral law, in circumcision, in the Sabbath, in short, in the law, but appears primarily and principally in the promise, in the covenant of grace, and in the gospel. Not law, but gospel, is in the Old and the New Testament alike the core of the divine revelation, the essence of religion, the sum total of the Holy Scriptures. Every other view fails to do justice to special revelation, effaces its difference from general revelation, degrades the Old Testament, rends apart the two economies of the same covenant of grace, and even gradually changes the gospel of the New Covenant into a law, and makes of Christ a second Moses. . . . The law thus is temporal, transitory, a means in the service of the promise, but the promise is eternal; it had its beginning in paradise, was preserved and developed by revelation in the days of the Old Covenant, received its fulfillment in Christ, and is now extended to the whole human race and all the peoples.[98]

This evangelical, promissory revelation is not a matter of course; it is not present in nature or creation, in reason or conscience. "But it is an historical product; the initiative came from God; he so reveals himself as, by the act of revelation,

---

96. Herman Bavinck, *The Philosophy of Revelation* (1909; repr., Grand Rapids: Baker, 1979), 188.
97. Ibid., 191.
98. Ibid., 192–93.

to receive a particular person and people into communion with himself."[99] The law was never confused with the promise nor did it replace it. God's covenant with Abraham was a gracious promise, so that even the moral law that attended it "was not a law of the covenant of works, but a law of the covenant of grace, a law of the covenant, a law of gratitude."[100] Jewish scholar Jon Levenson rightly sees the theme of the sacrifice of the firstborn as the heart of the biblical message: "The story of the humiliation and exaltation of the beloved son reverberates throughout the Bible because it is the story of the people about whom and to whom it is told. It is the story of Israel the beloved son, the first-born of God."[101]

As I pointed out in the introduction, two different types of covenants form distinct riverbeds cutting synchronically through the same biblical history: a purely promissory oath on God's part and a conditional suzerainty-vassal relationship on the other. As the story of Israel unfolds, it becomes increasingly clear (especially from the New Testament looking back) that this distinction can be generally applied to the Abrahamic and Mosaic (or Sinaitic) covenants, respectively. It is the inheritance of sons (in the ancient world, of course, the only real inheritance) that the Abrahamic covenant promises, while in the Sinaitic covenant Israel promises to be a loyal servant in God's land. The dialectic between law and gospel is never separated or confused in the biblical traditions. "Thus, when Luther spoke of the law both as a *lex implenda* and *lex impleta*," notes Childs, "he was not reflecting an allegedly 'tortured subjectivity,' but seeking to deal critically with the biblical material both exegetically and theologically."[102]

It is through Sarah's barren womb that an heir will come who will connect the universal solution to sin (Eve's seed) and Israel's particular solution to exile. The themes of son and servant, together with other metaphors (bride, city, hill), become interwoven in this narrative history. Like the Abrahamic covenant, the Davidic covenant is an unconditional adoption. He is promised that despite his own sins and those of his house, "your kingdom shall be made sure forever before me; your throne shall be established forever" (2 Sam. 7:11–17).

While the promissory oath runs from Adam and Eve (Gen. 3:15) through Seth and Noah to Abraham and Sarah (Genesis 12–17) and then to David and his everlasting dynasty (2 Samuel 7), the Sinai covenant, as we have seen in chapter one, is in a rather different form. It is a suzerainty treaty in which the people promise fealty to the Great King, and YHWH in turn imposes stipulations and sanctions. The Israelites are the subject of both covenants, but they are distinct arrangements and they should not be interpreted as simply representing two different emphases—law and grace—in a single covenant.

---

99. Ibid.
100. Ibid., 197.
101. Cited by William C. Placher, "Rethinking Atonement," *Interpretation* 53, no. 1 (1999), 11, from Jon Levenson, *The Death and Resurrection of the Beloved Son: The Transformation of Child Sacrifice in Judaism and Christianity* (New Haven, CT: Yale University Press, 1993), 67.
102. Childs, *Biblical Theology*, 533.

From Sinai on, Israel inherits the land by promise but remains in the land by obedience. In this respect, I can heartily concur with the thesis of E. P. Sanders regarding "covenantal nomism," just so long as we distinguish (as he does not) between the different types of covenant that we meet with in Israel's history, identified by Abraham and Sinai. The latter is anything but an unconditional oath (e.g., Deut. 7:12–14).

The language unmistakably echoes the creation narratives. Just as Israel has been brought out of the "darkness and void" of Egyptian bondage, so now Israel is to occupy the land as a new Adam under probation in anticipation of consummation. Israel's history is a trial within the larger trial of humanity. This specific aspect of Israel's covenant with God—the Sinaitic dimension—is a recapitulation of the original covenant with humanity in Adam. Israel interprets world history in the light of their own history because their covenant Lord is none other than the Alpha-Creator and Omega-Consummator of the whole created order. And, like Adam, Israel knows that their tenure in the land depends on their fidelity to the covenant. The passage just cited from Deuteronomy, and many others like it, draw on creation language to make this identification with the creation story. On this side of the curse—and in Israel's case, exile—there is flourishing: "Be fruitful and multiply." On the other side are closed wombs, fallow fields with thorns, famine, and death.

I must repeat the refrain that "eschatology antedates redemption."[103] In other words, creation was only the beginning for Adam and Eve. Called to imitate their creator and covenant Lord's pattern of working and resting, they were to enter in to God's everlasting rest according to the covenant of creation. "That door, however, was never opened," notes Kline.

> It was not the Fall in itself that delayed the consummation. According to the conditions of the covenant of creation the prospective consummation was either/or. It was either eternal glory by covenantal confirmation of original righteousness or eternal perdition by covenant-breaking repudiation of it. The Fall, therefore, might have been followed at once by a consummation of the curse of the covenant. The delay was due rather to the principle and purpose of divine compassion by which a new way of arriving at the consummation was introduced, the way of redemptive covenant with common grace as its historical corollary.[104]

Common grace opens up space for a delay of the consummation, in order to reverse the destiny of those thus fallen. "Consummation" after the fall would have proved the ultimate tragedy. The divine delay allows history to continue moving toward the consummation in God's eternal Sabbath as the fruit of God's own redemptive activity. And because of this stay of execution, there still remains the promise of entering his rest (Heb. 4:1).

103. Meredith Kline, *Structure of Biblical Authority*, 2nd ed. (Eugene, OR: Wipf and Stock, 1997), 155.
104. Ibid.

Throughout Israel's history, then, the themes of sonship and servant, Abrahamic promise (a messianic seed who will bring blessing to the nations) and Sinaitic compact ("We will do all these things!") appear side by side. Even in times of Israel's unfaithfulness to their oath at Sinai, YHWH suspends judgment "for the sake of the promise I made to Abraham, Isaac, and Jacob." It is this promissory oath that keeps Israel's history alive, moving toward its fulfillment. Without the Abrahamic covenant, Israel's hopes would have been aborted time and time again and would eventually have become altogether moribund.[105]

The eventual exile of Israel, however, also tragically echoes the fall of Adam. Psalm 78 recounts the whole history in terms of God's steadfast loyalty even in the face of Israel's persistent breaches of the covenant and their ingratitude. Beginning with God's liberating action, the psalmist then interjects, "They did not keep God's covenant, but refused to walk according to his law. They forgot what he had done, and the miracles that he had shown them" (vv. 10–11). Repeatedly in this psalm we read that God put Israel on trial, and they not only failed but instead put *God* to the test (vv. 18, 41, 56). Here the language of probation and trial echoes the original covenant with humanity in Adam. "How often they rebelled against him in the wilderness and grieved him in the desert!" (v. 40), and yet God continued to preserve Israel "for the sake of the promise to Abraham, Isaac, and Jacob." Israel's only hope appears to be the Davidic promise that ends the psalm:

> [God] rejected the tent of Joseph, he did not choose the tribe of Ephraim; but he chose the tribe of Judah, Mount Zion, which he loves. He built his sanctuary like the high heavens, like the earth, which he has founded forever. He chose his servant David, and took him from the sheepfolds; from tending the nursing ewes he brought him to be the shepherd of his people Jacob, of Israel, his inheritance. (vv. 67–71)

As Adam had been cast out of the garden, Israel was exiled by none other than YHWH himself, the suzerain whose treaty had been reduced to shattered tablets by his covenant partner. "Like Adam, they broke my covenant" (Hos. 6:7). Before and after the exile, the prophets take their place as prosecutors of the covenant lawsuit. YHWH announces to Jeremiah that he will "give this city [Jerusalem] into the hand of the king of Babylon, and he shall burn it with fire" (Jer. 34:2). While God had commanded the jubilees, liberating slaves and "proclaiming liberty to one another," Judah had come to ignore this stipulation and perpetuated slavery.

> Therefore, thus says the LORD: You have not obeyed me by granting a release to your neighbors and friends; I am going to grant a release to you, says the LORD—a release to the sword, to pestilence, and to famine. I will make you a horror to all the kingdoms of the earth. And those who transgressed my covenant and did not keep the terms of the covenant that they made before

---

105. Walther Eichrodt, *Theology of the Old Testament*, trans. J. A. Baker, 2 vols., Old Testament Library (Philadelphia: Westminster Press, 1961–67), 1:26–27.

me, I will make like the calf when they cut it in two and passed between its parts. (vv. 15–18)

We have seen this "cutting" ritual before, in Abram's vision (Genesis 15), but there God alone walks through the pieces, assuming upon his own head the curse-sanctions. Now, however, the Sinaitic covenant is in play with respect to the national status of Israel and the perpetuity of the theocracy. The nation will now have to bear the judgment by walking through the pieces: the ritual cutting now being invoked and executed in the form of Jerusalem's destruction and the exile of the inhabitants into slavery. When King Zedekiah of Judah inquired of Jeremiah whether he had received any word from the Lord, the prophet replied, "You shall be handed over to the king of Babylon" (Jer. 37:17). Further testimony to Israel's own realization that they had become the faithless servant of the covenant may be found in the Second Temple literature (e.g., Wis. 6:3–7). It is perhaps one of the few assumptions shared by such diverse Second Temple "revival" traditions as the Pharisees and the Qumran community. However, for them the new thing that God was about to do was basically a revival of the old covenant theocracy.

Yet, according to the Hebrew prophets themselves, the hope of entering God's Sabbath rest remains only on the basis of the Abrahamic promise rather than the Sinaitic covenant. This is the good news that survives amid the tragic circumstances about to be inflicted, and it is wholly rooted in the Abrahamic-Davidic promise (Jer. 33:14–22). It is an unconditional oath, a covenant that cannot be broken. "The word of the LORD came to Jeremiah: Thus says the LORD: If any of you could break my covenant with the day and my covenant with the night, so that day and night would not come at their appointed time, only then could my covenant with my servant David be broken." Notice especially the echo of the Abrahamic covenant in the last verse: while the Israelites will say that God has rejected his people, YHWH promises yet again, "Only if I had not established my covenant with day and night and the ordinances of heaven and earth, would I reject the offspring of Jacob and of my servant David and not choose any of his descendants as rulers over the offspring of Abraham, Isaac, and Jacob. For I will restore their fortunes, and will have mercy upon them" (vv. 25–26). As Adam and Eve heard after their rebellion, so too Israel heard: the covenant of law having been broken, God nevertheless has provided another way of entrance into his Sabbath rest through his own unconditional promise to unilaterally bring about redemption and restoration.

Jeremiah 31 is particularly explicit in founding God's promised future for his people on the Abrahamic-Davidic promise. The new covenant

will not be like the covenant that I made with their ancestors when I took them by the hand to bring them out of the land of Egypt—a covenant that they broke, though I was their husband, says the LORD. But this is the covenant that I will make with the house of Israel after those days, says the LORD: I will put my law within them, and I will write it on their hearts; and I will be their God, and they shall be my people. No longer shall they teach one another, or say to each other, "Know the LORD," for they shall all know me, from the least of them to the greatest, says the LORD; for I will forgive their iniquity, and remember their sin no more. (vv. 31–34)

The unconditional note ("I will . . . I will . . . I will"; "They shall be my people and I shall be their God") is striking, especially in light of the contrast that is explicitly made: "It will not be like the covenant that I made with their ancestors" at Sinai. Furthermore, it is not just restoration to a former condition that is promised, but a greater future and a wider hope, with Jerusalem rebuilt and enlarged (vv. 38–40). It will not be paradise regained, but the consummation that had been forfeited by Adam's and Israel's disobedience.

Isaiah 59 offers a particularly vivid courtroom scene. Although Israel has put God in the dock for failing to keep his promises, the prophet in his role as prosecuting attorney reverses the charges: "See, the LORD's hand is not too short to save, nor his ear too dull to hear" (v. 1). These are, after all, the usual charges brought by Israel and the nations against YHWH: either he is unable (his arm too short to save) or unwilling (his ears too plugged to hear) to do so. One must choose between God's sovereignty and goodness in developing an adequate theodicy. But in this trial, the tables are turned. "Rather, your iniquities have been barriers between you and your God, and your sins have hidden his face from you so that he does no hear" (v. 2). There follows the evidence: hands stained with blood, lying lips and perverse tongues, injustice, disregard for the law, and dishonesty. Even though the people try to cover themselves with cobwebs (notice the echo of Adam and Eve covering themselves), "they cannot cover themselves with what they make. Their works are works of iniquity" (v. 6)—a point also made in 64:6: "We have all become like one who is unclean, and all our righteous deeds are like a filthy cloth." After the prosecutor recounts Israel's transgressions before the bar, the accused are taken aback, acknowledging in an impassioned confession speech that they rather than YHWH have been the unfaithful party (59:9–13). This is why there is no righteousness, justice, and truth, they conclude: because *we* are unrighteous, unjust, and untruthful. But just as in the case with Adam and Eve, Israel's sin is not the last word. "The LORD saw it, and it displeased him that there was no justice. He saw that there was no one, and was appalled that there was no one to intervene; so his own arm brought him victory, and his righteousness upheld him" (vv. 15b–16). The judge becomes a warrior, donning "righteousness like a breastplate, and a helmet of salvation on his head," wrapping himself in a cloak of vengeance for the wicked but in mercy for his people.

And he will come to Zion as Redeemer, to those in Jacob who turn from transgression, says the LORD. And as for me, this is my covenant with them, says the LORD: my Spirit that is upon you, and my words that I have put in your mouth, shall not depart out of your mouth, or out of the mouths of your children, or out of the mouths of your children's children, says the LORD, from now on and forever. (vv. 17–21)

The enlargement of Jerusalem is anticipated elsewhere, some texts even recasting the traditional roles of the oppressor (Egypt and Assyria) as the oppressed who are delivered from bondage and taken as God's own people (Isa. 19:18–25). Isaiah 60 sets before us the vision of ships from all over the world entering Israel's harbor, laden not this time with implements of war but with rich treasures. "Nations shall come to your light, and kings to the brightness of your dawn" (v. 3). A royal procession of the nations and their kings, into gates that never close (v. 11), echoes the Sabbath enthronement of God in the beginning, with the parade of the creature-kings before the Lord in the day-frames of Genesis 1 and 2. Neither Adam nor Israel fulfilled this commission, but in the future YHWH himself will bring it about. One will come who will be both faithful Lord *and* servant of the covenant. God will bare his arm before all the nations and vindicate both himself and his people in the cosmic trial.

PART THREE
LORD AND SERVANT

Chapter Six

The Lord as Servant

So far we have seen that the story of Israel, like Hamlet's play-within-a-play, is the *petit récit* through which the larger narrative of humanity and the two covenants (creation and grace) is recapitulated. Like Adam, Israel was commissioned as the *imago Dei* in the world, the locus of God's communion and action. "But like Adam they transgressed the covenant" (Hos. 6:7). Just as the apostle Paul tells the story of Israel's condemnation within the larger plot of the human fall and curse, Isaiah 24 prophesies judgment on the whole earth. Here, not only has Israel sinned like Adam, but the judgment upon Israel in the form of devastation and the Babylonian captivity is described in the very language of a Paradise lost, a garden devoured by a curse. And this judgment in Eden and now in Israel is going to be extended to the whole earth. The trial will be brought to all people. Not only Israel, but "The earth lies polluted under its inhabitants; for they have transgressed the laws, violated the statutes, broken the everlasting covenant. Therefore a curse devours the earth, and its inhabitants suffer for their guilt" (Isa. 24:5–6). Israel and the gentiles are treated here, as in Romans 1 and 2, as united in the judgment for having transgressed God's law, the original covenant between God and humankind. Israel too had become a false witness and representative in this cosmic trial, yet for the sake of God's promise to Abraham, Isaac, and Jacob, also a republication of the covenant of grace announced to Adam, salvation will come to and from the Jews through the Abrahamic "seed." There is at last an Adam/Israel who is "the true and faithful witness" (Rev. 1:5). The theme of exile and restoration provides a common link for the world more generally in Adam, for Israel in the land, and for the cross and resurrection of Christ. This chapter marks the transition from the Lord (theology proper) and the Servant (anthropology) to christology (Lord and Servant). However, I will omit the biblical-theological development of the christological theme and move directly to the systematic-theological treatment, since the former is developed in relation to the work of Christ in the final two chapters.

THE TWO NATURES, OR WHAT HAS ANTIOCH TO DO WITH ALEXANDRIA?

Jesus as God and human is not simply the central affirmation of christology, but of covenant theology more generally: only YHWH can save, yet the covenant of our creation must be fulfilled. According to the covenantal model that we have been following, we cannot choose between a christology from above or from below. Martin Hengel reminds us, "This is a false alternative that goes against the course of New Testament christology, which developed in an indissoluble dialectic between God's saving activity and man's answering."[1] Christ is both the Lord of the covenant and its servant. Furthermore, as Moltmann writes, "The christology of Christ's single person in two natures is the condition which makes it possible to substantiate theologically the redemption of humanity through him. The fundamental concept here is the concept of incarnation."[2] It is in his relationship to others, especially the poor, the sick, women, and Israel, that the story unfolds. "If Jesus died as a private person, the significance of his death for salvation can only be ascribed to it subsequently. But he died as the brother of God-forsaken sinners, as head of the community of his followers, and as the Wisdom of the cosmos."[3] This returns us once again to the theme of covenant solidarity, which is nowhere disclosed as clearly—indeed, as the exclusive locus of *univocal* identity between the Creator and creation—as in the hypostatic union. Robert Jenson nicely captures the conclusion that the biblical narrative thus entails: "What Christology is—or ought to be—about is the Jesus who appears in the Gospels, as he is in fact the Son of God he was accused of claiming to be."[4]

An even-hundred survey of church history displays a remarkable consensus, not to be discounted, embodied in the churches of the Nicene and Chalcedonian confession. At the same time, as with the Trinitarian dogma, christological formulations of the ecumenical consensus are varied. Just as it has become fashion-

---

1. Martin Hengel, *The Cross of the Son of God*, trans. John Bowden (London: SCM, 1997), 89.
2. Moltmann, *Trinity and the Kingdom*, 50.
3. Ibid.
4. Jenson, *ST* 1:134.

able to overgeneralize differences in the formulation of the Trinity into "East" versus "West," the christological corollary is "Antioch" versus "Alexandria." According at least to the typology, the former leans toward the humanity of Christ and a distinction between the two natures, while Alexandrian christology tilts toward the divinization of Jesus. Not surprisingly, Nestorianism (the separation of the natures) arose in Antioch, while Eutychianism or Monophysitism (the confusion of the two natures) arose in Alexandria.

The triumph of Chalcedon was to proscribe both heresies in the affirmation that Jesus is "one person in two natures," the two natures being incapable of either separation or confusion.[5] Christology, particularly the charges of Nestorianism ("Antioch") and Eutychianism ("Alexandria"), was really the heart of the Lutheran-Reformed eucharistic debates. My purpose here is not to attempt to resolve those disputes, but to use them as an entry point for applying the exegetical treatment above to systematic-theological concerns. Leaving to my third volume the thesis that Zwinglianism rather than Calvinism and the confessional Reformed position reflects a Nestorian temptation, my purpose here is to point up the problem of failing to adequately distinguish the two natures, which often leaves the humanity of Christ underappreciated.

Platonic habits of thought are difficult to break, not only in Augustine and the Western tradition but also in Eastern christological reflection. As Hans Urs von Balthasar has observed, the corporeal reality of Christ's humanity is not, in Platonic fashion, a stepping stone to the incorporeal deity.[6] Once more we must recognize how important it is to go beyond the Logos christology of Justin Martyr, Origen, and even Augustine. It is especially when we recognize the covenantal context of christological development in Scripture that the unity of person and work and thus the salvific efficacy of Christ's humanity as well as his deity obtain an even clearer rationale. This will be a large part of the burden of this chapter to demonstrate.

Scripture everywhere treats the Word of God as active, bringing about its intended effects. As an illocutionary speech-act, the Logos is not only an externalization of divine thoughts but the incarnation of God's command and promise. "For in him every one of God's promises is a 'Yes.' For this reason it is through him that we say the 'Amen,' to the glory of God" (2 Cor. 1:20). In other words, it is because of the incarnation that we can join the rest of creation that

---

5. The Definition of Chalcedon, in John H. Leith, ed., *Creeds of the Churches: A Reader in Christian Doctrine from the Bible to the Present*, 3rd ed. (Atlanta: John Knox Press, 1982), 35–36: "[We also teach] that we apprehend [*gnōridzomenon*] this one and only Christ—Son, Lord, only-begotten—in two natures [*dyo physesin*]; [and we do this] without confusing the two natures [*asynchytōs*], without transmuting one nature into the other [*atreptōs*], without dividing them into two separate categories [*adiairetōs*], without contrasting them according to area or function [*achōristōs*]. The distinctiveness of each nature is not nullified by the union. Instead, the 'properties' [*idiotētos*] of each nature are conserved and both natures concur [*syntrechousēs*] in one 'person' [*prosōpon*] and in one *hypostasis*."

6. Hans Urs von Balthasar, *The Glory of the Lord: A Theological Aesthetics*, vol. 1: *Seeing the Form*, trans. Erasmo Leiva-Merikakis (San Francisco: Ignatius, 1982), 313.

we have led into bondage in answering back the creative, "Let it be!" with the covenantal response, "Here I am." The incarnation is thus understood as bringing about the proper covenantal conversation: the Lord speaking, and the servant answering back to God's glory. Christ both *says our* yes as our covenantal head in his active obedience, and *is God's* yes in embodied form. Affirming the distinct yet inseparable two natures of Christ is the basis for such an analysis.

In the sixteenth-century debates, Zwingli distinguished the humanity and deity of Christ to the point of practically reducing the former to an appendage. Any act of the human Jesus can only be regarded as salvific by virtue of the deity of the Logos; the Platonic antithesis of spirit and matter, the soul or intellect and the body, inner and outer, find an unmistakable echo in Zwingli's theology.[7] In modern theology Barth seems to have picked up on the weaknesses of this heritage, even to the point of carrying Augustine's (Neoplatonic) lack of interest in history still further in the particular way that he denied the historicity of the fall, faulted federal theology for its emphasis on successive historical covenants, and identified revelation proper exclusively with the deity of Christ.[8]

Closely connected to the *Logos asarkos* question (i.e., the existence of the Son before his incarnation) is the so-called *extracalvinisticum*, which stipulates that the finite cannot contain the infinite (*finitum non capax infiniti*). We are still very clearly within the ambit of the Lutheran-Reformed christological debates. The Reformed never interpreted the *non capax* to mean that the infinite could not be truly united to the finite, but only that the attributes of divine infinitude and of human finitude could not be "comingled or confused." For example, to the question, "If his humanity is not present wherever his divinity is, then are not the two natures of Christ separated from each other?" the Heidelberg Catechism responds, "Since divinity is not limited and is present everywhere, it is evident that Christ's divinity is surely beyond the bounds of the humanity he has assumed, but at the same time his divinity is in and remains personally united to his humanity."[9]

The *non capax* means for the Reformed not that the infinite cannot be united to the finite, but that it cannot be "comprehended"—that is, enclosed within the

---

7. Zwingli even displays some of these "Apollinarian" inclinations when he says under discussion of the sacraments, "We must note in passing that Christ is our salvation by virtue of that part of his nature by which he came down from heaven, not of that by which he was born of an immaculate Virgin, though he had to suffer and die by this part" (*Commentary on True and False Religion*, ed. Samuel Macauley Jackson and Clarence Nevin Heller [Durham, NC: Labyrinth, 1981], 204). W. P. Stephens concludes, "As the stress in Zwingli's theology as a whole is on God rather than on man, so the stress in his Christology is on Christ as God rather than on Christ as man" (*The Theology of Huldrych Zwingli* [Oxford: Clarendon, 1986], 111). It is no wonder that the christology and sacramentology of the Reformed confessions operate with significantly different categories than those employed by Zwingli. The extent to which Karl Barth is influenced more by Zwingli than by the subsequent Reformed tradition on this point is worth pondering.

8. For each of these claims, respectively, see Karl Barth, *Christ and Adam: Man and Humanity in Romans 5*, trans. T. A. Smail (New York: Harper & Bros., 1957), 36; idem, *Göttingen Dogmatics* (27.III; 24.IV); idem, *CD* I/1:165.

9. The Heidelberg Catechism, Lord's Day 18, Q. 48, in *Ecumenical Creeds and Reformed Confessions* (Grand Rapids: CRC Publications, 1988), 31. Cf. the Belgic Confession (1561), ibid., Articles 18 and 19.

finite without remainder. While Mary is rightly called *theotokos* (God-bearer), in view of the *person* whom she bore, this cannot mean that she is the origin of the Son's eternal deity. Even as he nursed at Mary's breast, the Son of God continued to fill the cosmos. The incarnation, in other words, brought about no change in the Logos; rather, the Logos assumed human nature: distinction without division. All of this is simply a repetition of the ecumenical consensus.

The problem is that, as I see it anyway, Barth is himself more Zwinglian than Calvinist in his interpretation of the *non capax*, and in some critical passages (were it not for his equally strong affirmations of the identification of Jesus and God) exhibits the lingering threat of Nestorianism, all in an effort to defend the glory of God. But defend God from what? This is the critical question that not only the Lutheran *capax* but Calvin's (and the confessional Reformed) version of the *non capax* helps us answer in ways not afforded, it seems to me, by Barth on one side or some of his Lutheran students on the other. God is a good deal more "haveable," according to Calvin and classical Reformed theology, than one finds him in Zwingli and Barth. But the place where this haveability occurs is not abstractly in Christ, but rather concretely in Christ *as he is given in the covenant of grace*. We truly possess Christ and all his benefits in the form of the promise that is heard and embraced through Word and sacrament according to the work of the Spirit.

The Nestorian temptation surely represents a hybrid christology, refuted by Chalcedon's stipulation, "without division." However, Luther's tendency to collapse the humanity into the deity of Christ is in its own way just as problematic, in view of the stipulation "without confusion." Although Luther's *communicatio idiomatum* spoke of the divine and human attributes being communicated in both directions, Lutheran theology came eventually to stress the divinization of the human nature rather than vice versa. But this too can easily lose sight of the importance of Jesus' genuine humanity in his development, death, resurrection, and ascension. As Berkhof points out, this version of the *communicatio* is incoherent: picking and choosing which attributes can be communicated from the divine to the human nature (viz., operative) and those that cannot (viz., quiescent). But surely if the communication is as they define it, all attributes of both natures would be communicated to the other. In the Lutheran view, the human nature is made "receptive for the inhabitation of the fullness of the Godhead and communicates to it some of the divine attributes," but this "virtually abrogates the human nature by assimilating it to the divine. Thus only the divine remains."[10]

Robert Jenson, however, does not seem to share Lutheran theology's reticence to embrace Monophysitism. Jenson offers a simultaneously learned and somewhat distorted account of the Nestorian-Monophysite controversy that led to the Chalcedonian definition.[11] To the Antiochenes, especially Theodore of Mopsuestia, Jenson attributes the doctrine of the two natures hypostatically united in

---

10. Louis Berkhof, *Systematic Theology*, 326.
11. Jenson, *ST* 1:125ff.

one person.[12] Even if he is not fair in his presentation of the Antiochene position, Jenson's own agenda is clear: the answer to Nestorianism is not Chalcedon, with its alleged capitulation to Antioch and Leo's Tome, but Cyril of Alexandria and Maximus the Confessor, both of whom become virtual Monophysites in Jenson's version of the story. In other words, the answer to the question, "How could the impassible suffer?" is best answered by divinizing the humanity.[13]

Jenson is unhappy with this compromise of what he regards as a robust Cyrillian christology, preferring "*from* two natures" to "*in* two natures."[14] While "Chalcedon accomplished much," it sacrificed logical coherence, not to mention Cyril's alleged rejection of a two-natures christology.[15] Those closest to Cyril's formulations became known as "Monophysites" and therefore separated from the imperial church, while those followers of Cyril remaining followed "an interpretation of Chalcedon that made it say what, in their view, it should have said." Meanwhile, the West's reading of Chalcedon has simply been a tragic reiteration of Leo's Tome.[16] Prejudicing the Monophysite cause, Jenson interprets Cyril of Alexandria as arguing for the Logos having been incarnated *from* rather than (as in Leo's Tome) *in* two natures.[17]

However, even some of the texts of Cyril and Maximus to which he appeals preserve the very distinction that troubles Jenson about the traditional Western (even Chalcedonian) position.[18] Jenson appears to announce a via media between the Alexandrians and Antiochenes, but only at the expense of making Cyril at least implicitly Monophysite, Leo (and the West) implicitly Nestorian, and the Chalcedonian creed confused on the subject.[19] Whatever the age-old suspicions between Lutheran and Reformed traditions, Jenson seems to move well beyond the consensus not only of Chalcedon but of Concord in a Hegelian absorption of distinction into sameness. Well beyond Cyril, Jenson's christology represents the deification of the human Jesus, locating that deification furthermore in his resurrection rather than in his incarnation. Ranging still further beyond the ecumenical consensus, Jenson rejects the *Logos asarkos* (the preincarnate Son), arguing that the Logos precedes his incarnation only by narrative anticipation (as a central character in a novel is anticipated before his or her actual arrival), rather than ontologically.[20] There is therefore no "unincarnate *Logos* lurking somehow before or behind or beyond Jesus the Son."[21] The consequence of his series of

12. Ibid., 127ff.
13. Ibid., 131.
14. Ibid., 132.
15. Ibid., 133.
16. Ibid.
17. Ibid., 128–29.
18. For example, he cites Cyril's letter to Nestorius, insisting that one "must even confess 'the death according to the flesh of the only-begotten Son of God,'" but "according to the flesh" is exactly the qualifier. "When he was formulating his own conceptual taste, Cyril's slogan for all this was that we are to confess 'one nature, of God the Logos, that has been enfleshed'" (ibid., 129).
19. Ibid., 132–33.
20. Ibid., 70–71, 139–43, 170.
21. Ibid., 142.

arguments is simultaneously to lose Jesus' humanity in his deity (a hyper-Alexandrian move) *and* the preincarnate Word in the temporal event of his resurrection. But, as Gunton points out in relation to Jenson's thesis, the *Logos asarkos* is Athanasian, not just Calvinist.[22] And the *extra calvinisticum* is simply Chalcedonian. Calvin writes, "Here is something marvelous: the Son of God descended from heaven in such a way that, without leaving heaven, he willed to be borne in the virgin's womb, to go about the earth, and to hang upon the cross; yet he continuously filled the world even as he had done from the beginning!"[23] George Hunsinger challenges Jenson on almost every point of this thesis, observing the odd convergence of seemingly antithetical transgressions of the ecumenical consensus.[24] "His view of the cross tends toward Socinus, of the incarnation toward Arius, and of the trinity toward Hegel in ways that seem subordinationist and tritheistic. One possible reason for this outcome is a rationalistic mindset that displays a low tolerance for paradox in dogmatic theology."[25] In addition, "For Jenson, the finite is not only capable of the infinite; in a certain sense, it is the infinite. The temporal is not only capable of the eternal; in a certain sense, it is the eternal. Given the metaphysical framework that thereby results, Jenson's understanding of Christ's person is so close to that rejected by the Council of Nicaea that it may fairly be called, if not 'Arian,' then certainly at least 'neo-Arian.'"[26]

But I would argue that Jenson's defense of such contradictory and rival christological errors is due not only to an impatience with paradox but to the Monophysite tendency itself. As we have seen, although in the official Lutheran position the *communicatio* moves in only one direction (divine attributes communicated to the humanity), nineteenth-century Lutheran (and some Reformed) christologies opened up the traffic in both directions. Hyper-Antiochene (semi-Arian) and hyper-Alexandrian (semi-Docetic) christologies can easily converge, particularly with the assistance of Hegelian sublation, in a Monophysitism that reduces the finite to the infinite and the infinite to the finite *simultaneously*.

Of great profit in Jenson's defense of a nearly Monophysite christology is that we do not have to wonder whether there is a *Logos* lurking behind the carpenter's son, Jesus, who might be someone other than Jesus. But the version of the *non capax* that the Reformed scholastics settled on makes this same point without surrendering the two natures or the *Logos asarkos*. Their version was essentially Chalcedon's: that which can be said, properly speaking, concerning either the deity or humanity of Christ can be attributed to the whole person. Thus Scripture speaks of *God* purchasing the church with *his own blood* (Acts 20:28). Conversely, "the

22. Colin Gunton, "Creation and Mediation" in *Time, Trinity, and Church*, ed. Gunton (Grand Rapids: Eerdmans, 2000), 83.

23. Calvin, *Institutes* 2.13.4.

24. George Hunsinger, "Robert Jenson's *Systematic Theology*: A Review Essay," *Scottish Journal of Theology* 55, no. 2 (2002): 168.

25. Ibid., abstract on 161.

26. Ibid., 170–71.

Son" does not know the schedule of his return in glory (Matt. 24:36). This is not a communication of attributes per se, but a predication of attributes proper to either nature as predicates concerning the one person. Only by properly distinguishing without separating the two natures are we able to avoid both the Nestorian and the Monophysite ways of getting around the significance of the humanity as well as the deity of Christ.

Ironically, these positions that seem so diametrically opposed (echoing the Antiochene/Alexandrian disputes) share a foundational agreement: the humanity of Christ as such is of less salvific significance than his deity. There is no discernible contrast between the Greek and Latin consensus on this point. According to John of Damascus, for example, Jesus' miracles are due to his divinity, while "the willing and the saying, 'I will, be thou clean,' are the energy of His humanity."[27] "It was as man, then, that He wished the cup to pass from Him: but these are the words of natural timidity." But as for the words, "Not my will, but Thine be done," "Now these are the words of a brave heart."[28] While we may differ on the presuppositions behind what is attributed to the humanity and the deity distinctly, the *distinction* is not only well attested across the ecumenical spectrum; it is also crucial for the affirmation of the true humanity as well as deity of the incarnate Son.

My thesis here is that despite their different ways of articulating it, both Alexandrians and Antiochenes tend to lodge the salvific significance of Jesus in his deity: either a divinized humanity or a divine nature as opposed to a human nature. I am attempting here to think anthropology and christology together (dialectically), without collapsing one into the other.

Irenaeus spends much of his treatise against the gnostics defending the unity of the Creator and Redeemer as one and the same God: the God of law and grace, giver of the Mosaic order and the fulfiller of the Abrahamic promise in Christ. In his deeply incarnational theology, he speaks of "the Gospel of His humanity" as well as "the winged aspect of the Gospel"—that is, the deity of Christ.[29] In one passage, after having attacked the view that the Logos "passed through Mary just as water through a tube" (3.11.3), he observes that although Jesus could have created the wine at Cana or the bread in John 6 ex nihilo, he wanted to show "that the God who made the earth and commanded it to bring forth fruit, who established the waters and brought forth the fountains, was He who, in these last times bestowed on mankind, by His Son, the blessing of food and the favour of drink: the Incomprehensible by means of the comprehensible, and the Invisible by the visible; since there is none beyond Him, but He exists in the bosom of the Father."[30] It is worth observing that Calvin used some of Irenaeus's arguments when he ran up against a similar Docetism of certain Anabaptists (especially

---

27. John of Damascus, "Exact Exposition," 61.
28. Ibid., 67.
29. Irenaeus, "Against Heresies" in *The Ante-Nicene Fathers*, vol. 1, op. cit., 3.11.8, 428.
30. Ibid., 3.11.3, 427.

Menno Simons).[31] God works through nature, not against it. God does not circumvent, overwhelm, or "saturate" the natural conditions of his revelation, but accommodates himself to our capacity. In this approach, then, the humanity of Christ is as essential as the deity not only as a prerequisite for, or visible manifestation of, but as the very locus of our redemption.

While denying Docetism, Apollinarius nevertheless represents this tendency. To be sure, the Logos became incarnate to some extent, but the Logos replaced the human soul of Jesus. Alan Spence contrasts the latent Apollinarian tendency in ancient and modern theology with the christology of John Owen, the seventeenth-century Oxford theologian whose work represents a distillation of the best of the Reformed scholastic consensus.[32] In ancient writers like Athanasius and modern ones like Barth, a formally rejected Apollinarianism nevertheless casts a certain spell, Spence argues. Athanasius, for example, spoke of the Son's embodiment even in somewhat Docetic terms in some places: "He was not bound to his body, but rather was himself wielding it."[33]

> The difficulty seems to lie in an inability to conceive of the incarnate Christ as "normative man." Although those who hold to his divine sonship are usually quick to affirm his true humanity, there has, nevertheless, been in the past an unwillingness to give due weight to the Gospel testimony to his growth in grace, wisdom and knowledge; to his continual need of divine comfort and empowering through the Holy Spirit; and consequently to the implication that as man he stood just as we do, a creature totally dependent on his God. . . . Other than in the actual assumption of human nature, is it proper to conceive of the Spirit, rather than the Word, as the divine agent acting directly on the humanity of Christ?

Owen thought so.[34] For writers such as Athanasius, the Logos becomes the "governing principle" of Christ, a relation "similar in some respects to that of the soul to the body," understood in a somewhat Platonic sense.[35] Thus the *real* person of Christ is the Logos. Apollinarius's answer was simple, Athanasius's more complex, but Owen emphasized the full human obedience of the incarnate Word.

---

31. *The Complete Writings of Menno Simons, 1496–1561*, ed. J. C. Wenger, trans. Leonard Verduin (Scottdale, PA: Herald, 1956). Menno Simons would not say that Jesus was conceived *of* but only "*in* the pure virgin" (428). "The Word became flesh (John 1:14). He does not say, The word too unto itself flesh" (431). Speaking of the "celestial flesh" of Christ, Simons writes, "He did not become flesh of Mary, but in Mary" (432). Part of this was due to Simons's adoption of the view that women were merely receptive and only men were active in procreation, to which Calvin replies, "Must we then say that women are nothing?" (*Institutes* 2.13.3). In fact, Calvin describes Simons's view as suggesting that the virgin was merely "a channel through which Christ flowed" (ibid.), a direct quote from Irenaeus.

32. Alan Spence, "Christ's Humanity and Ours: John Owen," in *Persons, Divine and Human*, ed. Christoph Schwöbel and Colin Gunton (Edinburgh: T & T Clark, 1991), 75–76.

33. Athanasius, "On the Incarnation of the Word," 45.

34. Spence, "Christ's Humanity and Ours," 75–76.

35. Ibid., 77–78. At the same time, as John of Damascus observed, "But the holy Athanasius in his discourse against Apollinarius says that He did actually feel fear" (*The Orthodox Faith*, 70).

Owen picked up on the better formula of Gregory of Nazianzus: "that which he has not assumed he has not healed." Yet "In the fourth century the emphasis on the Word's immediate or direct determination of the human life of Christ inclined naturally towards Apollinarianism," as in John of Damascus's *communicatio idiomatum*, in which the human will of Christ was "deified."[36] We may recall the quote from John of Damascus above, "His wonders were worked in His divine capacity, and His sufferings endured as man." "Almost without exception," says Spence, "the Fathers would not concede that Jesus grew in knowledge or needed to pray for himself."[37]

This tendency was bound to lead to the face-off between kenotic christologies and Apollinarian ones: "humanizing" God or "divinizing" humanity.[38] Leo's Tome marked an improvement: "For each nature retains its own distinctive character without loss; and as the form of God does not take away the form of a servant, so the form of a servant does not diminish the form of God," and "this in essence was the position maintained in the Definition of Chalcedon."[39] "In the seventeenth century John Owen reaffirmed the concept of Christ's human nature as 'autokineton,' that is as a self-determining spiritual principle, fully self-conscious and as a creature open and responsive to God, rather than as immediately or directly determined by the Son."[40] Christ's "dereliction," says Owen, "was possible, and proceeded from hence, in that all communications from the divine nature unto the human, beyond subsistence, were voluntary."[41] So Christ is the revelation and salvation of God in his humanity as fully as in his deity—and without the former being absorbed in the latter.

But Barth's doctrine of "self-revelation" "appears to undermine it radically." "The point at issue is whether Jesus Christ reveals God by his own divine nature or through his humanity as it is inspired by the Holy Spirit."[42] "But who can reveal God except God Himself?" asks Barth.[43] "The underlying concept is that revelation must be self-revelation and therefore only the divine nature can truly reveal God."[44] According to Owen, by contrast,

> The Lord Jesus Christ discharged his office and work of revealing the will of the Father in and by his human nature . . . for although the person of Christ, God and man, was our mediator . . . yet his human nature was that wherein he discharged the duties of his office and the "principium quod" of all his mediatory actings, 1 Tim 2.5.[45]

36. Spence, "Christ's Humanity and Ours," 79–80.
37. Ibid., 80.
38. Ibid., 81.
39. Cited ibid., 81–82.
40. Ibid., 82.
41. Cited ibid., 88, from John Owen, *An Exposition of the Epistle to the Hebrews*, vol. 2 (repr., Grand Rapids: Baker, 1980), 507.
42. Spence, "Christ's Humanity and Ours," 88–89.
43. Barth, *CD* I/1:406.
44. Spence, "Christ's Humanity and Ours," 89.
45. Cited ibid., 90, from *Hebrews* 3:30.

"In short," says Spence, "if we reject Apollinarianism there is no element of Christ's incarnate life which we can simply isolate as being that of God and not of man."[46] Barth asks, "Is the *humanitas Christi* as such the revelation? Does the divine sonship of Jesus Christ mean that God's revealing has now been transmitted as it were to the existence of the man Jesus of Nazareth, that this has thus become identical with it?"[47] No, says Barth, which "inevitably leads to the neglect of the historical life of Christ as the basis for our knowledge of God. Thus Barth argues . . . , 'We do not have the Word of God otherwise than in the mystery of its secularity. This means, however, that we have it in a form which as such is not the Word of God' . . . [I/1, 165]."[48] This means much for our own conformity to Christ.

> Our conformity is rather to Jesus Christ in the mundane experience of his historical existence, an existence marked by fears and trials, faith and hope, continually strengthened, comforted and inspired by the Spirit of God through suffering and temptation as he sought in loving obedience to accomplish the will of the Father. . . . Our destiny is not that we might be made divine but rather that we might at last become truly human.[49]

Spence has helpfully reminded us that the failure to distinguish sufficiently the two natures can lead to a *communicatio idiomatum* that loses either the divinity in the humanity or the humanity in the divinity. Either the Logos (or "God" generically) is absorbed into creatureliness (kenoticism) or vice versa (divinization). The former tendency we have seen in earlier kenotic christologies, but more radically today in kenotic doctrines of God (e.g., Moltmann). We could also appeal to further examples from Athanasius, although he was certainly not alone among both Eastern and Western writers. He interprets Ephesians 4:10 thus: "He descended in body, and He rose again because He was God Himself in the body. And this again is the reason why according to this meaning he brought in the conjunction 'Wherefore;' not as a reward of virtue nor of advancement, but to signify the cause why the resurrection took place. . . . He was highly exalted from earth, because He was God's Son in a body."[50] Whatever the different tendencies (separation or absorption), Zwingli and Athanasius end up at roughly the same place. Wherever Athanasius identifies Jesus as "He," the subject seems to be only the Logos. Ironically, Moltmann collapses Jesus into God just as thoroughly (even more so), yet redefines the nature of the God in view. This is also the criticism of Jenson by fellow Lutheran Gerhard Forde.[51]

---

46. Ibid., 91.
47. Cited ibid., from Barth, *CD* I/1:323.
48. Spence, "Christ's Humanity and Ours," 92; cf. Barth, *Christ and Adam*, especially 36.
49. Spence, "Christ's Humanity and Ours," 97.
50. Athanasius, "Four Discourses Against the Arians," *Nicene and Post-Nicene Fathers,* 2nd series, vol. 4: *Select Works and Letters,* ed. Philip Schaff and Henry Wace (Grand Rapids: Eerdmans, 1971), 332.
51. Gerhard O. Forde, "Robert Jenson's Soteriology," in *Trinity, Time, and Church,* ed. Gunton, 131.

With remarkable skill and nuance, Kathryn Tanner nevertheless basically affirms the Alexandrian emphases, even verging on an implicit Apollinarianism/Monophysitism. Clearly affirming and distinguishing Christ's divinity and humanity, she refuses either the kenotic christologies of Thomasius and especially other mid-nineteenth-century Lutherans and the historicizing (Hegelian) tendencies of Pannenberg, Moltmann, and Jüngel.[52] Yet, Tanner says that "the Word's assumption of [Jesus'] humanity is the immediate source of his whole human life."[53] But what about the Spirit? And what about his own faithful humanity as a true covenant partner? Is it just *God's* faithfulness acting in and through the humanity? Tanner speaks of Jesus as "the deified human." "Jesus is both the Word incarnate and deified or exalted humanity because these are just different descriptions of the same process from different points of view."[54] Although she warns against confusing the two natures, Tanner says that "the Word forms the character of Jesus' acts. . . . There are not two acts of will—a human will and the Word's direction of it—to be co-ordinated (or possibly fall out of sync), but one complex one—a human will shaped by the Word."[55] So the Logos is doing all of the work in the incarnation and life of Christ: this is why this human life is salvific. Again, I do not wish to take issue with the laudable defense of the deity of Christ as necessary for our salvation, but rather affirm the humanity as human (and not as deified or elevated humanity) as also salvific because in and through it the covenant of creation is fulfilled.

According to Tanner, the divinity is communicated to the humanity, but not vice versa (which is a traditional Lutheran approach to the *communicatio idiomatum*).[56] Jesus' reception of gifts beyond human capacity (e.g., immortality) cannot "become the properties of Jesus' humanity per se . . . they are attributable to the human works of Jesus only in so far as Jesus' works are united to the Word through the Word's assumption of his humanity."[57] The humanity seems merely to be the vehicle through which the Logos operates: "Whatever Jesus does for us, he does as the Word incarnate. . . . The humanity of Jesus himself is the first beneficiary of the new relation of humanity to divinity that is the incarnation."[58] Again, it is not that these expressions are unorthodox or threaten the Chalcedonian intention, but they do belong to a long history of interpretation that identifies the saving activity of God in the incarnation solely with the Logos as the subject of incarnation. We do not seem here to have moved beyond the famil-

---

52. Kathryn Tanner, *Jesus, Humanity and the Trinity* (Minneapolis: Fortress, 2001), 10.

53. Ibid., 16.

54. Ibid., 17; cf. Barth, *CD* IV/2:74–76, 98–99, 105–9.

55. Tanner, *Jesus, Humanity and the Trinity*, 31, 32 n. 75. Largely in reaction to Apollinarianism, the ecumenical affirmation of the two wills in Christ was seen as the corollary of his two natures.

56. Ibid., 48; cf. Thomas F. Torrance, *The Trinitarian Faith* (Edinburgh: T & T Clark, 1988), 221–27.

57. Tanner, *Jesus, Humanity and the Trinity*, 50.

58. Ibid., 51.

iar polarization between kenotic and apotheotic christologies, both of which reflect a Monophysite tendency to surrender the deity to the humanity or vice versa. While avoiding Nestorian separation, surely we must say that both are equally definitive of Christ's person: thus it is not only his body that is human, but his willing, feeling, thinking, and acting. The *Word* became flesh, it is true, but the Word became *flesh*. The humanity was active as well as the divinity for our salvation, and depended not only on the Logos, as if obedience was simply the ineluctable outcome of his being divine, but also on the conformity of his will to that of his Father through temptation and real struggle. According to Tanner, the Word brings the humanity along with it in "a covenant fellowship with God raised to a level otherwise unattainable for creatures: this covenant fellowship is the indivisible co-action of the members of the Trinity."[59] One may recall that in chapter one I challenged even Aquinas's view of revelation as a supernatural elevation of the human authors, along with Barth's even more radical refusal to identify revelation with any "givens" in nature and history. This presupposition carries over into christology, as we see here in Tanner's emphasis on the incarnation as the elevation of humanity rather than on the condescension of God. Once more, without denying the important truth in her point, viz., that the action of Jesus is the action of the second person of the Trinity, I must question the adequacy of simply reducing this "covenant fellowship" to an intra-Trinitarian exchange without remainder. She says that "Jesus' humanity saves in virtue of its being in the mode of the second Person of the Trinity."[60] Furthermore, "the Son of God was the subject of Jesus' acts" and "the human will of Christ simply is the will of the Son."[61] Where did the humanity go? And if the *communicatio* only runs in one direction (from the divine to the human), how can we regard the suffering of Christ, both in moral-spiritual and in physical terms, as not only real but inherently salvific?

While there has been a widespread tendency throughout church history to treat the victory of Christ almost exclusively as the victory of *God*, covenant theology—particularly in its insistence on the necessity of the original covenant being perfectly fulfilled—has underscored its significance also as the victory of a *human person*. To be sure, this person is the God-Man, but as the second Adam he is entrusted with a thoroughly human commission that must be fulfilled in thoroughly human terms, in reliance on the Spirit and not on his oneness with the Father. This emphasis of covenant theology has been challenged from time to time by what Alan Spence has identified as "Apollinarian" tendencies that fail "to conceive of the incarnate Christ as 'normative man,'" despite formal adherence to the humanity of Christ.[62] When we place the person and work of Christ in the context of the covenant of redemption (*pactum salutis*), we underscore his

59. Ibid.
60. Ibid., 54.
61. Ibid., 57.
62. Alan Spence, "Christ's Humanity and Ours," 77.

identity as the eternal Son, and in the context of the covenant of creation, his identity as the second Adam.

Jesus is therefore not merely the Son of God as to his divinity, but is the true and faithful Son of Adam who always obeys his Father's will in the power of the Holy Spirit. This meritorious human life lived in full dependence on the Spirit (recapitulation) is not extrinsic but intrinsic to redemption; it is not merely a necessary prerequisite of a sacrificial offering, but part and parcel of that offering. This is why the Son of Man claims victory for himself by right and not merely by gift, nor indeed by virtue of his deity (John 5:19–20, 26–27, 30, 36). "I glorified you on earth by finishing the work that you gave me to do. So now, Father, glorify me in your own presence with the glory that I had in your presence before the world existed" (John 17:4–5). So it is not only his suffering on behalf of sinners but his completion of the Father's commission that he has in mind when he cries out from the cross, "It is finished" (John 19:30). Because of this human achievement, Paul can say concerning Jesus, "being found in *human* form, he humbled himself and became obedient to the point of death—even death on a cross. Therefore God also highly exalted him and gave him the name that is above every name" (Phil. 2:7–9). Taking his cue from Daniel's vision of the four empires, Moltmann duly notes, "In the kingdom of the Son of Man man's likeness to God is fulfilled. *Through this human man* God finally asserts his rights over his creation" (emphasis added).[63]

It is appropriate at this point then to summarize the significance of this approach; at least three points may be mentioned: (1) It stresses the salvific significance of Jesus' human obedience as the second Adam/Israel; (2) it gives greater attention to the *suffering* humanity of Jesus' lifelong obedience in the context of the covenant drama of God's speaking and human answering, thus dialectically relating christologies from above and below instead of setting them in opposition; (3) it opens up a wider space for the role of the Spirit in christology. Let me unpack each of these points briefly.

1. Although not entirely consistent (i.e., attributing the miracles to Christ's deity), John of Damascus elsewhere makes the claim I am arguing for here: "For the very Creator and Lord Himself undertakes a struggle in behalf of the work of His own hands, and learns by toil to become Master."[64] He did not simply snatch humankind from its fall, but "rescued like by like, most difficult though it seemed: and His wisdom is seen in His devising the most fitting solution to the difficulty." He "bent the heavens and descended to earth. . . . And He becomes obedient to the Father Who is like unto us, and finds a remedy for our disobedience in what He had assumed from us, and became a pattern of obedience to us without which it is not possible to obtain salvation."[65] Thus the person, Jesus Christ, is one. Nevertheless, the Son, who according to his deity transcends time

---

63. Jürgen Moltmann, *Man: Christian Anthropology in the Conflicts of the Present*, trans. John Sturdy (Philadelphia: Fortress, 1974), 112.

64. John of Damascus, "Exact Exposition," 45.

65. Ibid., 46.

and space, "has a seat in the body, His flesh sharing in the glory."[66] The humanity is given its proper place (contrary to the Apollinarian and Nestorian tendency) without being absorbed into the deity (contrary to the Monophysite tendency).

> For the purpose of God the Word becoming man was that the very same nature, which had sinned and fallen and become corrupted, should triumph over the deceiving tyrant and so be freed from corruption, just as the divine apostle puts it, "For since by man came death, by man came also the resurrection of the dead." If the first is true the second must also be true.[67]

As I will argue in relation to the atonement, the Reformed emphasis on the active obedience reconciles the Greek emphasis on recapitulation and incarnation and the Latin emphasis on the cross. The person, life, and work of Christ is not therefore saving simply because of his divinity (whether referred to a divine nature or a divinized humanity), but because of both natures united in one hypostasis.

Jesus is therefore not only God turned toward God, but humanity turned toward God, a point that Barth rightly affirmed and even emphasized, but whose dualism between the sacred and the secular, the deity of God in revelation and the humanity of Jesus in history, he could not finally adequately account for.[68] The Gospels relate the story of one who was not a human shell whose inner impulses were determined by the Logos (Apollinarianism), nor a hybrid whose supernatural feats and victory over temptation and death could only be attributed to his divine nature (Nestorianism), nor a divinized human (Monophysitism). He is at last "the true and faithful witness," not only from heaven but also from earth (Rev. 1:5). Through its birth pangs, Israel has finally given birth to its messiah, the savior of the world (Rev. 12:1–17). It is in his humanity that the destinies of Israel and the world converge. At the same time, this human person is no less, has always been no less, than Israel's YHWH.

2. This emphasis on the salvific humanity of Christ allows us then to identify fully with our covenant head. Jesus' temptations, both religious-ethical and physical, were real (Matt. 4:1–11 and parallel passages; John 4:6; Heb. 2:17–18). Speculation about *how* this can be so of a man who was simultaneously God incarnate does not get us anywhere. In sharp contrast to the fanciful gnostic tales, such as the *Gospel of Thomas*, the canonical Gospels do not narrate the life of a noumenous child prodigy whose humanity is incidental if allowed at all. "The child *grew* and *became* strong, filled with wisdom; and the favor of God was upon him. . . . And Jesus *increased* in wisdom and in years, and in divine and human favor" (Luke 2:40, 52). His rejection in his hometown underscores that before he began his ministry Jesus was perceived as quite ordinary: "Is not this the carpenter's son? Is not his mother called Mary? And are not his brothers James and Joseph and Simon and Judas? And are not all his sisters with us? Where then did this man get all this?" (Matt. 13:54–56). Even his brothers did not believe in him

66. Ibid., 74.
67. Ibid., 56.
68. Cf. Barth, *CD* I/1:165 and 323.

until late in his ministry (John 7:1–9). How could the Son not have known the details to which he himself was a party in the eternal covenant (Matt. 24:36)? Such passages remind us not to pry into the secrets of the ontological Trinity and restrict our thoughts to the economic Trinity—specifically, the genuine humiliation endured by the one who called God "Father."

In Gethsemane Jesus agonizes over his destiny: "I am deeply grieved, even to death," he tells his disciples (Matt. 26:38a). In his prayer to the Father he famously petitions, "My Father, if it is possible, let this cup pass from me; yet not what I want but what you want" (v. 39). In one sentence we discern both Jesus' intimate unity with the Father ("My Father") and his differentiation ("not what I want but what you want"). While in trying to protect the deity of Christ the tradition has perhaps too often emphasized the latter—Jesus' unbroken fellowship with the Father—at the expense of the former, the opposite reduction is all too apparent in a number of recent christologies. It is not simply because the eternal Son cannot "die" and be "cut off" from the Father and Spirit that Jesus surrenders his spirit to the Father's guardianship. It is even Jesus as the fully human son who, though "cut off" in the Old Testament sense of bearing the covenant curse, is nevertheless still even in this very act in the very presence of his Father. In this way, he brings his own human blood into the heavenly sanctuary (Heb. 9:11–10:18).

Graham Ward endorses Augustine's spiritualizing or "Apollinarian" tendencies with respect to Christ's suffering, even verging on a Docetic christology that Augustine himself would have rejected:

> Augustine further makes plain that the infant Jesus was not born helpless and ignorant like other children: "that such entire ignorance existed in the infant in whom the Word was made flesh, I cannot suppose . . . nor can I imagine that such weakness of mental faculty ever existed in the infant Christ which we see in infants generally." Again, the logic here is theological—Augustine makes these suggestions on the basis of a doctrine of creation revealed through the incarnation in which materiality participates in God. Matter itself is rendered metaphorical within the construal of such logic.[69]

These reflections contrast sharply with those of Calvin on this subject. Defining Christ's "descent into hell" as his agony on the cross, suffering divine wrath, Calvin challenges those who try to explain away the cry of dereliction (Matt. 27:46, quoting Ps. 22:1). He meets the objection of certain critics that he is "doing a frightful injustice to Christ." "For they hold it incongruous for him to fear for the salvation of his soul. Then they stir up a harsher slander: that I attribute to the Son of God a despair contrary to faith."[70] But, Calvin replies, it is the evangelists themselves who "openly relate" this agony of soul as well as body.

---

69. Graham Ward, "Bodies: The Displaced Body of Jesus," in *Radical Orthodoxy: A New Theology*, ed. John Milbank, Catherine Pickstock, and Graham Ward (London and New York: Routledge, 1999), 165, citing Augustine, *On the Merits and Remission of Sins and on the Baptism of Infants*, pp. 63–64.
70. Calvin, *Institutes* 2.16.12.

After all, his humanity included his psychosomatic unity. His soul could not be equated with the Logos, as it was for Apollinarius and the Monothelites (much less the Monophysites). "To say that he was pretending—as they do—is a foul evasion. . . . His goodness—never sufficiently praised—shines in this: he did not shrink from taking our weaknesses upon himself." Hebrews 5:7, "He was heard for his *fear*," is related to this dereliction. This is not "reverence" or "piety," but *fear*, Calvin emphasizes, not only with Apollinarians and Docetists but perhaps with certain statements of Cyril and Athanasius as well as Augustine in mind.[71]

Weakness does not mean failure (Heb. 4:15), Calvin insists. Without referring specifically to the sources he is criticizing, he says the tearful wrestling in Gethsemane was not "a show for others' eyes," but a real torment verging on despair. "This banishes all doubt: he had to have angels descend from heaven to encourage him by their unaccustomed consolation [Luke 22:43]." All of this shows us that the sorrow, fear, and dread of death are not in themselves evil passions or "contrary to faith," as the vocative, "My God, my God . . . ," confirms. "Now this refutes the error of Apollinaris, as well as that of the so-called Monothelites. Apollinaris claimed that Christ had an eternal spirit instead of a soul, so that he was only half a man. As if he could atone for our sins in any other way than by obeying the Father! . . . This plainly appears to be a great paradox: '"Father, save me from this hour"? No, for this purpose I have come to this hour. Father, glorify thy name' [John 12:27–28]."[72] We could add that the Jesus who begins his life as a model of saintly passivity and stoic resolve (in the words of "Away in a Manger," "no crying he makes") could end his life only in perfect bliss, but we find the opposite in the Gospels. He was neither a divinized human nor a humanized God. The "great paradox" to which Calvin refers cannot be resolved in either a Nestorian or Monophysite direction.

This real agony, in contrast to the Apollinarian tendencies of Calvin's critics on this point, is set within the larger context not only of Christ's redemptive death but of his atoning life. "Now someone asks, How has Christ abolished sin, banished the separation between us and God, and acquired righteousness to render God favorable and kindly toward us? To this we can in general reply that he has achieved this for us by the whole course of his obedience. . . . In short, from the time when he took on the form of a servant, he began to pay the price of liberation in order to redeem us."[73] There are unmistakable echoes here of recapitulation, as we find it in Irenaeus. A strong emphasis on the active obedience of Christ as the second Adam necessarily entails an equally strong emphasis on the salvific value of Christ's humanity as such.

So when we look for the conquest of sin and death in the obedience of Christ, we should be directed not simply to the divine nature (as if Jesus could always

71. Ibid., 2.16.11.
72. Ibid., 2.16.12.
73. Ibid., 2.16.5. Yet Calvin concludes this section, "But because trembling consciences find repose only in sacrifice and cleansing by which sins are expiated, we are duly directed thither [to the cross]; and for us the substance of life is set in the death of Christ."

compensate for his human finitude by exercising his divine attributes), but to the Spirit. It is the Spirit who anointed David and his servant-son as messiah forever. Moltmannn too simply collapses Jesus into God in a manner that evacuates the human obedience of Jesus distinct from a generic humanization of God.[74] The humanity of Christ must not be submerged into an all-encompassing theory of the "suffering God," but must have its own space—our human space, as the site of God's redemptive activity.

It is easy to distort christology in a Nestorian direction by exaggerating the transcendence of God and God's immunity to the history of suffering and then applying this to the deity of Christ, all the while affirming the reality of his human suffering. But it is just as easy to distort christology in a Monophysite direction, either by divinizing the human or humanizing the divine. The doctrine of the two natures of Christ must be articulated within a thoroughly Trinitarian framework, without simply reducing one nature to the other. The paradox must never be resolved in any final synthesis: this, it seems, is precisely the point that Chalcedon makes. Pannenberg strikes just the right balance here: "The rule or kingdom of the Father is not so external to his deity that he might be God without his kingdom," even though the world itself is not necessary for that fact.

> But if he does create a world, his lordship over it is necessary to his deity. . . . [This] has its place already in the intratrinitarian life of God, in the reciprocity of the relation between the Son, who freely subjects himself to the lordship of the Father, and the Father, who hands over his lordship to the Son. Only on this basis can one speak of the trinitarian relevance of the cross of Jesus. The passion of Jesus Christ is not an event which concerned only the human nature that the divine Logos assumed, as though it did not affect in any way the eternal placidity of the trinitarian life of God. In the death of Jesus the deity of his God and Father was at issue. It is incorrect, of course, to speak point-blank of the death of *God* on the cross, as has been done since the time of Hegel. We can say only of the *Son of God* that he was "crucified, dead, and buried." To be dogmatically correct, indeed, we have to say that the Son of God, though he suffered and died himself, did so according to his human nature. Even to speak directly of the death of God in the Son is a reverse monophysitism. Nevertheless, we have to say that Jesus was affected by suffering and death on the cross in person, i.e., in the person of the eternal Son.[75]

3. Finally, this emphasis on the salvific humanity of Christ also opens up a wider space for pneumatology, pointing to the Spirit rather than merely the divine nature as the focus of Jesus' dependence. The same Spirit brooding over the waters of creation "overshadowed" Mary, joining the Father in declaring the benediction on the incarnate Son at his baptism. Throughout Jesus' ministry this same dependence on the Spirit as the perlocutionary effect of the Father's speaking is sustained in the Gospels. Raising Jesus from the dead, the Spirit was him-

---

74. See, for example, Moltmann, *Trinity and the Kingdom*, 77–79.
75. Pannenberg, *ST* 1, trans. G. W. Bromiley (Grand Rapids: Eerdmans, 1991), 313–14.

self vindicated as "the Lord and giver of life," and at Pentecost began to bring that same life to Jerusalem, Judea, and the furthest regions of the world. The pouring out of "the blood of the new covenant" (Matt. 26:28) is the presupposition of the pouring out of the Spirit at Pentecost (Acts 2). Because the Father gives the Son to us in the Spirit, the Son brings us into a relation to the Father by which we too, by and in the Spirit, can cry out, "Abba Father": "Our Father in heaven." What the Son is by eternal generation we are by adoption. Just as the Logos can only become flesh by the work of the Holy Spirit, believers cannot say "'Jesus is Lord' except by the Holy Spirit" (1 Cor. 12:3). The interdependence in all of this is as magnificent as it is obvious: apart from the Spirit, not only is it impossible for us to say "Jesus is Lord"; without the Spirit there would be no *Jesus* in the first place. It is just as true that the Spirit gives us Jesus as it is that Jesus gives us the Spirit. It was the *Spirit* who upheld Jesus and gave his mortal flesh the strength to cleave to every word that proceeds from his Father's lips, and it is the Spirit who unites us to Christ as our representative head.

To summarize, it is not via kenotic christologies but via a theology of divine accommodation that we are able to uphold the two natures of Christ in one person. Not only in the incarnation but throughout the history of God's covenant with his people God remains God while entering into solidarity with human beings and creation more generally. God is "haveable" because he has *given* himself, and yet he remains "other": free *from* as well as *for* the world. By uniting himself to our flesh, the Son executes in time the redemptive determination in eternity. The incarnation is therefore the culmination of covenantal accommodation. We have indeed met a stranger, but he is also flesh of our flesh, a mediator "who in every respect has been tested as we are, yet without sin" (Heb. 4:15). In this event, God is haveable without being fully possessed; given without being enclosed; brought into the most intimate solidarity with humanity without any loss to the deity that would place redemption beyond reach. As in all of God's analogical revelation, so too here—even in the univocal core that is Jesus Christ—there is more to God than meets the eye.

Chapter Seven

Suffering Servant

Challenges to Sacrificial Atonement

All along the way I have referred to Tillich's contrasting paradigms of "overcoming estrangement" and "meeting a stranger." In this chapter, I will evaluate some of the most significant challenges to a sacrificial motif under the rubric of "overcoming estrangement," and then turn in the final two chapters to a constructive elaboration of my own proposal, in which a revised (covenantal) sacrificial understanding is coordinated with emphases lacking in Anselm's satisfaction theory. At the risk of overgeneralization, I will nevertheless classify the dominant challenges under two subheadings: political liberation and ontological participation.

As with other chapters, here we walk in on a conversation in progress, assuming a certain familiarity with the various atonement positions in historical theology. Undoubtedly the most polemical chapter, its thesis is that the "ontological" way and the "covenantal" way give rise not only to two rather different metaphysics but also to different ways of approaching the human problem and its solution. In chapter one I elaborated on Tillich's typology by suggesting, for example, that the former approach tended to tell a story about a fall from being, while the latter speaks of a fall from original integrity into sin and ethical distance. It is quite understandable then that "overcoming estrangement" might view redemption as a means of reconciling "being."[1] This can take a host of forms, of course—everything from stoicism to panentheistic (or pantheistic) mysticism to dialectical historicism to therapy—but the common idea is that there is a problem in the very nature of things that needs to be overcome by a new awareness. By contrast, "meeting a stranger," I have argued, is an ethical enterprise. It is not a new awareness but a new creation that is required. New not in the sense that the material world is negated, but in the sense that ethical fault has to be atoned for and right relationships have to be established. The context for talking about this is the covenant, in which reconciliation is a matter of restoring the right relationships rather than overcoming conditions of ontological finitude. The theme of participation is crucial in both paradigms, but while the one views it in ontological terms, the other sees it in ethical-covenantal terms.

From the outset, I should at least make passing reference to the two typical and overgeneralized poles in atonement theory, the Anselmian and the Abelardian, since many of the critics of the sacrificial motif explicitly identify with the latter and treat the former as the foil for all versions of sacrificial atonement without distinction. A broad outline will have to suffice. In the ancient church, the event of Christ's mission was interpreted variously as incorporating the elements of sacrificial expiation, ransom (both to God and the devil), victory over the cosmic powers, and recapitulation (viz., the whole life of Christ, including his death, as undoing the sin of Adam and refashioning humanity in Christ's image). In his eleventh-century treatise, *Cur deus homo* ("Why the God-Man?"), Anselm articulated what has come to be called the satisfaction theory, according to which Christ's death was deemed appropriate compensation to God's offended dignity, much as a feudal lord might receive compensatory tribute from one who had slighted his person. Of course, Christ was not himself the guilty party, so his death could not have been punitive but was rather offered as a supererogatory settlement on behalf of humanity. An infinite indignity to an infinite person demands an infinite sacrifice.[2]

Abelard's rival account stressed that Christ's death was intended as a moving expression of God's love rather than a payment for sin or satisfaction of offended dignity. By contemplating the cross, therefore, one is moved to repentance and a new obedience. No satisfaction is needed because the cross is a demonstration of God's love. Obviously, these different atonement doctrines reflected deeper differences in understanding the human problem; and, I would argue, those differences are as deep as the divide between the ontological way and the ethical-covenantal approach. Nominalism carried forward Abelard's views by emphasizing that the atonement was rooted not in the necessity of God's nature but in an act of God's

1. For a recent example, see John Milbank, *Being Reconciled: Ontology and Pardon* (London and New York: Routledge, 2003).

2. Anselm, "Why God Became Man," in *A Scholastic Miscellany: Anselm to Ockham*, ed. Eugene R. Fairweather, Library of Christian Classics (Philadelphia: Westminster Press, 1956), 106, 119–24.

will. Rather than provide a satisfaction, the atonement was simply accepted as opening up the possibility for God to forgive those who "do what lies within them" (*facienti quod in se est deus non denigat gratiam*).[3]

The Socinians in the sixteenth century elaborated this moral or exemplary theory by arguing that retributive justice is unworthy of God and unnecessary. The goal of Christ's death in this view of the atonement is to provide an example for imitation (hence it is usually called the exemplary theory). Hugo Grotius and the Arminians elaborated what has come to be called the governmental view, in which the death of Christ is said to be a reestablishment of God's moral sovereignty rather than a substitution. All of these rivals to Anselm's theory have been traditionally classified as "subjective" theories because they maintain that the cross was necessary not as the basis for divine forgiveness but only in order to produce a moral change in humans.

The Enlightenment reflected a distinctly Pelagian anthropology, particularly in Kant's impatience with any notion of original sin that might impair moral duty. At the center of such criticism stood the doctrines of satisfaction and justification, which Kant regarded as morally debilitating.[4] Schleiermacher and especially Ritschl repeated the Socinian arguments against any judicial concept of the cross. "And so it came about," notes Gunton, "that various forms of exemplarism took the field, under the impulses provided by the rational criticism of traditional theologies by Kant, Schleiermacher, and Hegel. In place of an act of God centered in a historic life and death, towards the otherwise helpless, the emphasis came to be upon those who by appropriate action could help themselves."[5]

My aim in this chapter is not to defend Anselm's theory. Although I prefer it to the rivals just mentioned, the weaknesses are significant. As Louis Berkhof points out, "The theory of Anselm is sometimes identified with that of the Reformers, which is also known as the satisfaction theory, but the two are not identical."[6] Acknowledging its strengths, Berkhof nevertheless indicates the weaknesses that the Reformed tradition has typically observed in Anselm's theory. First, although it lodges the atonement in God's nature, it is God's dignity rather than justice that it addresses. "He really starts out with the principle of 'private law' or custom, according to which an injured party may demand whatever satisfaction he sees fit; and yet argues for the necessity of the atonement in a way which only holds on the standpoint of public law."[7] Second, his theory "really has no place for the idea that

3. See Heiko Oberman, *The Harvest of Medieval Theology: Gabriel Biel and Late Medieval Nominalism* (Durham, NC: Labyrinth, 1983), 135–36.

4. See, for instance, Kant, "Religion within the Boundaries of Mere Reason" in *Immanuel Kant: Religion and Rational Theology*, ed. and trans. Allen W. Wood and George di Giovanni (Cambridge: Cambridge University Press, 1996), see also 65–66, 70–96, 104–22, 134. For his own part, however, Kant was not motivated by a suspicion of the concept of divine judgment; on the contrary, the fear of final judgment was meant to motivate moral effort, which the substitionary satisfaction by Christ was thought to subvert.

5. Colin Gunton, "The Sacrifice and the Sacrifices: From Metaphor to Transcendental?" in *Trinity, Incarnation, and Atonement: Philosophical and Theological Essays*, ed. Ronald J. Feenstra and Cornelius Plantinga Jr. (Notre Dame, IN: University of Notre Dame Press, 1989), 211.

6. Louis Berkhof, *Systematic Theology*, 385.

7. Ibid., 386.

Christ by suffering endured the penalty of sin, and that His suffering was strictly vicarious. The death of Christ is merely a tribute offered voluntarily to the honor of the Father." It constitutes the "doctrine of penance applied to the work of Christ."[8] A third problem with Anselm's account is that it has no place for the active obedience of Christ. "The whole emphasis is on the death of Christ, and no justice is done to the redemptive significance of his life."[9] Finally, "In Anselm's presentation there is merely an external transfer of the merits of Christ to man. . . . There is no hint of the mystical union of Christ and believers, nor faith as accepting the righteousness of Christ. Since the whole transaction appears to be rather commercial, the theory is often called the commercial theory."[10]

Furthermore, these Western options do not take into account the important contributions of the early Greek church (viz., recapitulation and conquest of the powers) and the emphases of the Reformers and especially federal theology on Christ's life and resurrection as well as his death. But before I can lay out my own proposal in the next chapter I should offer some space to the challenges more recently placed before any notion of sacrificial atonement, Anselmian or otherwise. I will offer a running commentary on these proposals and a concluding summary response.

POLITICAL LIBERATION

Many of the recent challenges to the sacrificial motif explicitly draw on the Abelardian atonement tradition. Further, most (at least that we will consider) at least implicitly concur with the neo-Protestant rejection of the juridical element, and consequently focus their understanding of Christ's work on its impact upon us rather than on God. I would argue that it is not mere coincidence that a "subjective" theory of atonement corresponds to "new awareness" (overcoming estrangement), while a more "objective" view fits better with a covenantal model (meeting a stranger). This is not to dismiss such challenges as mere repristinations of earlier positions, however. As we will observe, there are impressive arguments against traditional atonement doctrine in recent treatments and they should be taken seriously on their own terms.

What brings together such diverse thinkers as René Girard, Rosemary Ruether, and some writers from the Anabaptist tradition is a critique of the sacrificial motif as engendering violence and an alternative understanding of Christ's work as chiefly concerned with bringing about political justice. I classify this as the "political" approach to atonement theory. While every atonement doctrine is political in an important sense, including my own, I use the label here to refer to the emphasis on liberation from social ills with intramundane resources. In other words, it is not simply that the concern is with a this-worldly redemption (as I would also

8. Ibid.
9. Ibid.
10. Ibid.

stress), but that this redemption is accomplished chiefly by us as we cooperate with the good within ourselves and one another. Thus overcoming estrangement is achieved by a new awareness of new possibilities for human flourishing. By realizing these new possibilities, we are free to pursue a more humane community.

René Girard: The Scapegoat Mechanism

A social theorist who has given a great deal of thought to the scapegoat mechanism at work not only in his own Jewish tradition but in the socioreligious consciousness at work across religions and cultures, Girard's main thesis is that cultures typically inscribe violence into their very fabric by finding a sacrificial victim to take their place. He allows that "Christ agrees to die so that mankind will live," but insists that this is not "sacrificial."[11] He also rejects the concept of the sacrificial meal, whether in Old or New Testament, since these all imply the scapegoat mechanism.[12] Accordingly, Jesus did not die as the sacrifice to end all sacrifice for sin, but as a victim on behalf of victims to say no to the sacrificial scapegoat once and for all. "To say that Jesus dies, not as a sacrifice, but in order that there be no more sacrifices, is to recognize in him the Word of God."[13] Apparently unable to salvage much of the Old Testament, Girard reinterprets the New as a radical critique of the scapegoat. But as Christopher Schroeder points out, this is a dangerous move: Girard pits the God of wrath and sacrifice (Old Testament) against the God of victims (New Testament).

> With this opposition . . . Girard follows the well-known tracks of Marcion. Eventually, the labeling of the God of the Old Testament as the "God of scapegoats, the barbaric God of the tribe," as the "God of lynchers" and the "God of executioners," supports the view of the Old Testament as "pre-christian" and fosters the latent anti-Judaism of Christianity. The main reason for this gloomy view of the Hebrew scriptures is that Girard sees divine wrath as inseparable from human violence against a scapegoat.[14]

But Girard's theory, though penetrating in its analysis, is yet another version of the moral theories we have encountered, theories that rest on an insufficiently realistic anthropology. As William Placher observes, this view amounts to "getting it." Once we get it, we should not be violent anymore. However, "The dominant Christian tradition has been less optimistic."[15] Placher points up this connection between anthropology and soteriology, or more concretely, sin and redemption. For Girard, these stories of crucifixion and sacrifice "are therefore

11. René Girard, *Things Hidden Since the Foundation of the World*, trans. Stephen Bann and Michael Metteer (London: Athlone, 1987), 241–43.
12. Ibid.
13. Ibid., 210.
14. Christopher Schroeder, "'Standing in the Breach': Turning Away the Wrath of God," *Interpretation* 52, no. 1 (1988): 17.
15. William C. Placher, "Rethinking Atonement," *Interpretation* 53, no. 1 (1999): 9. As Placher points out, Girard thinks that the book of Hebrews took the "wrong turn" in the NT.

good news for decent folks who can, with a good model to follow, figure out how to save themselves. . . . Can we make the story radical enough to be good news for *sinners?*" (emphasis added).[16]

> Girard says we must stop scapegoating the innocent, but then seems to claim that if only we see the truth, the problems of guilt will go away. The gospel, however, offers not just a revelation but a redeemer; whose love enables those who are guilty to know themselves to be forgiven. . . . The crucial difference, I think, lies in whether we urge the endurance of suffering that perpetuates injustice, or the acceptance of suffering in the service of justice, peace, and liberation. I do not think we need apologize for the latter. . . . For Paul, it is we who need to be reconciled to God, not the other way around. . . . In Calvin's words, "It was not after we were reconciled to him through the blood of his Son that he began to love us. Rather, he has loved us before the world was created."[17]

Radical Feminism

Beyond Moltmann's more modest approach, criticism of traditional atonement language has emerged in the various theologies of liberation associated with feminist reflection, where the traditional Christian understanding of the cross is taken as a valorization of passivity and violence.[18] "Divine child abuse is paraded as salvific and the child who suffers 'without even raising a voice' is lauded as the hope of the world."[19] Anselm's theory advances a view of justice that promotes the punishment rather than the righting of wrongs.[20] "We must do away with the atonement, this idea of a blood sin upon the whole human race which can be washed away only by the blood of the lamb."[21]

In a provocative chapter, "Can a Male Savior Save Women?" Rosemary Radford Ruether argues that the early messianic mission of Jesus to bring justice to the poor and oppressed had been transformed by the imperial church into a patriarchal religion that, among other things, concentrated on Christ's expiatory death as passive obedience.[22] Ruether asserts, "Jesus did not 'come to suffer and die,'" but to liberate the oppressed.[23] He never conceived of his death as redemptive,

---

16. Ibid., 12.

17. Ibid., 15–16.

18. It should be pointed out that Latin American liberation theology had a significant place for the justice of God in a sacrificial atonement. See, for example, Jon Sobrino, "Systematic Christology" in *Systematic Theology: Perspectives from Liberation Theology*, ed. Jon Sobrino and Ignario Ellacuria (Maryknoll, NY: Orbis, 1998), 124–45.

19. Joanne Carlson Brown and Rebecca Parker, "For God So Loved the World?" in *Christianity, Patriarchy, and Abuse: A Feminist Critique*, ed. Joanne Carlson Brown and Carole R. Bohn (New York: Pilgrim, 1989), 2.

20. Ibid., 7–8.

21. Ibid., 26.

22. However, it should be observed that it was the Pantocrator, not the crucifix, that dominated the Constantinian iconography.

23. Rosemary Radford Ruether, *Introducing Redemption in Christian Feminism* (Sheffield: Sheffield Academic Press, 1998), 104.

although he knew that his political mission might lead to that end. It is the undoing of the injustice that was redemptive. "The means of redemption is conversion."[24] As with earlier versions of the exemplary or moral influence theory, this is not really an atonement theory at all. Rather, it is a conversion theory. It is not about, among other things, how God and sinners are reconciled, but rather how people can become better and, consequently, engineer a more satisfying social and political order. At the same time, she raises important questions that I will take up again below.

Anabaptist Sources

Obviously, not all Anabaptists would subscribe to a radical critique of sacrificial atonement, much less endorse all of the views expressed under this section. Anabaptism, like other traditions, is diverse. Yet ever since the sixteenth century, this movement has suspected Luther, Calvin, and their heirs of compromising with Catholic theology (for instance, in its juridical emphasis) and practice (Christendom). Unlike the so-called magisterial Reformation, the Radical Reformation gave pride of place to discipleship and the imitation of Christ rather than to justification and union with Christ.[25] Many of the contemporary complaints against the so-called objective atonement doctrine are understandably brought from this quarter, even by some who would not identify themselves as Anabaptists.

According to Anthony Bartlett, the New Testament has no place for wrath and its propitiation.[26] Thus the atonement can only be "saved" if it is stripped of all "violent" implications. Borrowing from N. T. Wright, he thinks that church theologies have sometimes missed the eschatological significance of Christ's advent—a criticism that I readily accept and will attempt to address in the next chapter.

But Bartlett's arguments appear strained, and the obvious sacrificial references in the New Testament are relativized by alternative emphases instead of being correlated. So finally he adopts a line from Peter Lombard: "The death of Christ therefore justifies us, inasmuch as through it charity is excited in our hearts."[27] We begin to see not a new critique precipitated by a fresh exegetical harvest, but a familiar set of systematic-theological commitments that can be characterized as at least semi-Pelagian. This suspicion becomes even clearer: "The critique permits the so-called 'moral influence' theory to come to the fore with new, contemporary urgency."[28] The Augustinian violence begins with "the unconditioned violence of predestination. The violence also infects Luther, and to a greater

24. Idem, *Women and Redemption: A Theological History* (Minneapolis: Fortress, 1998), 279.

25. For example, see Kenneth Ronald Davis, *Anabaptism and Asceticism*, Studies in Anabaptist and Mennonite History 6 (Scottdale, PA: Herald, 1974); cf. *Anabaptism in Outline: Selected Primary Sources*, ed. Walter Klaassen (Scottdale, PA: Herald, 1981), especially 23–100.

26. Anthony Bartlett, *Cross Purposes: The Violent Grammar of Christian Atonement* (Harrisburg, PA: Trinity Press International, 2001), 203–16.

27. Cited ibid., 221.

28. Ibid., 223.

degree of spiritual crisis; and then continuing on through the Protestant tradition, up to and including the dialectical theology of Barth's *Church Dogmatics*."[29]

Similarly, Robert Hamerton-Kelly writes, "The Cross reveals this paradoxical wrath as God's acceptance of our free choice to destroy ourselves and each other, inasmuch as it is the supreme instance of this human rage against the good."[30] Though hardly paradoxical, that may be an interesting speculation with considerable intuitive appeal. God does not add insult to injury. Sin has already injured the sinner. The sin itself is punishment enough (a view we have already encountered in Moltmann). But can such a speculation be useful in explaining the actual passages in Scripture, narrative and didactic, that clearly portray God as acting in judgment not merely against sin in the abstract but against sinners? Why then would it come as bad news that someone has borne this for us—that in fact *God* has passionately accepted this burden for our salvation?

One of the most thoughtful recent studies of the atonement is by Anabaptist scholar J. Denny Weaver, *The Nonviolent Atonement*. Following John Yoder's lead, and fortified by Girard's critique of the scapegoat mechanism, J. Christiaan Beker's emphasis on resurrection, and the various feminist criticisms encountered above, Weaver advocates what he calls the "narrative Christus Victor" model. He distinguishes this from the "classic Christus Victor" view in that it is specifically designed to refute any violence in the Christian atonement doctrine. Conquest over the powers cannot occur through violence. "Thus proposing narrative Christus Victor as a nonviolent atonement motif also poses a fundamental challenge to and ultimately a rejection of satisfaction atonement."[31] According to Weaver, "Anselm's satisfaction atonement image likely originated as a reflection of the penitential system and the sacrament of private penance that was developed throughout the medieval era, and also reflected the image of a feudal lord who gave protection to his vassals but also exacted penalties for offenses against his honor."[32] As we have already noted from Berkhof, this is one of the typical Reformed objections, but Weaver does not see any distinctions. Although he does not provide citations, he says that Luther, Calvin, and "the divines of Protestant Orthodoxy" simply developed Anselm's theory in even more dangerous penal and juridical directions. "Common to this family of views in any of its versions is that the death of Jesus involved a divinely orchestrated plan through which Jesus' death could satisfy divine justice or divine law in order to save sinful humankind."[33]

Weaver appeals to the Apocalypse as the *locus classicus* for a nonviolent Christus Victor model, and I will return to this in the final chapter. To be sure, Jesus

29. Ibid., 224.

30. Robert Hamerton-Kelly, *Sacred Violence: Paul's Hermeneutic of the Cross* (Minneapolis: Augsburg Fortress, 1992), 102.

31. J. Denny Weaver, *The Nonviolent Atonement* (Grand Rapids: Eerdmans, 2001), 5.

32. Ibid., 16.

33. Ibid., 16–17. A recurring weakness of Weaver's study is its dependence, both in exegesis and the history of doctrine, upon secondary sources (critical of traditional atonement doctrine) with almost no evidence of firsthand knowledge of the views he judges inadequate.

touches on the theme of judgment, but in the Gospels, says Weaver, "Jesus made it clear that statements about the retribution of God were really a declaration of what those who reject the rule of God bring on themselves. Their sin turns upon them, and in effect, they judge themselves."[34] Of course, there is an important truth in this observation: they, rather than God, are responsible for their own sin. Nevertheless, does Jesus represent his judgment as merely passive in the parables, his "woes," and in the judgment of the nations in Matthew 25:31–46 (cf. Matt. 3:10; 5:22; Luke 3:16; 12:49)? For Weaver, "It was not a death, however, that was required as compensatory retribution for the sins of his enemies and his friends. It was a death that resulted from fulfillment of his mission about the reign of God."[35] Jesus died "in order to make the gift of the rule of God visible," essentially the same position as Ruether's above.[36]

At this point, Weaver anticipates the likely objection: "Is this narrative an atonement narrative?" "The answer is 'no,' if for atonement narrative one means a story that pictures Jesus' death as a divinely arranged plan to provide a payment to satisfy the offended honor of God or a requirement of divine law, or that understands Jesus as a the substitute bearer of punishment that sinful human kind deserves."[37] Jesus' death was categorically not "divine punishment that he suffered as a substitute for sinners."[38] Weaver follows through with the implications of this denial: "In narrative Christus Victor, the death of Jesus is anything but a loving act of God; it is the product of the forces of evil that oppose the reign of God."[39] But surely this is one-sided. While it is important to be reminded that Jesus was crucified "by wicked hands," it is also said in the same breath that he was "handed over to you according to the definite plan and foreknowledge of God" (Acts 2:23). To be sure, "both Herod and Pontius Pilate, with the Gentiles and the peoples of Israel, gathered together against your holy servant Jesus, whom you anointed"—but "to do whatever your hand and your plan had predestined to take place" (Acts 4:27–28).

As with much in this approach, the narrative drama is reduced to either-or choices. Instead, the biblical narrative involves God, Jesus, the Jews, the Gentiles—indeed all of us, in the passion of Jesus. If the atonement is founded in the intra-Trinitarian pact from all eternity, it cannot be an accident of his mission, something that just happens to Jesus along the way of doing something else. It is the reason he came into the world (John 12:27). Nobody takes his life; he gives it (John 10:18). It is by viewing the cross as God's plan to redeem even the perpetrators of the violence against him that we are able to look beyond the fault of those who crucified him and, though paradoxically, rejoice in his death. According to Weaver's model, Christ's death accomplishes nothing for the perpetrators

34. Ibid., 41.
35. Ibid., 42.
36. Ibid., 43.
37. Ibid., 43–44.
38. Ibid., 44.
39. Ibid., 45.

of violence. But even judged on its own premises (political/social reconciliation), this is hardly satisfactory.

Remarkably, Weaver does not regard the Old Testament sacrifices as substitutionary but as a rededication.[40] This is consistent with a moral influence view of the atonement, where the focus is subjective (viz., repentance) rather than objective (viz., propitiation and reconciliation). "The motif of sacrifice can of course be appropriated as an image for the death of Jesus. When it becomes clear, however, that the element of satisfying a legal penalty is not a dimension of the Hebrew ritual sacrifice, then mere use of sacrificial terminology or imagery should not be construed as evidence for satisfaction atonement."[41] Yet the only biblical evidence he cites against the notion of satisfying a legal penalty are passages that refer to sacrifices *other than* "the sacrifice of atonement," as it is called in the Levitical code. Weaver goes so far as to suggest, on the basis of Jeremiah 7, "Jeremiah even questioned whether sacrifices originated with God at all."[42] Yet the context of this passage is Israel's presumption that they can offer sacrifices instead of obedience. As I argue in the next chapter, this "obedience rather than sacrifice" is crucial in the prophets, but it is not represented as a repudiation of the sacrificial system, which God clearly had commanded and instituted *after* he brought them out of Egypt and yet still in perpetual need of forgiveness.

Even the book of Hebrews "has a nonsacrificial understanding of the death of Jesus," Weaver asserts. "While Hebrews obviously uses the language of sacrifice, the important questions concern how the rhetoric of sacrifice in Hebrews functions and 'which elements of the discourse are assumed, tolerated, modified, or embraced is another question.'"[43] Following Raymund Schwager once more, Weaver concludes that Jesus cannot be treated in Hebrews as the fulfillment of the Old Testament sacrifices, since that would constitute his "acquiescing to the violence of his enemies and voluntarily placing his own blood on the altar. This would be 'self-aggression in the service of a higher good.'" But this—again note the synthetic a priori— "would contradict God's nonviolence."[44] Not only does this present obvious challenges to most readings of Hebrews; it is open to a Marcionite interpretation, in which the Old Testament is repudiated by the New, which seems far remove from the writer's intention—to demonstrate that Jesus is the fulfillment of the old covenant types. Weaver realizes this problem: "If narrative Christus Victor does not appeal to the tradition of sacrifice in the Old Testament, does it have a connection to the Old Testament?" But he answers this by ignoring the motifs in question, changing the subject to the anticipation of the new creation in the prophets.[45]

40. Ibid., 59.

41. Ibid., 60.

42. Ibid., 61.

43. Ibid., 62, citing Loren L. Johns, "'A Better Sacrifice' or 'Better Than Sacrifice'? Michael Hardin's 'Sacrificial Language in Hebrews,'" in *Violence Renounced: René Girard, Biblical Studies, and Peacemaking*, ed. Willard M. Swartley (Telford, PA: Pandora, 2000), 121.

44. Weaver, *Nonviolent Atonement*, 64–65, referring to Schwager, *Jesus in the Drama of Salvation* (New York: Crossroad, 1999).

45. Ibid., 66–67.

According to the narrative Christus Victor model, "Since Jesus' mission was not to die but to make visible the reign of God, it is quite explicit that neither God nor the reign of God *need* [*sic*] Jesus' death in the way that his death is irreducibly *needed* in satisfaction atonement."[46] Thus the long shadow of nominalism reappears. "God did not send Jesus to die, but to live, to make visible and present the reign of God."[47] Rather, says Weaver, "Through the *resurrection*, God in Christ has in fact defeated these powers 'for us'" (emphasis added)[48]—even though, according to Colossians 2, this defeat is attributed to the *cross* (vv. 14–15). But Paul does not force us to choose between the cross and the resurrection. For him, they jointly resolve the problem of sin and death (cf. 1 Cor. 15:12, 17).

Like the others we have encountered, Weaver's account adopts what Weaver himself calls a "radicalized Abelardian" understanding of the cross as affecting not God's attitude toward us but our "perception of God."[49] He believes that, unlike the substitutionary model, his model encourages human activism in opposing the forces of evil. In other words, it is an exemplary doctrine of the atonement, eschewing the Chalcedonian Christology and Anselmian soteriology that derive from it.[50]

In a final chapter Weaver interacts "with Anselm and his defenders." "Many though by no means all these defense strategies are exercised by writers who reflect the Reformed tradition."[51] "Drawing on Martin Luther, [Thelma] Megill-Cobbler says that Christ is on our side, and in that location he is not a judge or angry tyrant. . . . 'Jesus has undergone and upholds the judgment of God, not in the sense of enduring retribution, but by intervening at great cost to set things right . . . taking on the consequences of human estrangement in order to make justice,'" so that there is, says Weaver, "*a change from understanding the work of Christ in passive to active voice*" (emphasis added).[52] Leanne Van Dyk adds that "the claim of 'divine child abuse' . . . 'implies that the relationship between the Father and the Son is one of domination, control, and punitive anger,'" while "correct atonement theology presupposes or emphasizes 'the inner trinitarian cooperation and gracious initiative of the Triune God.'"[53] These insights anticipate aspects of my proposal below: the understanding of Christ's work in an active rather than passive voice and locating the atonement ultimately in the "inner-Trinitarian cooperation" characterized by the covenant of redemption. However, all of these attempts to rehabilitate sacrificial theory are regarded by Weaver as reinscribing violence.

46. Ibid., 72.
47. Ibid., 74.
48. Ibid., 76.
49. Ibid., 78.
50. Ibid., 92–94.
51. Ibid., 179.
52. Ibid., 183, quoting Thelma Megill-Cobbler, "A Feminist Rethinking of Punishment Imagery in Atonement," *Dialog* 35, no. 1 (1996): 14.
53. Weaver, *Nonviolent Atonement*, 184, from Leanne Van Dyk, "Do Theories of Atonement Foster Abuse?" *Dialog* 35, no. 1 (1996): 24.

Since this is a common criticism, I add to my running commentary above a brief summary response. Before turning to criticisms, I should point out areas of potential agreement. Once again, these challenges are to be faulted more for what they deny than for what they affirm.

Responding to the "Political Paradigm"

First among my concessions is the relationship between *Christendom* and *violence*. While I will deal more thoroughly with this question in a third volume, its connection with atonement doctrine requires some comment. The very concept of religious violence is founded on the identification of cult (the kingdom of God) and culture (the kingdom of the world). (Anabaptism has similarly identified cult and culture but by associating the latter with groups withdrawn from the wider secular polities.) From crusades, inquisitions, and the slaughter of peasants and Anabaptists to the strife in Northern Ireland, it has not only been interreligious violence but interdenominational Christian violence that has been motivated by the prize of owning the brand "Christendom." In our world today, violence especially among Christians, Jews, and Muslims (and, especially in India, Muslims and Hindus) often comes down to the same factors that have confused the kingdom of God, however defined, with secular polities. Ironically, to borrow Peter Berger's distinction, secularization and secularism in the West have occurred alongside and with the collusion of the churches in order to retain some last vestige of imperial privilege. In reaction, many are turning to retrenchment of a nostalgic illusion of Christendom or a "Christian America" in an effort to recapture a time when the culture was supposedly "ours." Ideologies on the right and the left often confuse the great commission with national destiny.

It is not just the case that a lot of terrible things have been done in Christendom, but that the very idea is extremely bad for both the church and the world. It is false theology, not just false practice. As Weaver himself points out, the classical Christus Victor view is also capable of being appropriated for political violence. This fact alone should make us suspicious of sweeping indictments of sacrificial atonement theology. When "Christendom" is the dominant metaphor, anything and everything can become a weapon in the arsenal of violence. After all, the theme of "the people of God," so central to Anabaptist faith and piety, can be even more directly transposed into "Christendom," as it was in Thomas Müntzer's ill-fated experiment.[54] It is not an alleged violence inscribed within atonement doctrine, but the actual violence underwritten by empire that continues to require our collective efforts at deconstruction.

I also recognize the force of the criticism by feminist theologians and others that no atonement doctrine is complete that restricts the idea of justice to the vertical

54. See, for example, the description of the violent city-state under Thomas Müntzer in Eugene F. Rice, *The Foundations of Early Modern Europe* (New York: Norton & Norton, 1970), 138–39.

dimension, as if it is little more than an individualistic issue of "my personal relationship with God." Some of the criticisms rest on caricatures of the traditional view (especially those too dependent on R. W. Southern's widely contested thesis). Other criticisms are simply spurious, like the alleged connection between the preaching of the cross and the abuse of women and children in Western societies. Such treatments of the atonement often reflect neither competent social theory (my own limited research has yielded no actual studies of significant populations reared on the preaching of the cross correlating child abuse with such preaching) nor theology (most critiques resting on caricature and speculations about where a theory ought to or might lead, rather than actual exegesis of Scripture and wrestling with the tradition). Nevertheless, there has been in much of evangelical Protestant piety a tendency to reduce the atonement to a private transaction between God and the individual.

When we take a closer look at the civil laws of the Old Testament theocracy, a common theme emerges: the transgressor must make restitution. This is not a matter of chivalry but of justice, and not merely retributive but restorative justice—*rectitudo*. It is neither punishment nor reform of the criminal that is central in Israel's torah, but *ṣedeq*, "righteousness," the righting of wrongs and the consequent placement of enemies in the relation of friends, restoring the fruitfulness of the fallow earth by lifting the curse. Sometimes the righting of wrongs comes about by repaying a neighbor for the damage caused by one's bull. Other times, restitution meant that a life had to be exchanged for a life taken, on the basis that every person is God's image-bearer (Exod. 21:23). But in both cases, the judgment is not simply punitive. It is certainly not a matter of revenge. But it is also not simply done for the reform of the criminal. Rather, it is done to set things right: to bring about not only the sense that justice has been done, but actually to mend the fences broken by violence. But just for this reason the work of Christ must be seen to include at its heart this notion of vicarious sacrifice. Once we place the atonement in the context of the original covenant of creation, the work of Christ—beginning with his incarnation—becomes a matter of making restitution, fulfilling justice and not just being the victim of it, purchasing by his wholly voluntary obedience in life and death the participation of the whole creation in the consummation.

Another point I readily concede is that while Anselm recognized the importance of satisfaction, his formulation was weakened by his reduction of sin to a violation of divine honor rather than to a rebellion against God's covenant will, expressed in the law, and his person as judge of the earth. The relational element is almost entirely eclipsed by a mere commercial or legal transaction. God cannot simply forgive the way we are enjoined, because unlike us, he is not simply violated personally (which Anselm's formulation implies), but God's moral character that establishes and upholds the moral order of the cosmos must be sustained. It was not divine lust for personal satisfaction that moved God to send his Son, but the consideration of the human situation, motivated by both his love and justice. *God* made the satisfaction. He did not simply mete out punishment for his personal satisfaction but "gave his only-begotten Son." "*God* was in Christ reconciling the world to himself" (1 Cor. 5:12). There are parallels between the ancient Near Eastern treaty and Anselm's feudalism, but where Anselm appeals to the "tribute offering" that in both cases was brought by the vassal to the suzerain as a tax symbolic of subservience ("thank offering"), Christ's offering of himself was an *atonement*, a "guilt offering." It was not a payment to make God love us, but a payment made by God because of his love for us.

This is a point emphasized by Calvin, drawing on Augustine, that is often overlooked in sweeping criticisms. In *Institutes* 2.16.3–4, Calvin says that because the atonement is grounded in God's election ("In love he predestined us . . . in Christ" [Eph. 1:4–5]), God's love for us was the basis and not the goal of the Son's mission. He cites Augustine's comment:

> God's love is incomprehensible and unchangeable. For it was not after we were reconciled to him through the blood of his Son that he began to love us. Rather, he has loved us before the world was created, that we also might be his sons along with his only-begotten Son—before we became anything at all. The fact that we were reconciled through Christ's death must not be understood as if his Son reconciled us to him that he might now begin to love those whom he had hated. Rather, we have already been reconciled to him who loves us, with whom we were enemies on account of sin. The apostle will testify whether I am speaking the truth: "God shows his love for us in that while we were yet sinners Christ died for us" [Rom. 5:8].[55]

Here too there is an acknowledged paradox that we surrender only at the price of either the love or wrath of God. The cross establishes not God's love for us but the ground upon which God can justly accept those whom he has already loved in Christ "from the foundation of the world" (Eph. 1:4). Thus reconciliation is not first of all subjective but objective. We are reconciled to God (Rom. 5:10; 2 Cor. 5:19–20), but only because God has first found us acceptable in Christ.

The critics of Anselm are also correct to stress the importance of eschatology for atonement doctrine, as they are in their criticism that this element is often lacking in traditional accounts. It is my concern also, by using covenant and eschatology as a paradigm for constructive theology, to inject more eschatological thinking into every locus, including this one. Berkhof repeats familiar Reformed criticisms of Anselm's theory as reductionistic. It lodges the atonement in God's honor rather than justice and therefore there is no place for active obedience and "no hint of the mystical union of Christ and believers, nor of faith as accepting the righteousness of Christ"—it is just "commercial."[56] But the gospel focuses on the fact that God the Son laid aside his divine honor and dignity in order to bear God's righteous wrath against sinners. Not only is the resurrection missing from Anselm's theory; so too is the incarnation and the life of Christ.

55. Calvin, *Institutes* 2.16.3–4.
56. Berkhof, *Systematic Theology*, 386.

Aquinas improves on the theory somewhat, though with insufficient attention to the cosmic horizon.[57]

But criticisms of Anselm's formulation are not necessarily refutations of other versions of the sacrificial motif. My goal in the next two chapters will be to demonstrate how sacrifice fits within a wider covenantal framework that I hope obviates some of these weaknesses.

Having conceded some of the criticisms, I turn finally to areas of more obvious disagreement. The most basic issue is *the definition of violence*. It simply cannot be so broadly defined as "harm." According to the Anabaptist tradition, "just war" is an oxymoron. Passive suffering is the only properly Christian response to the evil of others. Yet passive suffering is precisely what feminist theologians (and even Weaver) found so troubling in the Anselmian atonement doctrine.

Beyond the principled arguments of the Anabaptist traditions, there is a quite different, often vague and sentimental reluctance to embrace an active suffering for righteousness' sake. Miroslav Volf offers an alternative to this pervasive tendency, which actually undermines the hope of justice for which victims cry out:

> My thesis that the practice of nonviolence requires a belief in divine vengeance will be unpopular with many Christians, especially theologians in the West. To the person who is inclined to dismiss it, I suggest imagining that you are delivering a lecture in a war zone (which is where a paper that underlies this chapter was originally delivered). Among your listeners are people whose cities and villages have been burned and leveled to the ground, whose daughters and sisters have been raped, whose fathers and brothers have had their throats slit. The topic of the lecture: a Christian attitude toward violence. The thesis: we should not retaliate since God is perfect noncoercive love. Soon you would discover that it takes the quiet of a suburban home for the birth of the thesis that human nonviolence corresponds to God's refusal to judge. In a scorched land, soaked in the blood of the innocent, it will invariably die. And as one watches it die, one will do well to reflect about many other pleasant captivities of the liberal mind.[58]

If the image of a son passively accepting a father's violence is a metanarrative for child abuse (or other forms of violence), then surely an approach that locates the significance of Christ's death in our imitation of his life is even more prone to that danger. But as Nancy Duff has argued, it is precisely by recognizing the uniqueness of the cross as an unrepeatable sacrifice—something that God did for us, not something designed for our imitation—that we can keep from valorizing passivity:

---

57. Even Aquinas maintains that God *could* (*de potentia absoluta*) have saved humankind in some other way than the incarnation and cross, but it was the most suitable route (*de potentia ordinata*) (*Summa theologiae* 3 q. 1, a.2). Here I am imputing categories that Aquinas himself defended but not in relation to the atonement. Condemnation befalls unbelievers not because original or personal sins are too serious (contra Anselm) but because they are without grace—i.e., remission of sins (1–2 87, 5). The focus is on justice, not honor.

58. Volf, *Exclusion and Embrace*, 304.

If faith does not acknowledge Christ as fully God and fully human, the connection between Christ's death on the cross and our involvement in suffering becomes distorted. When the church confesses the incarnation and the subsequent doctrine of Christ's two natures, the cross cannot rightly be interpreted as something God *required of* or *did to* Jesus, but something God *did for* us. Furthermore, because Christ is the Messiah, fully divine and fully human, the salvific nature of his death has a uniqueness and finality that cannot be repeated. No other person is required—or able—to do what Christ did. Therefore, the logic of the cross is not that we are to become victims consistent with Christ hanging on the cross, but that Christ became a victim to release us from the powers of sin and death. The abused wife does not "represent Christ" through exemplary self-sacrificial love. She is not the incarnate God suffering on behalf of sinful humanity. Rather, Christ on the cross represents her, reveals God's presence with her, and uncovers the sin of those who abuse or neglect her. Christ makes known to her and the world that her suffering represents *the opposite* of God's will.[59]

Furthermore, by recognizing that the cross is something that God did for us, and not merely something that we did to Jesus, it becomes a source of hope and not yet another example of what evil people do to those who try to bring about God's reign. If it rightly emphasizes the *active* obedience even of Jesus' death on the cross, it locates the place of ultimate judgment in God's hands, not ours. In other words, such a view is the best answer to the scapegoat mechanism, since even perpetrators of violence, like those who crucified Christ (both Jew and gentile), cannot be treated as such. This does not mean that there is no place for temporal judgment, so I at least would argue, since there is such a thing as the legitimate use of coercion for enforcing the law. However, it means that such judgments are always *only* temporal. Because the Lord has provided an offering for sin, "there is no longer any offering for sin" (Heb. 10:18).

Related to this point, it is this view of the atonement that guards most resolutely against anti-Semitic construals of the cross: first, by refusing to explain the Old Testament as the narrative of a violent deity in contrast to the New Testament; and second, by recognizing that it was ultimately God and not the Jews who sent Jesus to the cross. In Isaiah 53 YHWH is the one who offers up the Servant on behalf of Israel. It is he who "crushes" him and "cuts him off" from the land of the living in order to expiate their sins. The Good Shepherd himself says that *he* lays down his life for the sheep, even adding, "No one takes it from me, but I lay it down of my own accord. I have power to lay it down, and I have power to take it up again" (John 10:18). While those involved in carrying out the execution, both Jews and gentiles, can be blamed in one sense, ultimately they did "whatever [God's] hand and [God's] plan had predestined to take place" (Acts 4:28). As "a lamb without defect or blemish," Peter declares, "He was destined before the foundation of the world, but was revealed at the end of the ages for your sake" (1 Pet. 1:20–21). That God's wrath required punishment underscores

---

59. Nancy J. Duff, "Atonement and the Christian Life: Reformed Doctrine from a Feminist Perspective," *Interpretation* 53, no. 1 (1999): 27.

his justice, but that he himself gave what was required in the place of our punishment underscores his merciful love. In both cases it is the Father who gives up his Son to the cross and the Son who gives himself up in the Spirit. Thus Jesus can even cry from the cross, "Father, forgive them, for they know not what they do" (Luke 23:34). It is precisely because his death is propitiatory and substitutionary that he can say this—and by saying it, actually effect it.

Even more fundamentally, while the sacrificial motif cannot say everything, it presupposes as its basis a radical appraisal of human depravity and an equally radical view of God's holiness. While sin and divine holiness are not absent from critical reflection, rejection of sacrificial imagery often includes a strong antipathy to a radical view of human depravity and, correlatively, any concept of God's wrath or judgment as a consequence of God's holiness and righteousness. As a consequence, it is often the case that the vertical dimension is eventually lost entirely or at least eclipsed by purely horizontal questions. In other words, the two tables (love of God and love of neighbor) are separated.

In the alternatives to sacrificial atonement we are repeatedly left with possibilities for ethical transformation, when a more radical analysis of the human condition suggests that this will not suffice. In order even to bring about ethical transformation, something deeper needs to be done. So Christopher Schroeder, for instance, argues that Christ "stands in the breach" not by *bearing* God's wrath but by *turning it away*—and this opens up new possibilities for us to stand in the breach with him.[60] But can this thesis explain the cry of dereliction: "My God, my God, why have you forsaken me?" I find this cry impossible to reconcile with any of the alternative views I have surveyed. If curse-bearing is not central to Christ's death, we are led to ask why the Father's excommunication of the Suffering Servant is assumed here. And why does Jesus repeatedly, against the apostles' counsel, refer to his impending death as the reason for his mission? The clear testimony is that Christ's death *propitiates*—that is, appeases, satisfies, absorbs—God's wrath, so that there is nothing left of it for us. We are saved by the death of Jesus, "whom God put forward as a propitiation by his blood, to be received by faith . . . so that he might be just and the justifier of the one who has faith in Jesus" (Rom. 3:25–26 English Standard Version). "Since, therefore, we have now been justified by his blood, much more shall we be saved by him from the wrath of God" (Rom. 5:9 English Standard Version).

No sacrificial account is complete that forgets that God is both judge and the judged, justified and justifier. This is the cup that God himself took up when he elected us in Christ and walked alone between the severed halves in Abram's vision. This means that in a real sense God is the most violated victim in this whole story, a point that we often miss when we are preoccupied with our own victimization. Thus I must respectfully demur from Colin Gunton's judgment: "It has become fashionable in recent times to attack the doctrine of the impassibility of God, but in this context it proves its value. Sin is not a personal affront

---

60. Schroeder, "Standing in the Breach," 18–22.

to an anthropomorphically conceived deity; because he is impassible, he cannot be harmed, let alone offended by it."[61] Given my revised definition of impassibility (incapacity for being overwhelmed by suffering, not inability to enter into it), and the massive biblical witness to the fact that sin is chiefly an offense against God, I would argue that God is anything but aloof in this affair. Although the cross and resurrection declare God's ultimate triumph over sin and death in his world, it is a real struggle with the highest stakes. This is what we do with God when he comes to save us. It is not just his honor that has been offended, but his whole nature, which he has created the transgressor to reflect back in covenant faithfulness: his love, justice, holiness, righteousness, fidelity, goodness. It is only on these terms that humans can express the image of God. Transgressions are offenses and God is the foremost victim in these offenses—even when they involve other persons: "Against you and you alone have I sinned," said the psalmist after sinning against Bathsheba and Uriah (Ps. 51:4). The amazing irony in God's response is that instead of passing the appropriate sentence on the perpetrators (all of us), he bears the sentence himself. No atonement theory will approximate the witness of Scripture that fails to see sin first of all in its vertical dimension.

The very fact that God the victim of sin himself becomes the bearer of the victim's guilt is the undoing of the cycle of violence. When the concept of sin (which is in Scripture an undeniably juridical term) loses this vertical reference, however, it easily slips into merely horizontal categories of individual or collective therapy: either not living up to one's potential or failing to contribute adequately to human flourishing. The close connection between the first and second tables—love of God and love of neighbor—is key here. Without the vertical, we have only the horizontal dimension and sin can no longer be a valid concept. With it, however, we gain both, and sin against neighbor-love wears its truly awful specter. The "God-problem" is not metaphysical, but ethical.

While emphasizing only the aspect of justice can lend support to critics of the substitutionary theory that this sacrifice is cruel and vindictive, the question that remains without this aspect is far more sinister: What would a God be like who gave up his Son to such a death if it were *not* necessary? The answer that God did not give him up, but that the death is merely something that happened to Jesus, sets aside not only the atonement as a sacrifice but the death of Christ as valuable in any redemptive sense.

Once we see, however, that the death of Christ is rooted in God's justice as well as his love and mercy, it is possible to reconcile the sacrificial motif with the victory over the powers. Dorner expressed the point well: "Even a man would not be sufficiently zealous for the good if he thought only of his own good but was indifferent to the victory or defeat of the good outside him. How much more in God must it belong to his ethical self-affirmation that he will the good outside

---

61. Colin Gunton, *The Actuality of Atonement: A Study of Metaphor, Rationality and the Christian Tradition* (Grand Rapids: Eerdmans, 1989), 95.

himself with the same holy zeal as he will it in himself."[62] The cross answers not an offended dignity but the injustices that God will not endure precisely because of his love for the world. God's justice in relation to the atonement should not be reduced, as admittedly it often is, to accounting. It is not that juridical categories are wrong, but that our concept of the juridical itself must be broadened to include the wider scope that Scripture itself gives to it (i.e., the covenant). The goal of the cross is not simply forgiveness, but *ḥesed*—covenantal loyalty between God and humans, humans and humans, humans and the nonhuman creation, in the everlasting Sabbath of true righteousness, justice, freedom, and love. God is satisfied by the cross not merely as justice is served by the conviction and sentencing of a criminal, but because through the cross God is able to bring about for human beings what human beings, even *Christian* ones, have never brought about and will never bring about themselves.

In view of God's nature, sin requires punishment (Exod. 34:7; Num. 14:13; Nah. 1:3; Ps. 5:4–6; Rom. 1:18); in view of God's covenant, it requires death (Ezek. 18:4; Rom. 6:23). Sin is not represented simply as a weakness that could be reformed, but as guilt incurred, invoking sanctions (1 John 3:4; Rom. 2:25–27). So we read that human beings "are storing up wrath for [themselves] on the day of wrath, when God's righteous judgment will be revealed" (Rom. 2:5). God's law, whether written on the conscience in creation (for gentiles) or written on tablets (for Jews), is the basis for God's judgment (Rom. 2:1–29), and since "no one is righteous" (3:9–18), the law cannot reform or restore; it can only announce the guilty verdict over all humankind (vv. 19–20). "The law brings wrath" (4:15). At the same time, the atonement is not the result merely of strict justice, since far from compelling redemption it would actually entail universal condemnation. By definition, mercy need not be shown, but once God has decided to exercise mercy, he can only do so in a way that does not leave his righteousness, holiness, and justice behind.

Karl Barth speaks of Christ's "bearing of the eternal wrath of God. For the terrible thing, the divine No of Good Friday, is that there all the sins of Israel and of all men, our sins collectively and individually, have in fact become the object of the divine wrath and retribution."[63]

> But the real judgment of God is alone the crucifixion of Christ, and the terror of this event is that it is the reality which all other judgments upon Israel, the world and mankind can only foreshadow or reflect. . . . The only correct view, i.e., in harmony with the biblical interpretation, is that expressed in the 14th articles of the Heidelberg Catechism that "no mere creature can bear the burden of the eternal wrath of God against sin." In face of a real outbreak of God's avenging wrath, the creature would be annihilated.[64]

---

62. I. A. Dorner, *Divine Immutability: A Critical Reconsideration*, trans. and ed. Robert R. Williams and Claude Welch (Minneapolis: Fortress, 1994), 183.

63. Barth, *CD* II/1:395.

64. Ibid., 396.

But the wrath of God is not simply the no spoken by God to humanity. "The reason why the No spoken on Good Friday is so terrible, but why there is already concealed in it the Eastertide Yes of God's righteousness, is that He who on the cross took upon Himself and suffered the wrath of God was no other than God's own Son, and therefore the eternal God Himself in the unity with human nature which He freely accepted in His transcendent mercy."[65]

To any theology of the cross, therefore, we must relate a theology of the resurrection. Again echoing the Athanasian-Anselmian formulation, Barth adds, "God's wrath had to be revealed against the ungodliness and unrighteousness of men. But only God could carry through this necessary revelation of His righteousness without involving an end of all things. Only God Himself could bear the wrath of God."[66]

> For in Him who took our place God's own heart beat on our side, in our flesh and blood, in complete solidarity with our nature and constitution, at the very point where we ourselves confront Him, guilty before God. Because it was the eternal God who entered in in Jesus Christ, He could be more than the Representative and Guarantor of God to us. . . . He could also be our Representative and Guarantor towards God.[67]

No satisfactory refutation of the criticisms of sacrifice will probably be persuasive wherever a radical doctrine of sin and of God's righteousness and holiness are lacking. If God exists for us, for our happiness and moral reform, then the atonement can easily be conceived in therapeutic and social-political or individual-ethical terms alone. The fact that God has chosen to create us in covenant with him means that there *is* a "therapeutic" aspect (viz., the benefits of Christ), but that is not the whole story, because God does not finally exist for us, but we for God.

Further, any atonement theology therefore that claims to interpret Scripture must reflect substantial continuity with the albeit typological and therefore inferior character of the temple cult. I will return to this point in the next two chapters. As Martin Hengel observes, "dying for" is a Pauline formula rooted in the earliest Jerusalem community (cf. Acts 6:13).

> But what was the basis of these attacks on the sanctuary and the Torah? Presumably the certainty that the death of the crucified Messiah, who had vicariously taken upon himself the curse of the Law, had made the Temple obsolete as a place of everlasting atonement for the sins of Israel, and therefore the ritual Law had lost its significance as a necessary institution for salvation.[68]

So while Anselm's account is weakened by its own tendency to reduce the cross to a commercial transaction satisfying an offended monarch, the sacrificial motif

---

65. Ibid., 397.
66. Ibid., 400.
67. Ibid., 402.
68. Martin Hengel, *The Atonement: The Origins of the Doctrine in the New Testament*, trans. John Bowden (Philadelphia: Fortress, 1981), 36–38, 49.

itself is crucial throughout the Scriptures. Colin Gunton has attempted to rescue Anselm from the criticism that he reduces the atonement to the analogy of a feudal lord's demand of restitution to his affronted dignity. "In face of a tendency to mythologise the metaphor of ransom, Anselm's achievement is immense."[69] For Anselm, what really matters is "'the order and beauty of the universe,' for which God is responsible (I,xv)."[70] Both Hellenism and Christianity (e.g., Anselm) see justice as "good order" in cosmic as well as personal dimensions. "But their means of attaining it are opposite," as we see in Luther's famous lines about how he hated "righteousness" as the philosophers talk about it until he realized that it was "the passive righteousness with which merciful God justifies us by faith."

> It also encapsulates part of the difference between Christianity and paganism, as well as between Christianity as it was reshaped at the Reformation and the modern cult of autonomy. The Christian church still stands or falls by whether it proclaims and lives by the Gospel of the liberating grace of God, or whether its life degenerates into some form of self-salvation. For that reason, the doctrine of the atonement must continue to be at the heart of Christian theology, and the metaphor of the justice of God at the heart of the doctrine of the atonement, if Christianity's orientation to the action of God in re-establishing free human life is to be maintained and articulated.[71]

If that is so, it is also true, Gunton allows, that Luther's approach can also be one-sided, in a typically Western way: the cosmic dimension can get lost, especially in Kierkegaard and Bultmann as well as in some forms of mysticism and pietism. Further, overemphasis on penal aspects has sometimes shoved aside other important features.[72] Romans, for example, can be seen as a treatise on God's justice. "The centre is undoubtedly the justification of sinners, but they are seen in the context of a world which stands or falls with them." Thus God's justice is seen not only in relation to the justification of individuals, but the wider implications of God's justice vis-à-vis the godless (Rom. 1:22–25), the whole creation (8:19–23), and the Jews (chaps. 2, 9–11). "Then in the final chapters, which are largely concerned with Christian behaviour, he moves to the living out of the justice of God in daily life."[73] Referring to P. T. Forsyth's *Justification of God*, Gunton says, "The theme of the book is that the justice of God can be found only where he justifies himself, and that is in the act of atonement on the cross."[74] This is an important point, and this close connection between theodicy and soteriology has been especially brought out by Ernst Käseman, J. Christiaan Beker, and N. T. Wright more recently. Once more, this fits well with the character of the covenant, in which both partners are on trial for their fidelity. We cannot read the Psalms, for example, without noticing that God is not only finally extolled

---

69. Gunton, *Actuality of Atonement*, 87.
70. Ibid., 90.
71. Ibid., 100–101.
72. Ibid., 101.
73. Ibid., 102.
74. Ibid., 106.

for saving us in our troubles but is sometimes questioned for having caused them. "The cross is not a theological theme, nor a forensic device," Forsyth wrote, "but the crisis of the moral universe on a scale far greater than any earthly war. It is the theodicy of the whole God dealing with the whole soul of the whole world in holy love, righteous judgement and redeeming grace."[75]

While extreme feminist criticisms of the preaching of the cross offer somewhat new reflection in a postpatriarchal society, the broader liberationist interpretation itself has been maintained by various groups from the Maccabean revolt to the present. For many of the disparate parties of Jesus' day, the expectation of a political messiah who would restore the kingdom to Israel and drive out the Romans was one of the reasons for the transition from the triumphal entry to Good Friday. For many, like Saul of Tarsus, the proclamation of one who had been cursed by hanging on a cross was the contradiction of the righteousness and justice that the Messiah would establish. It was only when Saul became Paul as a result of seeing the cursed one exalted at the Father's right hand that the death of Christ as curse-bearing fell into place.[76]

First-century Judaism provides a necessary context for understanding Jesus and how he was heard by diverse groups but is hardly capable of exerting any normative role in interpreting either the Old or New Testament. Jesus' claim was that his contemporaries—even the most learned religious teachers—did not read the Scriptures correctly, largely due to their having missed him as Scripture's central figure and theme. Although he is uncomfortable with overly developed atonement theologies, N. T. Wright sees the sacrificial theme in Jesus' appropriation of the prophets. The following is a telling example of the proximity between his interpretation of the events and classic atonement theology:

> What then does the parallelism between the Temple-action and the Supper say about Jesus' understanding of his death? It says, apparently, that Jesus intended his death to accomplish that which would normally be accomplished in and through the Temple itself. In other words, Jesus intended that his death should in some sense function sacrificially. This should not surprise us unduly, or be regarded as necessarily meaning that the texts that suggest this viewpoint must be a later Christian retrojection.[77]

After all, even in his ministry, Jesus "regularly acted as if he were able to bypass the Temple system in offering forgiveness to all and sundry right where they were."[78] At this point Wright even says that the phrase, "When you make his life an offering for sin," in Isaiah 53, "by the first century was certainly taken to refer to a sacrifice."[79] But he also saw his death as a battle and the victory of God.[80]

75. Cited in ibid.
76. See Seyoon Kim, *The Origin of Paul's Gospel* (Grand Rapids: Eerdmans, 1981).
77. N. T. Wright, *Jesus and the Victory of God* (Minneapolis: Fortress, 1996), 604.
78. Ibid., 605.
79. Ibid.
80. Ibid., 606–10.

All of these themes are brought together at least in the Reformers, as I shall argue in the following chapters.

A final response concerns *social context*. Anselm, as has been recognized by "softer" critics in the Reformed tradition and "harsher" critics above, reflects his own location in a feudal economy. So too our reflections cannot help but be shaped to some extent at least by our own familiar form of life. Ironically, it is those of us who are relatively comfortable citizens of highly developed Western democracies, rather than those who are the brunt of injustice, who have the greatest trouble with the notion of radical sin and judgment.

Liberal bourgeois academic and popular culture breed a new kind of moralism verging on self-righteousness that divides the world into the "saved" and the "damned" just as surely as any fundamentalist preacher. One finds his or her own place very rarely among the "damned," but rather among those who can say, "God, I thank you that I am not like other people," inserting our own pariahs (Luke 18:11). It is not that some of us do this, but all of us reflect this tendency because we are all implicated in sin and self-justification. But what can break this cycle of self-justification? Surely it cannot be more instruction, ideology, awareness—the "wisdom" that, as important as it is, pertains only to the horizontal dimension. This may be good news for the well-adjusted and comfortable, but is it good enough for *sinners*? It may even be said that in the political paradigm the "others" are damned in the most ultimate sense, since they cannot be saved apart from their moral transformation, which includes the adoption of a particular ideology. There really is no redemption in this system for (real or imagined) perpetrators of violence and injustice, but only the imperative to "get it" and get with the program, whatever it happens to be, whether directed by ideologies of the left or the right.

The gospel of the cross, by contrast, holds out an objective redemption that is sufficient to save not only victims but perpetrators, even perpetrators who think that they are actually on the right side of things. The cross will not allow any of us to place ourselves in the safe category of those who, if not victims, are at least on their side. In the light of the law, revealed most fully in the person of Christ, we are all pretenders. We do not really love God or our neighbor the way we think we do.

Miroslav Volf has developed a similar line of thinking with much greater firsthand familiarity with the cycle of violence and despair. It is not only solidarity with victims that the cross affirms but atonement for the perpetrators.[81]

> If the claim that Christ "died for the ungodly" (Romans 5:6) is "the New Testament's fundamental affirmation," as Jon Sobrino rightly states in *Jesus the Liberator* (Sobrino 1993, 231), then the theme of solidarity, though indispensable and rightly rehabilitated from neglect by Moltmann and others, must be a sub-theme of the overarching theme of self-giving love. . . .

81. Volf, *Exclusion and Embrace*, 23.

To claim the comfort of the Crucified while rejecting his way is to advocate not only cheap grace but a deceitful ideology.[82]

Instead of valorizing the givens of modernity, Volf challenges them with the "inner logic of the cross," which "demands acceptance of two interrelated beliefs that are deeply at odds with some basic sentiments of modernity"—the irremediable character of evil from the human side and the covenant.

> First, modernity is predicated on the belief that fissures of the world can be repaired and that *the world can be healed*. It expects the creation of paradise at the end of history and denies the expulsion from it at the beginning of history (cf. Levy 1995, 91ff., 199ff.). Placed into the fissures of the world in order to bridge the gap that the fissures create, the cross underscores that evil is irremediable. Before the dawn of God's new world, we cannot remove evil so as to dispense with the cross. None of the grand recipes that promise to mend all the fissures can be trusted. . . . Second, modernity has set its high hopes in the twin strategies of *social control* and *rational thought*.[83]

But the weakness of the cross is "'stronger' than social control and this 'foolishness' is wiser than rational thought." In one and the same New Testament, sinners are at once identified as "children of hell" and yet embraced by grace. "Reflection on social issues rooted in the cross of Christ will have to explore what this interdependence of the 'universality of sin' and the 'primacy of grace' may mean when taken out of the realm of 'salvation' into the realm where we—many of us 'children of hell'—fight and wage wars against each other."[84]

In this light, the good news of the cross is that God's love and grace are great enough even to save an oppressor—even those of us who think we are not such a person. It is not only Paul, but Jesus, who says, "Did not Moses give you the law? Yet none of you keeps the law" (John 7:19). Our love of God and neighbor is often a cloak for our own self-interest.

Volf also brings together the themes of covenant and cross: "To place the new covenant at the center of theological reflection on social issues means for a Christian theologian to inquire about the relation between *the cross and the covenant*. On the cross we see what God has done to renew the covenant that humanity has broken."[85] This covenantal view of the cross entails that (1) God has made space in himself for others, and therefore has grounded the reality of both solidarity and difference; (2) "renewing the covenant entails self-giving." "On the cross the new covenant was made 'in blood' (Luke 22:20)." After referring to the sacrificial ceremony in which God passed through the halves, Volf says,

> For the narrative of the cross is not a "self-contradictory" story of a God who "died" because God broke the covenant, but a truly incredible story of God

82. Ibid., 24.
83. Ibid., 28.
84. Ibid., 85.
85. Ibid., 153.

doing what God should neither have been able nor willing to do—a story of God who "died" because God's all too human *covenant partner* broke the covenant. . . . The new covenant is eternal. God's self-giving on the cross is a consequence of the "eternality" of the covenant, which in turn rests on God's "inability" to give up the covenant partner who has broken the covenant.[86]

In line with my comments above, Volf concedes, "No doubt, there is more to divine judgment than setting the records straight; the One who judges at the end of history is the same One who 'justifies sinners' in the middle of history. But can divine judgment be anything less than setting the records straight."[87] Ironically, when we set aside divine judgment, we make ourselves the judges. "The attempt to transcend judgment—whether it be judgment of reason or of religion—does not eliminate but enthrones violence. The escape from the castle of (judging) conscience lands one in the castle of murderers."[88] Particularly persuasive in view of the criticisms mentioned above, Volf writes, "If Jesus had done nothing but suffer violence, we would have forgotten him as we have forgotten so many other innocent victims."[89] The death of a heroic reformer is tragic, but hardly redemptive—precisely because no matter how moving or exemplary, it cannot break the power of guilt and corruption in our own hearts or bring about an ultimate justice in the world. "A nonindignant God would be an accomplice in injustice, deception, and violence."[90] Volf concludes, "A 'nice' God is a figment of the liberal imagination, a projection onto the sky of the inability to give up cherished illusions about goodness, freedom, and the rationality of social actors."[91]

ONTOLOGICAL PARTICIPATION

If the theme of political justice is the criterion of the criticisms thus far reviewed, there is still one more significant perspective that should be mentioned. Ontological participation represents another challenge within a broader classification of "overcoming estrangement." Political and social liberation, at least as articulated by Moltmann, certainly stresses the ontological participation of all things in God ("trinitarian panentheism"). Many of the feminists who take a critical stance toward the sacrificial motif also adopt a pantheistic or panentheistic view of the God-world relation.[92] Moltmann insists, "The incarnation of God's Son is not an answer to sin. It is the fulfillment of God's eternal longing to become

---

86. Ibid., 155.
87. Ibid., 242.
88. Ibid., 290.
89. Ibid., 293.
90. Ibid., 297.
91. Ibid., 298.
92. Most notably, of course, is Sallie McFague, *Models of God.*

man and to make of every man a god out of grace; an 'Other' to participate in the divine life and return the divine love."[93]

Somehow we have to find a way to reconcile the cosmic dimensions of sin and redemption (beyond individualistic reductions) within a "meeting a stranger" paradigm that stresses difference, otherness, and ethical rather than ontological fault. "Overcoming estrangement," I have argued in relation to the atonement, downplays transgression of a covenant as the site of alienation and consequently views redemption chiefly in terms of a new awareness and/or a reconciliation that is conceived in ontic rather than ethical terms.

Even in quite typically Western treatments, the backlash against modern individualism has not only opened up space for the biblical emphasis on covenantal solidarity, but an all-encompassing concentration on community as defined by the horizon of philosophical abstraction or existing social praxis.[94] Among other implications, the many are again sacrificed to the one: the cosmic horizon simply absorbs the individual and his or her personal relation to the divine Other. I realize that this is a sweeping claim, but I will attempt to justify it.

Radical Orthodoxy

In the first chapter, I identified John Milbank and radical orthodoxy with the "ontological" paradigm, an association that Milbank at least seems quite happy to acknowledge with his avowed effort to retrieve Platonism and Eckhart for theology. Just as Tillich himself saw this approach as the best hope for reconciling religion and culture, Milbank and others seem similarly motivated. It is difficult to resist the temptation to see the radical orthodoxy project as yet another attempt to revive a Constantinian ideal. At the very least, when Milbank, Ward, and Pickstock do write theology (in the usual sense—i.e., doctrinal topics), ecclesiology swallows the whole horizon. "Christological and atonement doctrines are, I shall suggest, theoretically secondary to definitions of the character of the new universal community or Church," says Milbank.[95] Conflating Christ and his body, Milbank sees the work of Christ and the ongoing work of the church as a single act of atonement.[96] Furthermore, it is not at all clear that this atonement has reference to ethical breach; it has more to do with creating aesthetic beauty and cosmic harmony.[97] These aspects are not missing from my own account, as we will see, but they seem to be worked out more centrally and speculatively in Milbank's treatment.[98]

93. Moltmann, *Trinity and the Kingdom*, 46.

94. See, for example, John Milbank, "Postmodern Critical Augustinianism," in *The Postmodern God: A Theological Reader*, ed. Graham Ward (Oxford: Blackwell, 1997), 269–73, where the entire emphasis in his reference to the atonement is on the "community" (i.e., the church).

95. John Milbank, *The Word Made Strange* (Oxford: Blackwell, 1997), 148.

96. Ibid., 149, 150–52, 160–65.

97. Ibid., especially 148–75.

98. See particularly his most recent treatment, *Being Reconciled*, especially chaps. 3–6.

A suspicious mind might see Hegel lurking in the background of all of these diverse rivals. In any case, it is the ontological paradigm that, to my mind at least, brings them together.

Robert Jenson

Despite significant differences, Robert Jenson nevertheless displays a somewhat Hegelian turn in contemporary soteriological reflection as well, but in his particular case it is probably better called a turn east, even if in some respects he moves beyond it.[99] According to Jenson, Anselm's theory of the atonement has two difficulties (besides the absence of the resurrection).

> First, the idea that God cannot show mercy without the satisfaction of his justice, and that he views yet an additional crime as constituting such satisfaction, casts a most dubious picture of God, precisely by biblical standards. . . . Second, the central notion of vicarious debt-paying, of substitutionary "satisfaction," is difficult indeed: How can another's debt pay my debt, even if he *has* assumed a nature like mine—unless we assume an extreme Platonic realism of natures, which theology has otherwise much reason to reject? Perhaps the most notable enforcers of this second critique were the . . . "Socinians"—in general, vigorous precursors of Enlightenment critique.[100]

Yet critiques of Anselm's doctrine have reversed the effect of the atonement from God to humans, that is, to "subjective" theories, says Jenson. The problem with these theories, however, is that they cannot account for what the cross actually accomplishes that is different from before.[101] Even Gustav Aulén's revival of the "classic" theory "has the same flaws as the Anselmian doctrine. Here, too, the picture of God, who sends Jesus to his death to accomplish a victory easily attained otherwise, is dubious. Here, too, it is far from clear how what Christ does for himself—in this account, that he withstands Satan—is supposed to be actual for *us*."[102]

In recent treatments, the atonement has been reduced to relativism: who can really say what it means?—but this despair is unwarranted, Jenson insists. What if we begin by first of all questioning what all these theories affirm: "that the event's salvific efficacy must be an effect of what God does or the man Jesus does on humanity or on God," which is itself dependent on the christology of Leo's Tome.[103]

> Anselmian theories of atonement attribute the work to the human nature; subjectivist and "classic" theories attribute it to the divine nature, explicitly or implicitly. But if the Christology of our earlier chapter is right, we should

---

99. See Robert Jenson, *ST* 1:186–88, for his analysis of the different atonement theories.
100. Jenson, *ST* 1:186.
101. Ibid., 186–87.
102. Ibid., 188.
103. Ibid.

refuse both alternatives and attribute reconciliation to Christ according to neither nature but only according to both, jointly and simultaneously.[104]

Thus the cross is "itself an event in God's triune life." But this is not simply to affirm the unity of Christ's person; it is to collapse his humanity into his deity, which I have argued to be a more general weakness in Jenson's christology. "Its reconciling efficacy . . . is that this is the event in God that settles what sort of God he is over against fallen creation." But what about settling the sort of *human* he is?

> Just so the Crucifixion—given the Resurrection—settles also our situation as creatures. The Crucifixion put it up to the Father: Would he stand to *this* alleged Son? To *this* candidate to be his own self-identifying Word? Would he be a God who, for example, hosts publicans and sinners, who justifies the ungodly? The Resurrection was the Father's Yes.[105]

The cross does not seem to have its own distinct role in redemption. He asks a good question: "Why did Jesus have to die?" But instead of answering this question he quickly shifts the focus to a different one: Why do we keep handing over good servants to death? If Jenson does offer an answer to the first question, it seems to be nothing more than that whatever happened at the cross, God stood by his Son by raising him from the dead.

An advocate of the "new Finnish school" interpretation of Luther, Jenson has argued, citing Tuomo Mannerma,

> Justification is thus "a mode of deification." For Luther's strongest language, we again turn to the *Commentary on Galatians*: "By faith the human person becomes God." Carried along by the Scripture he is expounding, Luther can go beyond even his radical younger followers and make not only Christ but the believer, united with Christ, the subject of a real communion of divine attributes: "Every Christian fills heaven and earth in his faith." Yet this is not dissolution in God or even any usual sort of mysticism or idealism, for the Christ who is one with me so that I am one with God is precisely Christ in "flesh and bones."[106]

This is not the place to engage this interpretation of Luther, but to point up Jenson's appeal to it for his own understanding of atonement.[107] While Jenson

104. Ibid., 189.
105. Ibid.
106. Jenson, *ST* 2:296–97. In recent decades, not only has the substitutionary view been marginalized as "Lutheran" or "Calvinist"; Luther and Calvin have themselves been reinterpreted as torchbearers for views that their successors are said to have corrupted. (Aulén tried to recruit Luther especially for the Christus Victor cause.) In contemporary Luther studies, a circle of scholars identified as the Finnish school has gained growing support for the thesis that the reformer was, contrary to the conclusions of previous scholarship, not concerned with the question of how a sinner is declared right before God but with the deification of believers, in the sense generally understood by Eastern Orthodoxy's doctrine of theosis.
107. For a rebuttal of the Finnish circle see Carl R. Trueman, "Is the Finnish Line a New Beginning?" *Westminster Theological Journal* 65, no. 2 (2003): 231–44, with a response by Jenson, 245–46.

challenges Barth's tendency to collapse history into eternity, Jenson himself runs the risk, ironically, of pulling away from history by emphasizing the person over the work of Christ and then making ontological participation the principal soteriological theme. Again I would argue that this is a tendency whenever the humanity of Christ is engulfed in deity.

Avoiding both Nestorianism and Monophysitism is as difficult in considering Christ's work as in considering his person, since both are inextricably related. As Gerhard Forde comments concerning Jenson's approach, "The suspicion that salvation comes by participation lies near at hand, and salvation by participation slides too easily into salvation by *gratia gratum faciens*."[108] Furthermore, Jenson seeks to make the resurrection rather than the cross the central event in the life of God.[109] "It would seem to me," Forde concludes, "that Jenson's soteriology lacks something of the pathos that comes from a perception of faith's struggle with temptation, with the wrath of God, suffering and death."[110]

Furthermore, Jenson is rather vague in settling on any particular atonement theory, or even constellation of theories. Instead, he seems to lodge the real saving activity of God in Christ wholly in the resurrection. George Hunsinger judges, "Jenson's well-known reference to Jesus' resurrection—incessant throughout all his writings—is not finally so orthodox as it seems, because . . . it occurs at the expense of the cross."[111] Against Jenson's claim that there is no ecumenical consensus on the atonement, Hunsinger argues,

> The priestly work of Christ centers on the *admirabile commercium*, the wondrous exchange. Being both the priest and the victim in one, Christ has taken our sin to himself that we might receive his righteousness and life. As authorized by scripture, constitutive of tradition, and enshrined in every eucharistic liturgy worthy of the name, he is the Lamb of God that takes away the sin of the world. He has borne our sin on the cross and borne it away. He has suffered what sinners rightly deserved—the divine judgment, curse, condemnation and wrath—in order that they might be spared.[112]

After a number of citations, Hunsinger concludes, "The point is all too clear: Christ's death accomplishes nothing redemptive in itself," but is simply a prelude to the resurrection.

> The royal work of Christ fares little better. That by his perfect obedience as fulfilled in the cross Christ himself defeats, objectively, the powers hostile to God and that hold sinners in bondage, is dismissed as "mythology" ([*ST*]1.193). While Jesus achieved a personal victory that was "moral and spiritual" (1.193), the real saving event is again his resurrection, not his

108. Gerhard O. Forde, "Robert Jenson's Soteriology," 131.
109. Ibid., 135.
110. Ibid., 137.
111. George Hunsinger, "Robert Jenson's Systematic Theology: A Review Essay," *Scottish Journal of Theology* 55, no. 2 (2002): 162.
112. Ibid., 163.

death. . . . The gospel is not really so much that Christ died for our sins (1.179), he insists, but rather that Jesus is risen. . . . Jenson's rejection of anything like an objective atonement (1.192–3) tells us something important about his doctrine of sin. . . . In short, Jenson's God restores community without properly expiating sin. Although Jenson writes an entire chapter about "our place in God," he says nothing about "God in our place." He has almost completely lost sight of the perfect tense. He expressly rejects that "Christ fully accomplished our salvation at Golgotha" (1.179).[113]

The center of Jenson's theology seems to be "not Christ but the Spirit, or indeed not Christ but the church."[114] In short, despite occasional exceptions, salvation's present tense is "evacuated of all meaning along Socinian, liberal and existentialist lines."[115]

Gabriel Fackre draws out the implications of Jenson's version of the Lutheran *capax* in his understanding of the atonement. While Jenson says he is cutting a new path, it is really "a model with a long lineage in the Eastern tradition—the incarnation *as* the atonement." However, Fackre suggests,

> There is another kind of atonement model, with an ecumenical trail that runs through both Eastern and Western traditions but was developed in more detail than most by Calvin, one that attempts to honor and interrelate the partialities of the four standard models in the concept of the "threefold office"—prophet, priest, and king, the Work as carried through by the divine-human Person. . . . Its value also resides in the place given to the priestly office, indeed, its centrality in any full-orbed understanding of Christ's reconciling work. So both an ecumenical and a Reformed voice must ask Jenson: How in a systematics so focused on the resurrection does the cross get the attention it is due?[116]

It does seem that in "ontological" accounts of either stripe ("political" or "ecclesial"), the cross is submerged under other theologoumena, without its own place in the system. While there are dangers in a theology of the cross that mutes other essential themes such as incarnation and resurrection, the dangers appear even greater today of losing sight of the specificity of the cross in a general kenosis of God and theosis of the church.[117] The answer to both challenges, I would argue, lies at least partly in recovering the covenant as the site of creation, sin, incarnation, and atonement—the place, in other words, where we might meet a stranger. It is the covenant that incorporates both the individual and communal, personal and cosmic, *historia salutis* and *ordo salutis*, the soteriological and the ecclesiological—without allowing the one to overwhelm the other. It is to that proposal that we now turn.

---

113. Ibid., 163–66.
114. Ibid., 166.
115. Ibid., 167.
116. Gabriel Fackre, "The Lutheran *Capax* Lives," in *Trinity, Time, and Church*, ed. Gunton, 100.
117. The latter (unlike the former) I would wholeheartedly affirm, as will become clear in the third volume. Nevertheless, in Jenson it seems to swallow the horizon.

Chapter Eight

Prophet and Priest

I have argued that at least many of the alternatives to sacrificial atonement theory are wrong not in what they affirm but in what they deny. Conceding the usual Reformed objection that Anselm's theory is weakened by insufficient attention to the resurrection, the active obedience of Christ, recapitulation, covenant, and the cosmic dimensions of salvation, my goal in this chapter and the next is to develop a constructive proposal that attempts to do greater justice to these essential elements. I have adopted Calvin's rubric of the threefold office of Christ as the systematic structure of my own concluding presentation. One advantage of this approach is that it integrates the person and work of Christ.

PROPHET OF THE COVENANT LAWSUIT

It is certainly true that an individualistic soteriology that emphasizes the work of Christ in terms of personal benefits to the believer requires a correlative christology. Thus, especially in pietism, but also in some forms of Protestant orthodoxy (particularly the Puritan tradition), the person and work of Christ can easily be reduced to personal transactions between the sinner and God. Or, as recent

208

Reformed critics of this tendency have pointed out, the *historia salutis* (history of salvation) becomes eclipsed by the *ordo salutis* (logical order of salvation in the individual's experience).[1]

Nancy Duff has pointed out that too typically, when the only horizon is the salvation of the individual believer, the prophetic office of Christ is treated as the mediation of information. Understandably, it is easy then to correlate Christ's prophetic ministry to something like the moral influence theory of the atonement, while saving the discussion of Christ's sacrificial work for his priesthood.[2] It is an easy move to make when the "prophetic" is reduced to teaching or instruction, which even Calvin emphasizes far more than the eschatological, historical, and cosmic dimensions. The term *redemption* automatically makes us think of his priestly rather than his prophetic or royal ministry. Surely Christ is more than a prophet, but there is more to Christ as prophet than we often realize.

The Prophet as Mediator

In line with my comments above, we often think of the role of a mediator in priestly terms, with considerable justification. When we start with Christ's prophetic office, however, we begin to see that mediation is not only sacrificial but apocalyptic. A brief word at this point about eschatological assumptions is in order.

Jesus and Paul assume a "two-age" eschatology (Matt. 12:32; 1 Cor. 2:6; Gal. 1:4, etc.), and this may also have been a widely held view in Second Temple Judaism (Matt. 24:3). As I argued in *Covenant and Eschatology*, it is not two worlds but two ages that biblical eschatology has in mind when it speaks of heavenly realities and earthly shadows.[3] In Hebrews, the "heavenly realities" and their "earthly copies," far from a Platonic contrast, are given an eschatological content: "the age to come" and "this present age," respectively.[4] Typology, then, is not simply a preview of coming attractions: in every type, whether the clothing of Adam and Eve, Noah's ark, the exodus, the serpent in the wilderness, or the Mosaic theocracy on a grand scale, the reality is made present in a partly realized manner (1 Cor. 10:1–4, 9). In his study of Hebrews, Geerhardus Vos illustrates this as a triangle, with an arrow pointing downward from the heavenly realities ("the age to come") to both the left and right corners of the triangle, representing the

---

1. For a balanced (if somewhat in-house) discussion of this important subject, see Richard Gaffin Jr., "Biblical Theology and the Westminster Standards," *Westminster Theological Journal* 65, no. 2 (2003): 165–79.

2. Nancy Duff, "Atonement and the Christian Life: Reformed Doctrine from a Feminist Perspective," *Interpretation* 53, no. 1 (1999): 9.

3. Michael Horton, *Covenant and Eschatology*, chap. 1.

4. The appeal to "this age" and "the age to come," as employed by Jesus in the Gospels and by Paul, refers basically to the era of sin and death as well as the shadows of the old covenant distinguished from the era of eschatological judgment, justification, and renewal as the shadows give way to the reality. Hebrews emphasizes this latter aspect (old covenant/new covenant) more than the more general "before" and "after" Christ.

old and new covenants, respectively.[5] One more arrow points horizontally from old to new. The important point in that illustration is that whereas typology recognizes only the horizontal arrow, eschatology introduces the vertical "intrusions" of the age to come in a state of partial eschatological realization of heaven on earth. In other words, the kingdom is present not just by anticipation but really, though without yet being consummated. It is not only a forecast but a foretaste. "Yet all these [OT believers], though they were commended for their faith, did not receive what was promised, since God had provided something better so that they would not, apart from us, be made perfect" (Heb. 11:39–40). So concerned is YHWH to affirm the solidarity of all the saints under both administrations of the covenant of grace that they had to wait, as it were, for us to catch up with them. "All of these died in faith without having received the promises, but from a distance they saw and greeted them" (v. 13).

What is the point of this excursus on eschatology? It is to remind us of an important part of the background for our discussion of the three offices. Related to this office, it means that a prophet is not simply a conduit of divine information but a herald of the age to come. Indeed, the prophet mediates the age to come in this present age. The prophet is on trial for the testimony offered. This is why the true and false prophets in Jeremiah 23, for example, are distinguished by whether they have "stood in the council of the LORD," alternatively identified as having been "in the Spirit," that is, the Glory-Cloud that hovered over the watery abyss, led Israel through the wilderness, settled in the temple, and after having left the provisional temple, to settle on the heavenly temple made flesh, in order finally to indwell believers, raise them with Christ from the dead, and bring about resurrection of all living things. Are they through their human word uttering the divine Word—*bringing about* the age to come, in the Spirit? That is what distinguishes a true prophet ("true and faithful witness") from the rest. Their prophetic ministry is apocalyptic. Their word, as God's word, *brings about* what it threatens and promises: "Is not my word like fire, says the LORD, and like a hammer that breaks a rock in pieces?" (Jer. 23:29).

In the exodus narrative, Moses is made "like God to Pharaoh" as he, along with Aaron, brings God's word of judgment to the king. Even before we come to the priestly work of Aaron and the Levitical line, the prophet is treated as a mediator. The response of the people at Sinai to which Moses refers is recounted in Exodus 19 and 20, in the context of the giving of the Ten Words amid solemn signs: "'You speak to us, and we will listen, but do not let God speak to us, or we will die.' . . . Then the people stood at a distance, while Moses drew near to the thick darkness where God was" (20:18–21). Like Adam, Israel's first instinct is to take flight from God's holy presence. A mediator was needed: not only a priest to intercede for violation, but a prophet to mediate the Word that otherwise fills

---

5. Geerhardus Vos, *The Teaching of the Epistle to the Hebrews* (Grand Rapids: Eerdmans, 1956), 56–58.

the people with fear. The people asked for a mediator at Sinai and the Lord answered, "They are right in what they have said. I will raise up for them a prophet like you among their own people; I will put my words in the mouth of the prophet, who shall speak to them everything that I command," and all that he speaks will come to pass (Deut. 18:15–22). This prophetic mediation is more fully developed as the story unfolds, when Moses brings YHWH's judgment in the golden calf episode and yet restrains God's wrath, giving the people a stay of execution by his intercession (Exodus 32–34). This is the dual function of the prophetic ministry: representing the covenant Lord as prosecutor and the covenant people as a defense attorney. The prophet's blessings and curses are God's blessings and curses.

In this spirit of the covenant lawsuit, Ezekiel indicts the faithless nation. As Eichrodt observes in this connection,

> When Israel is restored to nationhood under her shepherd David, then Yahweh will conclude a covenant of peace with her, which will last forever and will set up an enduring relationship of grace between God and his people. The contrast with the Sinai covenant is here clear enough. For Ezekiel as for others the sense of standing amid the break-up of the old and the building of the new was much too strong to permit him to exempt any existing institution from the annihilation to come. All that survives the destruction of state and Temple is the God who is jealous for the honour of his Name; and it is solely in the knowledge of this God that the prophet sees a guarantee of the new covenant. The point of contact with the priestly ways of thinking is limited, as in Jeremiah, to this: that the *berît* of the future is seen as a relationship of pure grace. However, through the close association of the covenant with the new David, it follows that the new order of things acquires in addition a fairly strong character of rigid legal establishment.[6]

But, according to Eichrodt, "The prophetic interpretation of the covenant concept attains its greatest profundity in *Deutero-Isaiah*." The emphasis is not on Sinai but on the election of Abraham and divine faithfulness.[7]

> This manifestation of the *berît* in the last times is, however, no isolated act of a ritual character, no new constitution or organization but something embodied in the life of a human person, the Servant of God, who is defined as the mediator of the covenant to the nations. In him the divine will for the community is revealed as one of vicarious suffering, by which the covenant people with their messianic ruler are united in an indissoluble community and reconciled with God. At the same time, by this gathering of the people round a king raised to sovereignty from suffering, God's own purpose of absolute lordship receives unqualified acceptance.[8]

6. Walther Eichrodt, *Theology of the Old Testament*, trans. J. A. Baker, 2 vols., Old Testament Library (Philadelphia: Westminster Press, 1961–67), 1:60–61.

7. Ibid., 61.

8. Ibid., 61–62.

Thus the Servant Songs especially point toward the universalizing of the kingdom of God.[9] It becomes increasingly clear in the postexilic period that hope for the future consummation lies in the Abrahamic-Davidic-new covenant, and not in the shadows of Sinai.[10] It is as if the flaming sword guarding any reentry of Eden now stands guard against any return to the old covenant theocracy. If this interpretation is correct, it underscores that the New Testament eschatology briefly summarized above is at work already in the Old. The history of covenant-breaking by the people which has led to exile in the first place confirms this. We see this, for example, in Psalm 74:9–12:

> We do not see our emblems; there is no longer any prophet, and there is no one among us who knows how long. How long, O God, is the foe to scoff? Is the enemy to revile your name forever? Why do you hold back your hand; why do you keep your hand in your bosom? Yet God my King is from of old, working salvation in the earth. . . . Have regard for your covenant, for the dark places of the land are full of the haunts of violence. Do not let the downtrodden be put to shame; let the poor and needy praise your name. Rise up, O God, plead your cause. (vv. 9–12, 20–22)

All hope for the future began to focus on the unilateral promise to David and his seed.[11] In short, wherever the prophet announced judgment, it was on the basis of the failure to live up to the terms of the covenant at Sinai (the past and present), but whenever the announcement turns to good news it is always because of the seed promised to Abraham and David (the future). A hopeful future is established not on the covenant that the people made with God (at Sinai), "yet I will remember my covenant with you in the days of your youth, and I will establish with you an everlasting covenant . . . when I forgive you all that you have done, says the Lord GOD" (Ezek. 16:60, 63).

The Prophet as Messenger

Even angels (Greek *angeloi*, "messengers") can be prophets. They bring announcements from the throne of God, both of blessing and of judgment, and even execute God's announced intentions in some instances (Gen. 19:1; 24:7; 1 Kgs. 13:18; Luke 1:11–38). Centuries of exegesis have identified some of the angelic appearances as christophanies, especially where the angel is identified with YHWH himself (Gen. 18:1–33; 32:22–32; Exod. 23:23; 32:34; 33:2; 2 Sam. 13:20; 1 Chr. 21:16; Isa. 63:9; Zech. 3:1–10, etc.). In fact, the messianic figure who "will suddenly come to his temple" is "the angel [messenger] of the covenant" in Malachi 3:1.

If prophets are more than teachers, they are not less than that. In Isaiah 30:18–26 the Messiah is also named "Teacher," the most common name for the

9. Ibid., 62.
10. Ibid., 63.
11. Ibid., 65.

messianic Teacher of Righteousness in the Qumran texts. Not only in Malachi 3:1–3; 4:4–6, but in Sirach, as Richard Horsley points out, "The second-century B.C.E. scribe Ben Sira, in a recitation of the great heroes of the past, presents what looks like a common expectation that Elijah, who had performed wondrous deeds and 'sent kings down to destruction,' would return 'to restore the tribes of Jacob' (Sirach 48:1–10)."[12] Horsley underscores the parallels between the prophetic work of Moses, Elijah, and Jesus.[13]

> Clear reminiscences of Moses' founding and of Elijah's renewal recur through the first section on Jesus' inaugural mission in Galilee. Like Moses designating Joshua and Elijah summoning Elisha, Jesus calls those who will assist in his program of renewal. This program becomes unmistakable when he appoints them as the twelve representative heads of the renewed Israel (cf. Elijah's making an altar of twelve stones, representing the twelve tribes of Israel). Meanwhile, Jesus' declaration of forgiveness of sins and pronouncement about doing the will of God signal the renewal of the Mosaic covenant.[14]

However, I would argue that these announcements signal the renewal not of the Mosaic but of the Abrahamic-Davidic covenants, for reasons I have already argued.

The next section of the story unmistakably parallels the exodus under Moses "and Elijah's miraculous restorative deeds," Horsley says.

> As Moses engaged in sea crossings and wilderness feedings, so did Jesus. As Elijah healed people and brought a virtually dead child back to life and multiplied food, so did Jesus. . . . With all these clear parallels to Moses and Elijah, it is no surprise at all when Mark relates that people generally believed Jesus was a prophetic figure—either John the Baptist raised from the dead or Elijah or "a prophet like one of the prophets of old" (6:14–16; 8:27–28)—and that Jesus refers to himself as a prophet (6:4).[15]

The transfiguration confirms all of this. "Indeed, the command to 'listen to him' is a direct allusion to God's promise to raise up a prophet like Moses (Deut. 18:15)."[16] Then when he arrives at the temple, he is the prophet-as-critic, like Jeremiah's criticism of the temple, and Isaiah's critique of the Jerusalem rulers. "At the Passover, celebrating the exodus liberation of the people, he solemnly ceremonially renews the covenant at the last supper."[17] N. T. Wright adds,

12. Richard A. Horsley, *Hearing the Whole Story: The Politics of Plot in Mark's Gospel* (Louisville, KY: Westminster John Knox, 2001), 238.

13. Ibid., 238–40.

14. Ibid., 248.

15. Ibid.

16. Ibid., 248–49.

17. Ibid., 249–50. Yet this meal is certainly not a renewal of the Sinaitic covenant. Even in structure it is completely different from the renewal of vows evident in Ezra and Nehemiah. It is completely one-sided: he gives his life for them. Furthermore, Jesus *says* that it is the new covenant, which is said in Jeremiah to be "not like the covenant I made with your ancestors in the wilderness" (Jer. 31:32). Finally, although in one sense the institution of the Supper is a renewal of the Abrahamic covenant, it is not so much a renewal as an inauguration.

Moreover, John's family was priestly, and his activity of offering a baptism for forgiveness out in the desert presented a clear alternative to the Temple. Like Ezekiel, Jesus predicts that the Temple will be abandoned by the Shekinah, left unprotected to its fate. Like Jeremiah, Jesus constantly runs the risk of being called a traitor to Israel's national aspirations, while claiming all along that he nevertheless is the true spokesman for the covenant god.

Thus he is tried as a false prophet.[18]

This New Testament event is better illumined by its Old Testament background. In Exodus 24, after "the blood of the covenant" was sprinkled on the people in order to ratify their promise to keep the law, Moses, Aaron, Nadab, and Abihu, along with the seventy elders, went up the mountain to meet with God— "and they ate and drank" with God. The Lord tells Moses to come to the top of the mountain, where he will give the prophet the stone tablets.

> Then Moses went up on the mountain, and the cloud covered the mountain. The glory of the LORD settled on Mount Sinai, and the cloud covered it for six days; on the seventh day he called to Moses out of the cloud. Now the appearance of the glory of the LORD was like a devouring fire on the top of the mountain in the sight of the people of Israel. Moses entered the cloud, and went up on the mountain. Moses was on the mountain for forty days and forty nights. (vv. 15–18)

In reading Scripture from beginning to end, we are able to hear echoes of this event throughout Jesus' ministry. The blood of the new covenant is our salvation because the blood of the old covenant, which was sprinkled on the people as a threat should they violate their oath, was shed vicariously by Christ. The language and the actions (eating and drinking with God) in Exodus 24 reverberate in the upper room. Yet it is especially the transfiguration that echoes this ancient narrative. At Mount Sinai, heaven comes to earth; the top of the mountain is made the temple of the Shekinah-Spirit, the small-scale copy of the heavenly sanctuary. For forty days and forty nights Moses was in the Holy of Holies. Even the days are significant: after six days (echoing the creation narrative's workweek), Moses enters the "cloud" (the Spirit) on the seventh day. With this in mind, Matthew's account of the transfiguration reaches a dazzling fulfillment, with the future glory of the resurrection casting its rays forward proleptically. While Jesus converses with Moses and Elijah, representing the prophetic history, the familiar benediction from heaven is heard: "This is my Son, the Beloved; with him I am well pleased; listen to him!" (Matt. 17:1–8). Jesus is the "greater prophet" promised to Moses. This vision was part of the messianic secret that the disciples were not to divulge "until after the Son of Man has been raised from the dead" (v. 9). The whole prophetic tradition was brought to Jesus' feet in this vision. The quintessential prophet was also the content of all prophecy. Jesus not only brings the Word—he is the Word that he brings. As the Word spoken from eternity and

---

18. N. T. Wright, *Jesus and the Victory of God* (Minneapolis: Fortress, 1996), 161, 166.

spoken into creation, the Son of God as prophet appears in the flesh to speak a new creation out of the darkness and void of human sin.

On one hand, Jesus is like Elijah. "He too is announcing to the faithless people of YHWH that their covenant god will come to them in wrath. But at the same time he is also acting out a different message, one of celebration and inauguration, which bursts the mould of the Elijah-model."[19] We see this in Jesus' comparison of himself to John the Baptist, understood by Jesus to be the Elijah figure. Jesus was heralding the new age. But he was also, I should add, *bringing about* the reality that the message held forth. It is apocalyptic: the appearing of God's salvation in history. Jesus is both the preacher and the preached, the teacher and the lesson. As Wright expresses it, "He was not simply reshuffling the cards already dealt, the words of YHWH delivered in former times."[20]

> In the parable of the wicked tenants, Israel is the vineyard, her rulers the vineyard-keepers; the prophets are the messengers, Jesus is the son; Israel's god, the creator, is himself the owner and father. . . . Jesus is claiming to be developing a story already used by Isaiah (5.1–7); the present moment is the moment of crisis, the end of exile; behind the covenant stands a god who cannot be blackmailed by its supposed terms; Israel was made for YHWH's will and not vice versa, since he is after all the creator who called her into being in the first place; he will return to his vineyard, to judge his wicked tenants.[21]

These prophetic judgments were already part of Israel's history. In this respect, at least, there is nothing new. "To pronounce judgment on the present regime was not unusual; nor, it must be stressed, was it in the slightest degree a sign that one was being 'anti-Jewish' [see 1 Kgs. 18:17–18.]." This was typical of the Jewish prophets, and this warning was fulfilled in the destruction of the temple.[22]

> Jesus, in other words, was announcing that Israel's god was establishing his kingdom in a way which would leave the self-appointed guardians of Israel's tradition outside. Israel was being redefined; to be outside that company when the true god acted would mean total ruin. In that situation, Israel had better settle accounts quickly, before she was handed over to judgment [Matt. 5:25–26; Luke 12:58–59].[23]

There is the threatening reversal in Matthew 8: "I tell you, many will come from east and west and will eat with Abraham and Isaac and Jacob in the kingdom of heaven, while the heirs of the kingdom will be thrown into outer

19. Ibid., 167.
20. Ibid., 171.
21. Ibid., 178. Cf. 183–84 for his litany of prophetic "woes" by Jesus, which points up that Jesus was if anything more threatening in his prosecution of the covenant lawsuit than any of his prophetic predecessors.
22. Ibid., 324–25.
23. Ibid., 327.

darkness, where there will be weeping and gnashing of teeth" (vv. 11–12). Luke's Gospel adds to this account of Jesus' words, "Indeed, some are last who will be first, and some are first who will be last" (Luke 13:28–30). There is no doubt that in his *prophetic* office, Jesus was announcing imminent devastation.

> The master of the house is coming, and servants who are unready for him will be 'put with the unfaithful' ([Luke] 12.35–46). . . . From now on there will be division within Israel (12.49–53), while her citizens, not reading the signs of the times, do not recognize that her hour has come (12.54–6). If they did, they would come to terms with their enemies now, rather than risk total ruin (12.57–9).[24]

The parables are concentrated on this theme, despite the individualistic interpretation that is often given to them in preaching. In Luke 13, for example, the coming judgment is no respecter of persons as to their ethnic status: "No, I tell you; but unless you repent, you will all perish just as they did" (v. 5). This is followed by the parable of the barren fig tree that is about to be cut down if it fails to produce fruit (vv. 6–9).

Imminent judgment was not a new theme. "This, after all, was the basic hope of Israel: that the enemies of the chosen people would be destroyed, and the chosen themselves vindicated. Jesus seems to have been reaffirming, even though radically redrawing, this expectation."[25] "The plot is the same, the dramatis personae different," with the current regime under judgment.[26] In the "little apocalypse" of Mark 13, the Son of Man's "coming on the clouds" is "his 'coming' to Jerusalem as the vindicated, rightful king," even if it did not happen according to the usual expectations of his contemporaries, including his disciples.[27] Jeremiah 50:6–8, 28; 51:6–10, 45–46, 50–51, 57 and Zechariah 2:6–8, 14:2–9 are in the background of Mark 13. Jesus will be vindicated as Messiah and King when the temple is destroyed.[28] To be sure, it seems strange at first, if one were a Jew looking forward to a king who would restore Israel's national fortunes, but the point here is that the prophets themselves already correlated the triumph of the Messiah to the destruction of the temple. "The result of 'the vindication of the son of man'— exactly as it ought to be within the controlling story—is that exile will at last be over."[29] This is key to Jesus' prophetic message.

Repeatedly Jesus proclaims the same subversive themes as the prophets as well as Paul: Israel will be a "light to the gentiles," many of whom will be grafted into the covenantal tree of Israel in fulfillment of the promise made to Abraham, that he would be "the father of many nations" (Gen. 15:5–6; Gal. 3:6–9). To accept

24. Ibid., 331.
25. Ibid., 336.
26. Ibid., 338–39.
27. Ibid., 342.
28. Ibid., 360. That there is more to this prophecy than its immediate fulfillment is a question I will take up in my third volume.
29. Ibid., 363.

Christ is to accept the kingdom promised in the law and the prophets; to reject him is to place oneself under the ban of excommunication. Similarly, Wright remarks,

> Jesus' analysis of the plight of Israel went beyond the specifics of behaviour and belief to what he saw as the root of the problem: the Israel of his day had been duped by the accuser, the "satan." That which was wrong with the rest of the world was wrong with Israel too. "Evil" could not be located conveniently beyond Israel's borders, in the pagan hordes. It had taken up residence within the chosen people.

It is a different analysis of evil and its solution. Again, this was an intra-Jewish, not anti-Jewish, debate, as it had always been between the prophets and the wayward leaders and people.[30]

I turn, then, to the apostolic understanding of this prophetic office as fulfilled in Jesus. Christ's prophetic office was exercised even in the Old Testament (1 Pet. 1:11), and afterward, by his Word and Spirit. If we read the Old Testament christocentrically, that is, as the apostles read it, there is no reason why the angel of the Lord theophanies cannot be interpreted as christophanies—appearances of the preincarnate Logos. In Genesis 19, for example, three angels execute divine judgment on Sodom and Gomorrah, one of whom is distinguished by the title "angel of the LORD" and identified in the narrative as YHWH himself. As the other two angels execute the judgment on earth, this mysterious angel of the LORD returns to heaven to execute the judgment from his throne. It would be entirely consistent for the early Christians, like Jesus himself, to see the Son of Man as the final prophetic messenger bringing about the salvation and judgment that had been proleptically realized on earlier occasions.

The Prophet as Messiah

In Zechariah 3 there is the vision of Joshua the high priest, standing before "the angel of the LORD," and Satan standing at his right hand to accuse Joshua as he appears before God's throne in "filthy clothes." In this courtroom scene, we read, "The LORD said to Satan, 'The LORD rebuke you, O Satan! The LORD who has chosen Jerusalem rebuke you! Is not this man a brand plucked from the fire?'" Once again, the angel's speaking is identified as God's speaking. Like Moses interceding for the Israelites in the wilderness, the angel of the Lord is the defense attorney for Israel at it is representatively embodied in Joshua the high priest (vv. 1–10).

The prophets themselves share Moses' hope in the greater prophet to come, "one shepherd" who will gather his flock that has been scattered by the false shepherds (Ezek. 34:11–31). While the false prophets bring their own word of false comfort, God himself will lead his people according to the truth (Jeremiah 23). The difference between true and false prophets is that only the former have "stood

---

30. Ibid., 447.

in the council of the LORD" (v. 18). "Scattering" is always a sign of judgment, from the expulsion of humans from the garden to the scattering of the nations at Babel to the exile itself, but the gospel announces a "gathering" to take place under the true and faithful Shepherd, the prophet greater than Moses. Yet in this prophetic literature (particularly the texts cited: Ezekiel 34 and Jeremiah 23), the coming shepherd-prophet will be no less than YHWH himself.

Jesus calls himself a prophet (Luke 13:33), bringing his Father's message (especially in John). He proclaims future events (Matthew 24, etc.), speaks with an authority that is unlike that of the scribes (Matt. 7:29), authenticates his message with signs, and is thus recognized as a prophet by the people (Matt. 21:11, 46; Luke 7:16; 24:19; John 3:2; 4:19; 6:14; 7:40; 9:17). Jesus sees himself as the fulfillment of the prophetic writings (Matt. 5:17; cf. 1:22), and John the Baptist insists concerning himself that he was not "the prophet" but merely the forerunner (John 1:21–23). Jesus regularly attests, notably in the Fourth Gospel, that he has not only stood in the council of the Lord, but literally *comes from* the Father. He comes to fulfill the Father's eternal decree, ushering into the present the Spirit's "future."

The proper atonement correlate for the prophetic office of Christ then is not the exemplarist or moral influence theory (the revelation of proper behavior) but rather the active obedience of Christ and our union with him in that obedience. As the new Adam, Jesus comes as the "true and faithful witness" (Rev. 1:5), the "last word" from God (Heb. 1:2). As the embodiment of God's command and promise, he not only judges and justifies but is himself "born of a woman, born under the law, in order to redeem those who were under the law, so that we might receive adoption as children" (Gal. 4:4–5). In other words, even as prophet he takes his side not only with God in judgment but with us in listening to "every word that comes from the mouth of God" (Matt. 4:4). He is therefore not only our vicarious sacrifice in his priestly office, but in his prophetic office as well. The one who announces the covenant curses in the Gospels obeys the law in our place and bears them for us. He speaks both for God and for us, answering God's command (which is his own) representatively with a life consonant with our reply, "Here I am."

Judging Gustav Aulén's typology "limited in its usefulness," Nancy Duff turns instead to Calvin's "threefold office."[31] She concentrates her discussion of the atonement on the prophetic office, "for if the prophetic office is properly understood as the apocalypse (revelation) of God's act of reconciliation, then the stage will be properly set for interpreting Christ's priestly and royal offices."[32] Thus Duff shows the eschatological character of Christ's prophetic office. In him, the gospel—the wisdom of God—has not just been explained but has decisively *appeared.* "Divisions which reign in the Old Age such as those between Jew and Greek, slave and free, and male and female were brought to nothing by the advent

31. Duff, "Atonement and the Christian Life," 23.
32. Ibid., 26.

of the New Age in Jesus Christ."[33] Just because we live as if God had not reconciled the world to himself does not mean that he has not in fact done so.[34]

A theology of glory looks only at the appearance of things, their present shape, the givens, while a theology of the cross and resurrection relies on the promise that what God has said he would do he has in fact done in Christ. Not only in his priestly work but in his prophetic office Jesus sounds the indicative note: he has accomplished redemption, regardless of how determined we remain in our opposition to it. Adam and Israel failed, but Jesus himself fulfilled as the covenant Servant what he proclaimed as covenant Lord. This highlights the objectivity of the atonement within the context of the total life of Jesus Christ in a way that demonstrates its radical power to undo the tragic realities of everyday experience, if not for us, at least for many who find that they cannot bring about the transformation for which they long—in themselves, much less the political structures.

HIGH PRIEST OF THE ETERNAL COVENANT

Despite YHWH's faithfulness, God's people seem insistent on becoming strangers. "Presence" and "absence" therefore become ethical rather than ontological categories in the biblical traditions. In other words, it is the geography of relationship, not space, that is in view. "Presence" is typically synonymous with salvation and divine favor—righteousness ($\mathit{ṣĕdāqāh}$), Sabbath peace (shalom), while "absence" names the judicial curse for covenant-breaking (Lo-ammi, "not my people"). Similarly, gentile believers are described as those who were in the past separated from Christ, "being aliens from the commonwealth of Israel, and strangers to the covenants of promise, having no hope and without God in the world. But now in Jesus Christ you who once were far off have been brought near by the blood of Christ. For he himself is our peace," making of Jews and gentiles one family in Christ (Eph. 2:12–14). "Near" and "far" are therefore irreducibly ethical and relational terms, not spatial or substantial. The contrast between Neoplatonic (and more particularly, idealist) and Christian notions of reconciliation throws our contrasting typologies into even bolder relief. The biblical understanding of "reconciliation" is nowhere close to Hegel's, and the different definitions of that term, significant for both sources, throw open again the contrast between the ontological and ethical or covenantal approaches. What light then could this "meeting a stranger," in this covenant form, shed on the atonement?

The Covenantal Context: Meeting a Stranger

We have seen parallels between the biblical and secular cutting rituals in the ancient treaty form (making a covenant itself referred to as "cutting a covenant,"

33. Ibid.
34. Ibid., 29.

kārat bĕrît). Remembering Tillich's contrasting typology, overcoming estrangement versus meeting a stranger, it is intriguing that Israel's faith did not arise as a mythological symbol system expressing ultimate concern, a national spirit, or a worldview, but in the form of concrete covenants analogous to international treaties. In one sense, therefore, all the rumors are true: Jews and Christians are "atheists"; judged on pagan terms, not very "religious," as Paul somewhat sarcastically complimented the Athenians for being (Acts 17:22). Once more, the basis shifts from the ontological to the ethical: the image is an embassy, a commission, not a semidivine faculty or capacity distinguishing humans from nonhuman creation. The ethical definition of the *imago* is particularly recognized in the putting on of "the new self, created according to the likeness of God in true righteousness and holiness" (Eph. 4:24), being "predestined to be conformed to the image of his Son, in order that he might be the firstborn within a large family" (Rom. 8:29).

A Living Sacrifice: Recapitulation and Active Obedience

While the sacrificial-substitutionary motif is key, it is not the whole picture. The church has rightly seen in the work of Christ not only the legal but the transformative aspect as well. A covenant perspective emphasizes solidarity and therefore resists reduction to individualist theories of atonement. Inseparable from the substitutionary-vicarious work of Christ is his twofold obedience, typically distinguished as active and passive.[35] As we have already seen, the apostolic announcement is that God has done in Christ what Israel and the world could not ever achieve by their own obedience. With Irenaeus, Athanasius, and Anselm, the Reformers emphasized that the redeemer had to be God in order to achieve our salvation but had to be human because only a representative human being could pay what was owed to God's justice. It was the debt incurred by humanity in general and Israel in particular that engaged Jesus' compassionate ministry.

We also recall again the point that eschatology precedes soteriology: the goal of redemption is not simply restoration, "paradise restored," but the consummation; and for this not only forgiveness but the perfect fulfillment of the law was required. Jesus recapitulated in himself the history of Adam and Israel in order to bring us not only out of ruin into a state of innocence, or guilt into forgiveness, but to bring the whole creation into the everlasting Sabbath. Thus "the cross" can only be regarded synecdotally as standing for the whole of Christ's life and obedience. *Paradise restored* is the eschatological correlate of an atonement theology that concentrates on forgiveness through Christ's death without giving due weight to justification and glorification through Christ's life, before and after his death. What God is after in redemptive history is not merely the forgiveness of humanity and restoration to an original state but the fulfillment of the original commission for humanity and, through a successful outcome to its trial, entrance into God's own glory.

---

35. I will suggest below that the so-called "passive obedience" (his death) is just as active, so these are probably not the best terms. I use them here simply because of familiarity.

Thus we cannot sufficiently appreciate the servant theme apart from this active obedience or recapitulation. Jesus is baptized by John "to fulfill all righteousness" (Matt. 3:15). In contrast to Adam and Israel, the messianic Servant refused autonomy. Instead of passing the test, Adam and Israel put *God* to the test in their respective wilderness probations. While Adam and Israel "demanded the food they craved" (Exod. 16; Ps. 78:17–20), in Jesus' forty-day temptation by Satan he responds, "It is written, 'One does not live by bread alone, but by every word that comes from the mouth of God'" (Matt. 4:4). As the Servant, he refuses to reason with Satan and question God's ways in the midst of deep hunger. He refuses Satan's encouragement to turn the stones into bread because in doing so he would no longer be the Servant—fulfilling by his own obedience the covenant that Adam and Israel had broken. Satan then attempts to use Jesus' own tack of appealing to Scripture against him: "If you are the Son of God, throw yourself down; for it is written, 'He will command his angels concerning you,' and 'On their hands they will bear you up, so that you will not dash your foot against a stone.' Jesus said to him, 'Again it is written, "Do not put the Lord your God to the test."'" And when Satan offers Jesus the glory of the worldly kingdoms (we think also of Israel demanding a king, like the nations), Jesus replies, "Away with you, Satan! for it is written, 'Worship the Lord your God, and serve only him'" (vv. 3–10).

That this forty-day trial is intended to recapitulate Israel's forty years in the wilderness is more explicitly correlated to Deuteronomy 9, where Moses reminds Israel that it was only his intercession that stayed God's execution of wrath in the wilderness. When he ascended the mountain, he remained there "forty days and forty nights; I neither ate bread nor drank water" (v. 9). But already the people below were breaking the covenant with the golden calf. So he returned to the people, smashing the tablets. "Then I lay prostrate before the LORD as before, forty days and forty nights; I neither ate bread nor drank water, because of all the sin you had committed, provoking the LORD by doing what was evil in his sight." Again the Lord listened to Moses' intercession, which appealed to God's redemption of Israel from Egypt and—above all—the promise made to Abraham (vv. 17–18, 25–27). Given the similar pattern, we may perhaps assume that Jesus was not only fulfilling all righteousness by successful endurance of the temptation, but that he was all along using it as an opportunity to intercede for his people—perhaps even something like the so-called high priestly prayer in John 17. But while Moses could intercede for the people's transgressions, reminding God of his unconditional oath to Abraham, only the Servant of the Lord could fulfill the obedience to God's law that was requisite for obtaining the everlasting rest. Moses could intercede for forgiveness, but it was obedience that God required.

Beyond this temptation, Jesus' entire life was an extension of this Adamic and wilderness trial. When Peter attempts to distract Jesus from the cross, he receives the sharpest possible rebuke: "Get behind me, Satan! You are a stumbling block to me; for you are setting your mind not on divine things but on human things" (Matt. 16:23). Once more, as in the temptation, the choice is between a theology of glory ("setting your mind on human things") or the cross ("divine things").

While the disciples have set their mind on earthly glory as they approach Jerusalem, the Suffering Servant knows better what arrival in Jerusalem means. Once there, after the triumphal entry, Jesus finally announces what he had previously held at bay:

> "The hour has come for the Son of Man to be glorified. Very truly, I tell you, unless a grain of wheat falls into the earth and dies, it remains just a single grain; but if it dies, it bears much fruit. . . . Now my soul is troubled. And what should I say—'Father, save me from this hour'? No, it is for this reason that I have come to this hour. Father, glorify your name." Then a voice came from heaven, "I have glorified it, and I will glorify it again." The crowd standing there heard it and said that it was thunder. Others said, "An angel has spoken to him." Jesus answered, "This voice has come for your sake, not for mine. Now is the judgment of this world; now the ruler of this world will be driven out. And I, when I am lifted up from the earth, will draw all people to myself." (John 12:23–24, 27–32)

For the first time, the world has an Adam and Israel has a king who will do only what he hears the Father say (John 5:19–20, 30, 43–44; 6:38; 7:19; 8:26, 28, 50; 54; 10:37; 12:49–50). "I always do what is pleasing to him," Jesus could singularly say without arrogance or hypocrisy (John 8:29). Again it is crucial that we do not simply list such texts on the "deity of Christ" column. When Jesus utters such victory speeches, they are announcements that humanity in Adam was created to make after successful fulfillment of their commission. While neither Adam nor Israel drove idolatry and sin out of the temple-garden of God, a servant has finally arrived to make God's temple a house of prayer—indeed, as one greater than the temple (John 1:13–22). In his famous prayer in John 17 he is bold to declare, "Father, the hour has come; glorify your Son so that the Son may glorify you, since you have given him authority over all people, to give eternal life to all whom you have given him. . . . And for their sakes I sanctify myself, so that they also may be sanctified in truth" (John 17:1–2, 19). In the obedience of this servant YHWH in fact becomes his people's righteousness and sanctification (Jer. 23:6; 1 Cor. 1:30; Rom. 5:18; 2 Cor. 5:21). Further, it is because in Jesus Christ the Son has become Servant that the servants can become sons and daughters (John 15:15).[36]

Union with Christ is therefore the wider category for Christ's priestly work. In the last chapter I said, in relation to the challenge of "ontological" atonement ideas, that somehow we must find a solution that does justice to both the individual and cosmic that avoids the weaknesses of "overcoming estrangement." This solution is found at least in part in this notion of covenantal participation, which is not only legal but also ontological in the sense that we are not only externally related but become "one flesh" with Christ. The analogies employed by Scripture along these lines are suggestive. They are not analogies of ontological

---

36. Nevertheless, the apostles and believers in general are still called servants (Rom. 1:1 with 1 Cor. 4:1; 1 Pet. 2:16; Rev. 22:3), even as Jesus was simultaneously servant and son.

participation along Neoplatonic lines: the sun and its rays, for example. Rather, they are simultaneously juridical and organic analogies of marriage and of adoption. The organic analogies proliferate throughout the New Testament: vine and branches, tree and fruit, head and body, the temple and its living stones.

Through this motif Paul especially brings together the legal and organic aspects, as in Romans 5, where "in Adam" we inherit both corruption and guilt and in Christ both new life and justification. This is the basis for his transition from the more legal aspect (justification, Romans 3–4) to the more organic (baptismal) language of chapters 6 and 7. To be united to Christ in the likeness of his death (forgiveness) entails union with him in the likeness of his resurrection (new obedience) (chap. 6). And, we should note, this organic language expands to encompass not only the soul, but the body—and not only the individual person, but the whole creation (chap. 8).

This integration of legal and organic metaphors was already present in Jesus' teaching: in him we not only find forgiveness of sin but participate in his new creation, analogous to a vine and its branches (John 5:1–2). In covenant theology, the legal and relational aspects are never set at odds, as they typically are in modern theology. It would be a pitiful marriage that consisted merely in a legal ordinance, but neither can the piece of paper be despised in gnostic fashion as a mere external trapping or even obstacle to the simple love that one has for another. A marriage is surely more than a legal fact, but is cannot be less than that. Adoption would represent a similar analogy employed in Scripture as simultaneously legal and relational. The same is true of the atonement in its simultaneously legal and organic dimensions.

But union with Christ in his atoning work on the cross is only part of the story. Christ's sacrificial life precedes his sacrificial death. Although traditionally classified as his active and passive obedience, both should be seen together as one *active* self-offering. There is no passive suffering in Christ's ministry. Not only must sacrifice be correlated to the other important aspects of Christ's work; sacrifice itself cannot be reduced to Christ's death. Even in the most charitable reading of Anselm, the most the atonement accomplishes is forgiveness. This is largely due not only to the absence of the resurrection from his account but of Christ's incarnation and obedient life, the covenantal recapitulation of Adam and Israel. Yet ironically, "forgiveness" is part of the weakness of the law. E. P. Sanders is surely correct to remind us that Israel's faith cannot be reduced to "legalism"; there were provisions for transgression of the law, particularly the sacrifices.[37] As the writer to the Hebrews especially emphasizes, however, "forgiveness" is not the same as reconciliation, and the sacrifices could never bring about the positive obedience that God's covenant and character required.

We turn, then, to the "weakness" of the law (i.e., the old covenant cultus). We have seen that some critics of the sacrificial view highlight passages especially in the prophets where obedience is preferred to sacrifice. Such critics are correct to

---

37. E. P. Sanders, *Paul and Palestinian Judaism* (Minneapolis: Fortress, 1977).

point up these texts, which are often absent from defenses of the sacrificial view. However, they do not get to the heart of *why* the sacrificial economy was insufficient. In part, the sacrifices could not accomplish redemption precisely because expiation alone does not set things right. One may be forgiven and yet not be righteous. The requirement of the original commission given to humanity and reaffirmed in Israel, and by Jesus himself, is perfection—completion of the task for which humanity was created, not simply availing oneself of expiatory forgiveness or sacramental grace (Matt. 5:48). The problem with the law (which is really not a problem with the law, but with us) is that "The law made nothing perfect" (Heb. 7:19). By contrast, says the same writer, "Although he was a Son, [Jesus] learned obedience through what he suffered; and having been made perfect, he became the source of eternal salvation for all who obey him, having been designated by God a high priest according to the order of Melchizedek" (Heb. 5:8–9). Later in the argument we read,

> For it was fitting that we should have such a high priest, holy, blameless, undefiled, separated from sinners, and exalted above the heavens. Unlike the other high priests, he has no need to offer sacrifices day after day, first for his own sins, and then for those of the people; this he did once for all when he offered himself. For the law appoints as high priests those who are subject to weakness, but the word of the oath, which came later than the law, appoints a Son who has been made perfect forever. (7:26–28)

Although they could provide forgiveness in the outward administration of the covenant, such sacrifices could not substitute for the obedience that was required in order to fulfill God's original covenant with humankind or the Sinai treaty. So the psalmist prays, "Sacrifice and offering you do not desire, but you have given me an open ear. Burnt offering and sin offering you have not required. Then I said, 'Here I am; in the scroll of the book it is written of me. I delight to do your will, O my God; your law is within my heart'" (Ps. 40:6–8). Here is that "Here I am" language again, indicative of the faithful Son and Servant of YHWH. Jesus identifies with this when he says, "My food is to do the will of him who sent me and to complete his work" (John 4:34). Again, the contrast with Adam and Israel, demanding the food they craved rather than the Word of God, is obvious. Jesus has come not only to atone for human failure on God's behalf, but to "complete his work." Only in so doing is the creation able to be brought through the "six-day" ordeal into the "seventh day" of rest.

It is not simply forgiveness of sins that is required (and the sacrifices themselves could not even do this) for a right relationship with God, but obedience—conformity to God's righteous statutes, love of God and neighbor that is not abstract or generalized, but concrete and particular. God is looking for the holiness, righteousness, and justice that he created us to exhibit as image-bearers. It is the burden of the Epistle to the Hebrews to demonstrate the continuity of the New Testament with this Old Testament view of sacrifice, even citing Psalm 40:

Since the law has only a shadow of the good things to come and not the true form of these realities, it can never, by the same sacrifices that are continually offered year after year, make perfect those who approach. Otherwise, would they not have ceased being offered, since the worshipers, cleansed once for all, would no longer have any consciousness of sin? But in these sacrifices there is a reminder of sin year after year. For it is impossible for the blood of bulls and goats to take away sins. Consequently, when Christ came into the world, he said, "Sacrifices and offerings you have not desired, but a body you have prepared for me; in burnt offerings and sin offerings you have taken no pleasure. Then I said, 'See, God, I have come to do your will, O God' (in the scroll of the book it is written of me)." (Heb. 10:1–7)

It is not a sacrificial animal, but a body—in other words, a "living sacrifice" of obedience to God's will—that is required for redemption from the curse of the law.

When he said above, "You have neither desired nor taken pleasure in sacrifices and offerings and burnt offerings and sin offerings" (these are offered according to the law), then he added, "See, I have come to do your will." He abolishes the first [the Levitical priesthood] in order to establish the second [his own obedience]. And it is by God's will that we have been sanctified through the offering of the body of Jesus Christ once for all.

And every priest stands day after day at his service, offering again and again the same sacrifices that can never take away sins. But when Christ had offered for all time a single sacrifice for sins, "he sat down at the right hand of God," and since then has been waiting "until his enemies would be made a footstool for his feet." For by a single offering he has perfected for all time those who are sanctified. And the Holy Spirit also testifies to us, for after saying, "This is the covenant that I will make with them after those days, says the Lord: I will put my laws in their hearts, and I will write them on their minds," he also adds, "I will remember their sins and their lawless deeds no more." Where there is forgiveness of these, there is no longer any offering for sin. (vv. 8–18)

The New Testament sees these Old Testament sacrifices as prefiguring Christ's work—not only his death and resurrection but his faithful life, as shadow is related to the substance or type to fulfillment (2 Cor. 5:21; Gal. 3:13; Col. 2:17; Heb. 9:23–24; 10:1; 13:11–12; 1 John 1:7). The Christian claim is that Jesus is "the Lamb of God who takes away the sin of the world," the scapegoat caught in the thicket (John 1:29), "our Passover" (1 Pet. 1:9; 1 Cor. 5:7). It is typical of theology in the critical era (since Wellhausen) to dismiss whatever elements it finds at odds with its moralistic conception of religion by consigning it to a later development. Given the fact that the Old Testament precedes the New, however, the sacrificial-expiatory aspect of priestly ministry that Jesus inherits can hardly be so construed. Nor indeed can this paradigm be imposed upon the Old Testament any longer, contrasting an ostensibly primitive Yahwist faith (ethical monotheism, corresponding oddly enough to Kantian religion) and priestly obsession with expiatory sacrifice.

Thus it is through not only his sacrificial death but his perfect fidelity to God's covenant will that Christ's priestly work effects redemption. "Accordingly," wrote Calvin, "our Lord came forth as true man and took the person and the name of Adam in order to take Adam's place in obeying the Father, to present our flesh as the price of satisfaction to God's righteous judgment, and, in the same flesh, to pay the penalty that we had deserved."[38]

It is just this federal and organic union that is emphasized in Ireneaus's model of recapitulation, with Jesus as the "leaven" that makes the whole lump holy, beginning with his incarnation and then by filling up the years of human disobedience with his own obedience.[39] While Irenaeus may be a bit fanciful at times in elaborating recapitulation (viz., correlating each stage of Christ's life with the redemption of each stage of a human life to the point of suggesting that he must have died somewhere in his fifties), I agree wholeheartedly with his instincts. The further development of this theme in the East, as in the formula, "whatever he did not assume he did not redeem," is a close parallel with covenant theology and its particular understanding of union with Christ. It is a parallel that invites fruitful exploration and conversation between the two traditions.

If our atonement theology focuses only on the cross, we will be more likely to see Christ's work one-sidedly, in exclusively judicial-legal terms. Yet it was not only the case that Jesus was on trial throughout his ministry; he was in that lifelong trial recapitulating and restoring what was lost in Adam. That which he offered was not merely a sacrifice of atonement, but an obedient *life*. At the end of the day, it is not sacrifice but obedience (*ḥesed*, covenant love) in which God delights (Ps. 51:16–17; Isa. 1:11; Hos. 6:6). Yet these declarations in the old covenant did not mean that sacrifices should cease for Israel, which would leave the people without a means of forgiveness. Rather, the point being made is that such sacrifices are not in themselves God's delight. He does not require his pound of flesh at sunrise, the way the pagan deities required their human oblations. The shedding of blood was a means of forgiveness, but it did not make them love God and one another. It did not bring about justice and righteousness. In other words, the temple and its sacrificial cultus could in no way bring about the eschatological future that God had promised. There could be forgiveness, but no justification; divine restraint at least for the moment, but no guarantee, much less inauguration, of a new creation.

The sacrificial death of Christ is the necessary but not sufficient condition of that eschatological reality, as 2 Corinthians 5:17–21 underscores:

> So if anyone is in Christ, there is a new creation: everything old has passed away; see, everything has become new! All this is from God, who reconciled us to himself through Christ, and has given us the ministry of reconciliation; that is, in Christ God was reconciling the world to himself, not counting their trespasses against them, and entrusting the message of rec-

---

38. Calvin, *Institutes* 2.12.3.
39. See chapter two for Irenaeus on these points.

onciliation to us. . . . For our sake he made him to be sin who knew no sin, so that in him we might become the righteousness of God.

The covenant of creation envisioned a beautiful life, not a bloody death. Given the breach, the latter is necessary, but the former, realized representatively in Christ, establishes the basis for God's delight in us rather than a mere cancellation of debt. The contrast drawn in Jeremiah 31 between the Sinai covenant and the new covenant turns not only on the "once and for all" character of the divine forgiveness (v. 34); it will *bring about* the new obedience that the law could never accomplish (v. 33). This is the basis for the contrast in 2 Corinthians 3 between the ministry of Moses and that of Christ.

But we should not see forgiveness as something that happens because of Jesus, and the new obedience as something that happens because of us. Both occur precisely because in Christ as our federal head we are not only forgiven but justified, sanctified, and finally glorified. The work of Christ is different because Christ is different (note especially this contrast in Hebrews between Christ on the one hand and angels, Moses, animal sacrifices, the earthly sanctuary, and its priesthood on the other), and not only because of his divinity, but because of his perfect human obedience in dependence on the Spirit. He rendered that obedient life in which and for which humankind was created. He did not require forgiveness for himself. But it was more than not being a transgressor of the law; he was its champion, its lover, its fulfiller. Overcoming every temptation, he alone could sing with the deepest integrity,

> Your decrees are my delight, they are my counselors. . . . I run the way of your commandments, for you enlarge my understanding. . . . See, I have longed for your precepts; in your righteousness give me life. . . . I find my delight in your commandments, because I love them. . . . I have done what is just and right. . . . It is time for the LORD to act, for your law has been broken. Truly I love your commandments more than gold, more than fine gold. Truly I direct my steps by all your precepts; I hate every false way. (Ps. 119:24, 32, 40, 47, 121, 126–128)

In this perfect life and death, God was more satisfied than in all of the blood that had run down Israel's altars through the ages. It is this whole life, and not just his death, that is offered up to the Father as a sacrifice for sin (the negative aspect) and the justification of the ungodly (the positive aspect). In union with this life transgressors are not simply forgiven and justified but incorporated into the life that he lived and lives before the Father by the Spirit. The importance of the Spirit as the principal source of Jesus' active obedience, rather than (as traditionally emphasized) the Logos, is key, as I argued in chapter six. The humanity of Christ in his active obedience is dependent at every moment on the Spirit in order to be a faithful covenant servant. Thus the Spirit and not merely the Logos obtains his proper place in atonement formulation when the atonement itself is set within the larger context of the eternal covenant of redemption and the temporal covenants of creation and grace. In the covenant of redemption, the preincarnate Son is a partner within the Godhead; in his incarnate fulfillment of the covenant of creation, he is not only the divine partner but the human one as well. In the covenant of grace, he dispenses the success of his mission to the whole church.

Thus, as Gunton argues (drawing on Edward Irving), the work of Christ is not simply a matter of accounting ("the 'Stock-Exchange Divinity'"); it involves a renewed relationship between God and the sinner, not merely "an external transaction."[40] "Legal imagery, as a central theme in the New Testament, must be taken with due seriousness and has its place in the theology of atonement," but it must be placed within the context of "the altar of sacrifice," as Paul does in Romans 3:24ff. and elsewhere.[41] Like Irving, Gunton seeks to relocate the atonement in Trinitarian thought. "That is to say, Jesus as the eternal Son made flesh *is* the self-giving of the Father in expression and realization of his eternal will for covenant." Referring to Calvin on Hebrews 7:26; 8:2; and 9:14, Gunton adds:

> What is worth pursuing is that Irving, drawing on an old Calvinist tradition, and particularly, it seems to me, on insights contained in such writings as Calvin's commentary on the letter to the Hebrews, developed a view of the humanity of Christ in continuity with the use of the sacrifice metaphor in the New Testament. On such an understanding, Jesus as our representative offers to the Father a human life—the very sacrifice which the Psalmist described as 'a broken and contrite heart' and which, because of our sin, we refuse to give. Calvin sees in the life and death of Christ a human self-giving which is effective in giving life to others.[42]

Once more the similarities between recapitulation and union with Christ in his active obedience come through. Not only in his sacrificial death, but in his sacrificial life, beginning with the incarnation itself, Jesus accomplishes a complete redemption. The goal of the cross is not simply legal but relational, not simply judicial but eschatological, and not simply individual but cosmic. It is nothing less than communion with creation in everlasting shalom.

Criticisms of the substitutionary motif have often rightly insisted upon the ethical and relational character of Christ's work rather than reducing it to legal calculation. But they have usually done this by focusing not on the ethical and relational aspect of *Christ's* representative life before the Father and in the Spirit, but rather on our own. In other words, it is the atonement's effect on us (motivating holiness, love, perhaps even fear) rather than its effect on God (satisfying his just claims and bringing about true restoration) that is its vital concern. In a covenantal approach, where union with Christ is the encompassing soteriological theme, the objectivity of the atonement is maintained without simply reducing it to the satisfaction of God's dignity and justice. Furthermore, once the objective offering of a fulfilling human life (that is, one that is given to unbroken covenant loyalty) is made by Christ in the Spirit, that same Spirit unites us to

---

40. Gunton, "Sacrifice and the Sacrifices," 218.
41. Ibid., 218–19.
42. Ibid., 219.

Christ so that it is both objectively ours completely and subjectively ours definitively (in the new birth) yet imperfectly (in sanctification), and finally consummated (in glorification). As there are many opportunities for convergence between recapitulation and covenantal union, there is significant overlap between theosis and glorification, a point I will pursue in my third volume.

Gunton brings together sacrificial and restorative aspects similar to the arguments I have made above.

> Our sinfulness, then, is not conceived *mathematically* as the accumulation of wrong acts, but *relationally* as that which universally qualifies human existence in the flesh. If so, then, as the anti-Apollinarian theologians had argued, precisely *that* fallen flesh must be assumed by the savior. . . . The salvation of *this* representative piece of flesh becomes the basis for the salvation of the rest.

How is this accomplished? By reasserting "the place of the Holy Spirit in the theology of the Incarnation."[43] The Spirit makes possible both the perfect "living sacrifice" offered by Christ and the imperfect one offered by believers.[44] But what kind of gift is being offered here? First, rooted in the Trinity, it is "the expression and outworking of the inner-trinitarian relations of giving and receiving." Second, it is a representative offering on behalf of a humanity that because of its sin will not offer true worship.[45] Now we understand why "the blood of bulls and goats" cannot take away sin (Heb. 9:13).[46] Third, it emphasizes the relational: reconciliation. We are able to enter the precincts of God's holy presence.[47]

But what is it about this offering that accomplishes our entrance into God's presence? Here pneumatology returns.

> What the Spirit was to Jesus, he may be for us, because by virtue of his resurrection Jesus now becomes the one who gives the Spirit to those who believe. That is where we find the link between the Sacrifice and the sacrifices—between the once for all divine-human Sacrifice and the response of believers in the various sacrifices (e.g., sacrifices of worship and Christian living) that are realized through this Sacrifice.[48]

Thus, while we must not deny the insight that the Spirit applies the benefits of Christ's sacrifice to believers, "it tends to create an individualist apprehension of the work of the Spirit. . . . The missing dimensions are the eschatological and ecclesiological," including the cosmic.[49] The Spirit works to bring about the communion that he enjoys with the Father and Son, only finally achieved in the end. Yet,

---

43. Ibid., 220.
44. Ibid.
45. Ibid., 221.
46. Ibid., 221–22.
47. Ibid., 222.
48. Ibid., 222–23.
49. Ibid., 223.

as Gunton notes, "the promise of the Spirit is that—amidst the particularities of our worldliness—we shall be given anticipations of what is to come."[50] The Spirit works with Christ to bring about the community that is a sacrifice of worship.

> The Reformers were right to oppose any suggestion that the sacrifice of Jesus is in any way made or repeated by a churchly celebration. But the corresponding danger is that the metaphor should be deprived of its content insofar as it refers to the human response deriving from and made possible by the once and for all death of the savior. . . . Here both Catholic and Reformed have fallen short in stressing too strongly the notions of sin and forgiveness conceived legally, and the corresponding legal-institutional aspects of ecclesiology. . . . We might develop all this by saying that just as the humanity of Christ is the concentrated—and so representative—offering through the Spirit of true humanity to the Father, so the bread and wine become through the same Spirit the concentrated offering of all of the life of the creation.[51]

Gunton's point can be further established from Hebrews. After offering eleven chapters treating the once-and-for-all sacrifice of Christ for sin, including both his life and death, the writer, in chapter 13, relates this to the "living sacrifice" that Christ's life and death have made of us:

> Therefore Jesus also suffered outside the city gate in order to sanctify the people by his own blood. Let us then go to him outside the camp and bear the abuse he endured. For here we have no lasting city, but we are looking for the city that is to come. Through him, then, let us continually offer a sacrifice of praise to God, that is, the fruit of lips that confess his name. Do not neglect to do good and to share what you have, for such sacrifices are pleasing to God. (Heb. 13:12–16)

It is not that Christ's sacrifice (both of obedience and expiation) makes it possible for us to become living sacrifices by following his example, but rather that it makes us objectively and definitively such sacrifices, despite our own failures.

We have seen in the last chapter that John Milbank also seeks to integrate the atonement with ecclesiology, but consistent with the logic of Platonic participation, he regards the sacrifice of Christ as nothing more than the initiation of the atoning work of the church that completes that sacrifice. But this fatally ignores the "once and for all," unique nature of the cross. We are on safer ground with the writer to the Hebrews, who relates Christ's sacrifice to the sacrifices of his people, but distinguishes them as a completed *guilt* offering and an ongoing *thank* offering, respectively. Union with Christ never sacrifices the difference between Christ and his church.

Far from diminishing the significance of our own obedience, then, the covenantal approach I have been advocating affirms that the "alien righteousness" of Christ's active obedience is only "alien" in the sense that it is not the outcome

50. Ibid., 224.
51. Ibid., 225–26.

of our own obedience. But in an important sense, it is not alien at all: it is just as truly ours as if we had fulfilled our original mandate, since all that is Christ's belongs to us in the baptismal reality of both a legal and organic union. The new creation is something that God has brought about in Christ and by the Spirit, into which we have been inserted. Only on this basis can our lives, still wearing the scent of death, become a "fragrant aroma" to God: "For we are the aroma of Christ to God among those who are being saved and among those who are perishing; to the one a fragrance from death to death, to the other a fragrance from life to life. Who is sufficient for these things?" (2 Cor. 2:15–16). Thus the rubric of union with Christ in his sacrificial life and death keeps us from reduction on both sides of the atonement debate. On one hand, it refuses to reduce the atonement to the legal aspect, and on the other it refuses to reduce it to a moral example or influence.

The importance of including the neglected theme of Christ's active obedience in our atonement doctrine is also underscored by the criticism that the traditional sacrificial motif valorizes passive suffering. Jesus came to suffer not only on Golgotha but in the circumstances of his impoverished youth, the temptations of friend and foe alike, the common scourge of gentile oppression, as well as his own inner struggles, in the rejection of those he loved, the charges of blasphemy against the God he served, the abandonment of his closest comrades and even of his own Father. Yet, for all of that, he says, "For this purpose I have come to this hour" (John 12:27). No one *takes* his life; he *gives* it (John 10:18). Christ accomplished this reconciliation, as Calvin says, "by the whole course of his obedience," beginning with his incarnation and baptism. "In short, from the time when he took on the form of a servant, he began to pay the price of liberation in order to redeem us." This sacrificial life had to be made voluntarily. "Not, indeed, without a struggle; for he had taken upon himself our weaknesses, and in this way the obedience that he had shown to his Father had to be tested! And here was no common evidence of his incomparable love towards us: to wrestle with terrible fear, and amid those cruel torments to cast off all concern for himself that he might provide for us."[52]

To push this active character of Christ's self-giving further still, I must raise the controversial issue of merit. According to Anselm, Christ did not merit salvation by his obedience, since he was divine, but this reflects the Apollinarian tendencies I have already challenged. As Alan Spence shows, federal theologian John Owen "held that there was no value or efficacy in the sufferings and death of Christ considered in themselves":

> "For what excellency of the nature of God could have been demonstrated in the penal sufferings of one absolutely and in all respects innocent . . . ?" Its effectiveness can only be understood with respect to God's covenant to save sinful men, and it is in this context alone that these sufferings are made good and tend to God's glory. . . . But by recognizing that Christ's attitude

52. Calvin, *Institutes* 2.16.5.

in laying down his life is an integral part of the efficacy of his death, Owen effectively undermines what we might call an Apollinarian view of the atonement.[53]

The old federal theologians, as well as the Lutherans, also emphasized merit as a legitimate category as enthusiastically as any medieval theologian. The great difference was that in Reformation theology, it was Christ alone who could and did properly merit salvation for us. We cannot get rid of the concept of merit simply because of its erroneous application to *our* meritorious obedience, says Calvin.

> There are certain perversely subtle men who—even though they confess that we receive salvation through Christ—cannot bear to hear the word "merit," for they think that it obscures God's grace. Hence, they would have Christ as a mere instrument or minister, not as the Author or Leader and Prince of life, as Peter calls him [Acts 3:15]. Indeed, I admit, if anyone would simply set Christ by himself over against God's judgment, there will be no place for merit. . . . [But] it is absurd to set Christ's merit against God's mercy. . . . Both God's free favor and Christ's obedience, each in its degree, are fitly opposed to our works.[54]

"By his obedience, however, Christ truly acquired and merited grace for us with his Father."[55] Apart from the active obedience of Christ, it is easy to see the cross in purely punitive terms rather than as the culmination of that meritorious obedience that yielded the restoration of that original righteousness in which we were created and which we are still obliged to yield as God's image-bearers. The covenant of creation is not abrogated but fulfilled. There is no passive element at all in this account.

Union with Christ then not only provides a paradigm ample enough to include both the objective and subjective aspects of the so-called *ordo salutis* (i.e., how individuals are redeemed); it also provides a horizon wide enough to encompass the individual and the cosmic dimensions of this redemption. I will take up this cosmic aspect more fully below, but first I should give some space to the important theme of Christ's sacrificial death.

A Bloody Sacrifice: The Descent into Hell

Once more the priesthood emerges in the context of a covenant, and we have seen that in the secular treaties of the ancient Near East tribute offerings were brought annually in a renewal ceremony that reaffirmed the vassal state's loyalty (*hesed*) to the suzerain. The offerings the priest brought included thank offerings and tithes. This fits with the tribute offerings (usually firstfruits of the flock or harvest) brought by a vassal to a suzerain to renew the vassal's pledge. But Anselm,

---

53. Alan Spence, "Christ's Humanity and Ours," 86–87.
54. Calvin, *Institutes* 2.17.1.
55. Ibid., 2.17.3.

we have seen, reduces the sacrifice of Christ to this tribute offering as an appeasement of offended dignity, while I will argue that the proper cultic category for Christ's death is the sacrifice of *atonement*—in other words, the "guilt offering."

While we do not know exactly what sort of tribute might have been brought to God before the fall, we can eliminate the guilt offering from the list, since the shedding of blood has to do with the forgiveness of sins. After the fall God replaced Adam and Eve's homespun garments with the skins of an animal (Gen. 3:21). But of crucial significance for fallen humanity was the bringing of the guilt offering, a kipper (atonement). This question of what kind of sacrifice is acceptable to the Lord (the first from the flock or produce from the land) was the motive for Cain's murder of Abel is revealed (Gen. 2:4–7). It was the first "religious war." That these were intended as guilt offerings rather than tributes is supported by the fact that after the flood subsides Noah also offers a burnt offering that is atoning (Gen. 8:20–22).

The sacrificial economy of Moses and the theocracy does not arise ex nihilo but belongs to the progressive revelation of redemption in Christ. It is especially in Leviticus that we see the sacrificial system inaugurated in Israel. The clearly expiatory nature of the sacrifices in Israel is seen in Leviticus 1:4; 4:29–35; 5:10; 16:7; and 17:11, including transfer of guilt (1:4; 16:21–22). The burnt offering, singled out for atonement, was to be from either the flock or the herd, but in either case "a male without blemish" (1:3). Guilt would be transferred from the worshiper to the sacrifice by the laying on of hands, "and it shall be acceptable in your behalf as atonement for you" (v. 4). Further, the priest would sprinkle the blood of the sin offering on the altar and mercy seat, which covered the treaty tablets in the ark of the covenant. "Thus the priest shall make atonement on your behalf, and you shall be forgiven" (4:30–31; cf. 16:21–27).

It is Hebrews that interprets the whole Levitical priesthood as an imperfect copy of the heavenly priesthood of Christ ("in the order of Melchizedek," Ps. 110:4; see Heb. 3:1; 4:14; 5:5; 6:20; 7:26; 8:1). When we consider the centrality of the temple to the messianic concept as it was generally understood by first-century Jews, the claim that Jesus is the temple or somehow supplants the temple could only be regarded as incendiary—even if, as I have argued, such a vision had already been held out by the prophets. The theocracy was a parenthesis in God's plan for the world through Israel, a governess rather than the parent (Gal. 3:24–26). To put it simplistically, given the apocalypse of Jesus "in the fullness of time," Moses was now in Abraham's way, which is to say that to put one's hopes in the restoration of the temple cult when the true Temple had arrived is to mistake the signs for the reality they signify. It is to squander one's inheritance on the present age and miss out on the age to come, like Esau's infamous squandering of his inheritance for a bowl of soup.[56]

---

56. In Galatians 4 Paul actually reverses the roles along these very lines: The "Jerusalem that is below" is now a city of bondage (identified with Hagar), while the "Jerusalem that is above" is the offspring of the free woman (Sarah).

The temple cult, having served its essential function, could never actually take away sins but could only point to the place where atonement would be made once and for all. This is the running argument of Hebrews. Moses himself shared Abraham's faith, but the Sinaitic covenant had as its goal the land of Canaan, while Abraham longed for "a better country, that is, a heavenly one" (Heb. 11:16). The only way for the promise made to Abraham to find its ultimate fulfillment was for the parenthetical theocratic economy to be transcended. After all, Israel had shown repeatedly that it could not bring about its own, much less the world's, salvation by cooperating with God. No "covenantal nomism" could defeat sin and death. The provision for forgiveness in the sacrifices only deepened the sense of guilt and reminded worshipers that they could not live up to the expectations of the covenant.

"When questions of dealing with sin and enslavement were raised it was to the notion of sacrifice that Jews naturally turned," N. T. Wright explains.[57]

> If the exile itself was seen as a "death," and therefore return from exile as a "resurrection," it is not a long step to see the death of Israel as in some sense sacrificial, so that the exile becomes not simply a time when she languishes in Babylon, serving a forlorn sentence in a foreign land, but actually a time through which the sin she has committed is expiated. The exile, it seems, was to be seen both as a punishment for the nation in its wickedness, and as in some sense a vocation to a righteous bearing of sin and evil. This step was taken explicitly in the fourth of the Servant Songs in Isaiah 40–55 (52.13–53.12).

"The Servant, acting out the tribulation and future restoration of Zion (see the context in 52.7–10), dies and rises again as a sin-offering"; likewise, the death of martyrs in the Maccabaean revolt is expiatory.[58]

Equally clear, however, at least according to the New Testament, is that the sacrifices, including the nation's exile, could not themselves effect expiation. One important reason, as we have seen, is that they cannot make the worshiper perfect, but only atone for faults—and this only typologically and therefore repeatedly, rather than once and for all.

Before going further, I should point out the significance of blood in relation to the covenant idea, recalling the correlation between the Abrahamic covenant and secular treaties. We can compare this event to an example of an eighth-century (BCE) document, in which a ram is brought "to make the treaty of Ashurnirari, King of Assyria, with Mati²ilu. . . . This head is not the head of a ram; it is the head of Mati² ilu, the head of his sons, his nobles, the people of his land. If those named [sin] against this treaty, as the head of this ram is c[ut] off, his leg put in his mouth [. . .] so may the head of those named be cut off [. . .] (col. 1:10ff.)."[59] But in Abram's vision, YHWH himself takes a solitary

---

57. N. T. Wright, *New Testament and the People of God* (Minneapolis: Fortress, 1992), 274.
58. Ibid., 276.
59. Cited by Kline in *By Oath Consigned* (Grand Rapids: Eerdmans, 1968), 41, from McCarthy, *Treaty and Covenant*, 195.

self-maledictory oath, calling down upon his own head the curses of the law that he himself has imposed in the case even of the human partner's malfeasance.

Understandably, then, to *make* a covenant was to *cut* a covenant (*kārat bĕrît*). So close was the representative identification of the forswearer with the ritual animal and the sign with the thing signified that circumcision was called simply "the covenant," just as Jesus designated the cup he raised in the upper room as "the blood of the new covenant" (Matt. 26:25–28). No wonder Paul called the cross "the circumcision of Christ" (Col. 3:22).[60] It was he of whom Isaiah prophesied, "For he was *cut off* from the land of the living, *stricken* for the transgression of my people. . . . He bore the sin of many, and made intercession for the transgressors" (Isa. 53:8–12).

United to Christ in his circumcision-death, the baptized too come under God's sword of judgment. "It is a judicial death as the penalty for sin," says M. G. Kline. "Yet to be united with Christ in his death is also to be raised with him whom death could not hold in his resurrection unto justification."[61] And as Peter affirms, baptism, foreshadowed by the salvation of Noah and his family in the flood ordeal, "now saves" not by cleansing the body but "as an appeal to God for a good conscience, through the resurrection of Jesus Christ, who has gone into heaven and is at the right hand of God" (1 Pet. 3:21–22). As union with Christ brings together the legal and organic aspects, so too in Peter's interpretation of the covenant blessing, it unites the cross and the resurrection. But the forensic element is key. Kline adds, "Now conscience has to do with accusing and excusing; it is forensic. Baptism, then, is concerned with man in the presence of God's judgment throne."[62]

Here, as in the exodus, we are reminded by the prophet of the eschatological nature of both the water and fire ordeals as part of the testing of God's people:

> But now thus says the LORD, he who created you, O Jacob, he who formed you, O Israel: "Do not fear, for I have redeemed you; I have called you by name, you are mine. When you pass through the waters, I will be with you; and through the rivers, they shall not overwhelm you; when you walk through fire you shall not be burned, and the flame shall not consume you. For I am the LORD your God, the Holy One of Israel, your Savior" (Isa. 43:1–3a).[63]

---

60. In *By Oath Consigned*, 45, Kline reminds us that like Isaac, Jesus was circumcised as an infant, "that partial and symbolic cutting off"—the "moment, prophetically chosen, to name him 'Jesus.' But it was the circumcision of Christ in crucifixion that answered to the burnt-offering of Genesis 22 as a perfecting of circumcision, a 'putting off' not merely of a token part but 'of the [whole] body of the flesh' (Col. 2:11, *ARV*), not simply a symbolic oath-cursing but a cutting off of 'the body of his flesh through death' (Col. 1:22) in accursed darkness and dereliction."

61. Ibid., 47.

62. Ibid., 66–67.

63. See also ibid., 68: If Peter relates baptism to the deliverance through water, Paul relates it to a new exodus in 1 Corinthians 10. Here we see that the "fire-theophany," which also appeared to Moses in the burning bush, is judicial, as the pillar of fire. "In the exodus crisis the pillar served to shelter, guide, and protect the elect nation; it thereby rendered for Israel a favorable verdict (cf. Ex. 13:21f.; 14:19f.)," but was a fire of condemnation for the Egyptians. This fiery pillar "is a defense and glory" for Israel (Isa. 4:2–5). In the same way, after his baptism into death and condemnation, Christ "was raised for our justification" (Rom. 4:25).

The sprinkling of blood upon the people ratifying their oath at Sinai ("we will do all these things") was similarly an act of calling down divine judgment for transgression (Exod. 24:1–8). Both involve a ratification in blood, witnessing to and sealing the covenant with their own lives at stake. But the difference between the blood of the Sinai covenant and that of the Abrahamic covenant in the vision of YHWH walking alone through severed halves is made clear especially in Jeremiah 34, where God invokes the curses of the Sinai covenant. The ancestors all agreed to keep the law at Sinai, says YHWH, which included setting slaves free, but Israel is keeping slaves. Therefore, "those who transgressed my covenant and did not keep the terms of the covenant that they made before me, I will make like the calf when they cut it in two and passed between its parts: the officials of Judah, the officials of Jerusalem, the eunuchs, the priests, and all the people of the land who passed between the parts of the calf shall be handed over to their enemies and to those who seek their lives" (Jer. 34:8–20). The characteristic solidarity implied in all covenants is recognized by the fact that although generations have passed since the ratification of the Sinai treaty, "all the people of the land" are said to have "passed between the parts of the calf" with their ancestors in the wilderness.

Thus it is impossible to speak of a contrast between legal and relational arrangements when we are in the realm of covenant language. Basic to human relationships are mutual trust, dependability, righteousness, and justice. What kind of friendship can exist without these elemental characteristics? God's presence—nearness, in mercy and acceptance—is covenantally, which is to say, ethically, determined. But what happens when the fragile tissue of fidelity breaks down on either side? Can the relationship be repaired? Not without cost. "The wages of sin is death" (Rom. 6:23), and at least within the covenantal context established on God's terms, "there is no forgiveness of sins without the shedding of blood" (Lev. 17:11; Heb. 9:22).

The announcement therefore is that Christ "himself bore our sins in his body on the cross, so that, free from sins, we might live for righteousness; by his wounds you have been healed" (1 Pet. 2:24). "As for you also, because of the blood of my covenant with you, I will set your prisoners free from the waterless pit" (Zech. 9:11). It is not through the blood that was sprinkled on the Israelites at Sinai, the blood of their covenant with YHWH, but because of the blood of God's covenant with Abraham and his seed, that the blood of the new covenant can actually be referred to the intra-Trinitarian pact as "the blood of the eternal covenant" (Heb. 13:20). Jesus Christ was "cut off"—excommunicated from the people of God and thus from God's presence, cursed for us (Gal. 3:13), crucified for our sins (Rom. 4:25). He descended into hell and then entered the Holy of Holies with his own blood (Heb. 9:18–28).

Here Calvin is more helpful than some of his critics have alleged. At that consummate moment of paradox in which the Son cries out in dereliction, we can affirm with full seriousness the incomprehensible sorrow that Jesus experienced. Far from the violent picture of the Father "hating" his Son, which is oddly extended by Moltmann's notion of the Father "annihilating" the Son, Calvin cautions,

Yet we do not suggest that God was ever inimical or angry toward him. How could he be angry toward his beloved Son, "in whom his heart reposed" [cf. Matt. 3:17]? How could Christ by his intercession appease the Father toward others, if he were himself hateful to God? This is what we are saying: he bore the weight of divine severity, since he was "stricken and afflicted" [cf. Isa. 53:5] by God's hand, and experienced all the signs of a wrathful and avenging God. Therefore Hilary reasons: by his descent into hell we have obtained this, that death has been overcome. In other passages he does not differ from our view, as when he says: "The cross, death, hell—these are our life." In another place: "The Son of God is in hell, but man is borne up to heaven." And why do I quote the testimony of a private individual when the apostle, recalling this fruit of victory, asserts the same thing, that they were "delivered who through fear of death were subject to lifelong bondage"? [Heb. 2:15]. He had, therefore, to conquer that fear which by nature continually torments and oppresses all mortals. . . . Therefore, by his wrestling hand to hand with the devil's power, with the dread of death, with the pains of hell, he was victorious and triumphed over them, that in death we may not now fear those things which our Prince has swallowed up [cf. 1 Pet. 3:22 Vulgate].[64]

In this paragraph we begin to see the convergence of a revised sacrificial motif and a Christus Victor perspective, at once concerned with individual and cosmic redemption, legal and relational good—which is to say, *ḥesed*, covenant solidarity.

Therefore, while the law announces only condemnation to Jew and gentile alike, "now, apart from law, the righteousness of God has been disclosed, and is attested by the law and the prophets, the righteousness of God through faith in Jesus Christ for all who believe" (Rom. 3:20–22a). Christ's death brings peace with God (5:1, 6–10). Of first importance in the gospel is "that Christ died for our sins in accordance with the scriptures" (1 Cor. 15:3). He "loved us and gave himself up for us, a fragrant offering and sacrifice to God" (Eph. 5:2), "and he is the atoning sacrifice [propitiation] for our sins" (1 John 2:2; cf. 4:10). Jesus summarized his own mission in such terms: "The Son of Man came not to be served but to serve, and to give his life a ransom for many" (Mark 10:45). "I am the good shepherd [of Ezekiel 34]. The good shepherd lays down his life for the sheep" (John 10:11). It is his mission (John 12:27).

Nothing was more central to Jesus' own understanding of his mission than his priesthood, which would render him both vicar and victim, with no clearer instance than in the meal that inaugurated the new covenant: "Take, eat; this is my body," "Drink from [the cup], all of you; for this is my blood of the covenant, which is poured out for many for the forgiveness of sins" (Matt. 26:26–28). The cup that he drank was not the cup of human injustice, as some critics of a sacrificial atonement might have it, but the cup of the Father's wrath (Luke 22:42, with Isa. 51:17). In fulfillment of Abram's vision in Genesis 15, the Last Supper is the solemnization and ratification of a self-maledictory oath and because he was willing to drink this cup to its dregs, we are able to drink his blood as the

---

64. Calvin, *Institutes* 2.16.11.

cup of salvation. Jesus saw his crucifixion as the real "lifting up" that Moses' lifting up of the brass serpent on the pole only foreshadowed (John 3:14; 12:34). So Peter, who only after the fact now understands Jesus' obsession with the cross, adds, "He himself bore our sins in his body on the cross, so that, free from sins, we might live for righteousness; by his wounds you have been healed. . . . For Christ also suffered for sins once for all, the righteous for the unrighteous, in order to bring you to God" (1 Pet. 2:24; 3:18).

It is not the case that Jesus is only a priest symbolically. On the contrary: it is the officials of the Old Testament whose priesthood is figurative, deriving all of their force and efficacy from the true, eternal, and unfailing priesthood of Christ (Heb. 9:9). Every Levitical priest must sacrifice for his sins as well as for those of the people. However, Christ did not become a Levitical priest, "but was appointed by the one who said to him, 'You are my Son, today I have begotten you'; as he says also in another place, 'You are a priest forever, according to the order of Melchizedek.' . . . Although he was a Son, he learned obedience through what he suffered; and having been made perfect, he became the source of eternal salvation for all who obey him, having been designated by God a high priest according to the order of Melchizedek" (Heb. 5:5–10). Just as he is a Son and not just a servant (chap. 3), and ministers in the heavenly rather than the earthly sanctuary (chap. 9), he derives his priestly office from Melchizedek, according to an eternal oath (the covenant of redemption) rather than the shadows of the law (7:11–21). "Accordingly Jesus has also become the guarantee of a better covenant" (v. 22), since "he holds his priesthood permanently," without his intercession being interrupted by death (vv. 23–24) or by his own sins (vv. 26–28). His intercession is not merely superlative or consummate but is the reality that reduces the old economy to shadows. His mediation is established by the intra-Trinitarian *pactum* in eternity, not by a command at Sinai.

In Hebrews, as Vos notes, the divinity of Christ is emphasized in relation to the prophetic role (early in the letter), followed by an emphasis on his humanity in relation to the priestly role, since in the former he goes from God to us, and in the latter, from us to God.

> The priesthood is to him center and substance of the covenant, that in which the covenant actually subsists. . . . The author is so thoroughly convinced of the central place of the priesthood in both dispensations that in 7:11 he even represents the Levitical priesthood as the higher category under which the whole law is subsumed: "Under it the people received the law."[65]

It is no disqualification that Jesus' priesthood is not derived from the Levites (an earthly, perishable command), since "there arises a priest who owes His office to the power of an endless life."[66] Again, Jesus pulls heavenly reality (the age to come) down to earth (into this present age). They were made priests without an

---

65. Vos, *Hebrews*, 203ff.
66. Ibid., 221.

oath (just by law), he with one (Heb. 7:20). "In the legal ordinance God expresses His authority, in the oath He pledges Himself with the fullness of His prestige and all His divine resources." Hence his superiority—and also because he comes with "the blood of an everlasting covenant (13:20)."[67] The *latreia* (service) that Christ renders in the heavenly sanctuary is the perfect fulfillment of the vassal to the suzerain on behalf of his people.

While I will question certain aspects of N. T. Wright's view of justification in my third volume, this far I can wholeheartedly affirm with him that "It is one of Paul's chief points in Romans, especially in chs. 2, 3, 7 and 9, that Israel too is 'in Adam,' and that the law does not help her out of this plight but merely exacerbates it (2.17–3.20; 5.20; 7.7 ff.)."[68] In the light of Romans 5, Christ's "role was that of obedience, not merely in place of disobedience but in order to undo that disobedience. That is the point made in vv. 18–19 [of Romans 5], where the 'act of righteousness,' the 'obedience' of the one man Jesus Christ, undoubtedly includes a reference to his long pilgrimage to Calvary."[69] Paul definitely centers on a theology of the cross, Wright insists:

> The place "where sin abounded" (v. 20b) is undoubtedly Israel, the "place" where "the law came in that the trespass might abound." Adam's trespass, active though unobserved until Sinai (vv. 13–14, cf. 7.9a), found fresh opportunity in the arrival of the Torah. Again it could display its true colours as trespass, the flouting of the commands of God. And it was there that grace abounded. This point, thus far, is frequently noted. What is not usually seen is the line of thought which, beginning here in Romans, runs on through 7.13–20 and 8.1–4. Here, near the end of a key christological passage, we find perhaps the most important of all Paul's beliefs about Torah. . . . The Torah possesses, Paul asserts, the divinely intended function of drawing sin on to Israel, magnifying it precisely within the people of God (7.13–20), in order that it might then and thus be drawn on to Israel's representative and so dealt with on the cross (8.3). This is, as it were, the positive reason for the negative role of Torah. As a result, for our present purposes, it becomes clear that the obedient act of Jesus Christ was the act of Israel's representative, doing for Israel what she could not do for herself. Adam's sin and its effects are thus undone, and God's original intention for humanity is thus restored in the Age to Come, which has already begun with the work of Jesus Christ (v. 21).[70]

Thus the story of Adam (humanity generally) is concentrated in the story of Israel, particularly focused on the active obedience of Christ.

I would elaborate Wright's conclusion still further at this point by correlating the covenant of creation to both Adam's trial and that of Israel in the wilderness and in the land. The exegetical links that bind Adam, Israel, and Christ suggest that the covenant of creation and its renewal at Sinai (as a legal covenant) is the

---

67. Ibid., 221–22.
68. N. T. Wright, *The Climax of the Covenant: Christ and the Law in Pauline Theology* (Minneapolis: Fortress, 1992), 37.
69. Ibid., 38.
70. Ibid., 39.

valid category here. Jesus does not conquer death and receive the superlative name because of God's mercy and grace, but because he has fulfilled all righteousness.[71] His obedience, death, and resurrection are not accepted simply because Jesus is God nor as a gift of the Father's grace, but as a reward. "It is finished" announces not simply Jesus' relief at the conclusion of his own suffering but reflects that even here, even on the cross, he is overwhelmingly conscious of his mission, which his plea for the forgiveness of the perpetrators anticipated. He has finished his obedience as a representative substitute. Because he has finished running this race, doing the works of the Father and entering into the Sabbath rest not only as a private person but as a public official, we too are able to run the course, "looking to Jesus the author and perfecter of faith" (Heb. 12:1–2).

Further still, given the covenant of redemption, this suffering of the Son is not extrinsic to the inner-Trinitarian life. Even in our proclamation of the substitutionary death of Christ we must guard against the tendency to abstract the Father from the Son or the Son from the Spirit. It is the Father who sends him and the Spirit who makes him the first born of many brothers and sisters by raising him from the dead and creating new life in those "who were dead in trespasses and sins" (Eph. 2:1). Thus the important truth that "it was the will of the LORD to crush him with pain" can be understood properly only in connection with the goal that follows on that last statement's heels: "When you make his life an offering for sin, he shall see his offspring, and shall prolong his days; through him the will of the LORD shall prosper. Out of his anguish he shall see light; he shall find satisfaction through his knowledge. The righteous one, my servant, shall make many righteous, and he shall bear their iniquities" (Isa. 53:10–11).

Thus the atonement cannot be conceived as the causal action of a subject upon an external object. As I have argued, God does not suffer the same way we do. When we suffer, we can either prevail or be conquered, but God can only prevail over distress: Easter proves this. Because death could not contain him, "the second death has no power" over those who are united to him as their head (Rev. 20:6). Not only does God not suffer as we do; the Father and the Spirit cannot suffer the way the Son did. It was he who became flesh for our sakes, although the other persons were at work in his incarnation, life, death, and resurrection. If we take one more step, we can say that precisely because of the earlier premises,

71. This should challenge Wright's contention, everywhere in his writings assumed but nowhere actually argued, that "The reformers had very thorough answers to the question 'why did Jesus die?'; they did not have nearly such good answers to the question 'why did Jesus live?' Their successors to this day have not often done any better. . . . It would not, then, be much of a caricature to say that orthodoxy, as represented by much popular preaching and writing, has had no clear idea of the purpose of Jesus' ministry." If his life is simply a means of getting himself crucified to put into effect an atonement theology, it all seems contrived (*Jesus and the Victory of God*, 14). Wright routinely challenges "the reformers," "their succesors," and "orthodoxy" as abstract opponents for positions that are easily refuted. I hope that on this specific point (viz., that active obedience of Christ) as others, I have illustrated not only that the Reformers and their successors had quite clear conceptions of why Jesus lived but that at least some of these views actually anticipate several of Wright's observations by centuries.

the divinity of the Son cannot suffer like the humanity. To suggest otherwise opens the door to either an Arian or a Docetic christology.

Yet having said all of this I can still affirm in a qualified sense, with Moltmann, "What happens on Golgotha reaches into the innermost depths of the Godhead, putting its impress on the trinitarian life in eternity."[72] The qualification is this: in view of the covenant of redemption (i.e., *pactum salutis*), the victory of God over, in, and through the cross was never in doubt. The Father did not annihilate and cast out the Son, as Moltmann suggests. The Son who cried out, "Why have you forsaken me?" also committed his soul to the Father. Even on the cross the King was driving out the serpent from his garden, crushing his head, putting an end to sin and death. Even in the Father's excommunication of the curse-bearing Son, his work was being done on earth as in heaven. Just as paradoxical as enthronement on a cross is the Father's simultaneous disdain and pleasure in the sacrifice Jesus offered. There was a real "giving" of the Son by the Father that cannot be understood otherwise than involving the most active "mobility" and passionate involvement, to the point of causing grief and anguish—even if understood of God analogically. Because of this eternal pact, the divine persons were never overcome by the fact of the cross. It was their common will from the beginning. They were not overwhelmed by sorrow, because they were not awaiting Easter morning in doubt. For the triune God, the cross and resurrection were distinct but united realities in an eternal decree, equally ultimate, equally decisive, equally accomplished. Even as he walked the shores of Galilee and hung on the cross, Jesus was ministering in the heavenly sanctuary. His priesthood therefore is finally effective, once and for all, not only in securing "eternal redemption" (Heb. 9:12) but in inaugurating the new age. The reality of heaven (the age to come) was now and is now made present in the realities of our world (this present age). My treatment of the work of Christ in the light of his person as prophet, priest, and king must now turn, in the concluding chapter, to that last "office."

---

72. Moltmann, *Trinity and the Kingdom*, 81.

Chapter Nine

King of Glory

The Servant Who Is Lord

My approach to the resurrection emphasizes with Oliver O'Donovan that Christ's resurrection is representative not in a symbolic way of independent and prior truths, but inasmuch as it effects its concrete results representatively for a people.[1] "Not that the created order has changed, or was ever anything other than what God made it, but that in Christ man was able for the first time to assume his proper place within it, the place of dominion which God assigned to Adam."[2] To be sure, there is an already–not yet character to this, as Hebrews reminds us, after quoting Psalm 8: "Now in subjecting all things to them [humans], God left nothing outside their control. As it is, we do not yet see everything in subjection to them, but we do see Jesus, who for a little while was made lower than the angels, now crowned with glory and honor because of the suffering of death, so that by the grace of God he might taste death for everyone" (Heb. 2:8–9).

In the incarnation, the Lord of the covenant becomes its servant; in the resurrection, the servant takes up his rightful lordship, both as Son of God and Son of Adam. Having considered Christ's offices of prophet and priest, I now turn to

---

1. Oliver O'Donovan, *Resurrection and Moral Order: An Outline of Evangelical Ethics* (Grand Rapids: Eerdmans, 1986), 15.
2. Ibid., 24.

the resurrection and ascension, concentrating especially on the royal office. Jesus' kingdom announcement involved three central features: "the return from exile, the defeat of evil, and the return of YHWH to Zion."[3] It is not overinterpreting this pattern to suggest that each of these central features can be correlated to the three offices and the integration of sacrifice, recapitulation by active obedience, and the conquest of the powers bringing about the universal reign of Israel's God in history.

THE KING ON A CROSS: CONQUEST OF THE POWERS

In his seminal work to which I have referred in passing, Gustav Aulén gave renewed attention to the patristic theme of conquest over the powers.[4] The typology is strained, and alternative conceptions (particularly the sacrificial) are somewhat caricatured. Furthermore, as Gunton surmises, his own articulation of the Christus Victor model leaves us "hanging in the air," without making any real connection between Christ's victory and our struggles with the powers not yet apparently defeated.[5] Nevertheless, Aulén has reminded us that an account of the atonement that does not include the theme of cosmic conquest is inadequate.

Where Aulén's heavy typecasting tended to set sacrifice and conquest in opposition, a covenantal approach as suggested here at least would seek their integration. Furthermore, it would give more concrete form to the cosmic conquest by orienting it to the progress of redemption in history, rather than leaving it hanging in the air. Apocalyptic, which is the genre in which we find most of the references to conquest over the powers, is not an otherworldly preoccupation, but rather a redescription of this world as it becomes the theater of a heavenly battle. It is analogical revelation in the fullest sense, expressing the inexpressible in terms drawn from everyday life.

I considered Dennis Weaver's revision of Aulén's model in chapter seven. Narrative Christus Victor takes its bearings from the Apocalypse, among other places, in which the cosmic battle is won by Christ and his saints through nonviolent means, particularly through death, resurrection, and testimony. But Weaver's exegesis even of his principal text, the Apocalypse, is strained. There is no way of getting around the warrior theme and its obvious references to a cosmic judgment that eventuates in cataclysmic defeat for the powers—and not just in abstraction, but in the concrete reality of political action taken against the enemies of God. There is a real and historical cleansing of God's world, not only by sympathetic suffering with, but by triumphant victory over, all who have set their faces against YHWH and his Messiah. Picking up on various prominent threads in the Old Testament, Childs notes, similarly to Wright above, three basic trajectories when

---

3. N. T. Wright, *Jesus and the Victory of God*, 477.
4. Gustav Aulén, *Christus Victor*, trans. A. G. Herbert (New York: Macmillan, 1931).
5. Gunton, "Sacrifice and the Sacrifices," 211.

it comes to the question of Christ's sacrificial work: "(1) restoration, righteousness, justification; (2) atonement, sacrifice, forgiveness; (3) victory, defeat, warfare."[6] "Yahweh's righteousness consists, above all, in acts of the saving deeds of redemption (*ṣidqōt YHWH*) by which he maintains and protects his promise to fulfil his covenantal obligations with Israel (Ps. 36:7 ET 6)."[7]

As H. H. Schmid argues, there is a common ancient Near Eastern (Canaanite) background in which "righteousness" denotes a cosmic harmony, but Childs adds that this must be seen, in its use by Israel, as a personal rather than impersonal notion.[8] Appealing to Gerhard von Rad, Jenson says, "Throughout Scripture, the central moral and historical category is 'righteousness.'"[9] I have emphasized this in my treatment of the various covenants. Where there is no righteousness, there can be no blessing but only judgment. This is the background, or at least part of it, for the royal office of Christ. He comes not only to atone for injustice, but to establish justice throughout the earth (Num. 14:21; 1 Sam. 2:10; Ps. 22:27; Isa. 6:3), so that God's will is done on earth as it is in heaven (Matt. 6:10).

It is undeniable that both Old and New Testaments give significant development to the warrior theme in reference especially to the conquest of Canaan, the Davidic monarchy, and the prophetic expectation of David's heir, with the New Testament fulfillment in Christ as the warrior-servant who not only drives the serpent from the Holy Land but finally crushes its head.[10] An earlier "Jesus" (= Joshua) had led the Israelites across the Jordan and into the land of promise in conquest, driving the nations out before him. But like Adam, the kings failed to "cleanse the temple" thoroughly, always leaving the door open to idolatry. The Servant will set everything right by waging the last battle, making the whole earth the temple-garden of YHWH. The seed of the woman will crush the head of the serpent at last. This warrior-servant theme is given messianic overtones especially in Psalm 91:7–13. It is not surprising, then, that Satan takes this psalm on his lips during Jesus' temptation, although it is ironic that he uses it as a means of enticing Jesus to abandon his warrior-servant role, as if he could assume his sabbath enthronement without defeating darkness.

In Luke 10 the seventy are sent out on a mission to every town ahead of Jesus: "Whenever you enter a town and its people welcome you, eat what is set before you; cure the sick who are there, and say to them, 'The kingdom of God has come near to you'" (vv. 1–9). After the seventy return from announcing Jesus' blessing for believers and woes against unrepentant cities, they joyfully report, "Lord, in your name even the demons submit to us!" Jesus replies, "I watched Satan fall from heaven like a flash of lightning. See, I have given you authority to tread on snakes and scorpions, and over all the power of the enemy; and nothing will hurt

---

6. Childs, *Biblical Theology*, 486.
7. Ibid., 488.
8. Ibid., 490, referring to H. H. Schmid, *Gerechtigkeit als Weltordnung* (Beitrage zur historischen Theologie, Tübingen 40, 1968).
9. Jenson, *ST* 1:71, citing von Rad, *Theology*, 1:368.
10. For holy war more generally, see Kline's *Structure*, 158ff.

you. Nevertheless, do not rejoice at this, that the spirits submit to you, but rejoice that your names are written in heaven" (vv. 17–20). No longer is the kingdom merely typological, a clash of swords and warhorses, but the future reign of God actually dawns in this present age. Jesus says that he has come to cast out Satan. "But no one can enter a strong man's house and plunder his property without first tying up the strong man; then indeed the house can be plundered" (Mark 3:27). The apostles recognized that at the cross the "strong man" thus bound was finally "crushed." As harbingers of the age to come breaking into this present evil age, already the blind see, the deaf hear, the poor are blessed, and life is restored. This, and not the restoration of the merely typological theocracy, was the kingdom that Christ promised and announced as present in his person. It is a kingdom in which the old taboos no longer apply: the outcasts long regarded as "unclean" take their place at the table with Abraham and Sarah.

Another important aspect of the Christus Victor theme and Christ's royal office is the jubilee theme, which is closely related to the Sabbath. In chapter six we explored the "framework" view of the creation narratives in which each creature-kingdom, with its own ruler, culminates in the creation of humankind as the representative of the whole created order, entrusted with the task of bringing it with him into the seventh day of God's royal enthronement, as the various creature-kings are paraded behind the *imago Dei* in tribute. Protology turns to eschatology in the institution of the Sabbath as the pattern for Israel as God's new servant: six days of labor, followed by the day of rest. Not only is this a weekly pattern; every seventh year the whole creation—land, animals, aliens—will participate with Israelites in a rehabilitative rest (Exod. 23:10–12). This is not only to provide refreshment but to imitate God's pattern of work and enthronement. Furthermore, according to the law, every fiftieth year, after "seven times seven years, . . . on the day of atonement," a trumpet will sound announcing a "jubilee," providing rest to the land and liberty to all of the inhabitants, even to the stranger and debtor (Lev. 25:8–12). The sabbath eschatology is deepened, as if Israel were Adam in the garden, commissioned to work "six days" and then enter into the sabbath consummation even as God had after his successful work.

The land does not belong to Israel, but to YHWH, and here once more the ecological significance of God's sole lordship is important: "for the land is mine; with me you are but aliens and tenants. Throughout the land that you hold, you shall provide for the redemption of the land" (Lev. 25:23–24). There are still more benefits of this jubilee year. Their homes lost in various commercial transactions will be redeemed back for them, interest on loans will not be exacted, anyone forced into service as a result of debt will go free with their debts cancelled. Furthermore, "resident aliens" who have become slaves may be redeemed. "And if they have not been redeemed in any of these ways, they and their children with them shall go free in the jubilee year. For to me the people of Israel are servants; they are my servants whom I brought out from the land of Egypt: I am the LORD your God" (vv. 54–55).

Both the original covenant of creation and the oath God made to Noah on behalf of the whole creation are in the background, as well as the Mosaic covenant. But this jubilee institution not only looks back to creation and Sinai; it looks forward to the everlasting sabbath rest anticipated and partly realized every fiftieth year. In Isaiah 42 Israel's jubilee becomes universalized, exported, as it were, to the nations.

> Here is my servant, whom I uphold, my chosen, in whom my soul delights; I have put my Spirit upon him; he will bring forth justice to the nations. He will not cry or lift up his voice, or make it heard in the street; a bruised reed he will not break, and a dimly burning wick he will not quench; he will faithfully bring forth justice. He will not grow faint or be crushed until he has established justice in the earth; and the coastlands wait for his teaching. (vv. 1–4)

The jubilee echoes become more distinct in the unfolding verses, where the Servant is given "as a covenant to the people, a light to the nations, to open the eyes that are blind, to bring out the prisoners from the dungeon, from the prison those who sit in darkness" (vv. 6–7).

The jubilee theme is also sounded in Daniel 9: "Seventy weeks are decreed for your people and your holy city: to finish the transgression, to put an end to sin, and to atone for iniquity, to bring in everlasting righteousness, to seal both vision and prophet, and to anoint a most holy place" (v. 24). With the Day of Atonement at its heart, the jubilee year will be an eschatological intrusion of God's eternal sabbath in which business as usual is turned on its head and the kingdom of God is partially realized within fallen creation. Atonement is central even to this calendar, but it is not an end in itself: it is the means of bringing about a restoration of the land as God's temple-garden.

With this background we come to Luke 4, where Jesus returns to his hometown of Nazareth. After reading the scroll of Isaiah 42:1–4 cited above, adding that this servant has come "to proclaim the [jubilee] year of the Lord's favor," he announces to the congregation, "Today this scripture has been fulfilled in your hearing" (Luke 4:16–21). When questioned as to why he and his disciples were picking grain on the Sabbath, Jesus gave the example of David entering the sanctuary with his companions to eat the bread of the Presence, "which it is not lawful for any but the priests to eat." The justification is that Jesus is not only equal to but greater than David: "Then he said to them, 'The Son of Man is lord of the sabbath'" (Luke 6:3–5). The episode is more amply recounted in Matthew's Gospel—intriguingly inserted just after Jesus' invitation, "Come to me, all you that are weary and are carrying heavy burdens, and I will give you rest" (Matt. 11:28). In Matthew's version of the dispute, Jesus adds, "I tell you, something greater than the temple is here. But if you had known what this means, 'I desire mercy and not sacrifice,' you would not have condemned the guiltless. For the Son of Man is lord of the sabbath" (Matt. 12:6–7).

We find this jubilee theme explicitly mentioned also in 2 Corinthians 6: "For [God] says, 'At an acceptable time I have listened to you, and on a day of salvation I have helped you' [Isa. 49:8]. See, now is the acceptable time; see, now is the day of salvation!" (v. 2). The more general sabbath theme is found in Hebrews 4, where Jewish believers are warned not to return to the types and shadows of the law now that the true sabbath rest has arrived. The wilderness generation was barred from God's rest "because of unbelief" (3:19).

> Therefore, while the promise of entering his rest is still open, let us take care that none of you should seem to have failed to reach it. For indeed the good news came to us just as to them; but the message they heard did not benefit them, because they were not united by faith with those who listened. For we who have believed enter that rest, just as God has said, "As in my anger I swore, 'They shall not enter my rest,'" though his works were finished at the foundation of the world. (4:1–3)

But since they failed to enter God's rest, "again he sets a certain day—'today'— saying through David much later, in the words already quoted, 'Today, if you hear his voice, do not harden your hearts.' For if Joshua had given them rest, God would not speak later about another day. So then, a sabbath rest still remains for the people of God; for those who enter God's rest also cease from their labors as God did from his" (vv. 7–10).

In other words, the door to the everlasting sabbath is not Moses but Jesus. It is not by returning to Sinai, although Sinai is not repudiated but rather fulfilled. "All who came before me"—that is, the recent claimants to the messianic throne—"are thieves and bandits; but the sheep did not listen to them. I am the gate. Whoever enters by me will be saved, and will come in and go out and find pasture. The thief comes only to steal and kill and destroy. I came that they may have life, and have it abundantly" (John 10:7–10). Again, the cosmic battle comes through clearly enough: those who came before are not just misled would-be messiahs, but agents, witting or not, of the Servant's age-old enemy.[11]

Throughout the old covenant, Israel was looking for a greater sabbath rest. In his resurrection and ascension, Jesus bursts through heaven's gates as "the pioneer of [our] salvation," with the announcement, "Here am I and the children whom God has given me" (Heb. 2:10, 13, appealing to Isa. 8:18). Jesus is the Lord of the Sabbath, Alpha-Creator and Omega-Consummator. In him the restless find the shalom held out in the beginning to humanity in Adam. Like Adam, the generation under Moses forfeited the rest. Even afterward the rest into which Joshua brought the Israelites was partial and only typological, but the door is still open to the seventh day. "Cut off from the land of the living" for the sins of his people (Isa. 53:8), Christ and those who are in him can now say, "I walk before the LORD in the land of the living" (Ps. 116:9). The warning of the writer to the Hebrews, therefore, like Jesus' and Paul's warnings, is that the contemporary generation is in danger of being "cut off"—ironically, to the extent that they return to the shadows of the law now that the true Prophet, Priest, and King has arrived. Again, as noted before, the one who builds the temple is legitimized as king, as

---

11. For a chronology of these Second Temple claimants, see Josephus, *Antiquities* 17.271–81.

in the tradition of David and Judas Maccabeus.[12] The New Testament announcement is that in the resurrection, the Temple has been raised after three days. The exile is over, giving way to the ultimate exodus.

These jubilee strains are heard every time we encounter in the Gospels one of Jesus' healings or his association with the outcasts, not to mention the kinsman-redeemer theme, as when he announces that he has come "not to be served, but to serve and to give his life a ransom for many" (Matt. 20:28). It is heard when two blind men follow Jesus, "crying loudly, 'Have mercy on us, Son of David!'" and are healed (Matt. 9:27–30; Luke 18:35–40). So when the Baptist's disciples inquire of Jesus as to whether he is "the one who is to come," Jesus replies, "Go and tell John what you hear and see: the blind receive their sight, the lame walk, the lepers are cleansed, the deaf hear, the dead are raised, and the poor have the good news brought to them" (Matt. 11:2–6). The King has arrived at last to conquer sin and death and to bring about the everlasting and cosmic jubilee that Moses, Joshua, and David could experience only by promise and type.

Interestingly, this assumes that those for whom Christ lived, died, rose, and now intercedes are victims as well as sinners. Christus Victor must be part of our atonement doctrine, and it includes this element of sinned-against as well as sinners. His life, even before his death, is already a covenantal identification with sinners, the outcasts. As Jesus walked along, "he saw a man blind from birth. His disciples asked him, 'Rabbi, who sinned, this man or his parents, that he was born blind?' Jesus answered, 'Neither this man nor his parents sinned; he was born blind so that God's works might be revealed in him. . . . As long as I am in the world, I am the light of the world'" (John 9:1–5). Jesus repeatedly demonstrated throughout his ministry that there is not a one-to-one correspondence between one's sin and sickness, poverty, or other forms of suffering; in other words, sin is a condition that makes sinners victims as well as perpetrators. This was not a new teaching, of course, but according to the contemporary interpretation of the law, those who were sick, diseased, or in some way physically challenged were regarded as cursed or at least "unclean."[13] By welcoming these untouchables to the table, Jesus was inaugurating a kingdom in which not only the guilt of sin but its power, and not only its individual-ethical but its cosmic-physical effects, would be undone. Everyone is equally "unclean" and, in Christ, equally "clean": sin and grace democratized God's new society.

This is a compassionate king, one who overthrows the powers of evil and yet turns to the weakest of his sisters and brothers to embrace and protect them. In his conquering campaigns, he does not break bruised reeds or snuff out smoldering candles. It is not a kingdom like the gentiles', too often imitated by Israel and expected by Jesus' contemporaries. Presupposing a theology of glory and a kingdom of power, the mother of James and John entreats Jesus to enthrone her sons at his right hand and left hand when they arrive in Jerusalem. Of course, the

---

12. N. T. Wright, *The New Testament and the People of God* (Minneapolis: Fortress, 1992), 309.
13. Wright, *Jesus and the Victory of God*, 191–93, referring to 1QSa 2.3–11.

"sons of thunder" were thinking about thrones of geopolitical power, while Jesus knew that the thrones on either side of him would be crosses: "You do not know what you are asking. Are you able to drink the cup that I am about to drink?" Not surprisingly, given their overrealized eschatology, they answer, "We are able" (Matt. 20:20–22). Jesus tells the other ten disciples, angry at the brothers upon hearing the request, "You know that the rulers of the Gentiles lord it over them, and their great ones are tyrants over them. It will not be so among you; but whoever wishes to be great among you must be your servant" (vv. 25–26).

Having now elaborated at least some of the major patterns of a Christus Victor interpretation, can we see lines of correlation with the prophetic and priestly work we have already considered? The close connection between sacrifice and conquest has already been pointed out in relation to the Gospels. If I had sufficient space, I would also survey the book of Acts, where the kingdom of Christ unfolds more dramatically still in the wake of Pentecost. But I should reflect briefly on some of these areas of overlap in the Pauline Epistles, where the themes of conquest over the powers and substitutionary atonement are interwoven into one fabric:

> And when you were dead in trespasses and the uncircumcision of your flesh, God made you alive together with him, when he forgave us all our trespasses, erasing the record that stood against us with its legal demands. He set this aside, nailing it to the cross. He disarmed the rulers and authorities and made a public example of them, triumphing over them in it. (Col. 2:13–15)

If we look closely, we can even discern in this passage a passing reference to recapitulation in the first sentence: union with Christ, in whom both victory over the powers of sin and death as well as legal acquittal are integrated. The same can be seen, for example, in 2 Corinthians 5:16–19, where we no longer regard people "from a human point of view," that is, from the perspective of this passing evil age. The "new creation" has dawned in Jesus Christ. But this Christus Victor theme is correlated with, even dependent upon, the fact that God has reconciled enemies to himself through Christ's death, "not counting their trespasses against them."

Second, Paul shows considerable interest in bringing the cross and the resurrection together under the rubric of conquest, especially in 1 Corinthians 15. With the Adam-Christ typology once again in view, Paul shows the one-to-one correspondence between death coming through a human being and resurrection from the dead also through a human being (vv. 21–22). The covenantal motif of union with Christ is once again crucial, with Christ being "the first fruits" of the full harvest. In his resurrection, we see the shape of our own future. In other places, of course, the organic imagery is that of the head and its body (viz., Eph. 1:22–23; 4:15–16), but the point is the same: as goes the king ("first fruits"), so goes his kingdom ("harvest"). Just as he is dead to sin and alive to righteousness, so too are we to regard ourselves (Romans 6). Although his resurrection is definitive for our own, this cosmic event will not be completed until the corporate body is raised with its federal head. There really is only one resurrection of the dead with two phases: head and body.[14] But the individual is not swallowed up in the community. The whole people of God are raised with Christ as one temple because each member is a "living stone" in it (1 Pet. 2:1–10). So Paul can say, "When this perishable body puts on imperishability, and this mortal body puts on immortality, then the saying that is written will be fulfilled: 'Death has been swallowed up in victory.'" But again, this cosmic conquest of death is immediately integrated with the individual and judicial aspect: "The sting of death is sin, and the power of sin is the law," but both have been defeated in Christ's death and resurrection (1 Cor. 15:54–56). In fact, a similar statement in 2 Corinthians 5:4— "so that what is mortal may be swallowed up by life"—reminds us of yet another somewhat neglected and, admittedly, not widely attested, motif summarized by John of Damascus: "Wherefore death approaches, and swallowing up the body as bait is transfixed on the hook of divinity, and after tasting of a sinless life-giving body, perishes, and brings up again all whom of old he swallowed up."[15]

Third, Paul relates this cosmic battle (royal) theme to the sacrificial (priestly) motif in Ephesians 6, a lodestar for reflection on Christus Victor: "For our struggle is not against enemies of blood and flesh, but against the rulers, against the authorities, against the cosmic powers of this present darkness, against the spiritual forces of evil in the heavenly places" (v. 12). On one hand, this description of the cosmic battle will not allow Christ's royal office to be exploited for our own ideological purposes, as it had been by Jesus' false messianic rivals. Yet if it resists reduction to secular utopianism, it also does not underwrite a spiritualized or otherworldly interpretation. As the Gospels narrate so vividly, the contest *is* political in an important sense: the kingdoms of this world are in conflict with the kingdom of God and his Christ. While the polity of the kingdom of grace in this age is never to be confused with that of the kingdoms of power, the struggle "against the cosmic powers of this present darkness" takes this world as its theater. This "spiritual warfare," as it is often called, is not a fanciful battle for individual well-being, taking back our health, wealth, and happiness from the devil. This is a significant theme in some radical and immensely popular versions of Pentecostalism, but Paul's argument resists such speculation as strenuously as it does exploitation for struggles against "flesh and blood." The real character of this cosmic warfare is seen in the "armor" that Paul identifies for our defense: the belt of truth, the breastplate of righteousness, as shoes readiness "to proclaim the gospel of peace," the shield of faith, the helmet of salvation, and "the sword of the Spirit, which is the word of God" (vv. 14–17). Could not all of these pieces of defense be summarized in Paul's encouragement elsewhere to clothe themselves with Christ—itself a probable allusion to being "clothed with the garments of salvation" (Isa. 61:10) and the "robe of righteousness" (61:10), especially

---

14. Richard Gaffin Jr., *Resurrection and Redemption* (Phillipsburg, NJ: Presbyterian and Reformed, 1987), 35.

15. John of Damascus, "Exact Exposition," 72.

since the "breastplate of righteousness" comes from Isaiah 59:17? Believers have "clothed [themselves] with the new self, which is being renewed in knowledge according to the image of its creator. In that renewal there is no longer Greek and Jew, circumcised and uncircumcised, barbarian, Scythian, slave and free; but Christ is all and in all!" (Col. 3:10–11). Thus the cosmic warfare, at least in this age, is chiefly concerned with the proclamation of the gospel, received through faith, on the basis of the truth of God's Word, "with which you will be able to quench all the flaming arrows of the evil one" (Eph. 6:16).

Fourth, we see this apocalyptic victory of the seed of the woman over the powers of darkness also in Paul's understanding of the mystery revealed: "But we speak God's wisdom, secret and hidden, which God decreed before the ages for our glory. None of the rulers of this age understood this; for if they had, they would not have crucified the Lord of glory" (1 Cor. 2:7–8). Indeed, throughout the Old Testament the enmity between the serpent and the woman's seed is the big story behind all of the headlines. The historical books highlight the threat posed to the covenantal line. From Abel to the last of the prophets, Jesus said, the heavenly battle between the serpent and the Messiah is played out below even by unwitting human actors (Matt. 24:33–36). Cain slays Abel, but God raises up Seth. The Sethites intermarry with those outside the covenant almost to the point of being lost altogether, only to be finally brought into the promised hope through Abraham and Sarah, despite barrenness. This tug-of-war, as we have already seen, became particularly violent in the contest between the "firstborn" of Egypt and Israel, with the infant Moses barely snatched from the massacre. Repeatedly, the covenant promise is hanging by a thread during the era of the kings. For example, when Ahaziah of Judah died, his mother, Athaliah, ordered the execution of the entire royal family. Recalling that it is from Judah that the Messiah was to come, one realizes that the whole of redemptive history was at this point hanging on one child, Joash, who was hidden away by one of Ahaziah's sisters. In solemn assembly, the leaders of Israel eventually declared the boy king: "Jehoiada said to them, 'Here is the king's son! Let him reign, as the LORD spoke concerning the sons of David'" (2 Chr. 22:10–23:3). This cosmic warfare played out on the historical stage culminates in the massacre of the newborn male infants under Herod (Matt. 2:16–18), which is marvelously captured in apocalyptic form in Revelation 12. The defeat of Herod, Pilate, Caiaphas, even the overcoming of his abandonment by the disciples and Peter's denial of him (as well as our own), was the defeat of Satan and the demonic "principalities and powers" that conspire to keep the world under sin, death, and judgment. The trial is over. The new humanity has triumphed in Christ, crossing the river of judgment into the kingdom of grace and finally one day, the kingdom of glory.

The so-called givens of the kingdom of power, in whatever regime of it we happen to live, are exposed as the "elemental principles of the universe" (Col. 2:8), a sham, childish playacting gone terribly wrong, something no longer in any way determining the obligations, loyalties, and destinies of those who are in Christ. Yet, once more, what brings these motifs together in this passage (Colossians 2), what *effects* the recapitulation (alive together with him) and the conquest of the powers, is the cancellation of the legal sanctions against us by virtue of their having been carried out in and upon Christ. The case against us before God in the cosmic courtroom has been settled in our favor, leaving no basis for the accusations of Satan and therefore no final claim of the demonic powers over our lives. Paul's courtroom cannot simply be dismissed as an influence of Roman jurisprudence; it is the courtroom in which Adam was convicted and pardoned. It is the courtroom of the altar's sacrifices and the Holy of Holies, where Isaiah, beholding God's enthronement in a vision, was "undone" and atonement was made for his cleansing (Isaiah 6), and where Joshua the high priest was declared righteous and clothed in royal splendor despite his filthy clothes and Satan's prosecution of the case against him (Zechariah 3).

I might even add the truth in the governmental theory here: once Christ has entirely satisfied the claims of justice, the cosmic trial in which God has not only been the judge but judged by mortals, clears *God* of all charges. We now understand how God could (and still does) patiently endure injustice and evil. God is not aloof to the cry, "How long?" but "is not willing that any should perish but that all should come to repentance" (2 Pet. 3:9). God's government not only of the cosmos but of history is upheld: both God and his people are vindicated in the sight of all the nations. The same integration of the sacrifice, recapitulation, and conquest motifs is found, for example, in Hebrews 2:

> Since, therefore, the children share flesh and blood, he himself likewise shared the same things, so that through death he might destroy the one who has the power of death, that is, the devil, and free those who all their lives were held in slavery by the fear of death. For it is clear that he did not come to help angels, but the descendants of Abraham. Therefore he had to become like his brothers and sisters in every respect, so that he might be a merciful and faithful high priest in the service of God, to make a sacrifice of atonement for the sins of the people. (vv. 14–17)

The dependence is asymmetrical. Neither recapitulation nor a Christus Victor model can establish the vicarious-substitutionary formula, but the third provides the basis for the other two.

This is even more the case in relation to the various other theories put forward, such as the moral influence (exemplarist) theory and the theory of moral government. Of course, there are many different versions of the exemplarist account, but they are all basically subjective. They do not announce any new state of affairs obtaining between God and creatures, but only a new state of awareness. Thus they cannot issue in a new creation but only in our rededication to the old. This was the problem with those who wanted to go back to the types and shadows of the old covenant (i.e., the law) when the new creation had arrived. Synergism, whether inspired by the "covenantal nomism" of Sinai or the Pelagian assumptions of the gentiles, belongs to "this fading age," and cannot achieve their own goals. Exemplarist views of Christ's work assume an optimistic anthropology—as if the only thing standing in the way of our being reconciled to God was information or a moving example. The result of a pelagianizing anthropology is a soteriology in which human repentance rather than divine redemption becomes the basis for forgiveness and reconciliation.

Yet it is only because the offering of Christ is expiatory that the cross is a symbol of love (John 3:16). In fact, "In this is love, not that we loved God but that he loved us and sent his Son to be the atoning sacrifice [*hilasmon*, 'expiation'] for our sins" (1 John 4:10). Only on the basis of this indicative can the imperative follow: "Beloved, since God loved us so much, we also ought to love one another" (v. 11). Note that precisely because of the uniqueness of Christ's sacrificial death and its value, the imperative is to imitate not his sacrificial death but his obedient life. Once we sufficiently appreciate the sacrificial character of the atonement, we can indeed recognize the cross as the most obvious demonstration of God's love and an example of true friendship in our ethical relationships with others. Apart from its expiatory character, the cross exhibits not God's love but an arbitrary will.

Finally, if, as the so-called governmental theory has it, Christ's death simply reestablishes God's justice as the ruler of the world, apart from rendering a payment for sin on behalf of human beings, how could this be anything more than the mere assertion of justice by an arbitrary act of will? Yet in the substitutionary work of Christ, as prophet, priest, and king, both as divine and human, in his obedient life and death, God himself plays by the rules. God establishes justice throughout the earth by submitting himself to that justice which he himself is in his very being. The cross does not ignore that everything must be set right but in fact accomplishes it. In short, if, as subjective theories of the atonement generally maintain, the cross is *not* somehow necessary for God to reconcile sinners, then it is not an example of anything but arbitrary divine power. Yet when Jesus prayed, "Father, if you are willing, remove this cup from me; yet, not my will but yours be done" (Luke 22:42), the answer to that question came on Good Friday. "Yet it was the will of the LORD to crush him with pain. When you make his life an offering for sin, he shall see his offspring, and shall prolong his days; through him the will of the LORD shall prosper. Out of his anguish he shall see light. . . . The righteous one, my servant, shall make many righteous, and he shall bear their iniquities" (Isa. 53:10–11). It was not merely because God needed to vindicate his justice that this sacrifice was the only way forward, but because God wanted to vindicate his people.

It is only within the broader context of sacrificial analogies, then, that the cross can be seen both to encompass and to satisfy the whole being of God and the need of humankind. Honor at the expense of justice reduces God to a petty fief whose only concern is to restore his pride, not his people. Justice at the expense of love reveals a deity who can be feared but never trusted by the unjust. Love at the expense of justice worships love as God instead of God as love. According to such a sentimental theology, the cross can hardly be seen as a lesson of anything but arbitrary cruelty.

A weakness of the usual division of Christ's life into the states of humiliation and exaltation is that it typically attributes the cross to the one and the resurrection to the other. However, the Gospels treat the death of Christ in a more paradoxical fashion. It is precisely because the cross is not the end but the valley through which Jesus must pass to glory that it can be treated as simultaneously tragedy and triumph. The Son of Man must be "lifted up," Jesus tells Nicodemus, "that whosoever believes in him may have eternal life" (John 3:14). Not only in the resurrection but at the cross, "When you have lifted up the Son of Man, then you will realize that I am he" (8:28). "And I, when I am lifted up from the earth, will draw all people to myself" (12:32). This is said in the context of his conquest of the powers: "Now is the judgment of this world; now the ruler of this world will be driven out" (v. 31). The "lifting up" is paradoxical: simultaneously humiliation and exaltation. The picture of a victim dying the death of a criminal according to Roman law and of a cursed member of the covenant according to Jewish law, nevertheless "lifted up" in the language of enthronement is as paradoxical as the image of the Lamb sitting on a throne in the Apocalypse. The point to be made here then is that the humiliation and exaltation of Christ are dialectically related throughout Christ's work, not simply accorded to different phases. Christ is king on the cross, as the inscription rightly read. Even there he was not passive, but was defeating the powers that hold us (and in our wake, all of creation) in bondage to sin, despair, and death. Even on the cross, he was wrestling with his ancient foe, as he had done throughout his ministry, beginning with the temptation. While Satan promised him a glorious kingdom of power here and now, avoiding the cross, Jesus embraced the cross precisely as a king embraces a scepter. Or, to change the metaphor slightly, Jesus is *enthroned* on a *cross*.

When we see the cross in the light of Christ's threefold office, reflecting both his life and death, the cross and the resurrection, his divinity and humanity, the legal and the relational, the individual and the cosmic, we are better able to affirm with John of Damascus,

> Every action, therefore, and performance of miracles by Christ are most great and divine and marvelous: but the most marvelous of all is His precious Cross. For no other thing has subdued death, expiated the sin of the first parent, despoiled Hades, bestowed the resurrection, granted the power to us of contemning the present and even death itself, prepared the return to our former blessedness, opened the gates of Paradise, given our nature a seat at the right hand of God, and made us the children and heirs of God, save the Cross of our Lord Jesus Christ. For by the Cross all things have been made right.[16]

THE KING IN GLORY

Jesus' messianic claim had to do primarily with his relationship to the temple, since the claimants to the title "king of the Jews" had taken action to attempt a public show of the royal and priestly roles being fused in their person. With his

16. Ibid., 80.

triumphal entry into Jerusalem, Jesus was claiming to be the messiah identified in Zechariah 9. Now Jesus enters the temple in royal state, to cleanse it: "there shall no longer be traders in the house of the LORD of hosts on that day" (Zech. 14:21). No wonder the Hasmonean line found such actions so threatening, since those actions repeated the sequence of Judas Maccabeus: "victory over the pagans, cleansing the Temple, fulfilment of the promises, and establishment of the new dynasty."[17]

"In Mark and Matthew," notes Wright, "Jesus' Temple-action is closely linked with the cursing of the fig tree." The "mountain" to be removed and cast into the sea is the temple mount, echoing Zechariah 4:6–7, which itself echoes Isaiah 40:4 and 42:16.[18] Zechariah 4 anticipates this day, with the angel telling the governor of Judah, "This is the word of the LORD to Zerubbabel: Not by might, nor by power, but by my Spirit, says the LORD of hosts. What are you, O great mountain? Before Zerubbabel you shall become a plain; and he shall bring out the top stone among shouts of 'Grace, grace to it!'" (vv. 6–7). The present temple and its mount are in the way, just as the theocracy itself, though once the sanctuary of God, is in the way of the true Temple who has now arrived. As David's lord as well as son (Mark 12:35–37, from Psalm 110), Jesus claimed authority over the temple as a greater king than David and a greater priest than Aaron (both anticipated in Psalm 110). While earlier (and later) claimants represented themselves as the rescuers of the temple and its cultic life, Jesus places his messianic mission in direct conflict with it. It is one of the reasons why even early on Jesus is such a "rock of offense."

There simply is not room enough in the world, much less in Israel, for two temples. The earthly copy cannot pretend to be the real thing and when the latter comes, the former must be joyfully and respectfully left behind. As Wright adds, "In the eschatological lawcourt scene, he has pitted himself against the Temple. When his prophecy of its destruction comes true, that event will demonstrate that he was indeed the Messiah who had authority over it." It will be a replay of the Maccabean crisis, though ending in utter destruction."[19] Wright turns to the parable of the Prodigal Son as a recapitulation of this overarching story of exile and restoration.

> And the story of the prodigal says, quite simply: this hope is now being fulfilled—but it does not look like what was expected. Israel went into exile because of her own folly and disobedience, and is now returning simply because of the fantastically generous, indeed, prodigal, love of her god. But this is a highly subversive retelling. The real return from exile, including the resurrection from the dead, is taking place, in an extremely paradoxical fashion, in Jesus' own ministry. Those who grumble at what is happening are cast in the role of the Jews who did not go into exile, and who opposed the returning people. They are, in effect, virtually Samaritans. The true Israel is

17. Wright, *Jesus and the Victory of God*, 493.
18. Ibid., 494.
19. Ibid., 511.

coming to its senses, and returning to its father, as Jeremiah had foretold [31:18–20]; and those who oppose this great movement of divine love and grace are defining themselves as outside the true family.[20]

It seems obvious enough that "Jesus himself believed that he was the great agent of this strange return from exile, and that he lived and acted accordingly."[21]

> If this is the new exodus, those who are objecting to it are cast as Pharaoh. If it is the real return from exile, the objectors are the Samaritans. If Jesus is in some sense building the real Temple, the objectors—ironically, since their own worldview focuses so strongly on the Temple in Jerusalem—are cast as those who resolutely opposed its rebuilding. They, in their turn, are saying to Israel's covenant god that they wish he were dead.[22]

Again, the view that the Messiah would restore the status quo of the Mosaic theocracy could justify the separation of "clean" from "unclean." The Messiah would come, said the Pharisees, by more rigorous obedience to the details of the Sinaitic code, including punctilious concern with the layers of scribal tradition interpreting the Torah.

Not only a new creation and a new exodus, this prophecy will fulfill the unconditional promise made to David for his seed to sit on an everlasting throne. This messianic seed of David will be anointed by the Spirit for his tasks, righteously judging and defending the cause of the weak. Again the new creation/sabbath language is evident: "The wolf shall live with the lamb, the leopard shall lie down with the kid, the calf and the lion and the fatling together, and a little child shall lead them. . . . They will not hurt or destroy on all my holy mountain; for the earth will be full of the knowledge of the LORD as the waters cover the sea" (Isa. 11:1–9). Micah 4 and 5 envision the nations streaming to the hill of the Lord, with God's Word going out to the world. The Messiah will judge the nations and bring peace to the earth, and he will be born in Bethlehem (5:2). In Zechariah 9 the king riding on the foal of a donkey will bring everlasting peace. "As for you also, because of the blood of my covenant with you, I will set your prisoners free from the waterless pit." It will be a time of festival, with new wine and grain (vv. 9–17). There are other clear parallels in the Second Temple literature, as in *1 Enoch* (especially 48:10) and *4 Ezra* (especially 13:32ff.). Thus the greater exodus from bondage occurs not simply in the *ordo salutis* (with individual regeneration and acquittal), but in the cosmic drama of history and eschatology: God did not abandon his messiah to the grave (Ps. 16:10).

As Herman Ridderbos puts the matter, "The early church did not create the story; the story created the early church! . . . Without the resurrection the story

---

20. Ibid., 127. Wright sees a parallel between Luke 15 (the parables of the lost sheep, the lost coin, and the prodigal and his brother) and Acts 15 (the council at Jerusalem at which gentiles were accepted as full members of the new covenant community) (128).
21. Ibid., 128.
22. Ibid., 130.

would have lost its power. It would have been the story of the life of a saint, not the gospel."[23] In his Pentecost sermon, Peter cited Psalm 16:8–11 as the proof text for his announcement of God's saving work in Christ: "But God raised him up, having freed him from death, because it was impossible for him to be held in its power" (Acts 2:24–28). (Thus the truth in that odd patristic notion that at the cross Satan swallowed the bait only to be swallowed himself reflects a profound insight.) Since David's tomb is not empty, Peter said in his first recorded sermon, Scripture could only have been referring to "the resurrection of the Messiah."

> This Jesus God raised up, and of that all of us are witnesses. Being therefore exalted at the right hand of God, and having received from the Father the promise of the Holy Spirit, he has poured out this that you both see and hear. . . . Therefore let the entire house of Israel know with certainty that God has made him both Lord and Messiah, this Jesus whom you crucified. (vv. 29–36)

It is the proclamation of the resurrection and ascension of Christ as the fulfillment of the work of the cross that constitutes the kerygma or gospel that the apostles proclaim. Although they crucified "the Author of life," it is he "whom God raised from the dead."

> To this we are witnesses. . . . And now, friends, I know that you acted in ignorance, as did also your rulers. In this way God fulfilled what he had foretold through all the prophets, that his Messiah would suffer. Repent therefore, and turn to God so that your sins may be wiped out, so that times of refreshing may come from the presence of the Lord, and that he may send the Messiah appointed for you, that is, Jesus, who must remain in heaven until the time of universal restoration that God announced long ago through his holy prophets.

In fact, this Jesus is himself the great prophet promised through Moses.

> You are the descendants of the prophets and of the covenant that God gave to your ancestors, saying to Abraham, "And in your descendants all the families of the earth shall be blessed." When God raised up his servant, he sent him first to you, to bless you by turning each of you from your wicked ways. (Acts 3:15–26)

This pattern, "whom you crucified, [but] God raised from the dead," appealing to Old Testament prophecies, and announcing salvation in no other name, marks many of the sermons in Acts (2:24–36; 3:14–15; 4:10–12, 24–30; 5:30–32; 7:1–53; 10:39–43; 13:16–39; 17:30–32; 25:19; 26:4–8, 22–23; 28:20, 23–24). Before the Jewish council Paul noted with some irony, since the Pharisees were distinguished by their belief in the resurrection of the dead, "Brothers, I am a Pharisee, a son of Pharisees. I am on trial concerning the hope of the resurrection of the dead" (23:6).

---

23. Herman Ridderbos, *Studies in Scripture and Its Authority* (Grand Rapids: Eerdmans, 1978), 42.

As already argued, we should not allow the threefold office of Christ to be too rigidly tied to the so-called *states*: humiliation and exaltation, since at no point was Jesus without a kingdom even in his ministry under the cross and is even now "ever-living" at God's right hand to intercede for us. The crucifixion itself can be seen as a kind of exaltation, as we find in the Fourth Gospel: "And I, when I am lifted up from the earth, will draw all people to myself" (John 12:32). We might be inclined at first to take this as a reference to Jesus' ascension, but the next verse corrects that impression: "He said this to indicate the kind of death he was to die" (v. 33). So we see not simply a progression from the state of humiliation to that of exaltation, or from prophet to priest and finally king, but a dialectic of cross and glory.

The transfiguration recounted in Mark 9 is a prolepsis of the exaltation of the Messiah in the middle of Jesus' earthly ministry, much as the whole old covenant economy was a typological prolepsis of the consummation it could never itself realize. Second Corinthians interprets this as hiding the fading glory of the old covenant as it gives way to the new—more specifically, the ministry of Moses (the letter that kills) giving way to "the ministry of the Spirit " that has now arrived in surpassing glory (2 Cor. 3:3–9). "For if there was glory in the ministry of condemnation, much more does the ministry of justification abound in glory! Indeed, what once had glory has lost its glory because of the greater glory; for if what was set aside came through glory, much more has the permanent come in glory!" (vv. 3–11). Only in Christ is Moses' veil removed (vv. 14–16). "Now the Lord is the Spirit, and where the Spirit of the Lord is, there is freedom. And all of us, with unveiled faces, seeing the glory of the Lord as though reflected in a mirror, are being transformed into the same image from one degree of glory to another; for this comes from the Lord, the Spirit" (vv. 17–18). Jesus is called "the Lord of glory" (1 Cor. 2:8), "the reflection of God's glory" (Heb. 1:3).

Nevertheless, for good reason Reformed as well as Lutheran theology has typically followed the eschatological distinction of Christ's kingship between the reign in grace (*regnum gratiae*) and his reign in glory or power (*regnum gloriae/potentiae*). God has installed his king on his holy mountain and now demands universal homage (Ps. 2:6; 45:6–7, the latter quoted in Heb. 1:8–9; Ps. 132:11; Isa. 9:6–7; Jer. 23:5–6; Mic. 5:2; Zech. 6:13; Luke 1:33; 19:27, 38; 22:29; John 18:36–37; Acts 2:30–36). But this kingdom is not simply an extension or reinvigoration of the kingship in Israel, as many of Jesus' erstwhile followers had expected, including the disciples after the resurrection (Acts 1:6). During the trial Pilate asked Jesus,

> "Are you the King of the Jews?" Jesus answered, "Do you ask this on your own, or did others tell you about me?" Pilate replied, "I am not a Jew, am I? Your own nation and the chief priests have handed you over to me. What have you done?" Jesus answered, "My kingdom is not from this world. If my kingdom were from this world, my followers would be fighting to keep me from being handed over to the Jews. But as it is, my kingdom is not from here." Pilate asked him, "So you are a king?" Jesus answered, "You say that

I am a king. For this I was born, and for this I came into the world, to testify to the truth. Everyone who belongs to the truth listens to my voice."
Pilate asked him, "What is truth?" (John 18:33–38)

A kingdom of truth and grace rather than a kingdom of power and glory: this
regime surely confused the Romans even more than the Jews. With the concrete
Truth standing before him, Pilate can only retreat into the supposedly ethically
neutral space of the abstract: "What is truth?"

The kingdom of Christ, then, is in its present phase, before the second advent,
empirically weak and foolish. There is nothing abstract about it: the kingdom is
present. Yet despite the fact that this kingdom is more global in its reach than any
empire has ever been and claims a deeper allegiance from its subjects than the
powerful rulers of the world have ever attained, it can hardly compare in outward
pomp and glory with the kingdoms of the world that it nevertheless outlasts (cf.
Daniel 7). The kingdom lives not only from the cross but from the resurrection,
and yet it is very much in a state of humiliation when empirical criteria are
applied. While in the old covenant the kingdom was typologically concentrated
in the outward glory of Israel's cultic and civil structures, in the kingdom of
Christ during "this present age" its glory is hidden under the cross. It claims
hearts, not geopolitical lands. It brings new birth (John 3:3–7) from the future
reign of the Spirit and as a prolepsis of the consummation that the "Lord and
giver of life" will bring in "the resurrection of the body and the life everlasting."
Regeneration is but the first phase of the new creation.

Christ as king, like the other titles we have explored, involves both a human
and a divine aspect. The king greater than David is so not only because he is God,
while David was a mere human. He is greater also because as a human being he
actually achieves what neither David nor Adam and Israel could accomplish: he
fulfills the embassy that humanity in Adam was created for. He restores, not only
in the name of God, but in the name of Adam and Israel, the reign of God in the
world. In the mystery of the incarnation, a human being, our brother, restores
God's righteousness in the world, as Hebrews explains in the light of Psalm 8.
"As it is, we do not yet see everything in subjection to [humanity], but we do see
Jesus, who for a little while was made lower than the angels, now crowned with
glory and honor because of the suffering of death, so that by the grace of God he
might taste death for everyone" (Heb. 2:8–9). "As it is" right now, we see a world
at odds with itself: humans against nonhuman creatures, humans against one
another, creatures against creatures, and the sinful domination and exploitation
that mark the distorted power regimes of this present order.

Although definitively transferred from "darkness into his marvelous light"
(1 Pet. 2:9), believers too are caught in this ongoing struggle against "powers and
principalities" not only external but also internal to them. Humankind does not
seem to be the liberator of creation to its divinely given genetic potential but
exploits creation for its own selfish ends. "As it is," the world appears to be poorly
run indeed. The power that God delegated to humankind has been abused and

manipulated for sinful purposes, and thus human authority over creation has become not only a parody of its original intention but dangerous to both the human and nonhuman creation. "As it is," things do not seem to be working. "But we do see *Jesus*," who has fulfilled the Adamic commission, bearing the curse in his own body and raised to glory at God's right hand of authority. He entered heaven as a conquering king not only in his own person, for himself, but as "the pioneer" or "forerunner" of our salvation and the restoration of the proper dominion to humanity. By his sanctification we are sanctified, and by his reign the world is assured its participation in the cosmic glory that he has already inherited in his investiture as "King of kings and Lord of lords" (1 Tim. 6:15). His investiture at the right hand of God is a reward for his meritorious obedience (Ps. 2:8–9; Matt. 28:18; Eph. 1:20–22; Phil. 2:9–11).

The already–not yet dialectic is at work in this understanding of Christ's kingly office, in relation to both the cosmos and the church. The concept of the kingdom of God is broader than that of the church, but in this present age it is especially in the church that the "body of Christ" comes to visible expression. There, at least in principle, Christ's heavenly reign is openly acknowledged, embraced, and experienced as a living reality. There, at least in principle, through the waters of baptism, the breaking of bread, the hearing of the Word, and the guidance of Christ's people through the ministry of pastors, elders, and deacons, the Spirit makes "dry land" appear for God's dwelling in the world. Just as the regeneration and justification of the wicked anticipates or, better, is in fact the "first fruits" of the bodily resurrection and glorification that awaits us, the existence of the church is the down payment on "the time of universal restoration that God announced long ago through his holy prophets" (Acts 3:21). As Paul confirms, the resurrection of Christ is not distinct from the resurrection of believers, but the "first fruits" of the whole harvest (1 Cor. 15:21–26, 45, 49). These organic analogies reflect not a model of sheer domination of one person over another, but an intimate union. Christ rules *over* by ruling *within* those who are identified as part and parcel of his own body.

> God put this power to work in Christ when he raised him from the dead and seated him at his right hand in the heavenly places, far above all rule and authority and power and dominion, and above every name that is named, not only in this age but also in the age to come. And he has . . . made him the head over all things for the church, which is his body, the fullness of him who fills all in all. (Eph. 1:20–23)

In the resurrection of Christ, then, we see the power of the age to come exercised by the Spirit in the present. It is a power that reigns over every other power and authority (a general sovereignty in creation and providence) in the service of his covenant people (cf. Eph. 4:15; 5:23; 1 Cor. 11:3). It is therefore not surprising that immediately after describing Christ as "the image of the invisible God" through whom and by whom all things exist and "hold together" in creation, Paul says, "He is the head of the body, the church; he is the beginning, the

firstborn from the dead, so that he might come to have first place in everything"
(Col. 1:15–20; cf. 2:19). Thus he rules organically and spiritually. He rules *in*
(communicatively and covenantally), not just *over* (causally), his church through
the ministry of the keys as well as the fellowship of believers. The Spirit justified
Jesus Christ by raising him from the dead, and so "he was crucified for our sins
and raised for our justification" (Rom. 4:25). As one who was "declared to be Son
of God with power according to the Spirit of holiness by resurrection from the
dead" (Rom. 1:4), Jesus, as it were, traded places with the Holy Spirit in the economy of redemption. Indeed, the Spirit justified Christ on his way to Pentecost,
to justify the Jews and gentiles whom he would make into one body with him.

Therefore, as Berkhof summarizes, the kingdom of grace is founded upon his
redemption, not creation.[24] It is not a geopolitical kingdom as in the theocracy
(Matt. 8:11–12; 21:43; Luke 17:21; John 18:36–37). The children of this kingdom do not lord it over others as the gentiles do, but serve one another sacrifi-
cially (Matt. 20:25–28). Yet the kingdom will one day be revealed in power and
glory. Just as the empirical reality that we see all around us, epitomized by the
decay of our bodies, speaks against the claim that the new creation has truly
dawned, the weakness of a church "by schisms rent asunder, by heresies dis-
tressed," witnesses against the participation of the earthly body, the church, in its
heavenly head. Yet the resurrection of Christ makes it so, not only because it sets
the rest of the redemptive economy in motion, but because it is already now the
first installment on the full consummation.

The principle that Paul applies to the physical body, "sown in mortality, raised
in immortality, sown in dishonor, raised in glory, sown in weakness, raised in
power" (1 Cor. 15:42–43), is illustrative of the already–not yet scheme involved in
the manifestation of the kingdom in history. Entered by the new birth (John
3:3–5), this kingdom nevertheless cannot remain a merely spiritual reality. It must
one day become as tangible and complete as the resurrection itself will be for the
human person. But for now, it is a mustard seed (Mark 4:30), leaven being worked
into the dough of the wider matrix of earthly powers (Matt. 13:33). The kingdom
is present (Matt. 12:28; Luke 17:21; Col. 1:13), yet not consummated (Matt.
7:21–22; 19:23; 22:2–14; 25:1–13, 34; Luke 22:29–30; 1 Cor. 6:9; 15:50; Gal.
5:21; Eph. 5:5; 1 Thess. 2:12; 2 Tim. 4:18; Heb. 12:28; 2 Pet. 1:11). The kingdom
of God cannot be circumscribed by the church, and the church cannot be identified wholly with the kingdom of God. The already–not yet dialectic in this exercise of Christ's royal office remains in play until those who are being sanctified are
glorified, the church militant is made the church triumphant, the dead are raised,
and the announcement is finally heard that the cities of oppression and violence
have been destroyed and "The kingdom of the world has become the kingdom of
our Lord and of his Messiah, and he will reign forever and ever" (Rev. 11:15).

As I have argued, the claim "Jesus is Lord" is not simply identical to saying,
"Jesus is God." It is that and more. The important eschatological point that this

---

24. Louis Berkhof, *Systematic Theology*, 407.

claim makes is that in Jesus Christ the threats to God's promises being fulfilled have been conquered objectively and will be realized fully in the age to come. To say *Christos kyrios* is to witness to the fact that the advent of God's lordship visibly in history has occurred, and it is located in the person of Christ. There are no powers, authorities, thrones, or dominions that can thwart his purposes, although they may present fierce opposition until they are finally destroyed. All things have been subjected to humanity. The original commission is fulfilled, so that the so-called great commission in Matthew 28:18–20 brings the original "creation mandate" to fruition: "All authority in heaven and on earth has been given to me. Go therefore and make disciples of all nations, baptizing them in the name of the Father and of the Son and of the Holy Spirit, and teaching them to obey everything that I have commanded you. And remember that I am with you always, to the end of the age."

Moltmann reminds us,

> Anyone who sees the risen Christ is looking in advance into the coming glory of God. He perceives something which is not otherwise perceptible, but which will one day be perceived by everyone. . . . In talking about a resurrection of Jesus *from the dead*, the Christians have altered the old apocalyptic hope in quite a decisive way. In making this alteration, what they are saying is this: in this one person, ahead of all others, the End-time process of the raising of the dead has already begun. With Jesus' resurrection from the dead, history's last day is beginning: "The night is far gone and the day is at hand" (Rom. 13.12). That is why they proclaim him as "the first fruits of those who have fallen asleep" (I Cor. 15.20), "the first-born from the dead" (Col. 1.18), "the pioneer of salvation."[25]

And the resurrection sheds new light on the cross as well:

> For the symbol of resurrection from *the dead* allows us to take Jesus' death seriously. It excludes every notion that Jesus revived after death, or that his soul went on living . . . for it excludes all notions of a projection. . . . Paul did not see this as being in any way a contradiction of the statement that Jesus is God's own Son in eternity. The temporally marked beginning of Jesus' ministry as "the Son of God in power" and the statements about the pre-existence of the Son (Phil. 2.6; Col. 1.15) stand side by side, without any attempt to reconcile them.
> . . . The kingdom of the Son is the kingdom of brothers and sisters, not a kingdom of the lord and his servants. . . . He was raised through the creative *Spirit* (Rom. 1.4; 8.11; I Peter 3.18; I Tim. 3.16). He was raised through *the glory of the Father* (Rom. 6.4). He was raised through *the power of God* (I Cor. 6.14). . . . Jesus is risen into the coming kingdom of God.[26]

Accordingly, "Wherever people confess that Jesus is the Christ of God, there is living faith. Where this is doubted or denied or rejected, there is no faith."[27]

25. Moltmann, *Trinity and the Kingdom,* 85.
26. Ibid., 85–86, 87, 88.
27. Jürgen Moltmann, *The Way of Jesus Christ: Christology in Messianic Dimensions,* trans. Margaret Kohl (Minneapolis: Fortress, 1990), 39.

Anyone who pares the theme of christology down to "the Jesus of history," anyone who reduces the eschatological person of Christ to the private person of Jesus, and anyone who historicizes his presence to the time of his life on earth, must not be surprised to discover that christology is no longer a subject that has any relevance at all. For who could still get up any interest after 2,000 years in a historical Jesus of Nazareth who lived a private life and then died?[28]

To say "Jesus is Lord," one must try to hear it with Jewish ears. It means that the God of Israel—the one who won the duel with Egypt's gods and led his people through the sea and wilderness into the promised land—is the one who raised Jesus from the dead and, in turn, gave the human person thus raised the name above every name. It is to say that he is the one who will restore Israel's fortunes, not by reinvigorating a typological theocracy but by bringing about the universal judgment of sin and vindication for his people that the Mosaic economy could only foreshadow. To hear "Jesus is Lord" as a slogan for nothing more than "my personal relationship with Jesus" is not to hear it as it is meant to be heard. It is to truncate the message that Jesus both *is* and *proclaims*. Against the temptation to reduce salvation to an inner, personal experience, Moltmann rightly suggests, "It is therefore more appropriate to present the salvation which Christ brings in ever-widening circles, beginning with the personal experience of reconciliation and ending with the reconciliation of the cosmos, heaven and earth."[29] There is exegetical precedent for this in Romans 8, where not only the soul but the body, and not only human beings but the whole creation is swept into the train of the second Adam (vv. 18–25).

Lordship and redemptive love are not at odds in the one who holds the titles prophet, priest, and king in one office. Henceforth, we cannot think YHWH as "Lord" apart from YHWH as "servant." In YHWH's action culminating in Christ, the very meaning of lordship undergoes a radical revision from the depraved analogies with which we have become all too familiar. Christ rules the world *for us* as well as for his own and his Father's glory, since he has made both to be interdependent. Because he is Lord, "Who will bring any charge against God's elect? . . . Who shall separate us from the love of Christ?" Name a person, power, influence, cause, principle, or force in the world—anything at all that plays on our fears, saps us of vitality, and dries up our hope. "No, in all these things we are more than conquerors through him who loved us." Things *as they are* may witness against this hope, but what God has done and is doing in Christ, by the Spirit, is the countertestimony that nothing can separate us from the love of God in Christ Jesus (Rom. 8:33–39). Since Jesus is Lord, he calls us out of the bondage to sin and the law into the new obedience in the Spirit that the new covenant promised (Jer. 31:31–34). Furthermore, to say "Jesus is Lord," the speaker must be a qualified confessor—a "witness." One can only say this, in fact,

---

28. Ibid., 40–41.
29. Ibid., 45.

"by the Spirit" (1 Cor. 12:3). That is, the new creation of which Jesus is the fore-runner requires a new birth that none can effect for oneself (John 1:12–13; 3:5).

"Who Is This King of Glory?": Atonement and Ascension

While I have rejected the "ontological" way as defined by Tillich and as reflected in the various approaches I have identified, there is an ontological aspect to the work of Christ in the more technical sense of that term. This is a point that I will develop more fully in the third volume, but will use as a transition to a brief mention of the ascension, which marks a turning point from the priesthood to the kingship of Christ. I discuss it here as well as under the royal office because it is as frequently linked in Scripture to Christ's intercession as to his rule. Furthermore, as Douglas Farrow has argued at length, the ascension is far more important to atonement theology—and the rest of theology, for that matter—than we often realize.[30]

In answer to the question concerning the relevance of the ascension for us, the Heidelberg Catechism offers a Trinitarian reply:

> First, he pleads our cause in heaven in the presence of his Father. Second, we have our own flesh in heaven—a guarantee that Christ our head will take us, his members, to himself in heaven. Third, he sends his Spirit to us on earth as a further guarantee. By the Spirit's power we make the goal of our lives, not earthly things, but the things above where Christ is, sitting at God's right hand.[31]

Jesus prepared his followers for his absence by promising "another *paraklētos*," a defense attorney whom he will send when he ascends to the Father (John 14:16). In this unfolding eschatology, the Son returns to the Father so that they may send the Spirit to complete the earthly work that needs to be done in order to bring about the consummation of all things in God.

Again, there was prophetic precedent for the anticipation of this as for the other events in the life of Christ. In Psalm 2 YHWH installs his king on his holy hill, demanding universal homage in the face of the world's rulers, who would overthrow him. The New Testament appeals to this battle hymn repeatedly (Matt. 3:17; 17:5; Acts 4:25–27; 13:33; Rom. 1:4; Heb. 1:5; 5:5). Pursuing this unabashedly political theme, Psalm 68 is a war psalm attributed to David, quoted in Ephesians 4:8, in which YHWH in his lead chariot descends upon his enemies in sweeping victory.

> With mighty chariotry, twice ten thousand, thousands upon thousands, the Lord came from Sinai into the holy place. You ascended the high mount, leading captives in your train and receiving gifts from people, even from

30. Douglas Farrow, *Ascension and Ecclesia: On the Significance of the Doctrine of Ascension* (Grand Rapids: Eerdmans, 1999).

31. The Heidelberg Catechism, Lord's Day 18, Q. 49, in *Ecumenical Creeds and Reformed Confessions* (Grand Rapids: CRC Publications, 1988), 32.

those who rebel against the LORD God's abiding there. Blessed be the Lord, who daily bears us up; God is our salvation. Our God is a God of salvation, and to GOD, the Lord, belongs escape from death. . . . Your solemn processions are seen, O God, the processions of my God, my King, into the sanctuary. (Ps. 68:17–20, 24)

The theme of military victory is seen also in Psalm 24, also attributed to David, a psalm of ascent that would be sung antiphonally as the Israelites made their pilgrimage up the steps of Jerusalem to the hill of the Lord:

The earth is the LORD's and all that is in it, the world, and those who live in it; for he has founded it on the seas, and established it on the rivers. Who shall ascend the hill of the LORD? And who shall stand in his holy place? Those who have clean hands and pure hearts, who do not lift up their souls to what is false, and do not swear deceitfully. They will receive blessing from the LORD, and vindication from the God of their salvation. Such is the company of those who seek him, who seek the face of the God of Jacob. Lift up your heads, O gates! and be lifted up, O ancient doors! that the King of glory may come in. Who is the King of glory? The LORD, strong and mighty, the LORD, mighty in battle. Lift up your heads, O gates! and be lifted up, O ancient doors! that the King of glory may come in. Who is this King of glory? The LORD of hosts, he is the King of glory. (vv. 1–10)

It is not the people themselves who are in view in this psalm—"those with clean hands and pure hearts," who thereby command the royal doors to open. It is the King of glory himself who returns from conquest, and it is on the basis of that conquest that he commands the doors to open.

Thus the New Testament presents Jesus of Nazareth as the Son of David, the Messiah, whose origin is "from of old," and yet whose life will be unending, guaranteeing the security of David's house and throne forever. No thanks to his people, YHWH has himself ensured the fulfillment of his promise. It was this royal title to which the two blind men appealed, "crying loudly, 'Have mercy on us, Son of David!'" (Matt. 9:27; cf. Luke 18:35–40). And Luke's Gospel is eager to make this connection in the birth narrative (Luke 2:4). The Son of David theme is raised finally in Revelation 5. In this heavenly scene, no one is able to break the seals of the scroll and open it. Only one person—the Lamb who was slain, "the Lion of the tribe of Judah, the Root of David"—is qualified to explain the mystery of history, because he is its fulfillment. The "new David" becomes the catalyst finally for the unending "new song" of the saints (vv. 8–10).

The people arrive with him in his train, like captives who have been set free by his victory. It is with such texts as Psalm 24 in mind that we read,

But each of us was given grace according to the measure of Christ's gift. Therefore it is said, "When he ascended on high he made captivity itself a captive; he gave gifts to his people." (When it says, "He ascended," what does it mean but that he had also descended into the lower parts of the earth? He who descended is the same one who ascended far above all the heavens, so that he might fill all things.) (Eph. 4:7–10)

The consequence is that he has now, through his Spirit, poured out his gifts on his people, establishing the various offices of the church for the edification of the saints and the swelling of their ranks (Eph. 4:7–13). The Psalms make their way through the Gospels (especially John 14) to Pentecost: "Being therefore exalted at the right hand of God, and having received from the Father the promise of the Holy Spirit, he has poured out this that you both see and hear" (Acts 2:33).

So the priestly office remains central to Christ's heavenly session, as John reminds his readers: "My little children, I am writing these things to you so that you may not sin. But if anyone does sin, we have an advocate [*paraklētos*] with the Father, Jesus Christ the righteous; and he is the atoning sacrifice for our sins, and not for ours only but also for the sins of the whole world" (1 John 2:1–2). The angel of the LORD who stood in the heavenly courtroom to justify Joshua the high priest (Zechariah 3) is the same who intercedes at the Father's right hand, but now without Satan admitted into the chamber. He has been bound, and his house looted, with the victor leading captives in his train.

As we have seen above, Hebrews emphasizes the undying priesthood of Christ as providing the only sure foundation for our acceptance in the courtroom: "Consequently he is able for all time to save those who approach God through him, since he always lives to make intercession for them" (Heb. 7:25). While his sacrifice has been offered "once and for all" (Heb. 10:1–18), his intercession upholds the saints in the faith that unites them to his priestly work. Again, that the kingly reign of Christ exists to serve his priestly work is seen in Revelation 12:10, with the song of the defeat of the dragon: "Then I heard a loud voice in heaven, proclaiming, 'Now have come the salvation and the power and the kingdom of our God and the authority of his Messiah, for the accuser of our comrades has been thrown down, who accuses them day and night before our God.'" It is in this intercession that believers take their assurance of never being "cut off" by God:

> What then are we to say about these things? If God is for us, who is against us? He who did not withhold his own Son, but gave him up for all of us, will he not with him also give us everything else? Who will bring any charge against God's elect? It is God who justifies. Who is to condemn? It is Christ Jesus, who died, yes, who was raised, who is at the right hand of God, who indeed intercedes for us. Who will separate us from the love of Christ? (Rom. 8:31–35)

It is the same love manifested on the cross with which Jesus continues his unfailing intercession.

HERE I AM: THE SERVANT WHO IS LORD

In chapter four I traced the development of a covenantal anthropology that depends not on a few slender exegetical threads in the creation accounts for the *imago*, but rather to the wider biblical theme of the servant of the Lord. One of the most important messianic titles is *servant*, and no theme better underscores the covenantal character of the Messiah's mission. In any divine-human covenant, "servant" names the human partner. It is among the earliest biblical traditions to answer God's call with the words "Here I am" or "Behold your servant." The servants of the Lord do not presume to take up their office as one might choose a vocation. Rather, they are called away from their ordinary labors, family, friends, and customs. They leave their father and mother, as Abraham did and Jesus required of his disciples. In the face of God's call, they leave their flocks, nets, and bonds of kith and kin to answer, "Here I am." This response stands in contrast to Adam's flight from God's presence, hiding from judgment. The servant's role is to listen to God's word and relay it to his covenant people (Exod. 3:4; 1 Sam. 3:9; 1 Kgs. 3:9; Ps. 116:16; Isa. 44:1; Jer. 7:25). Servant, Son of Man, and Son of David are related themes (Ps. 78:70; Ezek. 34:23; Zech. 3:8–9). The royal servant speaks in his own person but also as the representative of the whole nation, "O LORD, I am your servant; I am your servant, the child of your serving girl. You have loosed my bonds. I will offer to you a thanksgiving sacrifice and call on the name of the LORD" (Ps. 116:16–17). The Servant Songs in Isaiah deepen this theme, as we have already seen.

But in the resurrection especially we see the other side. Not only has the Lord of the covenant been *made* Lord in his resurrection, but he has been *declared* in this event to be the Lord that he has always been (Rom. 1:4). This approach is given exegetical support by Christopher Seitz in his exploration of the handing over of the name (YHWH) to Jesus in the New Testament.

> Ironically, an act intended to guard a personal name, with corollary, indeed massive, implications for what it means to address Jesus this way, has at the end of our era been heard as an act of oppression. The most charitable thing to say is that those who feel oppressed have forgotten, if they ever knew, that the practice of referring to God's personal name by this convention coincided with the joy and bracing confession of seeing in Jesus of Nazareth the very face of God, the LORD, the Maker of Heaven and Earth.[32]

Jesus appropriates for himself this name that he has received from the Father:

> The "I am" statements of Jesus in John's Gospel and his statement that "before Abraham was, I am" appear to direct us to the "I am who I will be" divine (first-person) explanation for the name, as this is found in Exodus 3:14.... The "I am" statements assert through the simple force of their declaration what later theologians sought in the term "of one substance" (*homoousia*) to describe the relationship between Jesus and the LORD, the God of Israel, Maker of Heaven and Earth.[33]

32. Christopher Seitz, "Handing Over the Name," in *Trinity, Time, and Church*, ed. Colin Gunton (Grand Rapids: Eerdmans, 2000), 25.
33. Ibid., 31.

In Revelation 1:8 the ascended Christ declares, "'I am the Alpha and the Omega,' says the Lord God, who is and who was and who is to come, the Almighty." This reference combines Isaiah 44:6 ("I am the first and I am the last; besides me there is no god") and the revelation of the name YHWH in Exodus 3:14.

Therefore, Seitz observes, Christian theology in its most basic form is "commentary on the divine name YHWH-*kyrios*."[34] While *ĕlohîm* is generic for "God," "The sentence 'I am the LORD your God,' is a dense confession, combining two things: the personal and the sovereign."[35]

> The phrase "say to them, 'I will be has sent me to you'" (Exod. 3:14) harks back to the response of God to Moses at verse 12 about his own adequacy ("I will be with you") before the formal explanation is given at verse 14. . . . The name is presence and testimony to a specific shared history that will continue with this people. . . . God's name is himself; God's name expresses his promise and his faithfulness to that promise, to his elected people.[36]

As a gloss on Isaiah 45:14, 23–24, then, Philippians 2 announces, "The promise is sealed by an oath that cannot be revoked. It is sworn by God in his own name."[37] But it is not the case that the Christians now name the name that Israel would not name out of reverence. Rather, as Isaiah prophesied, the irrevocable oath has been fulfilled eschatologically in Christ, "that at the name of Jesus every knee shall bow and every tongue confess that Jesus Christ is Lord, to the glory of God the Father" (Phil. 2:10–11). YHWH has been true to his name.

> The name of the LORD would stand. This has taken place to the glory of God the Father. . . . It is not the case that the text seeks to conflate the name of Jesus and the name of "the LORD." The name of Jesus is not a vocalization of YHWH! God has a name, and it is the name above every name. He gives this name to Jesus. . . . The name of God is God's very self, and by giving it to Jesus, maximal identity is affirmed. Jesus Christ is Lord. He who will be as he is is this One raised by God.[38]

But this one raised as Lord is also Servant. The titles "Son of Man" and "Last Adam" must be included under this general theme. The role of humanity, as understood by Israel, was to answer back to God's speech, with the reply of the covenant servant, "Here I am." It is the reply of the prophets: those who hear God's word and then declare it and witness to it in the covenant lawsuit that YHWH brings against his people in the great trial of history under this present age ("in Adam"). Isaiah, for example, exclaims, "Here am I. Send me!" (Isa. 6:8). As the Lord's earthly representative, the messiah figure is also designated "Son of Man (Adam)." While in the canonical texts of Psalm 8:4, Ezekiel, and Daniel,

---

34. Ibid., 32.
35. Ibid., 33.
36. Ibid., 34–35.
37. Ibid., 37.
38. Ibid., 38–39.

"one like a son of man" appears as a description, by the time of *1 Enoch* it appears to become a messianic title (see *1 Enoch* 46 and 62; *2 Esdras* 13).[39]

"Here I am and the children whom God has given me" (Heb. 2:13). This gloss on Isaiah 8:18 reveals the covenantal form of Jesus' ascension in glory. This faithful reply to the summons of the other, with open palms, placing oneself at God's disposal, summarizes Jesus' life, death, and resurrection. Because of this, "God also highly exalted him and gave him the name that is above every name, so that at the name of Jesus every knee should bend, in heaven and on earth and under the earth, and every tongue should confess that Jesus Christ is Lord, to the glory of God the Father" (Phil. 2:9–11). With these open hands, the Son received a kingdom from his Father in the Spirit. With the same hands, filled with the bountiful harvest of his labors, he will hand the kingdom back to the Father. He will do this not only as Son of the Father, but as the faithful representative of the new humanity in an exchange without reserves.

In Christ we find the servant together in whom and with whom we owe the debt and the Lord who by death conquers death and makes us not only servants but sons and daughters. He was Servant even at the same time as he was the Son in that he was under a covenant of *works*. It was by his merit that we are then able to receive the benefits of his undertaking within a covenant of *grace*. As Delbert Hillers reminded us in the first chapter,

> There could not be any clearer evidence of the great gulf that is fixed between this and the intention of the Sinai covenant, where the stress is on Israel's responsibility. The statement here, shaped no doubt by Israel's experience of what David did to Uriah, of Solomon's apostasies, and so on, attests that God is bound to this promise no matter what. But at the same time, although this contrasts sharply with Sinai, there is a transfer from the older covenant pattern. If the older covenant spoke of blessings for obedience and curses for disobedience on the part of all Israel, this covenant now strikes the motif that Israel's history will henceforth be determined by the character of her king.[40]

Here is the genuinely ontological ingredient of a covenantal paradigm: union with Christ as the "leaven" who makes the whole lump holy. Perhaps the best conclusion to this section and indeed summary of this volume can be taken from Isaiah 43–44:

> I, I am He who blots out your transgressions for my own sake, and I will not remember your sins. Accuse me, let us go to trial; set forth your case, so that you may be proved right. Your first ancestor sinned, and your interpreters

---

39. This is one instance where the inclusive language of the NRSV does not do justice to the original text, translating Hebrew *ben ʾādām*/Aramaic *bar ʾĕnāš* as "human being," while retaining it as a title in the New Testament (Greek *hyios tou anthrōpou*). While this may be an appropriate rendering on one level, the fact that Second Temple Judaism raised the description to a title suggests a closer connection between Ezekiel and Daniel and the NT.

40. Delbert Hillers, *Covenant: The History of a Biblical Idea* (Baltimore: Johns Hopkins University Press, 1969), 112.

transgressed against me. Therefore I profaned the princes of the sanctuary, I delivered Jacob to utter destruction, and Israel to reviling. But now hear, O Jacob my servant, Israel whom I have chosen! Thus says the LORD who made you, who formed you in the womb and will help you: Do not fear, O Jacob my servant, Jeshurun whom I have chosen. For I will pour water on the thirsty land, and streams on the dry ground. I will pour my spirit upon your descendants, and my blessing on your offspring. They shall spring up like a green tamarisk, like willows by flowing streams. This one will say, "I am the LORD's," another will be called by the name of Jacob, yet another will write on the hand, "The LORD's," and adopt the name of Israel. Thus says the LORD, the King of Israel, and his Redeemer, the LORD of hosts: I am the first and I am the last; besides me there is no god. (43:25–44:6)

Index of Subjects and Names

271

70424823R00166

Made in the USA
Middletown, DE
13 April 2018